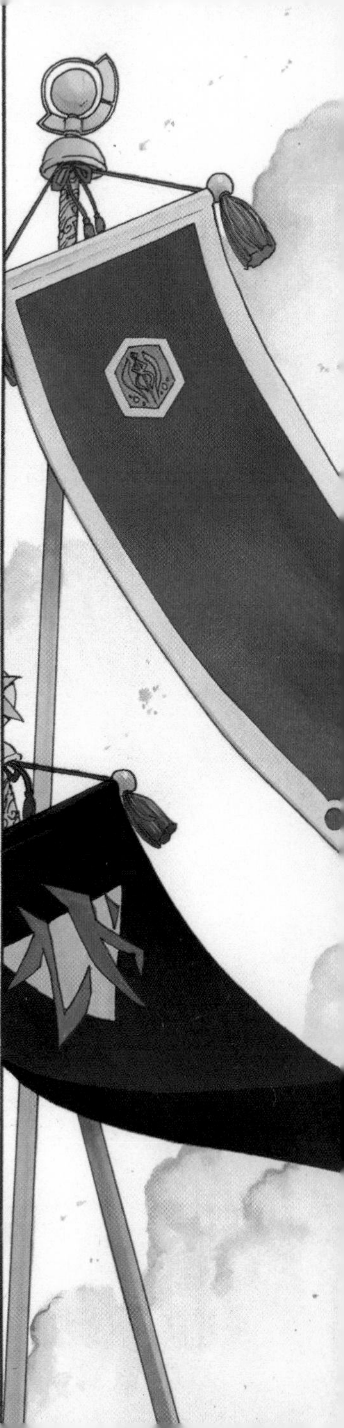

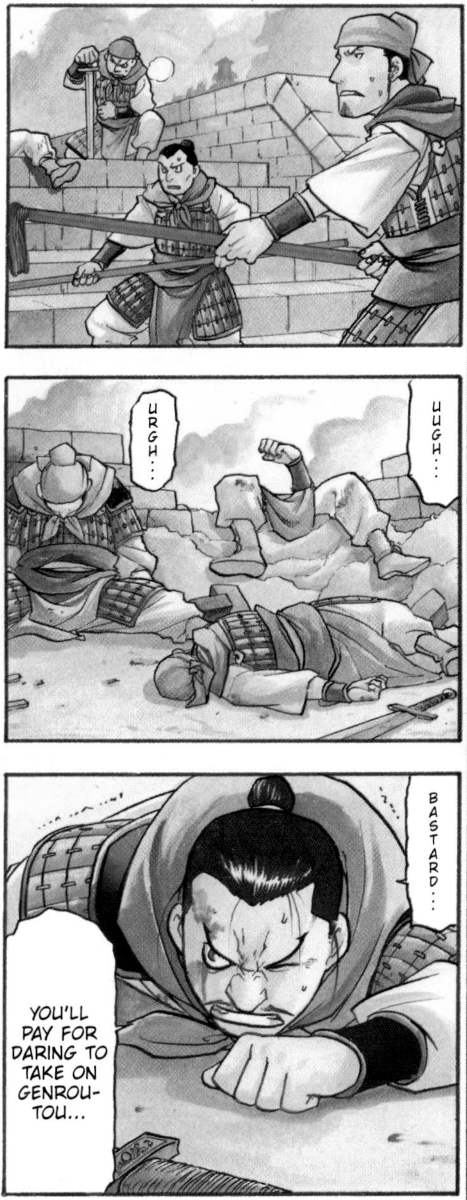
UGH...
URGH...
BASTARD...
YOU'LL PAY FOR DARING TO TAKE ON GENROU-TOU...

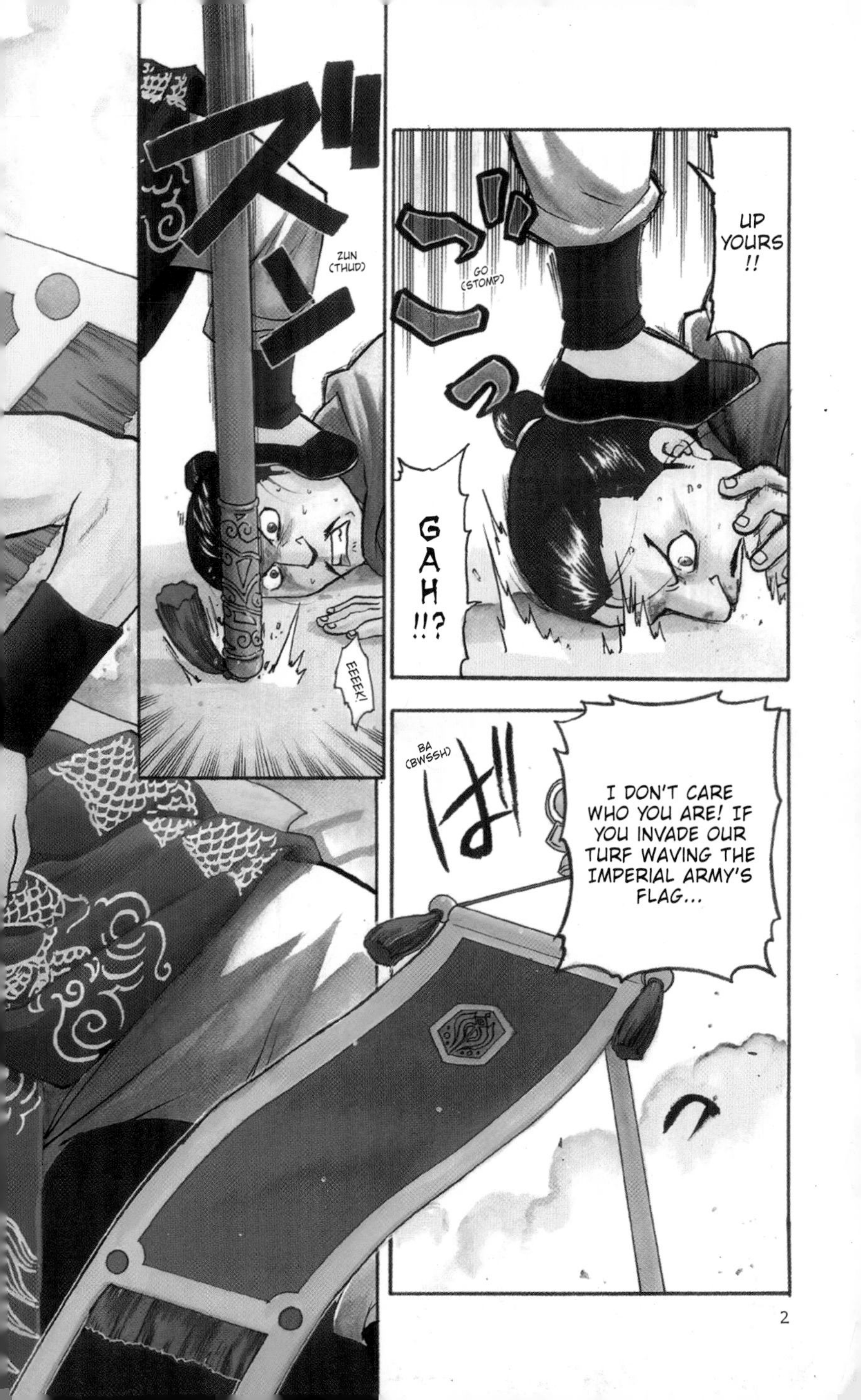
ZUN (THUD)
EEEEK!
UP YOURS !!
GO (STOMP)
GAH !!?
BA (BWSSH)
I DON'T CARE WHO YOU ARE! IF YOU INVADE OUR TURF WAVING THE IMPERIAL ARMY'S FLAG...

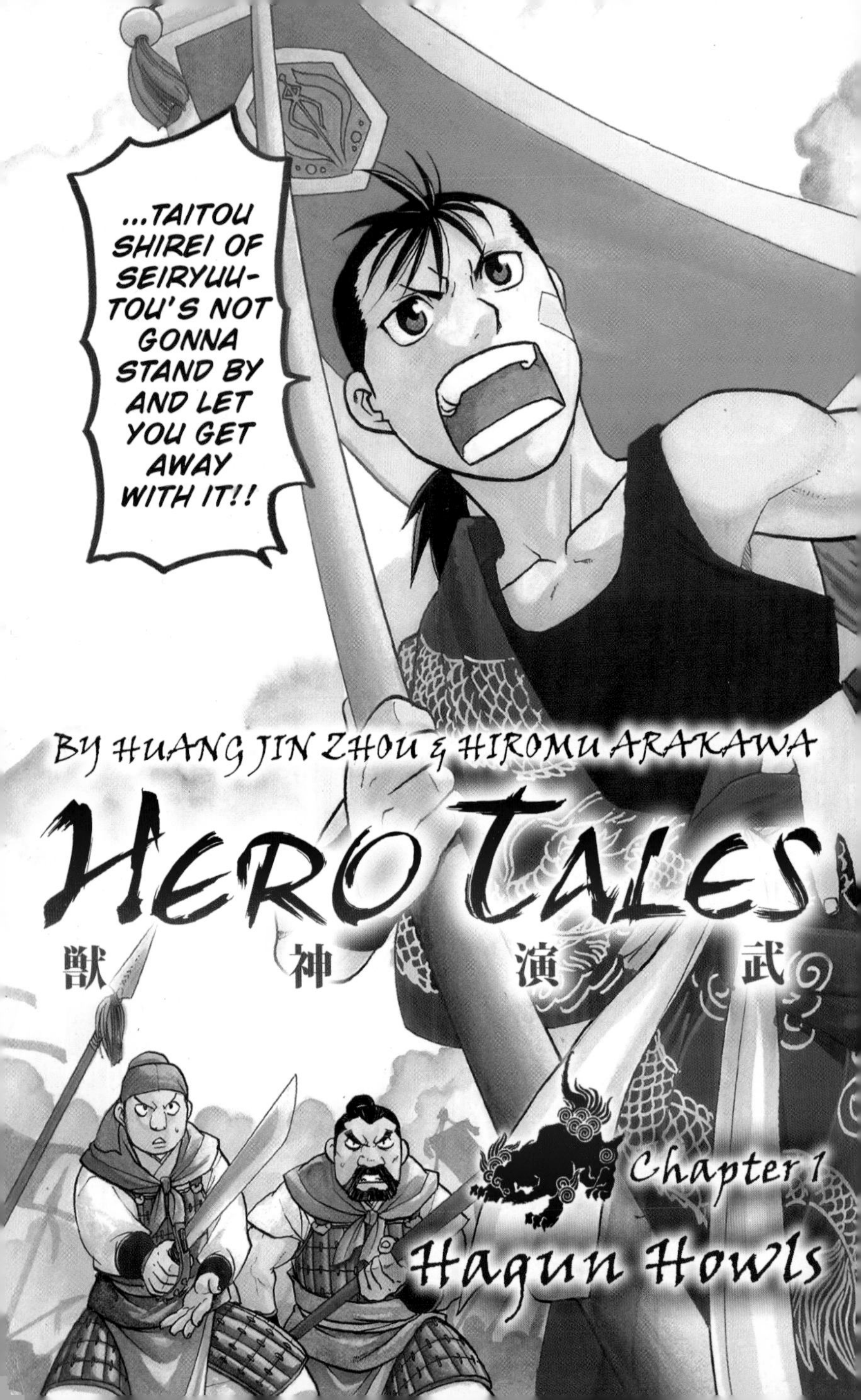
...TAITOU SHIREI OF SEIRYUU-TOU'S NOT GONNA STAND BY AND LET YOU GET AWAY WITH IT!!
BY HUANG JIN ZHOU & HIROMU ARAKAWA
HERO TALES
獣 神 演 武
Chapter 1
Hagun Howls

HERO TALES 獸神演武

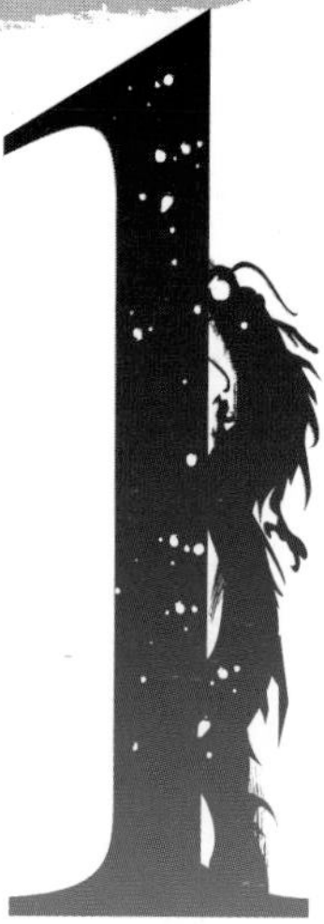

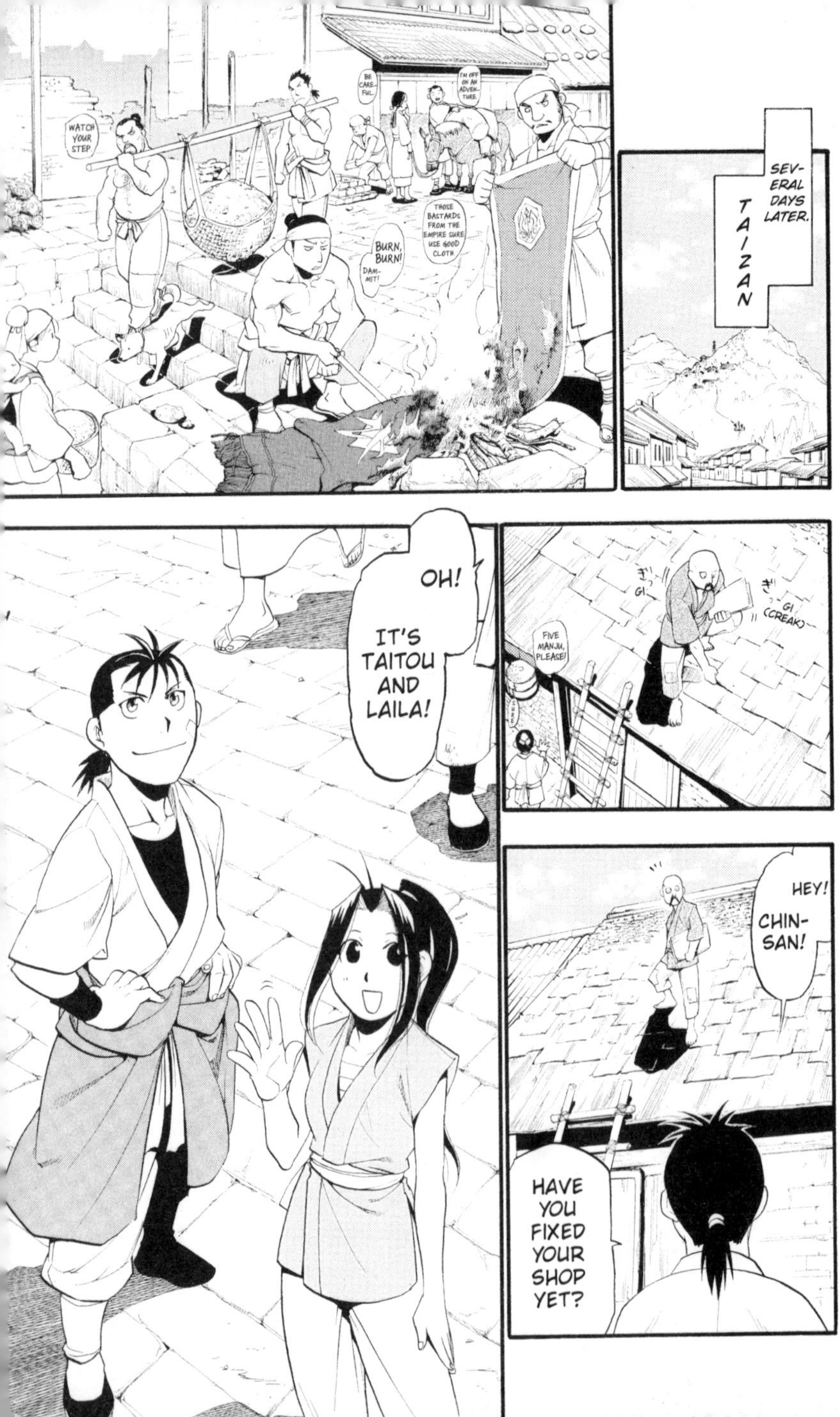

SEVERAL DAYS LATER.
TAIZAN
I'M OFF ON AN ADVENTURE.
BE CAREFUL.
WATCH YOUR STEP.
THOSE BASTARDS FROM THE EMPIRE SURE USE GOOD CLOTH
BURN, BURN!
DAMMIT!
ぎっ GI
ぎっ GI (CREAK)
FIVE MANJU, PLEASE!
HEY!
CHIN-SAN!
HAVE YOU FIXED YOUR SHOP YET?
OH!
IT'S TAITOU AND LAILA!

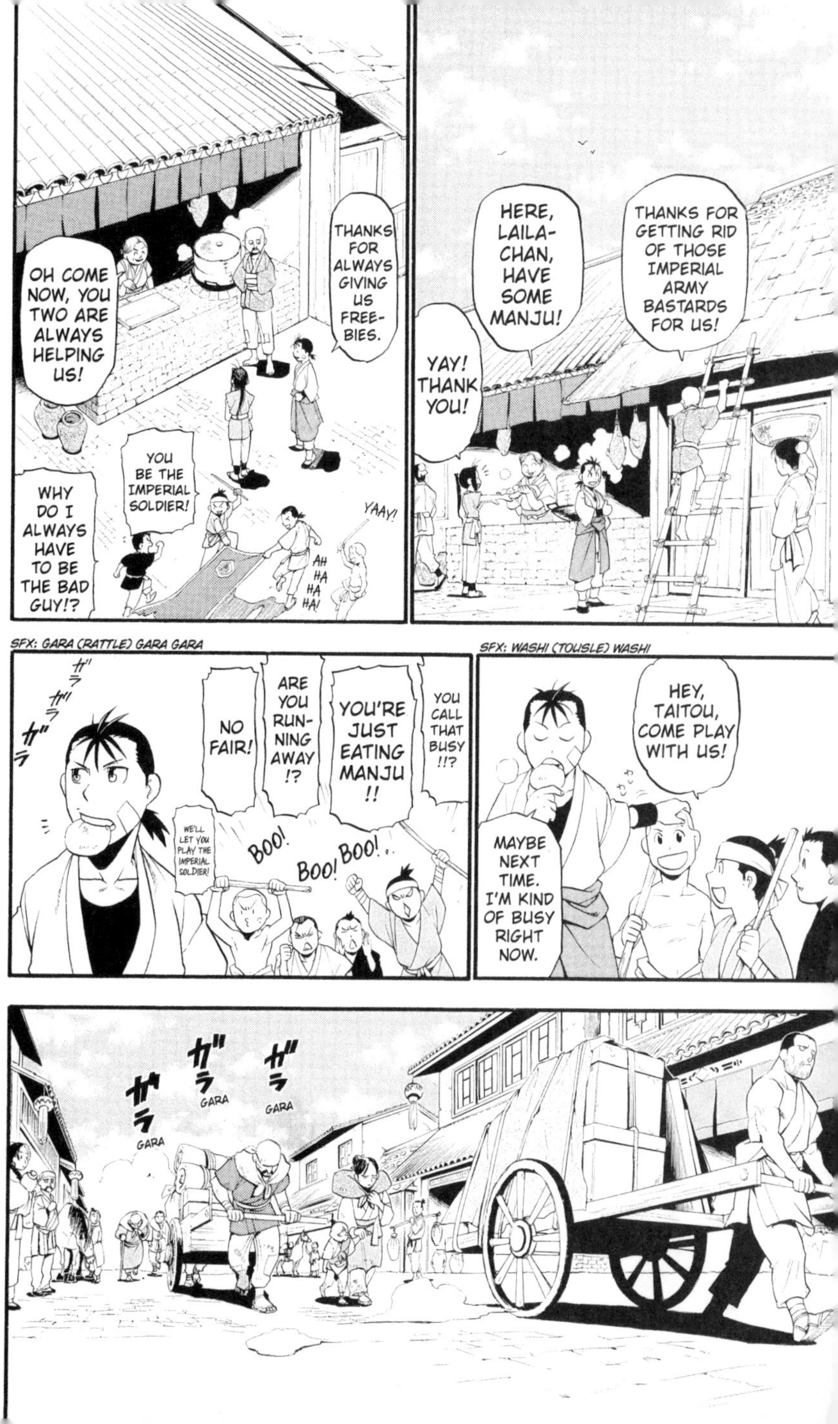
THANKS FOR GETTING RID OF THOSE IMPERIAL ARMY BASTARDS FOR US!
HERE, LAILA-CHAN, HAVE SOME MANJU!
YAY! THANK YOU!
THANKS FOR ALWAYS GIVING US FREE-BIES.
OH COME NOW, YOU TWO ARE ALWAYS HELPING US!
YAAY!
AH HA HA HA!
YOU BE THE IMPERIAL SOLDIER!
WHY DO I ALWAYS HAVE TO BE THE BAD GUY!?
SFX: WASHI (TOUSLE) WASHI
HEY, TAITOU, COME PLAY WITH US!
MAYBE NEXT TIME. I'M KIND OF BUSY RIGHT NOW.
SFX: GARA (RATTLE) GARA GARA
YOU CALL THAT BUSY !!?
YOU'RE JUST EATING MANJU !!
ARE YOU RUN-NING AWAY !?
NO FAIR!
BOO! BOO! BOO!
WE'LL LET YOU PLAY THE IMPERIAL SOLDIER!
ガラ ガラ ガラ
GARA GARA GARA

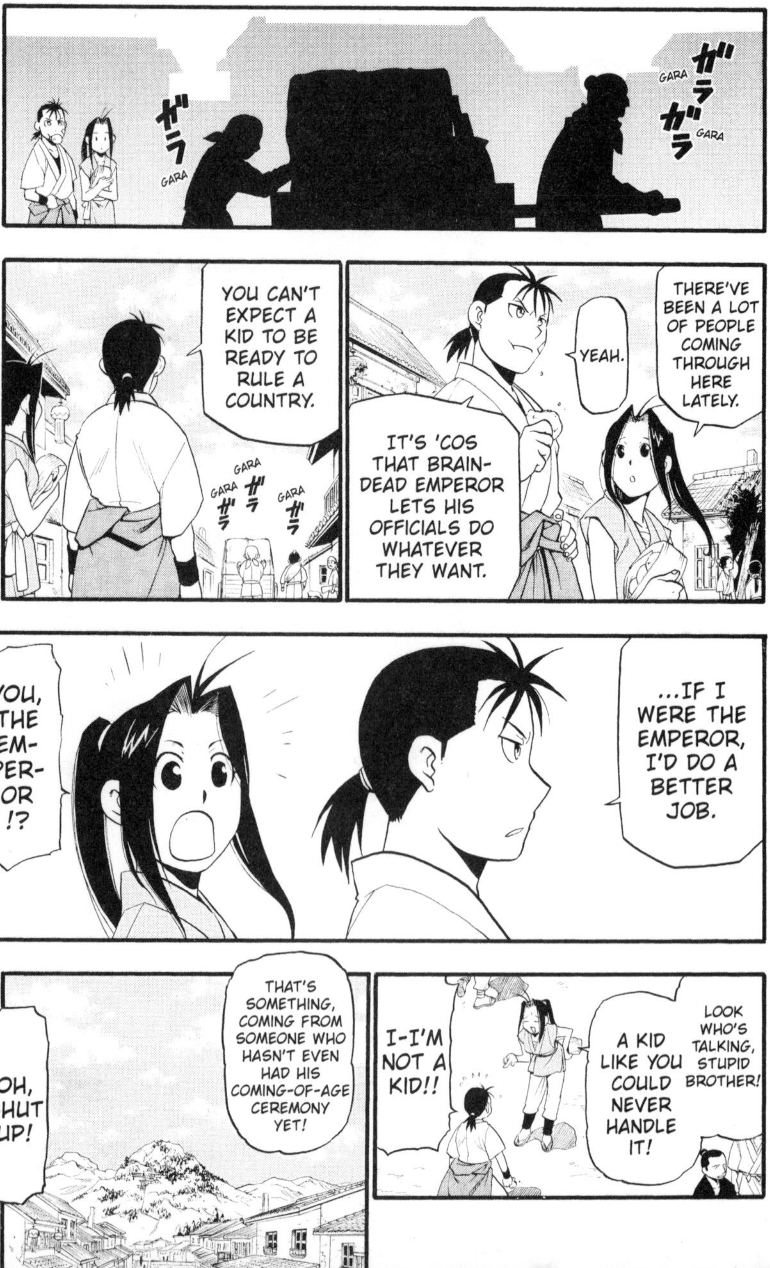
ガラ
GARA
ガラ
GARA
ガラ
GARA
THERE'VE BEEN A LOT OF PEOPLE COMING THROUGH HERE LATELY.
YEAH.
IT'S 'COS THAT BRAIN-DEAD EMPEROR LETS HIS OFFICIALS DO WHATEVER THEY WANT.
YOU CAN'T EXPECT A KID TO BE READY TO RULE A COUNTRY.
GARA
ガラ
GARA
ガラ
GARA
ガラ
...IF I WERE THE EMPEROR, I'D DO A BETTER JOB.
YOU, THE EM-PER-OR!?
LOOK WHO'S TALKING, STUPID BROTHER!
A KID LIKE YOU COULD NEVER HANDLE IT!
I-I'M NOT A KID!!
THAT'S SOMETHING, COMING FROM SOMEONE WHO HASN'T EVEN HAD HIS COMING-OF-AGE CEREMONY YET!
OH, SHUT UP!

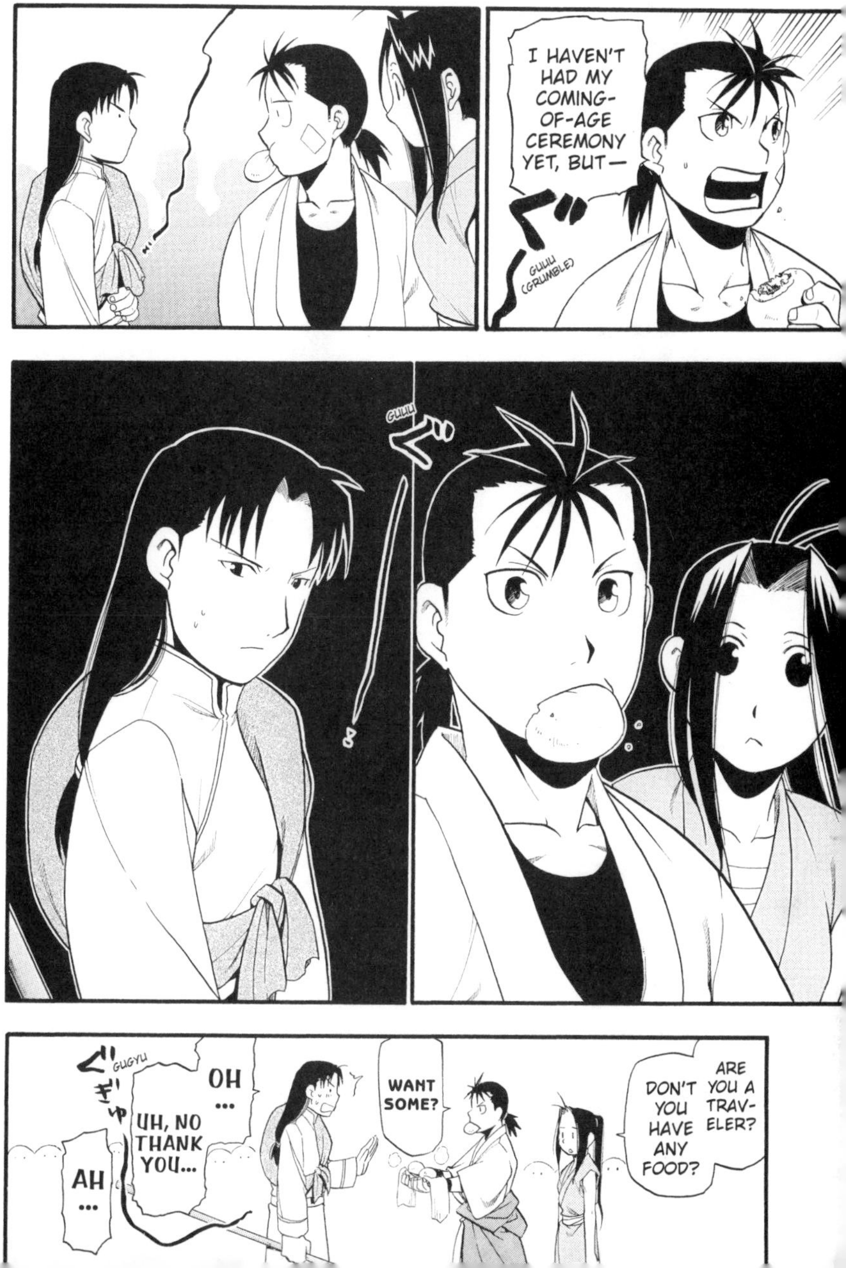
I HAVEN'T HAD MY COMING-OF-AGE CEREMONY YET, BUT—
GUUU (GRUMBLE)
GUUU
ARE YOU A TRAV-ELER?
DON'T YOU HAVE ANY FOOD?
WANT SOME?
OH ...
UH, NO THANK YOU...
GUGYU
AH ...

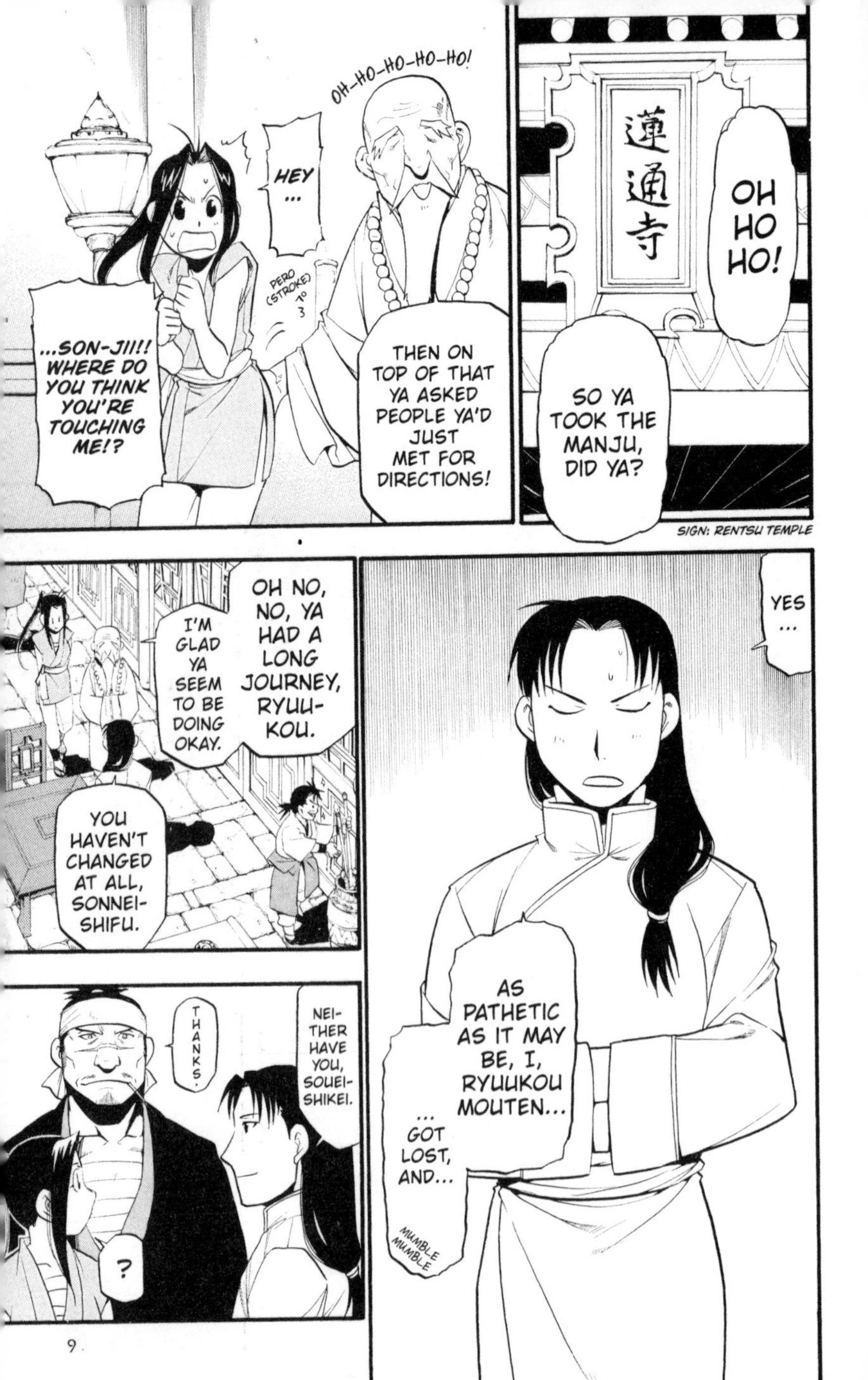

蓮通寺
OH HO HO!
SO YA TOOK THE MANJU, DID YA?
SIGN: RENTSU TEMPLE
OH-HO-HO-HO-HO!
THEN ON TOP OF THAT YA ASKED PEOPLE YA'D JUST MET FOR DIRECTIONS!
HEY ...
PERO (STROKE)
...SON-JII!! WHERE DO YOU THINK YOU'RE TOUCHING ME!?
YES ...
AS PATHETIC AS IT MAY BE, I, RYUUKOU MOUTEN...
... GOT LOST, AND...
MUMBLE MUMBLE
OH NO, NO, YA HAD A LONG JOURNEY, RYUU-KOU.
I'M GLAD YA SEEM TO BE DOING OKAY.
YOU HAVEN'T CHANGED AT ALL, SONNEI-SHIFU.
NEI-THER HAVE YOU, SOUEI-SHIKEI.
THANKS.
?

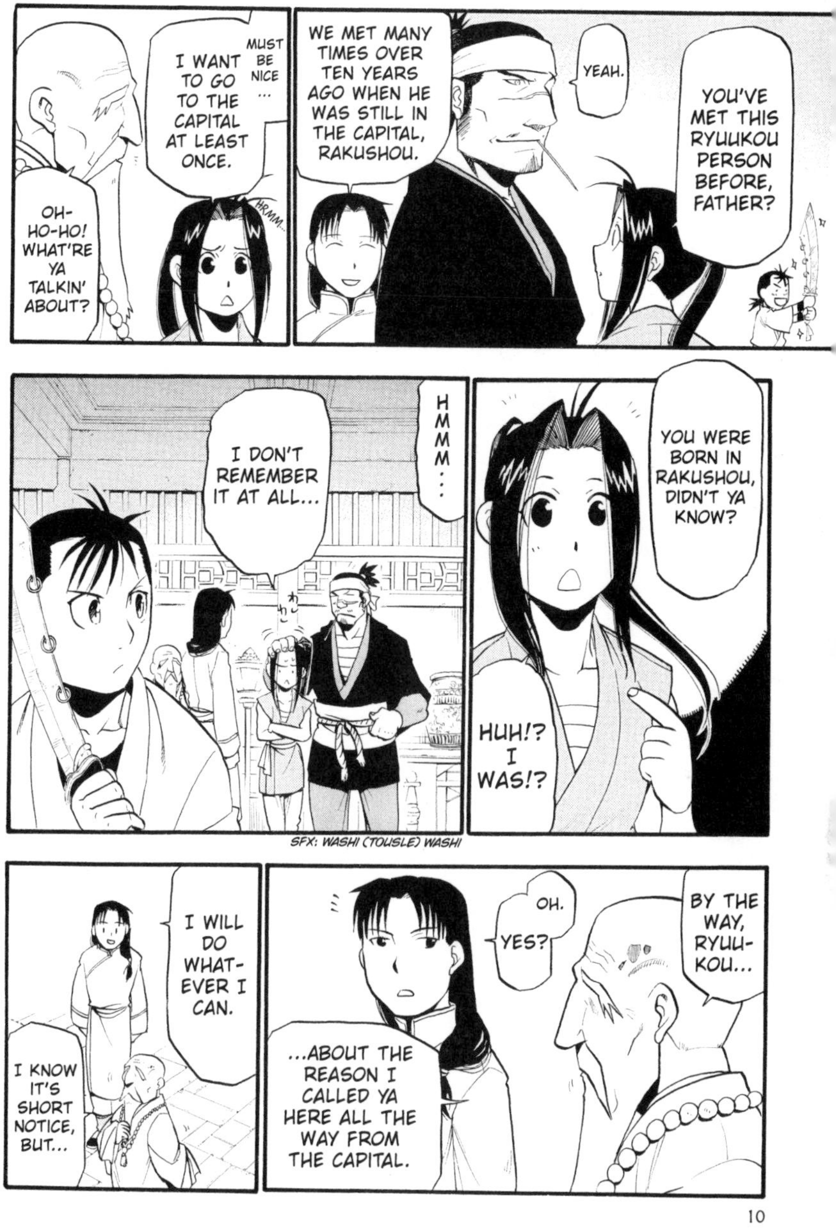
YOU'VE MET THIS RYUUKOU PERSON BEFORE, FATHER?
YEAH.
WE MET MANY TIMES OVER TEN YEARS AGO WHEN HE WAS STILL IN THE CAPITAL, RAKUSHOU.
I WANT TO GO TO THE CAPITAL AT LEAST ONCE.
MUST BE NICE...
HRMM...
OH-HO-HO! WHAT'RE YA TALKIN' ABOUT?
YOU WERE BORN IN RAKUSHOU, DIDN'T YA KNOW?
HUH!? I WAS!?
HMMM...
I DON'T REMEMBER IT AT ALL...
SFX: WASHI (TOUSLE) WASHI
BY THE WAY, RYUUKOU...
OH. YES?
...ABOUT THE REASON I CALLED YA HERE ALL THE WAY FROM THE CAPITAL.
I WILL DO WHATEVER I CAN.
I KNOW IT'S SHORT NOTICE, BUT...

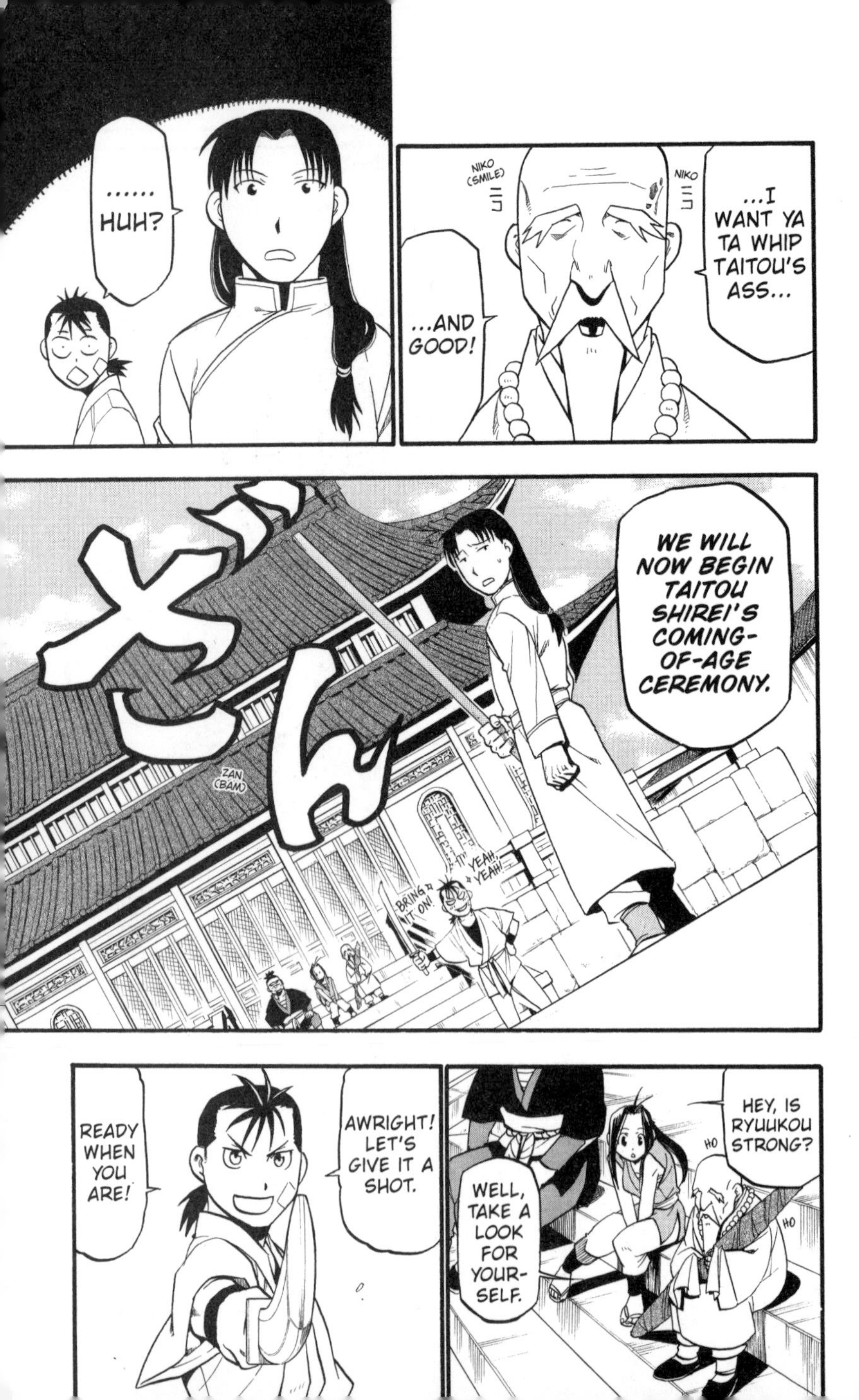
NIKO (SMILE)
NIKO
...I WANT YA TA WHIP TAITOU'S ASS...
...AND GOOD!
...... HUH?
WE WILL NOW BEGIN TAITOU SHIREI'S COMING-OF-AGE CEREMONY.
ZAN (BAM)
YEAH, YEAH!
BRING IT ON!
HEY, IS RYUUKOU STRONG?
HO
HO
WELL, TAKE A LOOK FOR YOURSELF.
AWRIGHT! LET'S GIVE IT A SHOT.
READY WHEN YOU ARE!

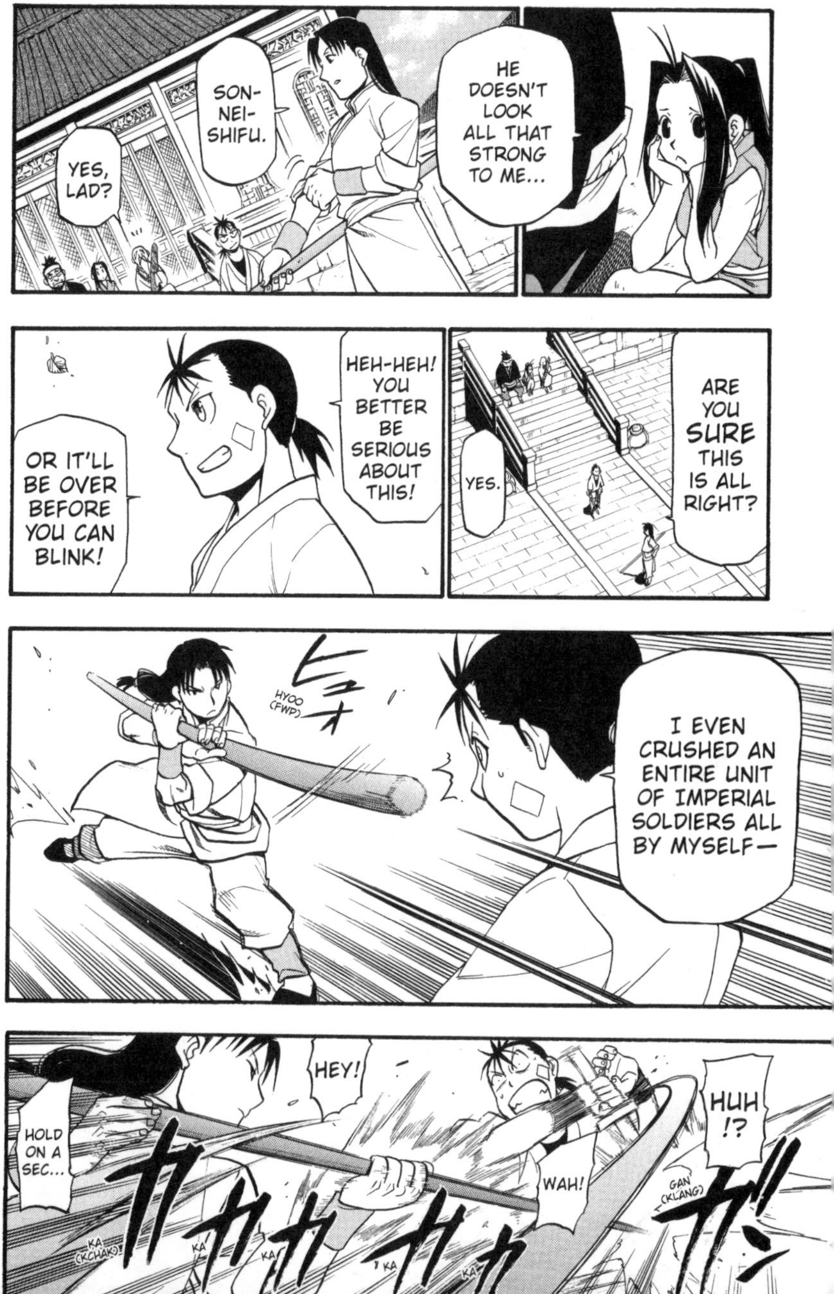
HE DOESN'T LOOK ALL THAT STRONG TO ME...
SON-NEI-SHIFU.
YES, LAD?
ARE YOU SURE THIS IS ALL RIGHT?
YES.
HEH-HEH! YOU BETTER BE SERIOUS ABOUT THIS!
OR IT'LL BE OVER BEFORE YOU CAN BLINK!
I EVEN CRUSHED AN ENTIRE UNIT OF IMPERIAL SOLDIERS ALL BY MYSELF—
HYOO (FWP)
HUH!?
GAN (KLANG)
WAH!
HEY!
HOLD ON A SEC...
KA
KA
KA
KA
KA (KCHAK)!

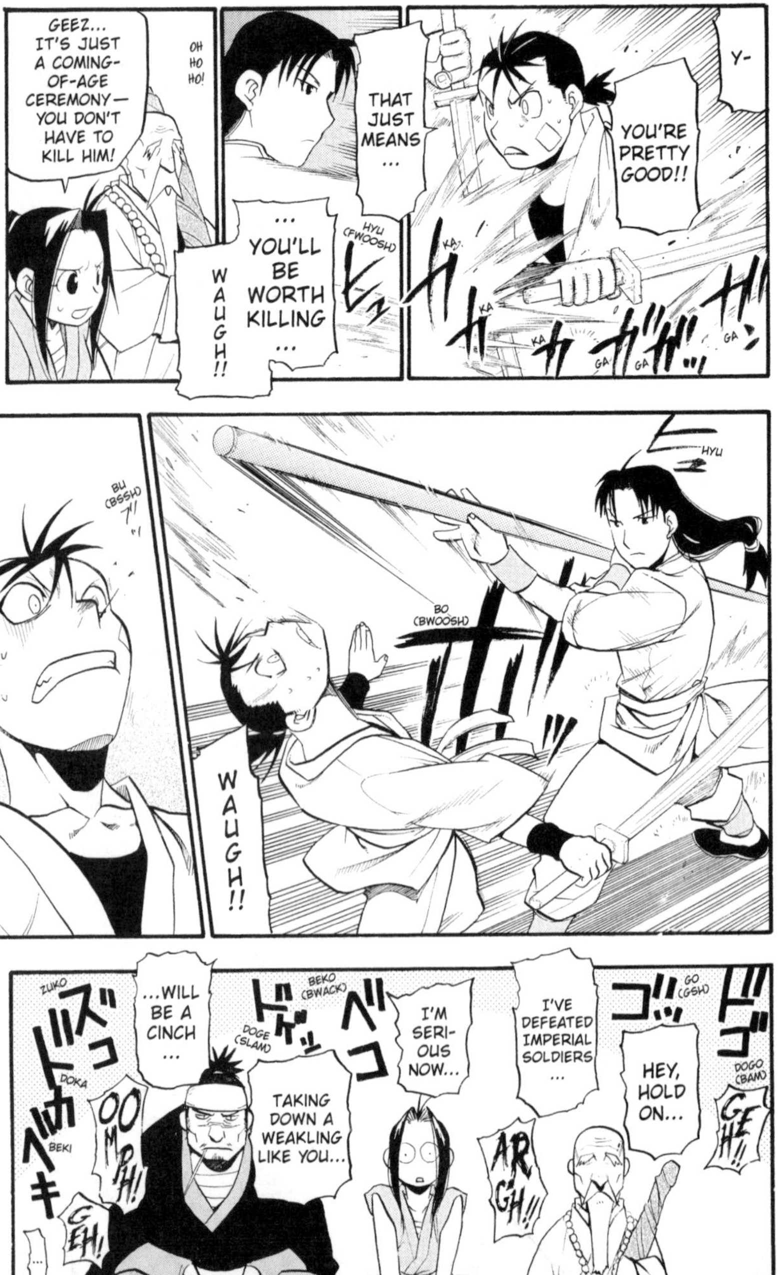
Y-
YOU'RE PRETTY GOOD!!
KA
KA
KA
GA
GA
GA
THAT JUST MEANS ...
... YOU'LL BE WORTH KILLING ...
HYU (FWOOSH)
WAUGH!!
OH HO HO!
GEEZ... IT'S JUST A COMING-OF-AGE CEREMONY— YOU DON'T HAVE TO KILL HIM!
HYU
BO (BWOOSH)
WAUGH!!
BU (BSSH)
DOGO (BAM)
GO (GSH)
GEH!!
HEY, HOLD ON...
I'VE DEFEATED IMPERIAL SOLDIERS ...
ARGH!!
I'M SERIOUS NOW...
BEKO (BWACK)
DOGE (SLAM)
TAKING DOWN A WEAKLING LIKE YOU...
...WILL BE A CINCH ...
ZUKO
DOKA
OOMPH!
BEKI
GEH!
...

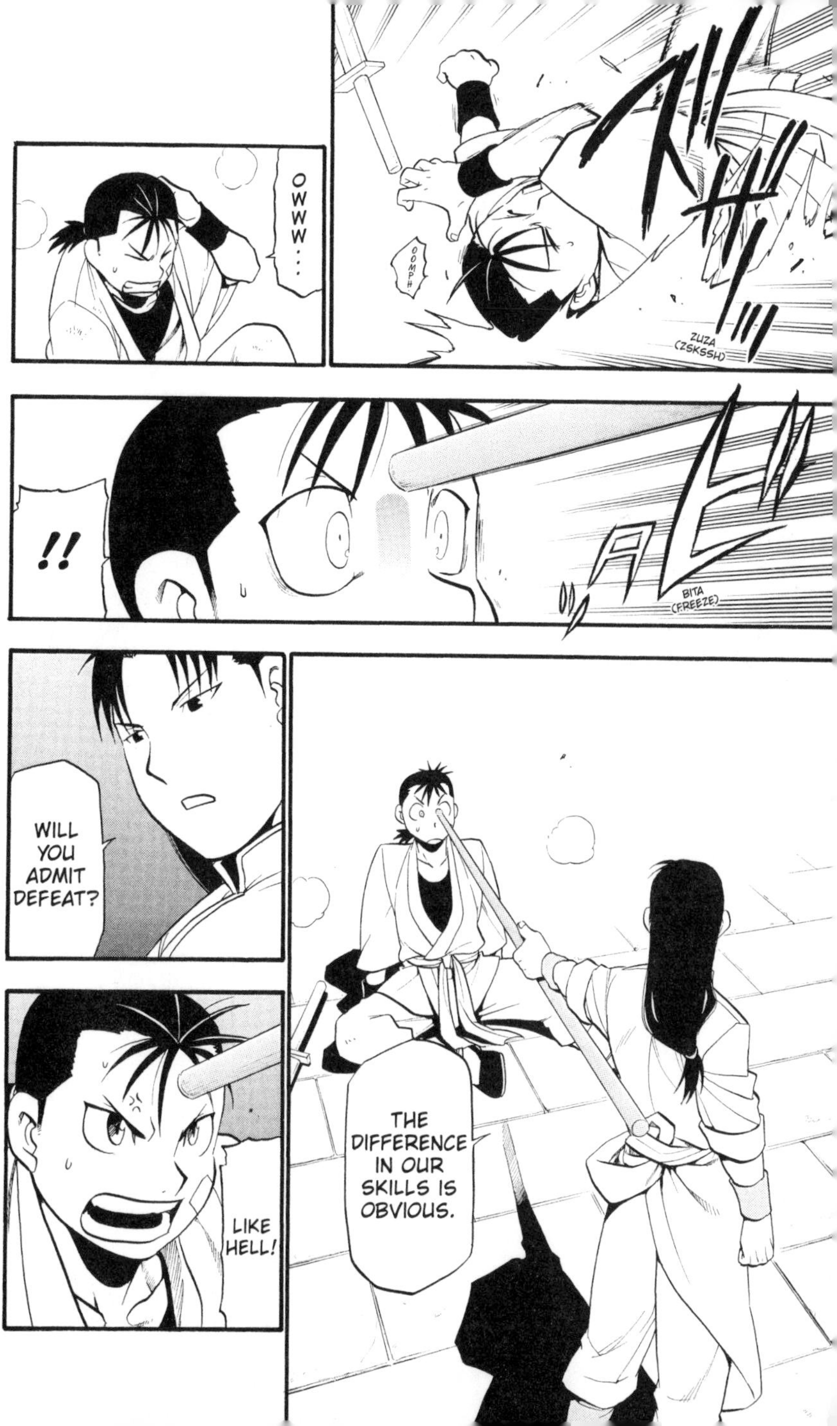
OOMPH
ZUZA (ZSKSSH)
OWWW...
!!
BITA (FREEZE)
THE DIFFERENCE IN OUR SKILLS IS OBVIOUS.
WILL YOU ADMIT DEFEAT?
LIKE HELL!

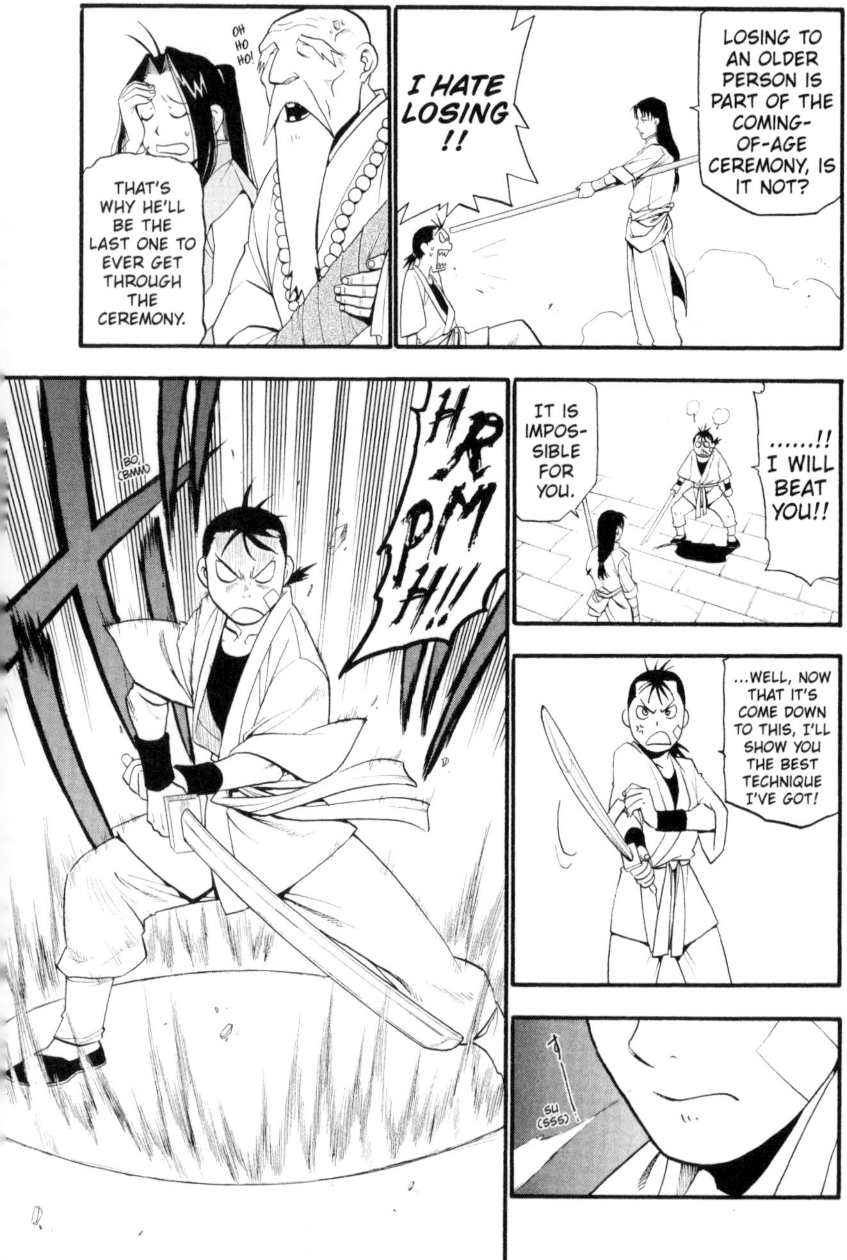
LOSING TO AN OLDER PERSON IS PART OF THE COMING-OF-AGE CEREMONY, IS IT NOT?
I HATE LOSING!!
OH HO HO!
THAT'S WHY HE'LL BE THE LAST ONE TO EVER GET THROUGH THE CEREMONY.
IT IS IMPOSSIBLE FOR YOU.
......!! I WILL BEAT YOU!!
...WELL, NOW THAT IT'S COME DOWN TO THIS, I'LL SHOW YOU THE BEST TECHNIQUE I'VE GOT!
SU (SSS)
HRPMPH!!
BO (BMM)

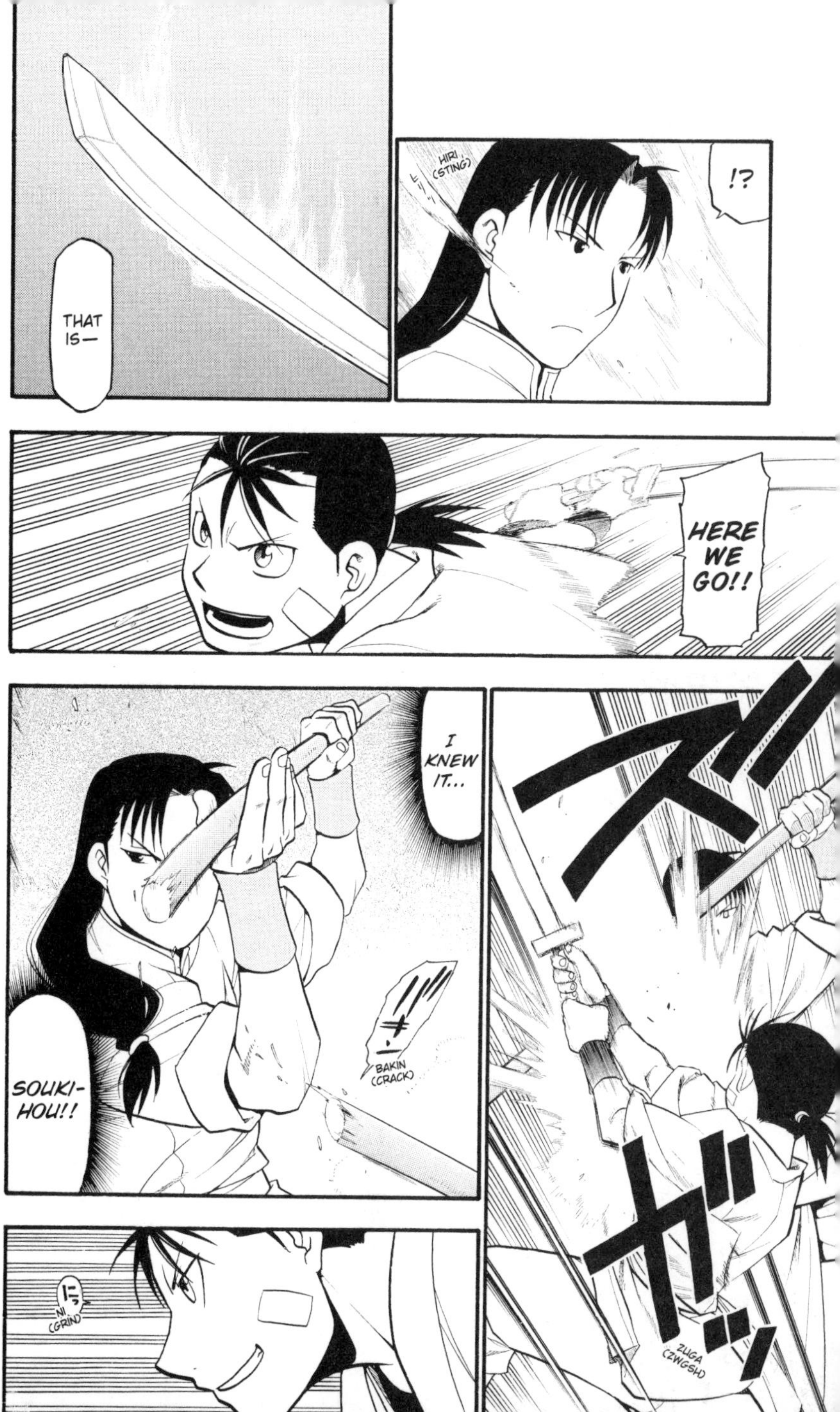
HIRI (STING)
!?
THAT IS—
HERE WE GO!!
ZUGA (ZWGSH)
I KNEW IT...
BAKIN (CRACK)
SOUKI-HOU!!
NI (GRIN)

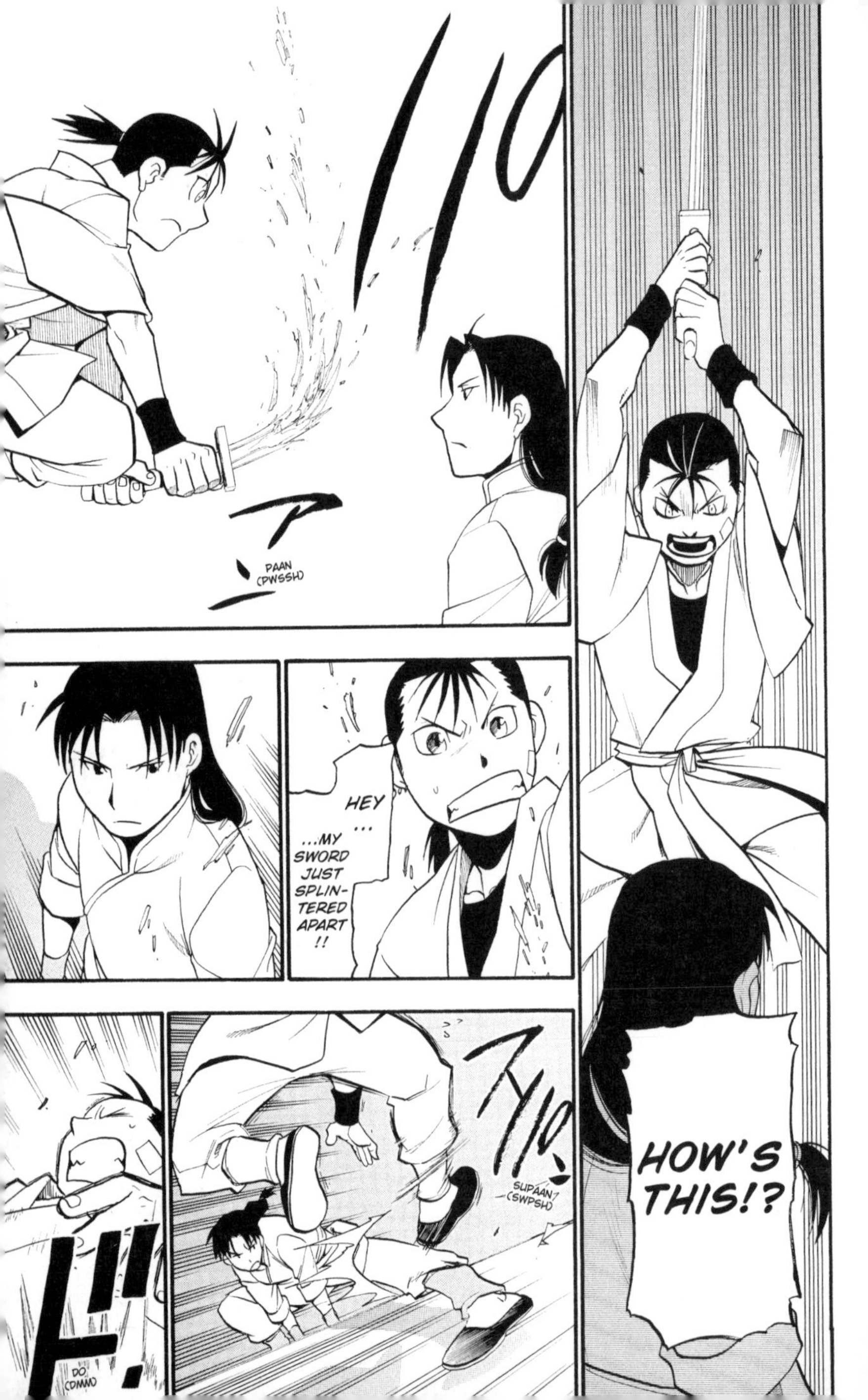
HOW'S THIS!?
PAAN (PWSSH)
HEY ...
...MY SWORD JUST SPLINTERED APART!!
SUPAAN (SWPSH)
DO (DMMM)

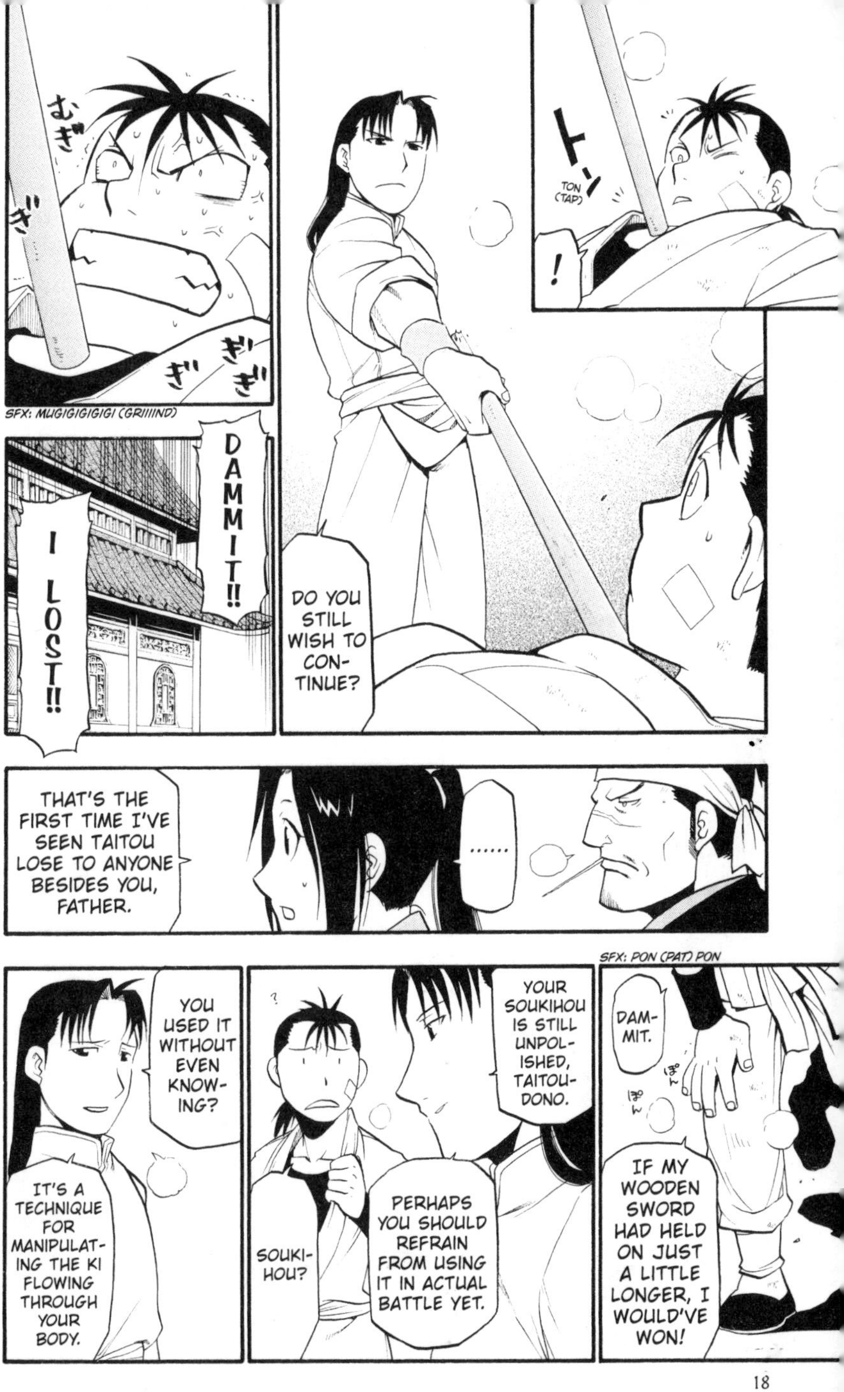
トッ
TON (TAP)
!
DO YOU STILL WISH TO CON-TINUE?
むぎぎ
ぎぎぎ
SFX: MUGIGIGIGIGI (GRIIIND)
DAMMIT!!
I LOST!!
......
THAT'S THE FIRST TIME I'VE SEEN TAITOU LOSE TO ANYONE BESIDES YOU, FATHER.
SFX: PON (PAT) PON
DAM-MIT.
ぽん
ぽん
IF MY WOODEN SWORD HAD HELD ON JUST A LITTLE LONGER, I WOULD'VE WON!
?
YOUR SOUKIHOU IS STILL UNPOL-ISHED, TAITOU-DONO.
PERHAPS YOU SHOULD REFRAIN FROM USING IT IN ACTUAL BATTLE YET.
SOUKI-HOU?
YOU USED IT WITHOUT EVEN KNOW-ING?
IT'S A TECHNIQUE FOR MANIPULAT-ING THE KI FLOWING THROUGH YOUR BODY.

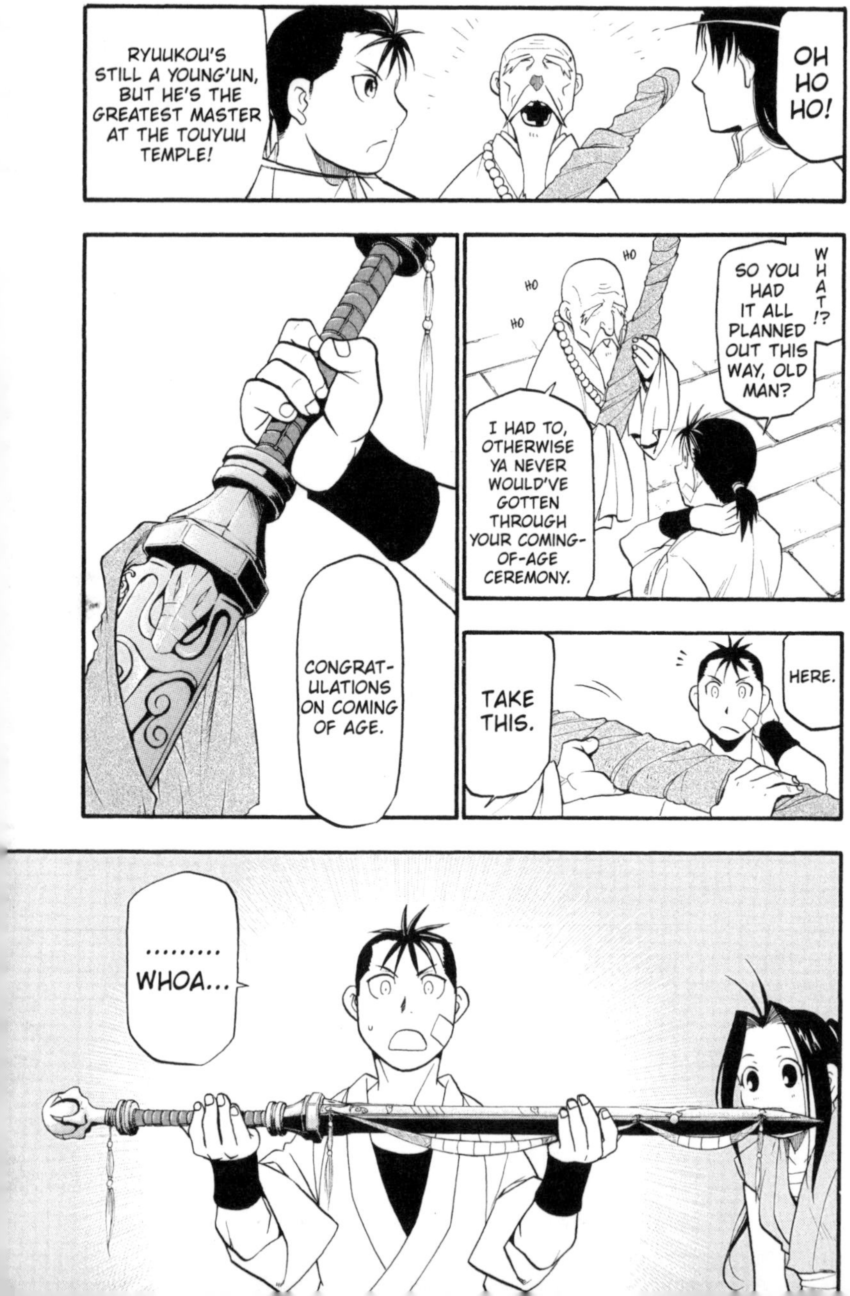
OH HO HO!
RYUUKOU'S STILL A YOUNG'UN, BUT HE'S THE GREATEST MASTER AT THE TOUYUU TEMPLE!
WHAT!?
SO YOU HAD IT ALL PLANNED OUT THIS WAY, OLD MAN?
HO HO HO
I HAD TO, OTHERWISE YA NEVER WOULD'VE GOTTEN THROUGH YOUR COMING-OF-AGE CEREMONY.
HERE.
TAKE THIS.
CONGRAT-ULATIONS ON COMING OF AGE.
.... WHOA...

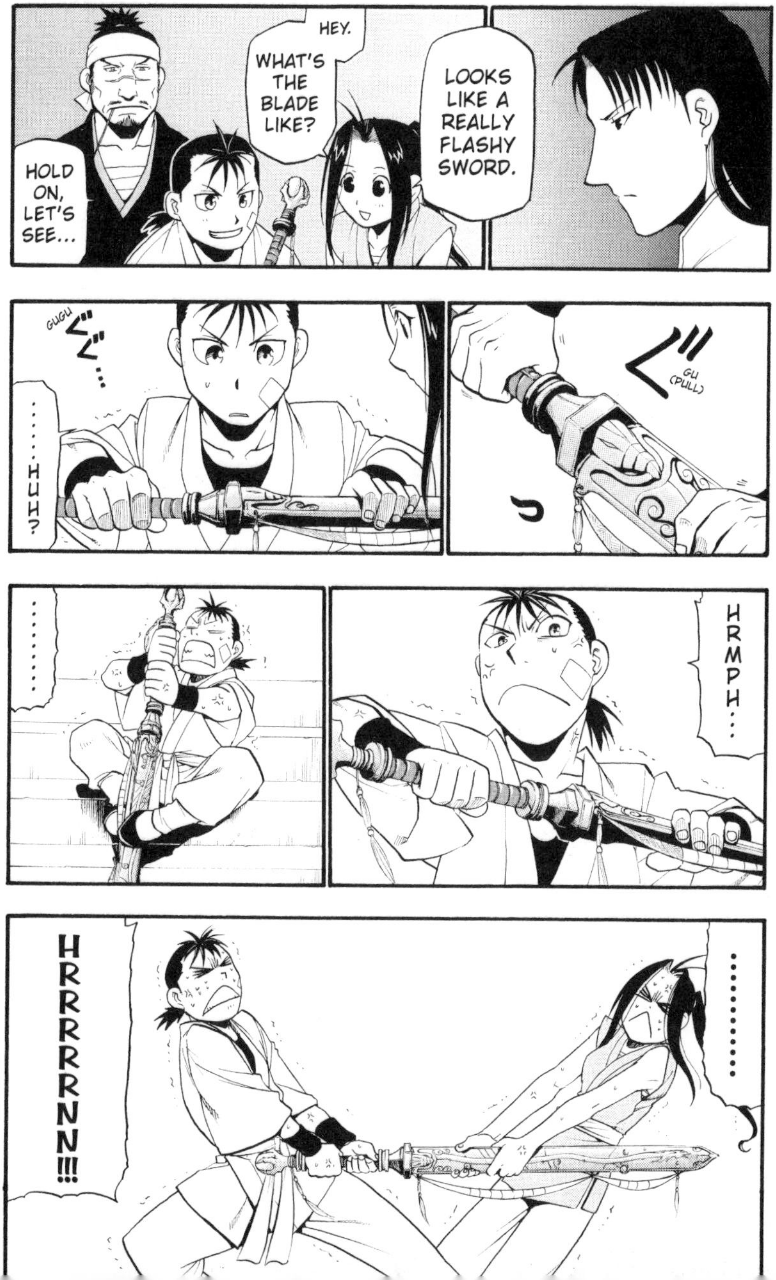
LOOKS LIKE A REALLY FLASHY SWORD.
HEY.
WHAT'S THE BLADE LIKE?
HOLD ON, LET'S SEE...
GU (PULL)
GUGU
......HUH?
HRMPH...
....
....
HRRRRRNN!!!

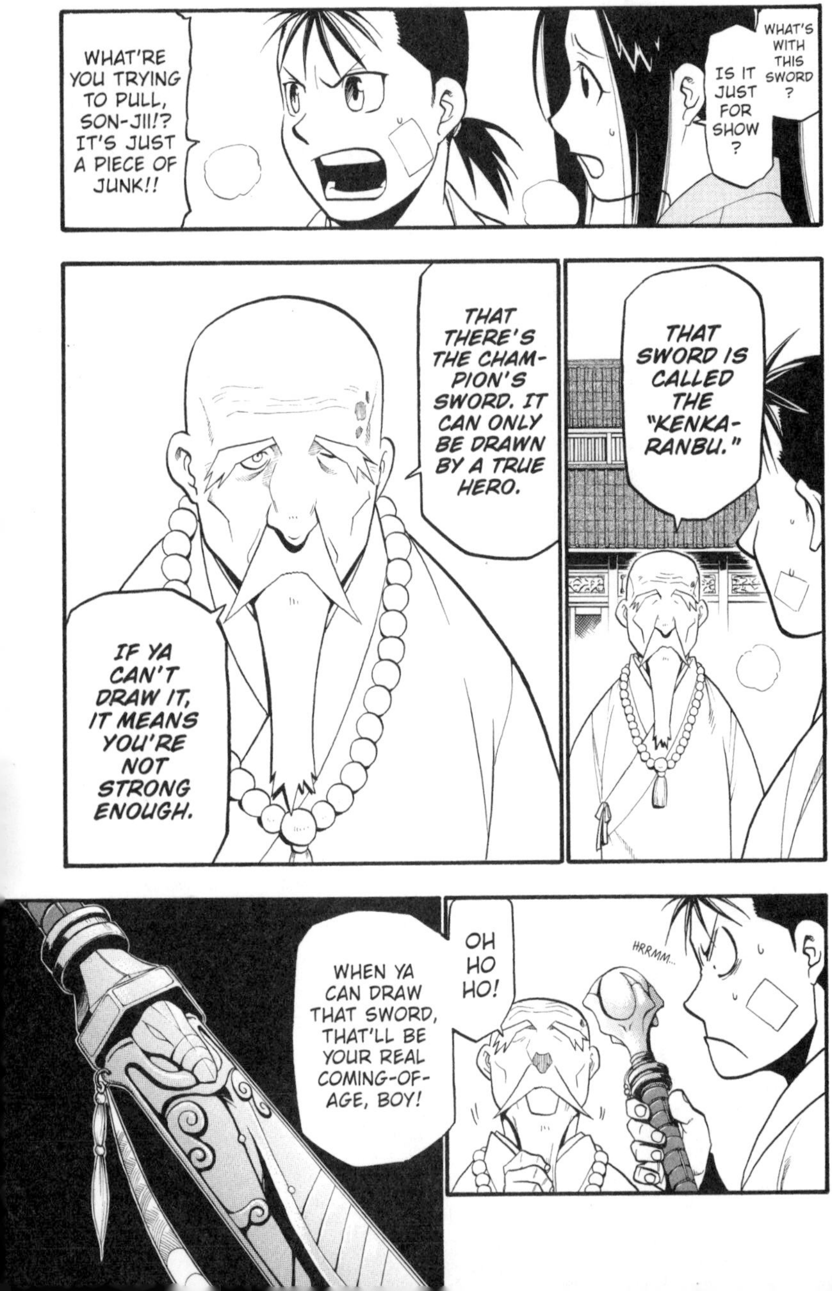
WHAT'S WITH THIS SWORD?
IS IT JUST FOR SHOW?
WHAT'RE YOU TRYING TO PULL, SON-JII!? IT'S JUST A PIECE OF JUNK!!
THAT SWORD IS CALLED THE "KENKA-RANBU."
THAT THERE'S THE CHAMPION'S SWORD. IT CAN ONLY BE DRAWN BY A TRUE HERO.
IF YA CAN'T DRAW IT, IT MEANS YOU'RE NOT STRONG ENOUGH.
HRRMM...
OH HO HO!
WHEN YA CAN DRAW THAT SWORD, THAT'LL BE YOUR REAL COMING-OF-AGE, BOY!

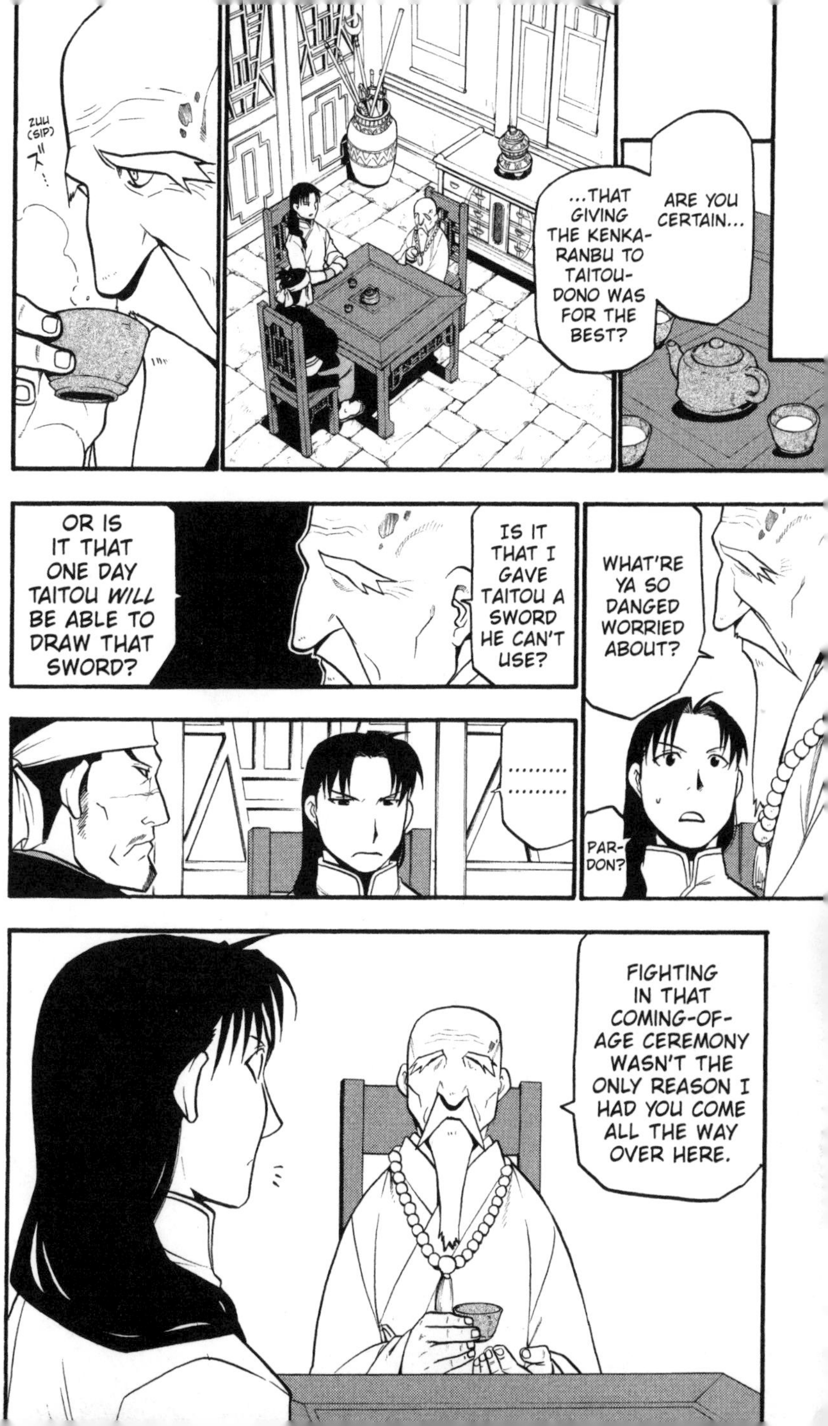
ARE YOU CERTAIN...
...THAT GIVING THE KENKA-RANBU TO TAITOU-DONO WAS FOR THE BEST?
ZUU (SIP)
ズ
WHAT'RE YA SO DANGED WORRIED ABOUT?
PARDON?
IS IT THAT I GAVE TAITOU A SWORD HE CAN'T USE?
OR IS IT THAT ONE DAY TAITOU *WILL* BE ABLE TO DRAW THAT SWORD?
....
....
FIGHTING IN THAT COMING-OF-AGE CEREMONY WASN'T THE ONLY REASON I HAD YOU COME ALL THE WAY OVER HERE.

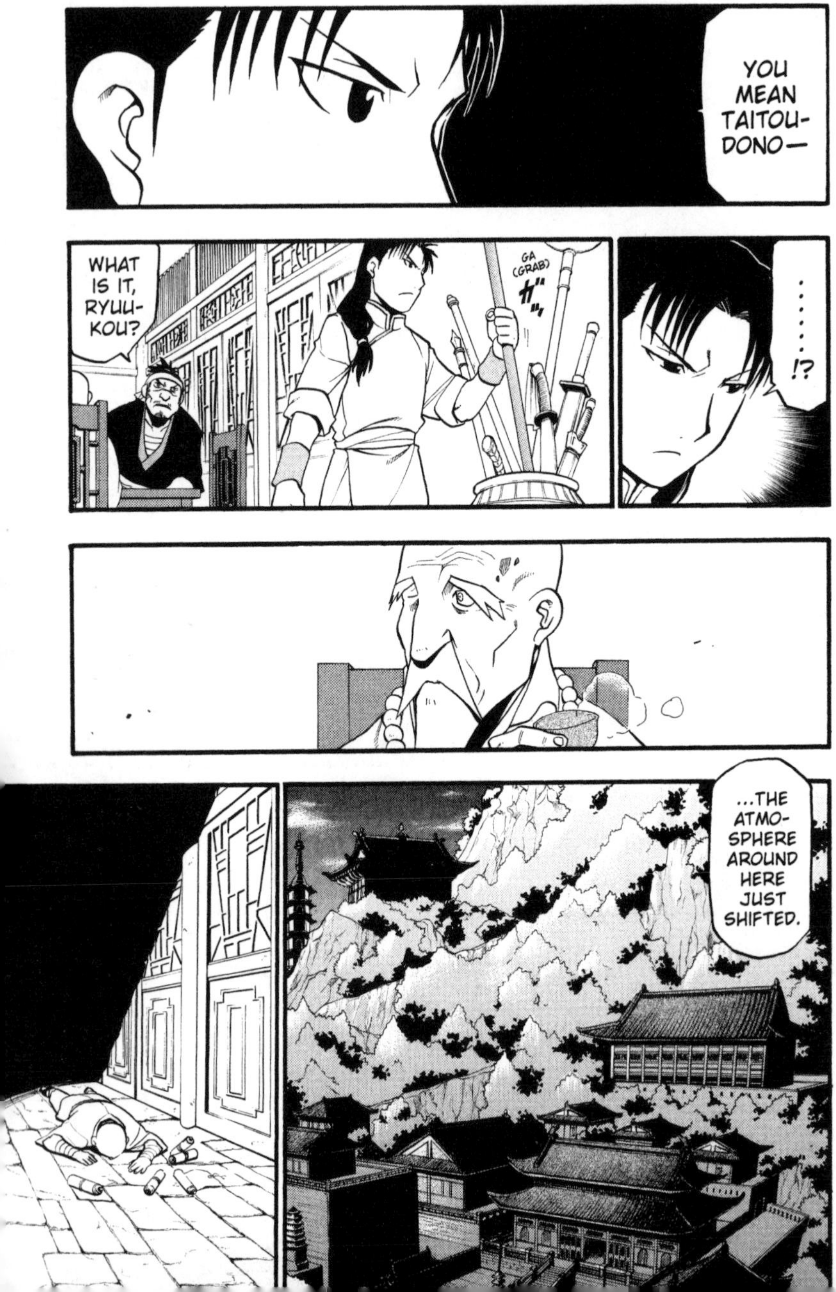
YOU MEAN TAITOU-DONO—
......!?
GA (GRAB)
ガッ
WHAT IS IT, RYUU-KOU?
...THE ATMOSPHERE AROUND HERE JUST SHIFTED.

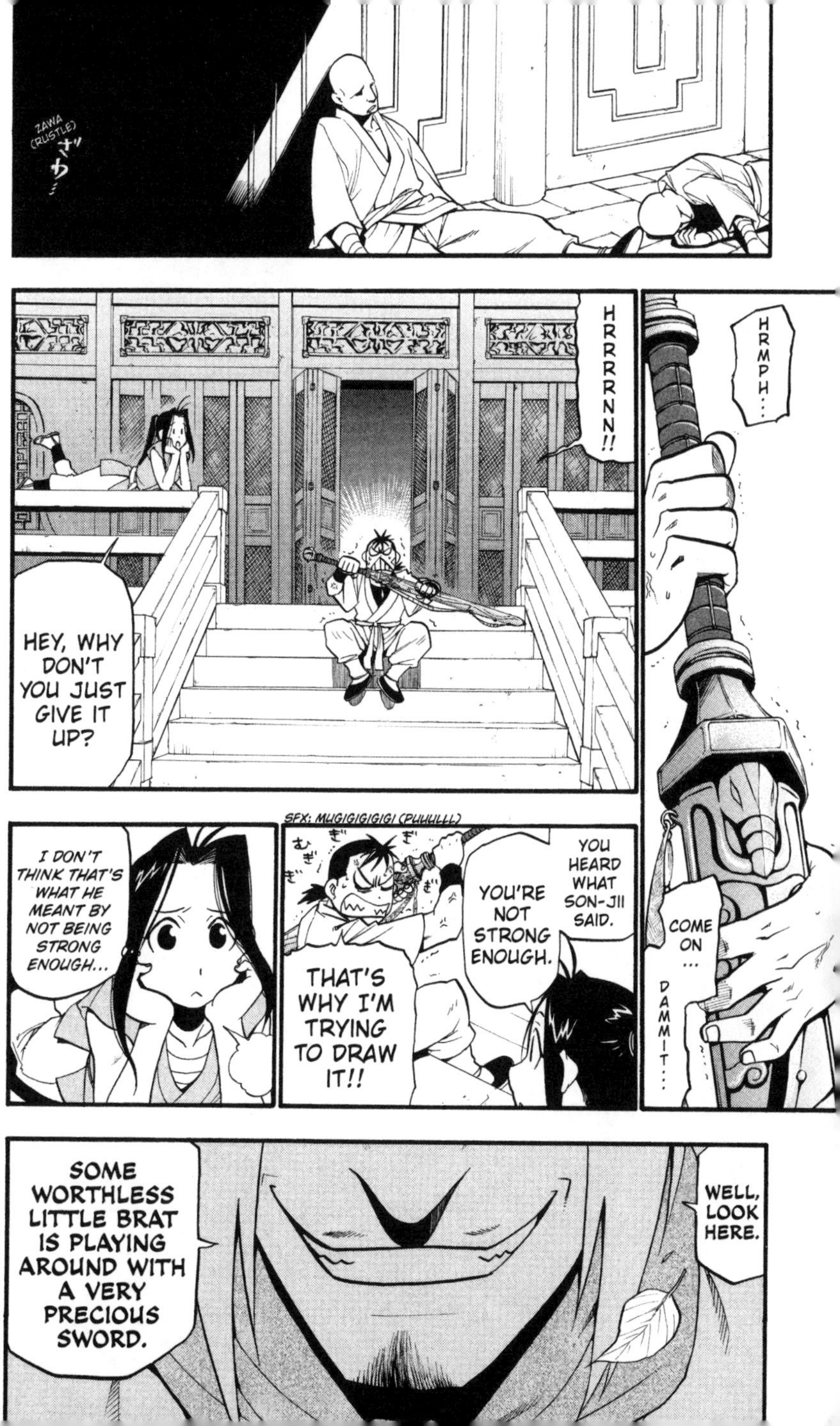
ZAWA (RUSTLE)
ざわ…
HRMPH…
COME ON… DAMMIT…
HRRRRNN!!
HEY, WHY DON'T YOU JUST GIVE IT UP?
SFX: MUGIGIGIGIGI (PUUULLL)
YOU HEARD WHAT SON-JII SAID.
YOU'RE NOT STRONG ENOUGH.
THAT'S WHY I'M TRYING TO DRAW IT!!
I DON'T THINK THAT'S WHAT HE MEANT BY NOT BEING STRONG ENOUGH…
WELL, LOOK HERE.
SOME WORTHLESS LITTLE BRAT IS PLAYING AROUND WITH A VERY PRECIOUS SWORD.

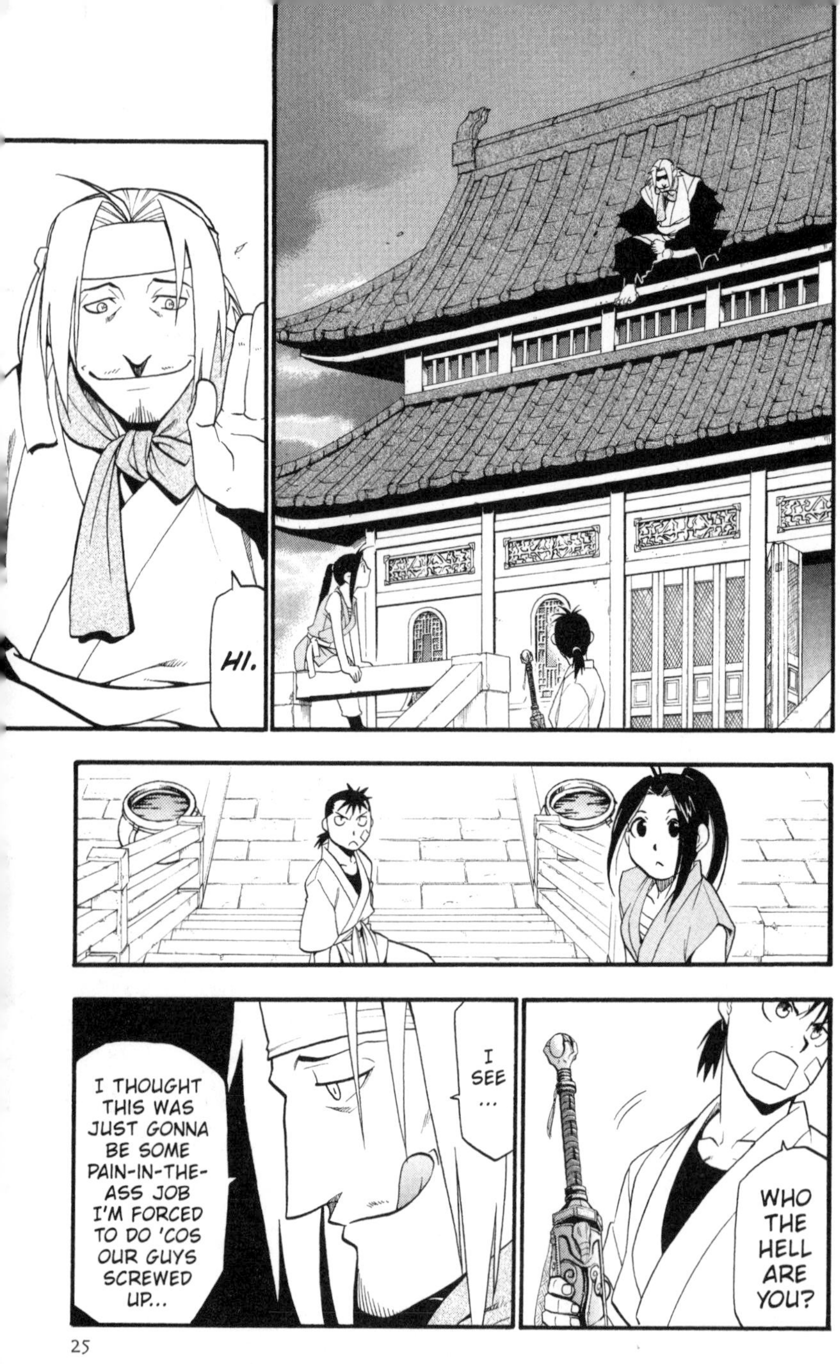
HI.
WHO THE HELL ARE YOU?
I SEE...
I THOUGHT THIS WAS JUST GONNA BE SOME PAIN-IN-THE-ASS JOB I'M FORCED TO DO 'COS OUR GUYS SCREWED UP...

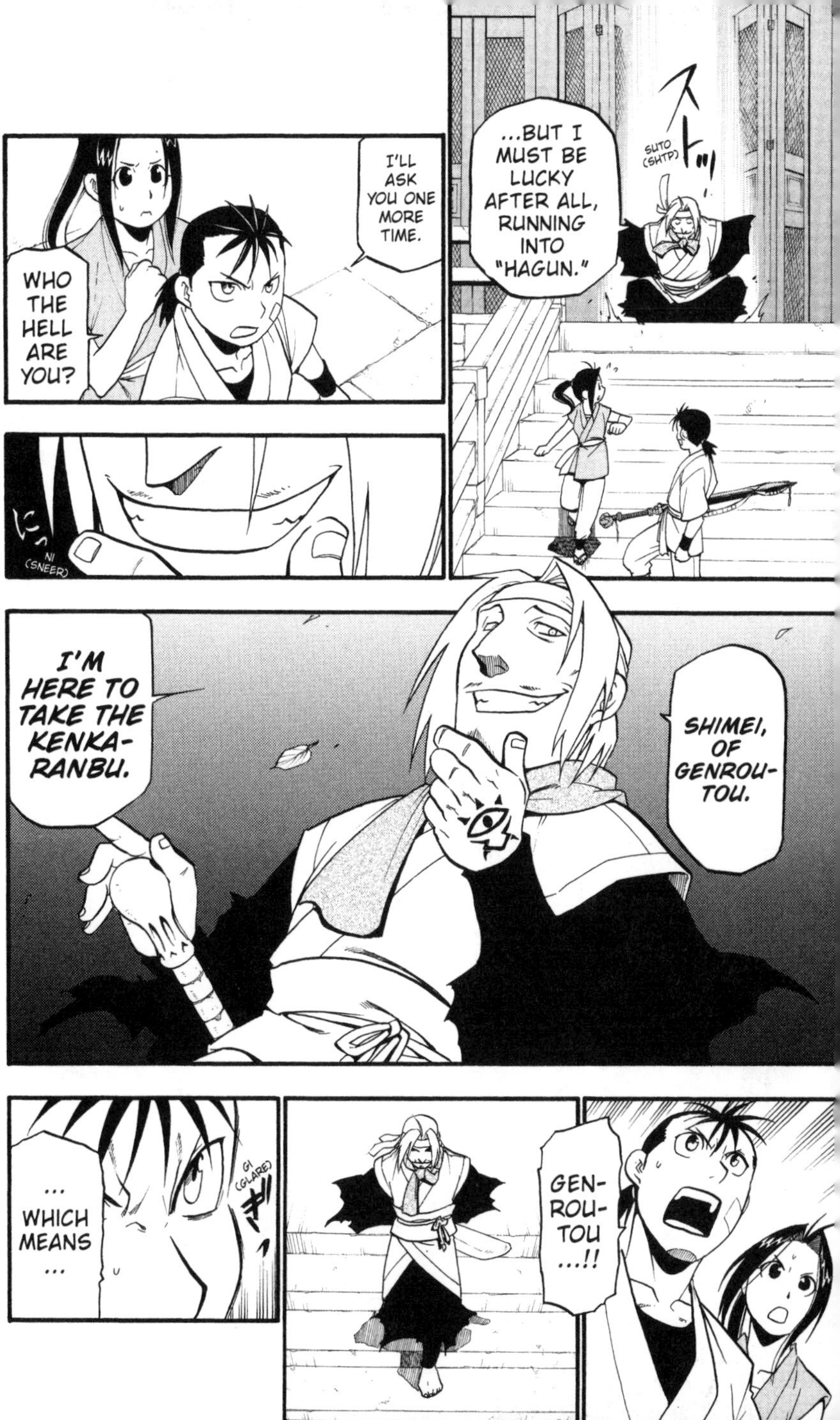
SUTO (SHTP)
...BUT I MUST BE LUCKY AFTER ALL, RUNNING INTO "HAGUN."
I'LL ASK YOU ONE MORE TIME.
WHO THE HELL ARE YOU?
NI (SNEER)
SHIMEI, OF GENROU-TOU.
I'M HERE TO TAKE THE KENKA-RANBU.
GEN-ROU-TOU ...!!
GI (GLARE)
... WHICH MEANS ...

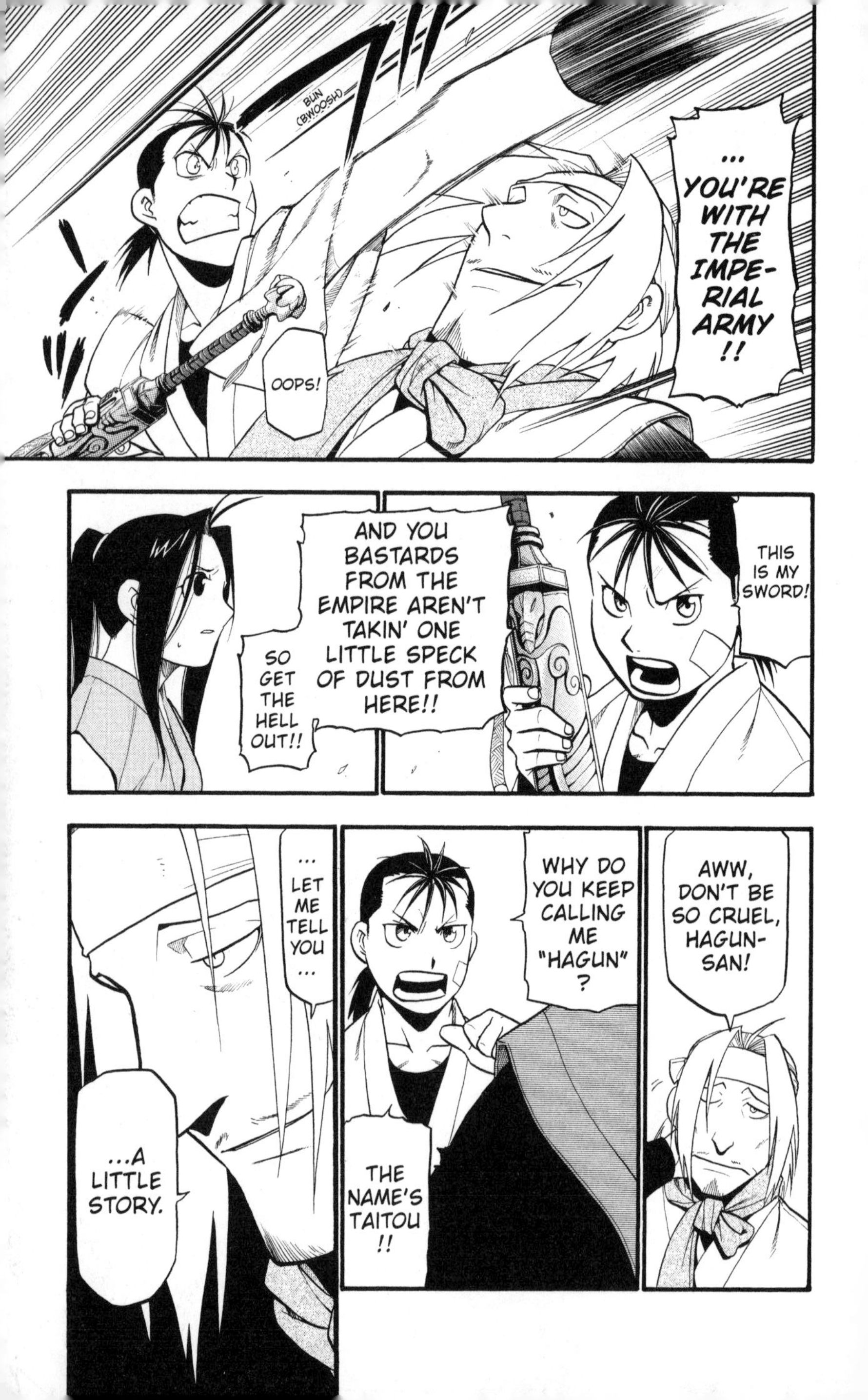
... YOU'RE WITH THE IMPERIAL ARMY !!
BUN (BWOOSH)
OOPS!
THIS IS MY SWORD!
AND YOU BASTARDS FROM THE EMPIRE AREN'T TAKIN' ONE LITTLE SPECK OF DUST FROM HERE!!
SO GET THE HELL OUT!!
AWW, DON'T BE SO CRUEL, HAGUN-SAN!
WHY DO YOU KEEP CALLING ME "HAGUN"?
THE NAME'S TAITOU!!
... LET ME TELL YOU ...
...A LITTLE STORY.

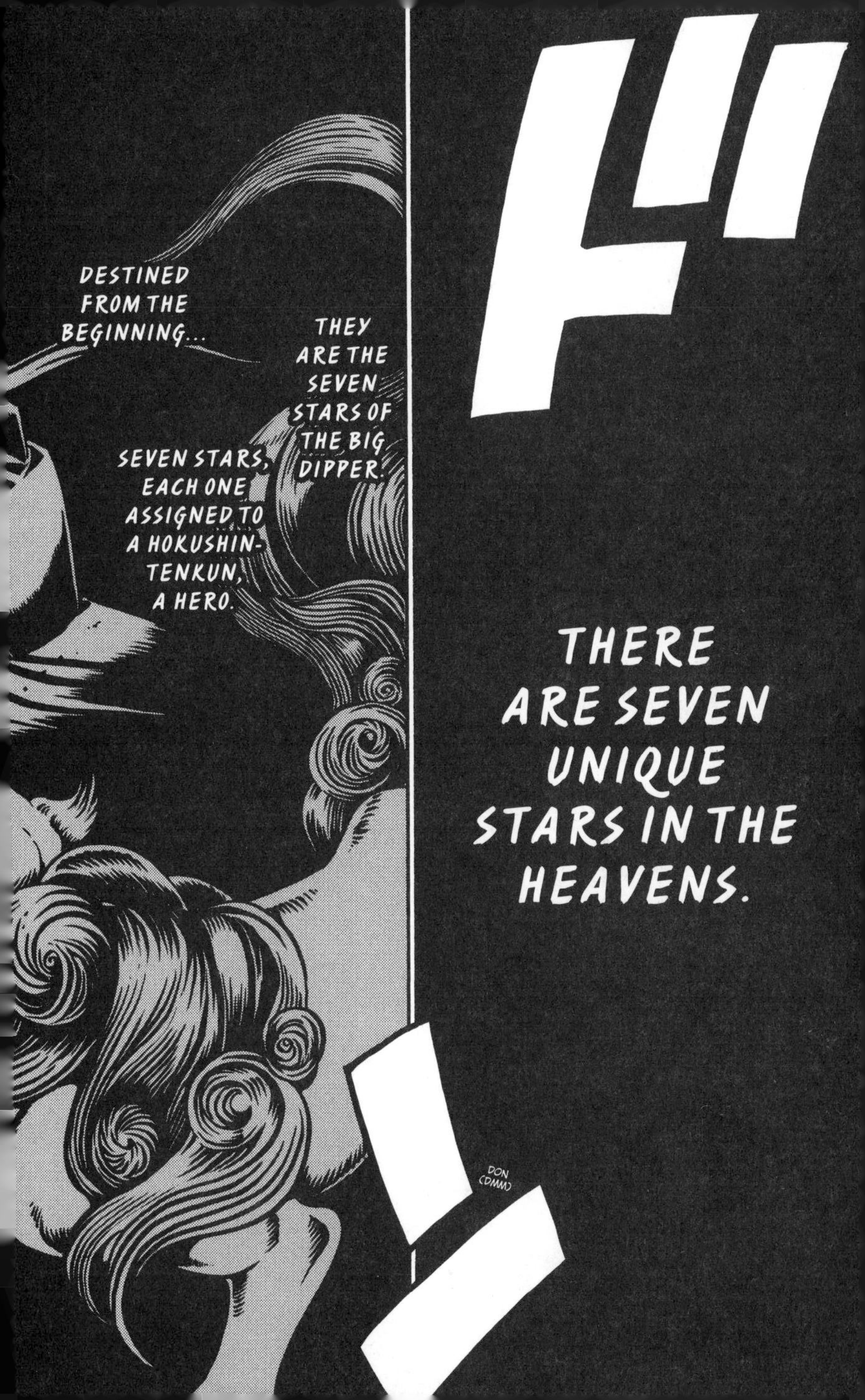
THERE ARE SEVEN UNIQUE STARS IN THE HEAVENS.
DON (DMM)
THEY ARE THE SEVEN STARS OF THE BIG DIPPER.
SEVEN STARS, EACH ONE ASSIGNED TO A HOKUSHIN-TENKUN, A HERO.
DESTINED FROM THE BEGINNING...

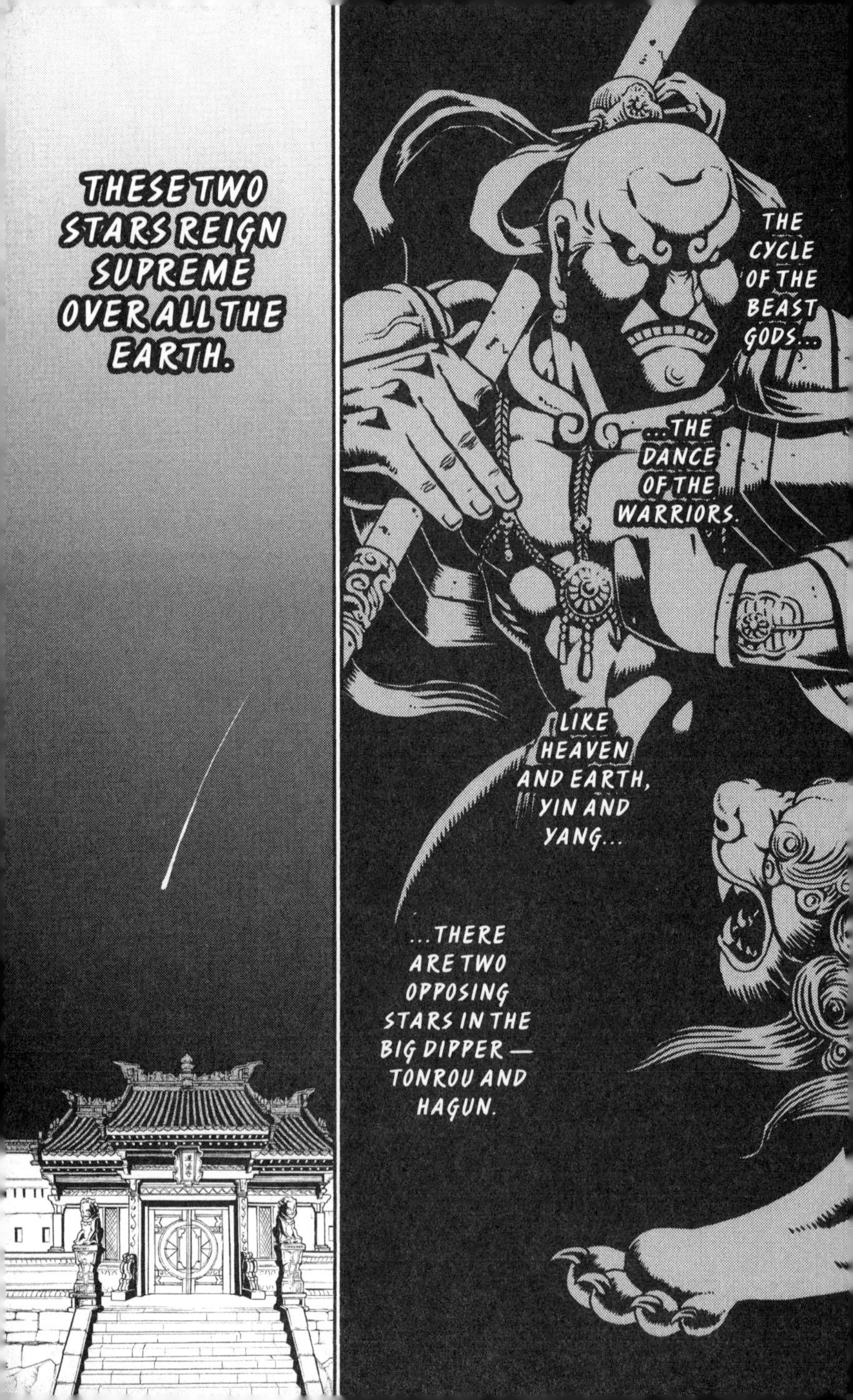
THE CYCLE OF THE BEAST GODS...
...THE DANCE OF THE WARRIORS.
LIKE HEAVEN AND EARTH, YIN AND YANG...
...THERE ARE TWO OPPOSING STARS IN THE BIG DIPPER— TONROU AND HAGUN.
THESE TWO STARS REIGN SUPREME OVER ALL THE EARTH.

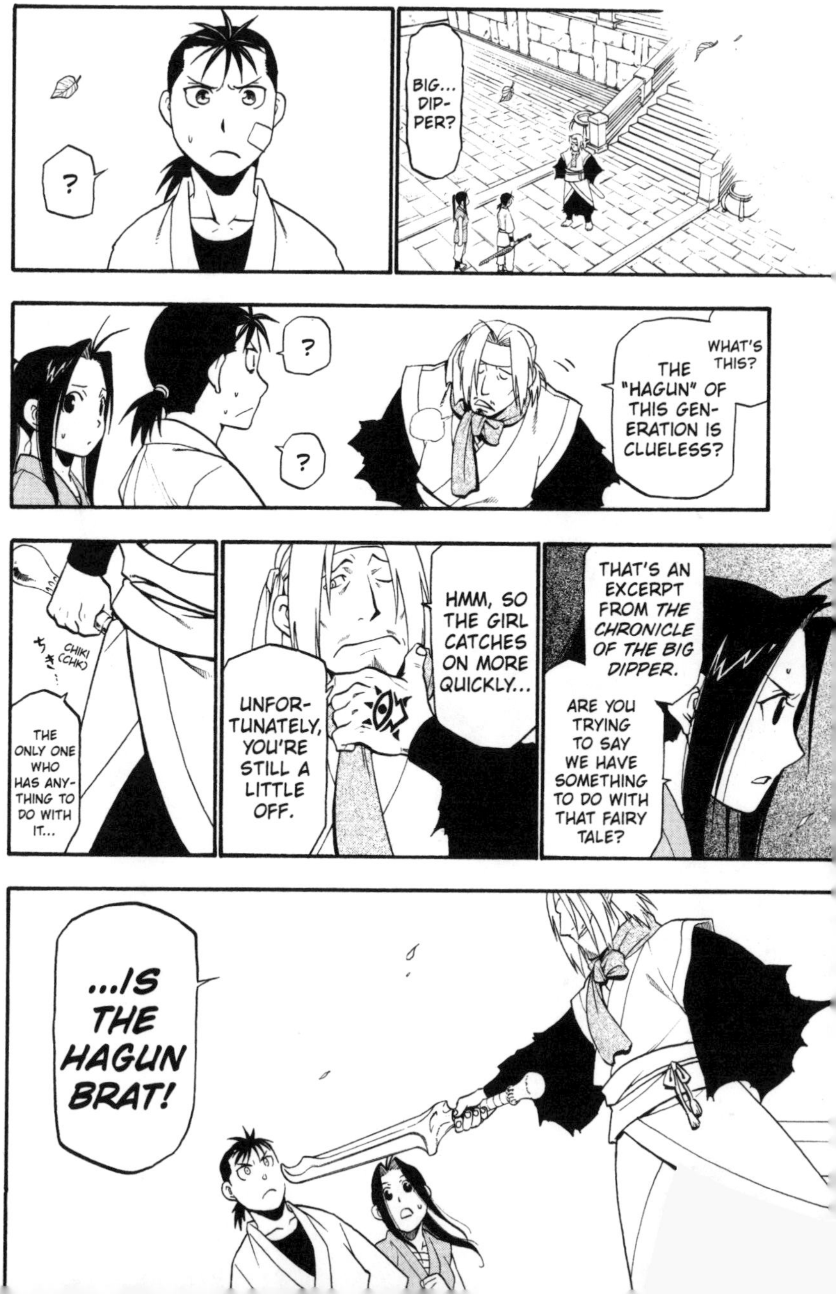
BIG... DIPPER?
?
WHAT'S THIS? THE "HAGUN" OF THIS GENERATION IS CLUELESS?
?
?
THAT'S AN EXCERPT FROM *THE CHRONICLE OF THE BIG DIPPER.*
ARE YOU TRYING TO SAY WE HAVE SOMETHING TO DO WITH THAT FAIRY TALE?
HMM, SO THE GIRL CATCHES ON MORE QUICKLY...
UNFORTUNATELY, YOU'RE STILL A LITTLE OFF.
ちき CHIKI (CHK)
THE ONLY ONE WHO HAS ANYTHING TO DO WITH IT...
...IS THE HAGUN BRAT!

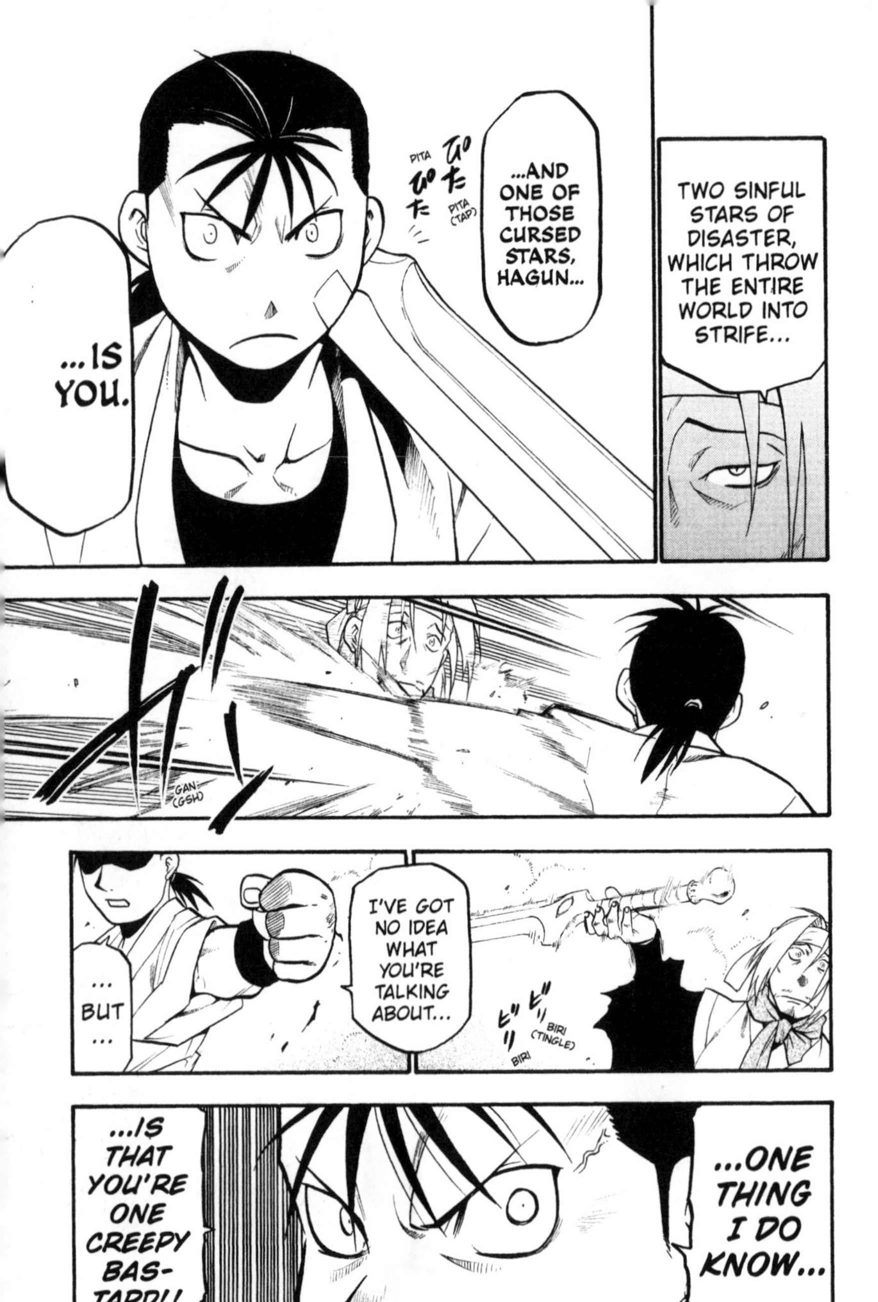
TWO SINFUL STARS OF DISASTER, WHICH THROW THE ENTIRE WORLD INTO STRIFE...
...AND ONE OF THOSE CURSED STARS, HAGUN...
ぴた ぴた
PITA PITA (TAP)
...IS YOU.
GAN (GSH)
ビリ ビリ
BIRI BIRI (TINGLE)
I'VE GOT NO IDEA WHAT YOU'RE TALKING ABOUT...
... BUT ...
...ONE THING I DO KNOW...
...IS THAT YOU'RE ONE CREEPY BAS-TARD!!

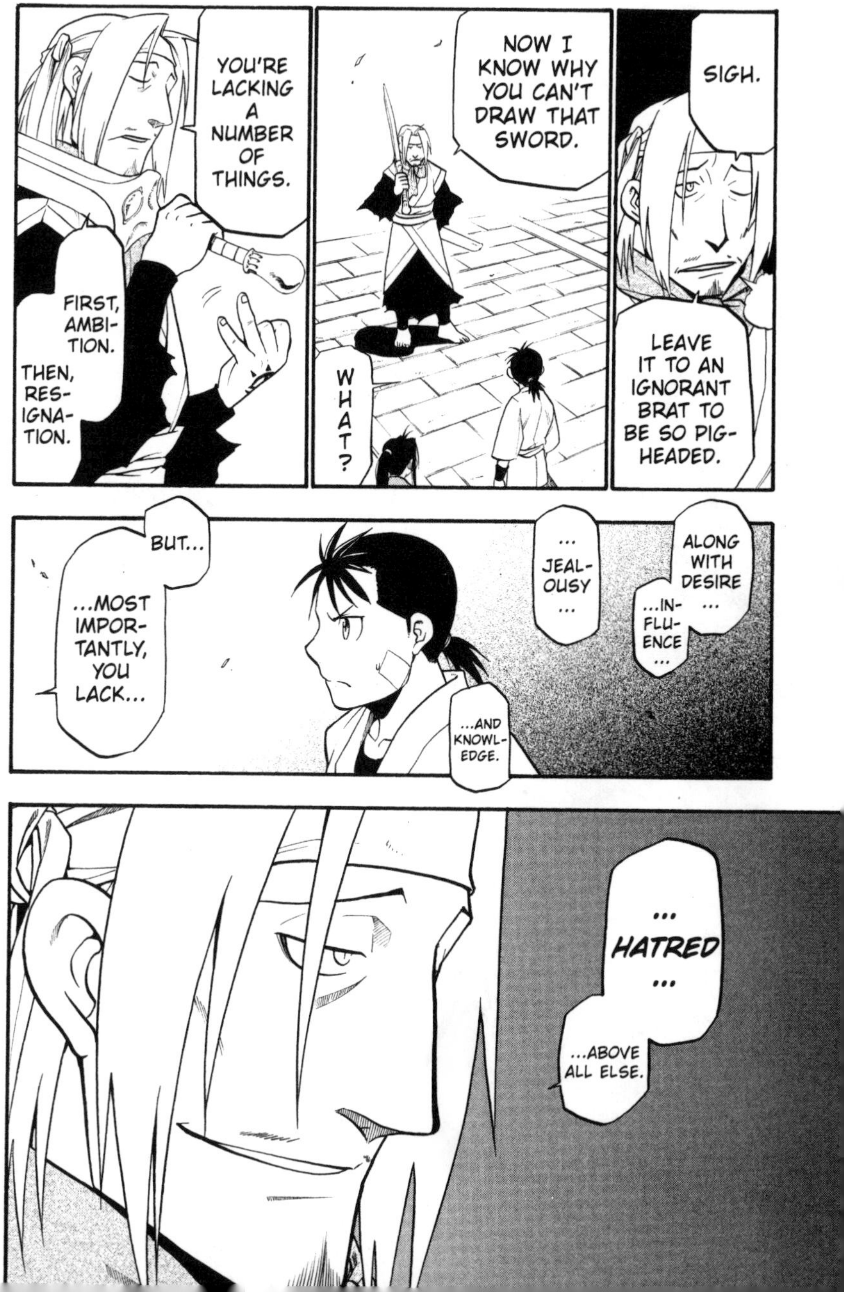
SIGH.
LEAVE IT TO AN IGNORANT BRAT TO BE SO PIG-HEADED.
NOW I KNOW WHY YOU CAN'T DRAW THAT SWORD.
WHAT?
YOU'RE LACKING A NUMBER OF THINGS.
FIRST, AMBITION.
THEN, RESIGNATION.
ALONG WITH DESIRE...
...INFLUENCE...
...JEALOUSY...
...AND KNOWLEDGE.
BUT...
...MOST IMPORTANTLY, YOU LACK...
...HATRED...
...ABOVE ALL ELSE.

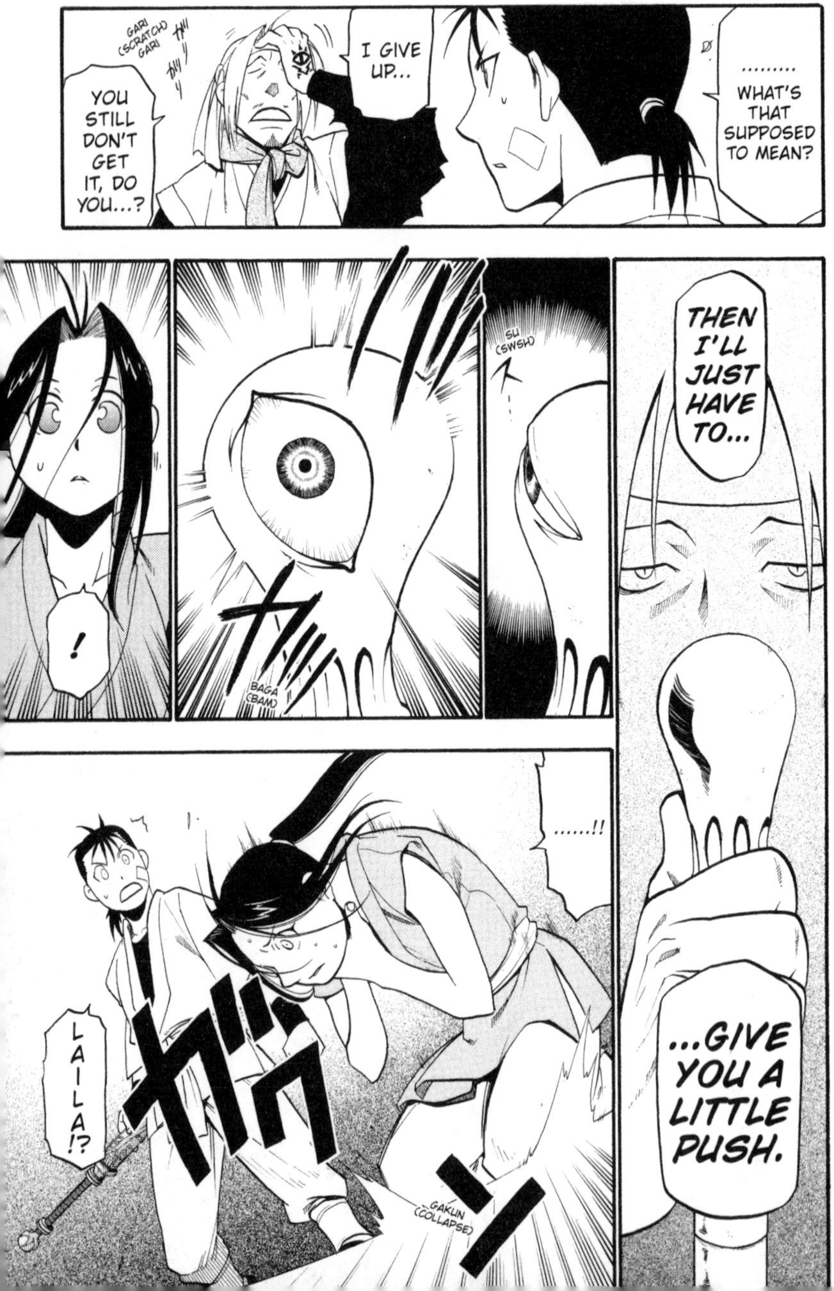
....
WHAT'S THAT SUPPOSED TO MEAN?
I GIVE UP...
GARI (SCRATCH) GARI
YOU STILL DON'T GET IT, DO YOU...?
THEN I'LL JUST HAVE TO...
...GIVE YOU A LITTLE PUSH.
SU (SWSH)
BAGA (BAM)
!
......!!
GAKUN (COLLAPSE)
LAILA!?

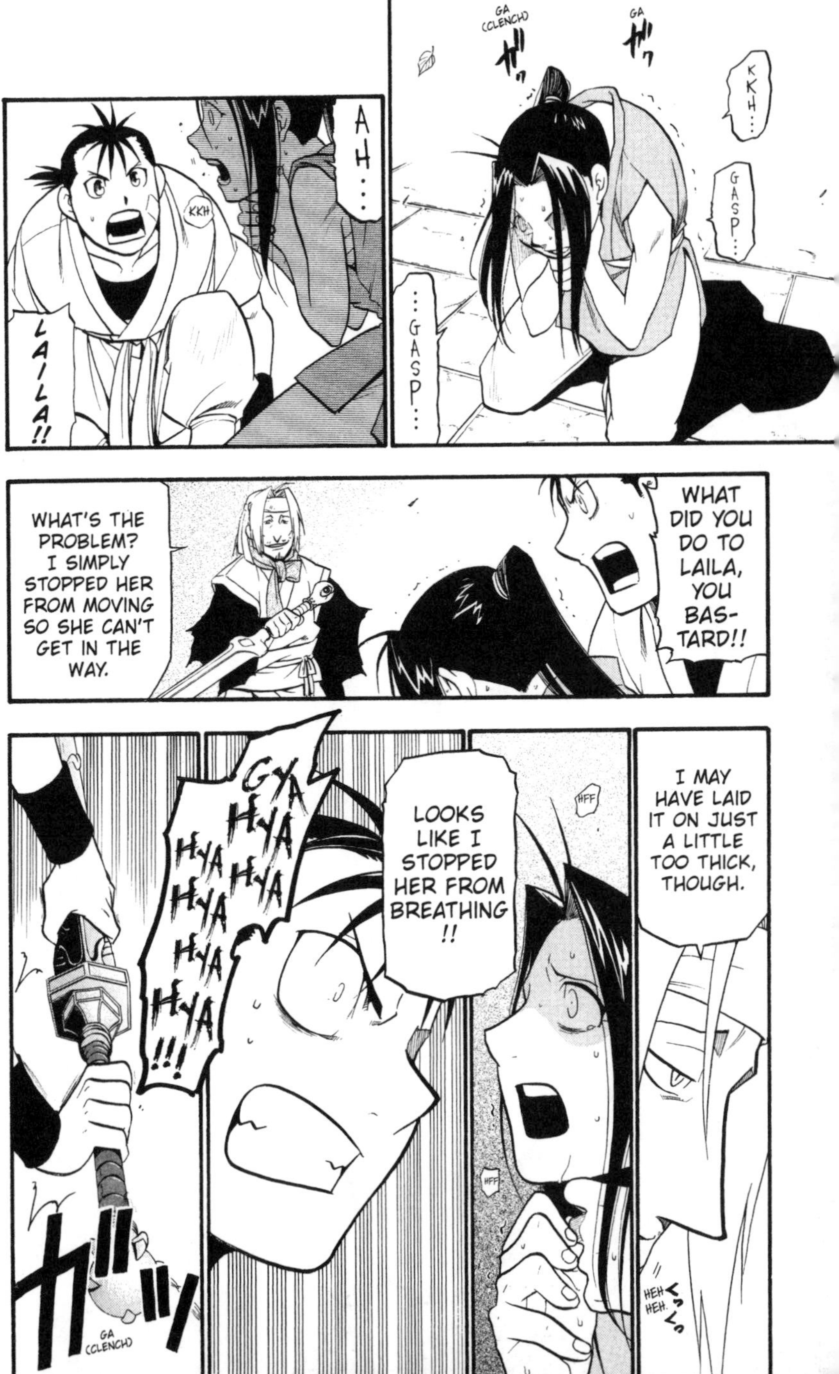
KKH...
GA
GASP...
GA (CLENCH)
...GASP...
AH...
KKH
LAILA!!
WHAT DID YOU DO TO LAILA, YOU BASTARD!!
WHAT'S THE PROBLEM? I SIMPLY STOPPED HER FROM MOVING SO SHE CAN'T GET IN THE WAY.
I MAY HAVE LAID IT ON JUST A LITTLE TOO THICK, THOUGH.
HEH HEH.
HFF
HFF
LOOKS LIKE I STOPPED HER FROM BREATHING!!
GYAHYA HYA HYA HYA HYA HYA HYA!!!
GA (CLENCH)

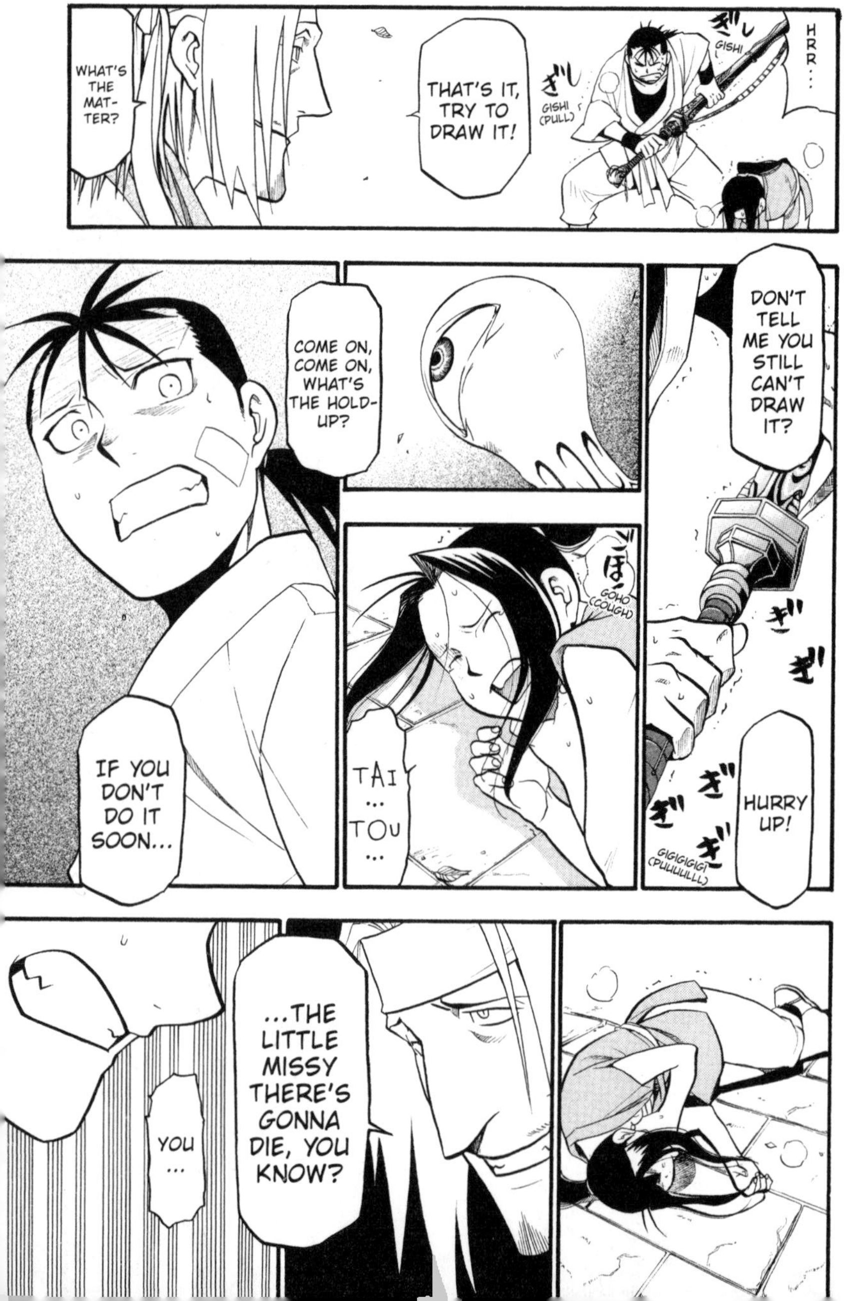
HRR...
GISHI
GISHI (PULL)
THAT'S IT, TRY TO DRAW IT!
WHAT'S THE MAT-TER?
DON'T TELL ME YOU STILL CAN'T DRAW IT?
GIGIGIGIGI (PULLLLLLL)
HURRY UP!
COME ON, COME ON, WHAT'S THE HOLD-UP?
GOHO (COUGH)
TAI... TOU...
IF YOU DON'T DO IT SOON...
...THE LITTLE MISSY THERE'S GONNA DIE, YOU KNOW?
YOU...

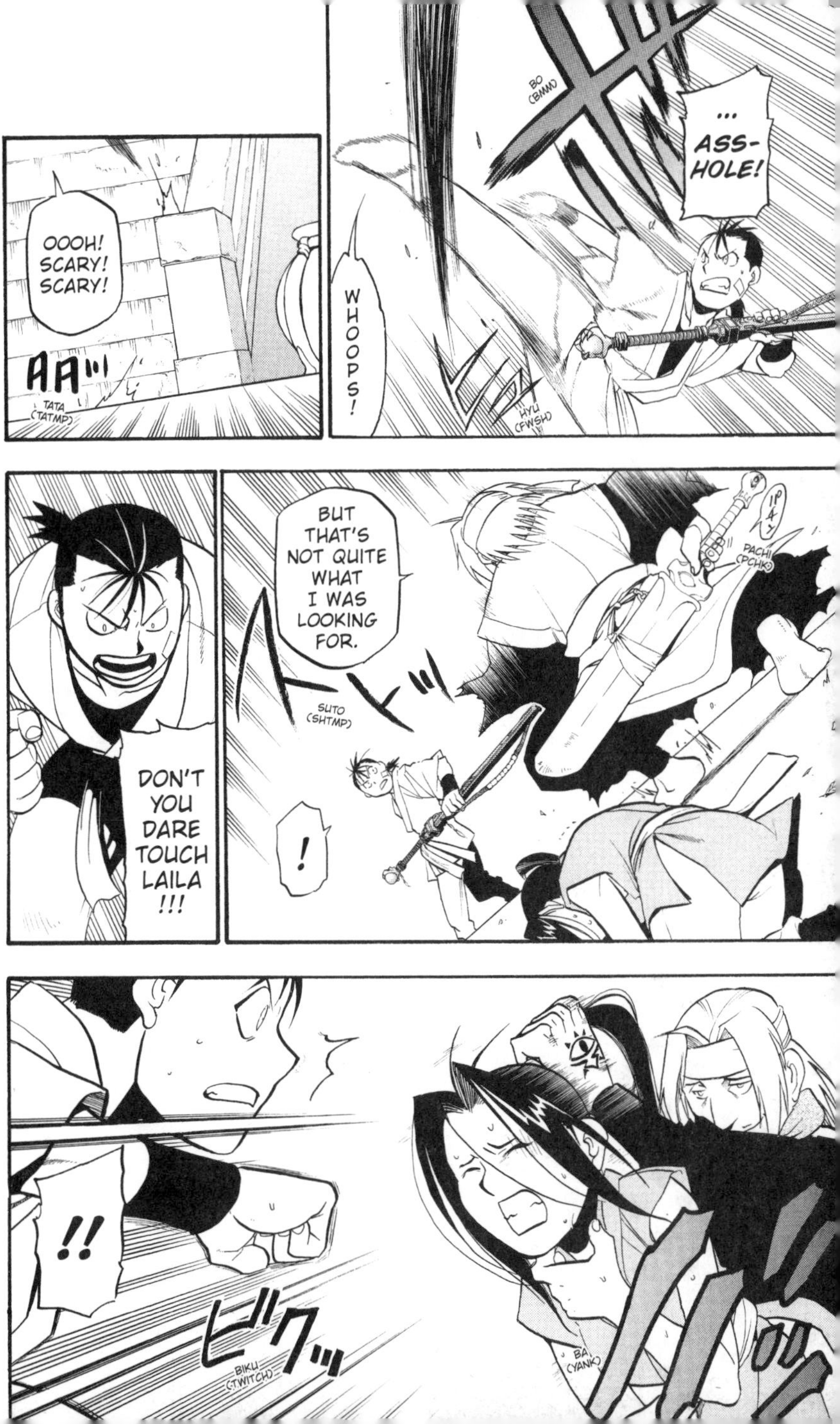

BO (BMM)
... ASS-HOLE!
WHOOPS!
HYU (FWSH)
OOOH! SCARY! SCARY!
TATA (TATMP)
PACHI (PCHK)
BUT THAT'S NOT QUITE WHAT I WAS LOOKING FOR.
SUTO (SHTMP)
!
DON'T YOU DARE TOUCH LAILA!!!
BA (YANK)
!!
BIKU (TWITCH)

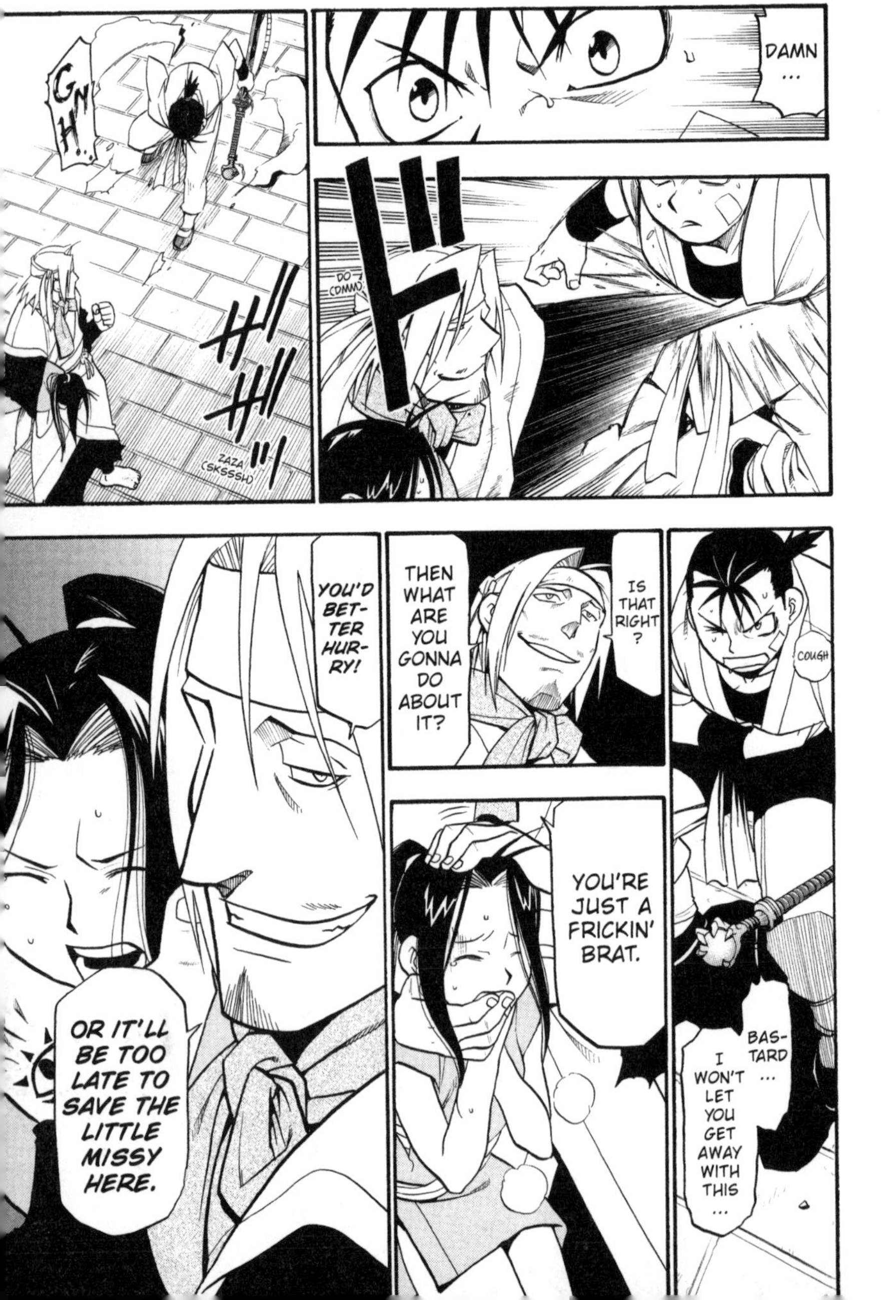
DAMN ...
DO (DMM)
ド
GNH!..
ZAZA (SKSSSH)
COUGH
BASTARD ...
I WON'T LET YOU GET AWAY WITH THIS ...
IS THAT RIGHT?
THEN WHAT ARE YOU GONNA DO ABOUT IT?
YOU'RE JUST A FRICKIN' BRAT.
YOU'D BETTER HURRY!
OR IT'LL BE TOO LATE TO SAVE THE LITTLE MISSY HERE.

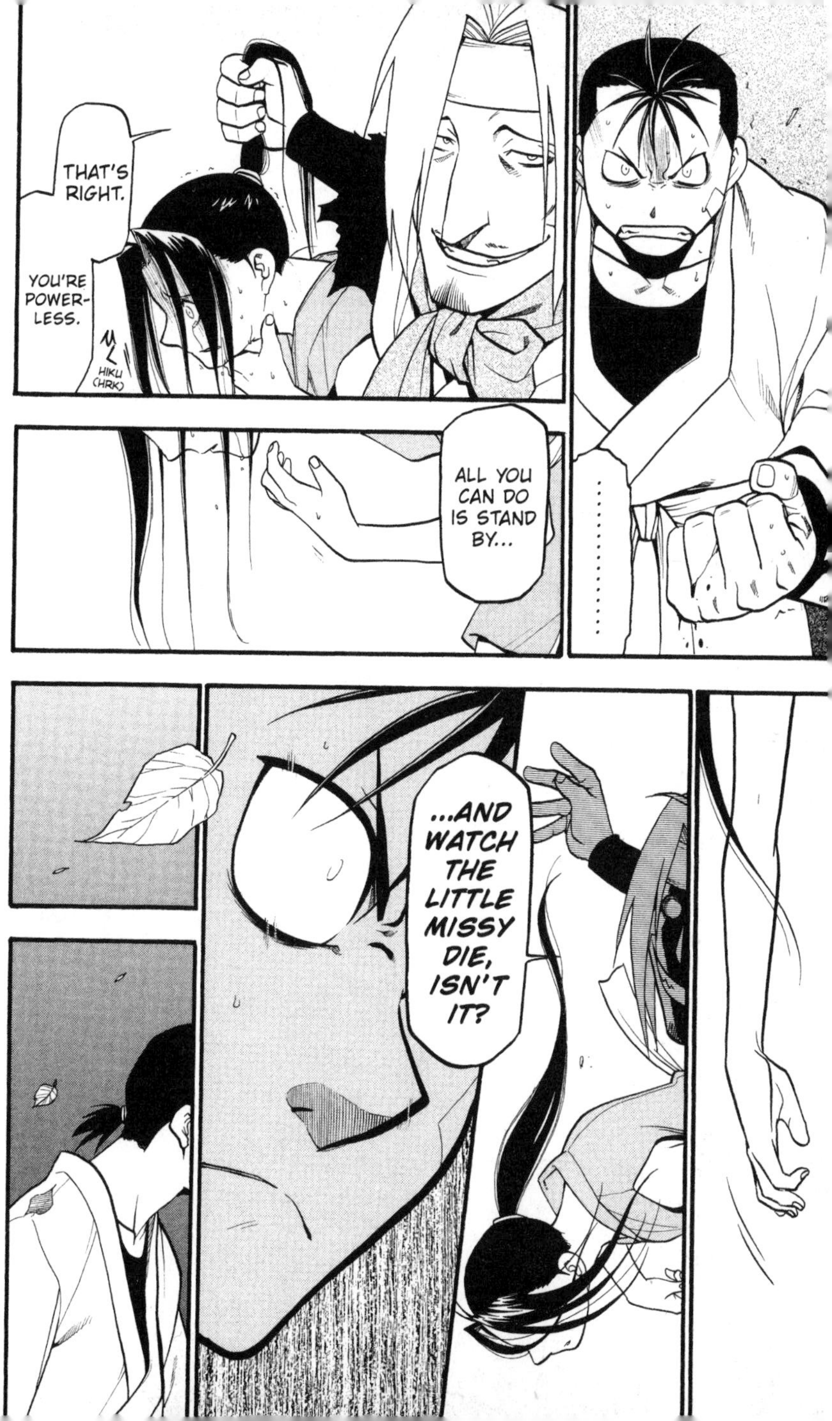
THAT'S RIGHT.
YOU'RE POWER-LESS.
HIKU (HRK)
....
ALL YOU CAN DO IS STAND BY...
...AND WATCH THE LITTLE MISSY DIE, ISN'T IT?

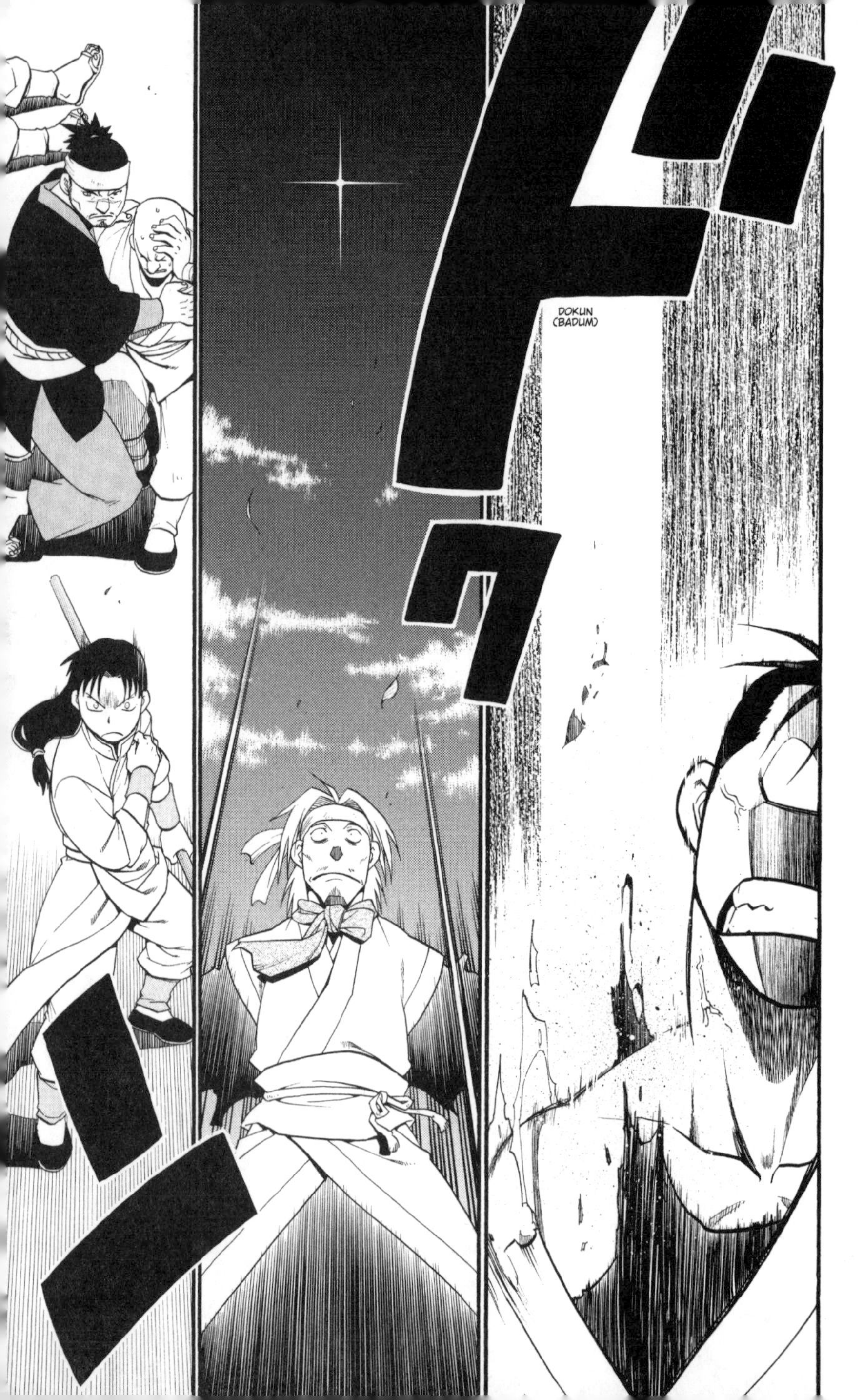
DOKUN
(BADUM)

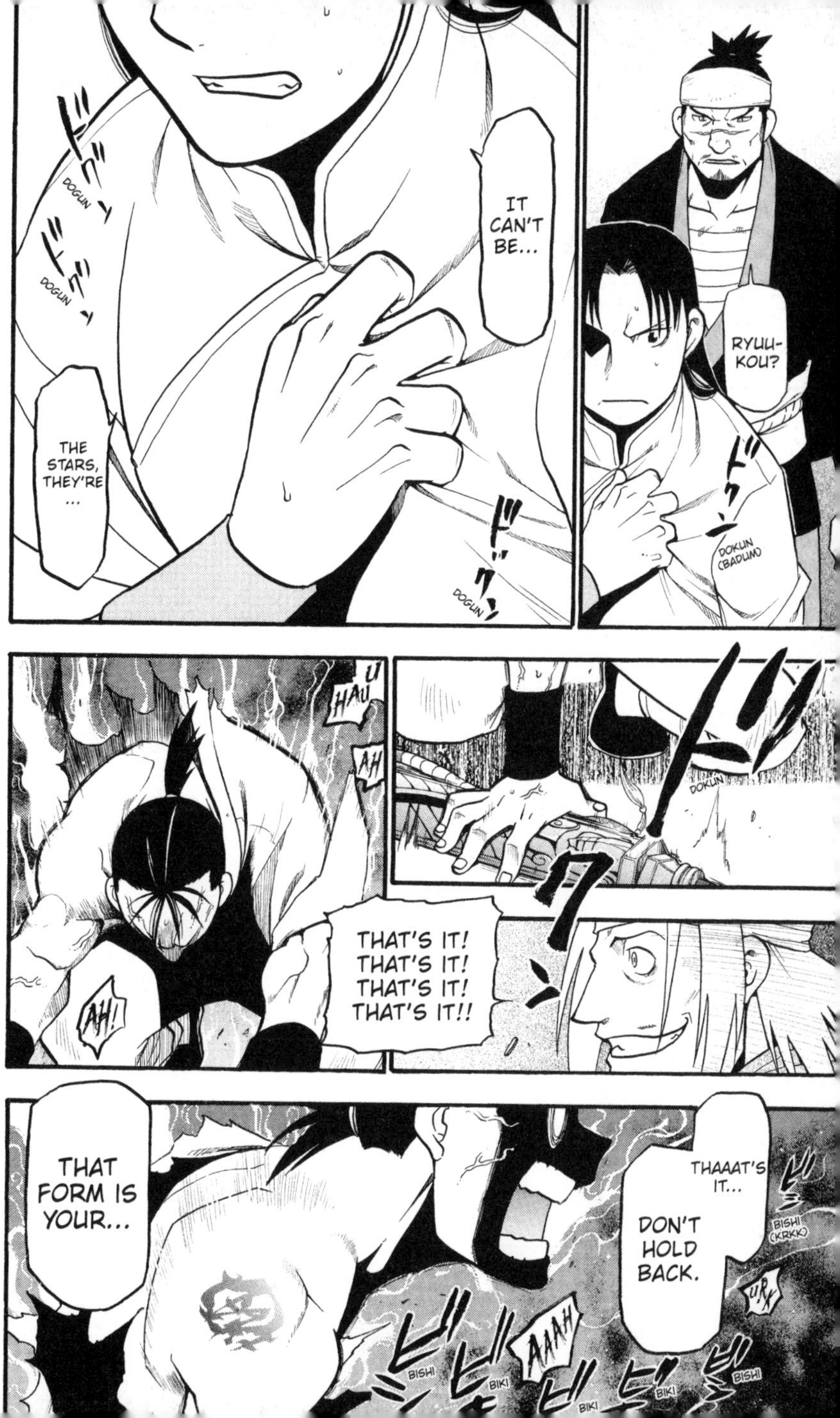
RYUU-KOU?
DOKUN (BADUM)
IT CAN'T BE...
DOGUN
DOGUN
DOGUN
THE STARS, THEY'RE ...
DOKUN
THAT'S IT! THAT'S IT! THAT'S IT! THAT'S IT!!
HAU U
AH
AH!
THAAAT'S IT...
DON'T HOLD BACK.
BISHI (KRKK)
URK
THAT FORM IS YOUR...
AAAH
BISHI
BIKI
BIKI
BIKI
BISHI

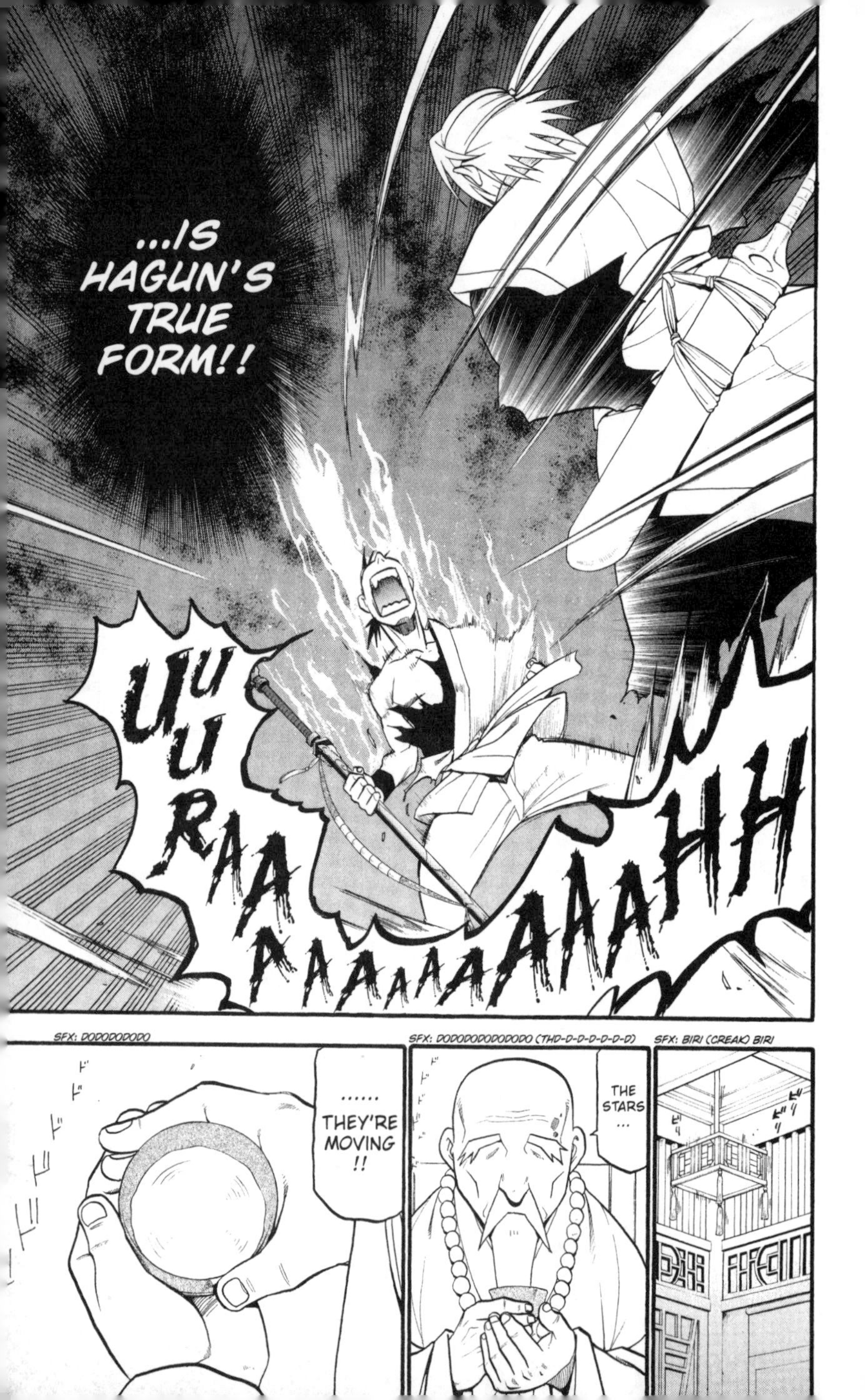
...IS HAGUN'S TRUE FORM!!
UUURAAAAAAAAAAAHH
SFX: BIRI (CREAK) BIRI
SFX: DODODODODODODO (THD-D-D-D-D-D)
THE STARS...
SFX: DODODODODO
...... THEY'RE MOVING!!

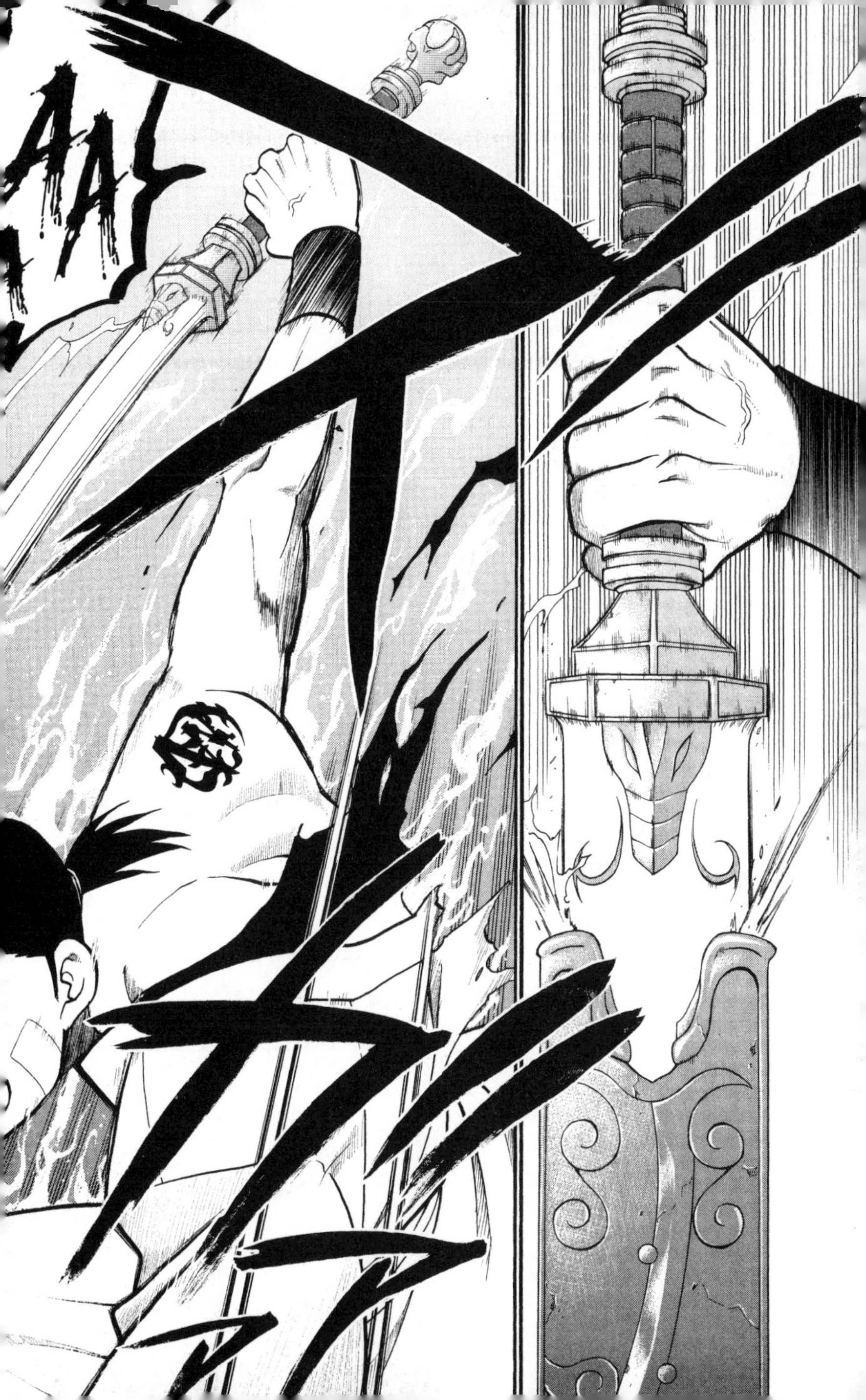
AA

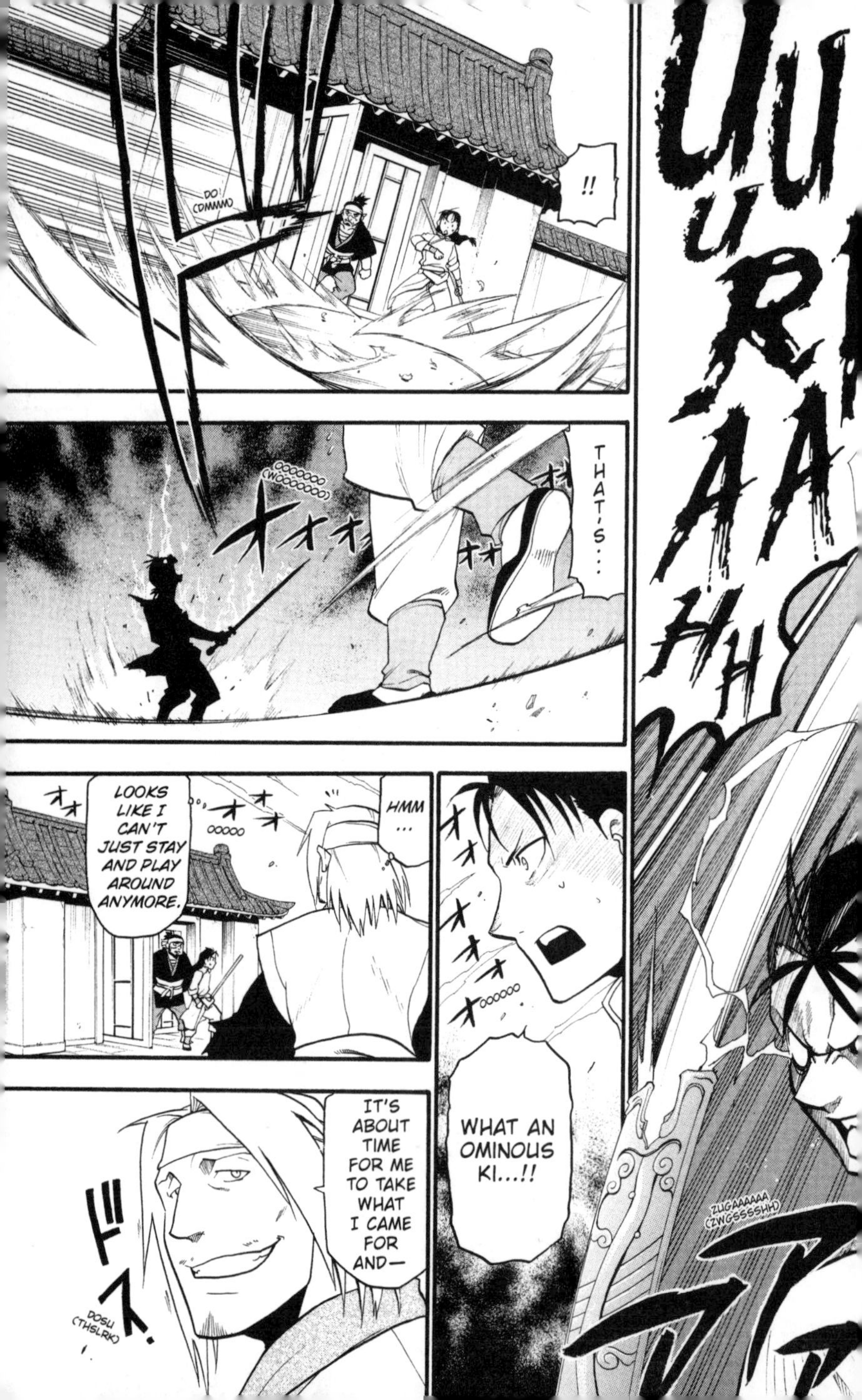

UUURAAHH
ZUGAAAAAA (ZWGSSSSHH)
!!
DO! (DMMMM)
THAT'S...
OOOOOOO (WOOOOOOOO)
WHAT AN OMINOUS KI...!!
OOOOOO
HMM...
LOOKS LIKE I CAN'T JUST STAY AND PLAY AROUND ANYMORE.
OOOOO
IT'S ABOUT TIME FOR ME TO TAKE WHAT I CAME FOR AND—
DOSU (THSLRK)

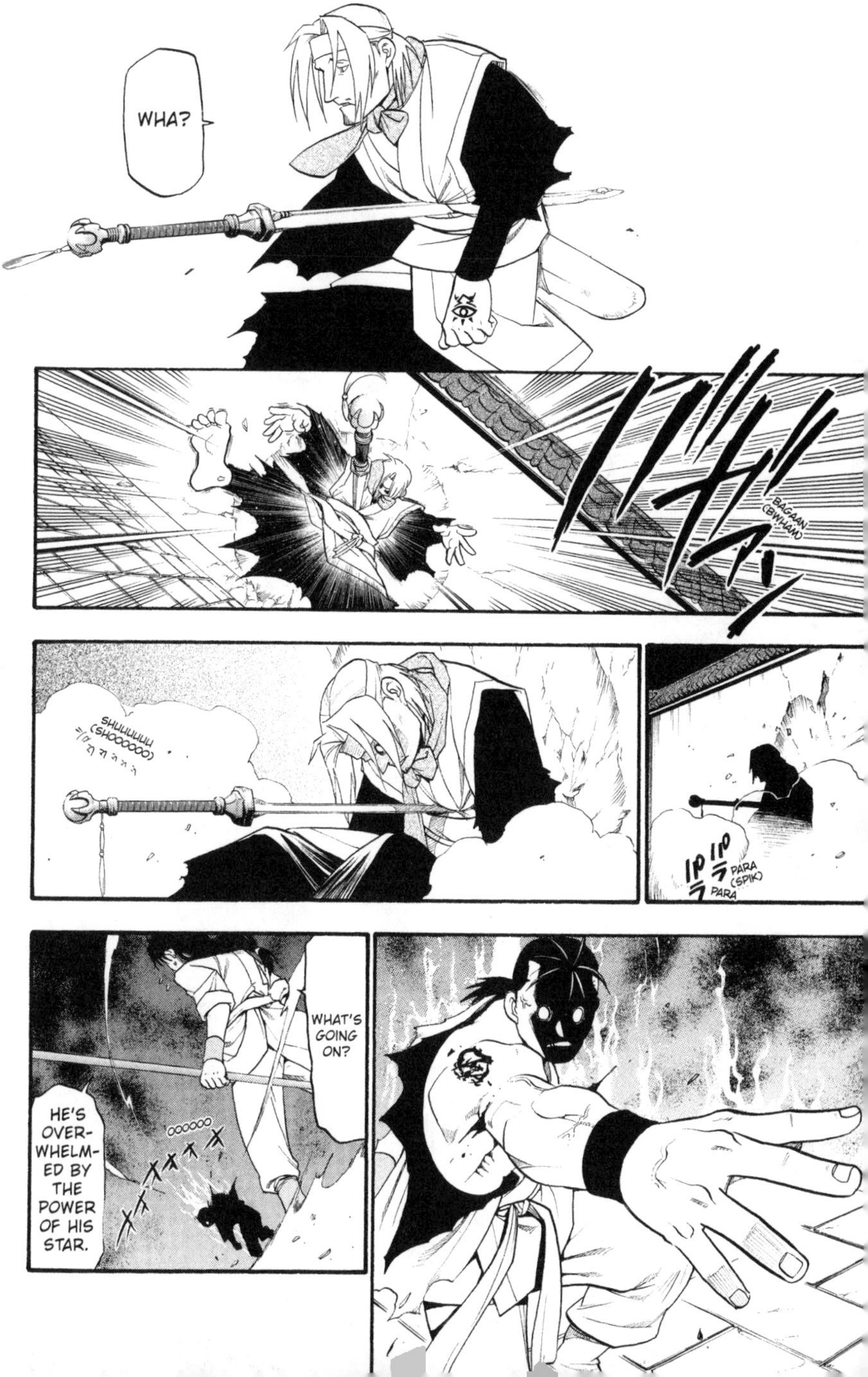
WHA?
BAGAAN (BWHAM)
PARA PARA (SPIK)
SHUUUUUU (SHOOOOOO)
WHAT'S GOING ON?
HE'S OVERWHELMED BY THE POWER OF HIS STAR.
OOOOOO

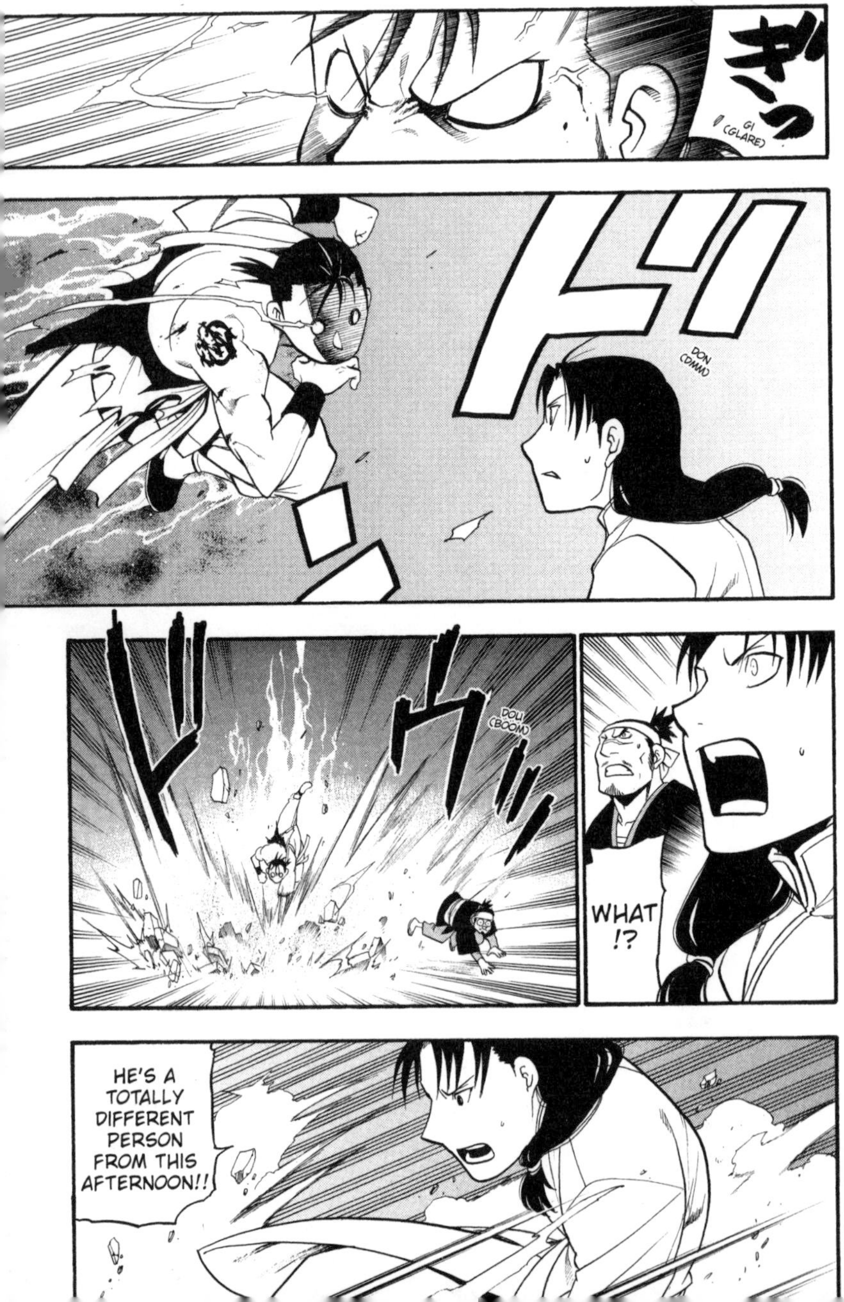
ぎっ
GI (GLARE)
ドン
DON (DMM)
ドゥ
DOU (BOOM)
WHAT !?
HE'S A TOTALLY DIFFERENT PERSON FROM THIS AFTERNOON!!

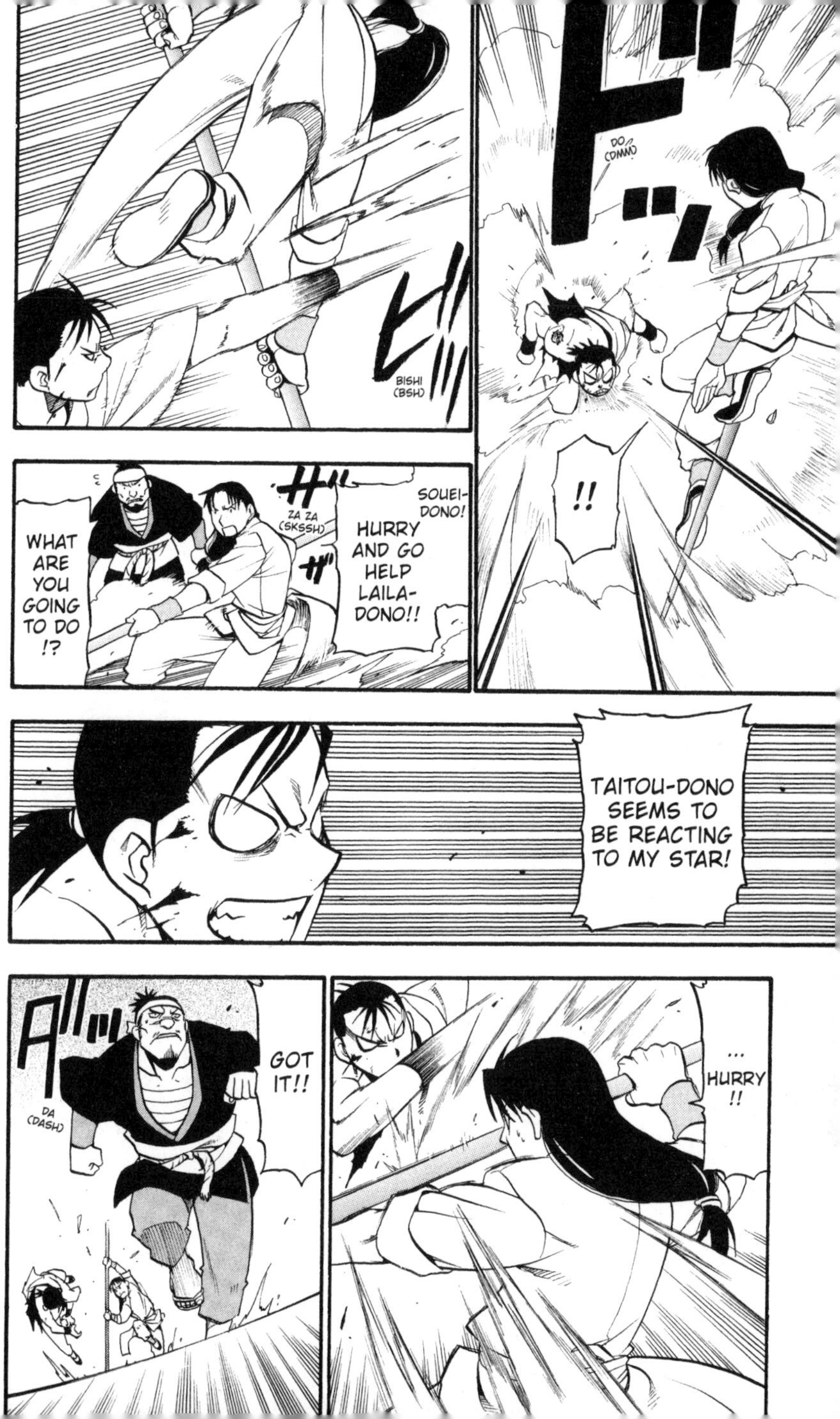
DO (DMM)
!!
BISHI (BSH)
SOUEI-DONO!
HURRY AND GO HELP LAILA-DONO!!
ZA ZA (SKSSH)
WHAT ARE YOU GOING TO DO !?
TAITOU-DONO SEEMS TO BE REACTING TO MY STAR!
... HURRY !!
GOT IT!!
DA (DASH)

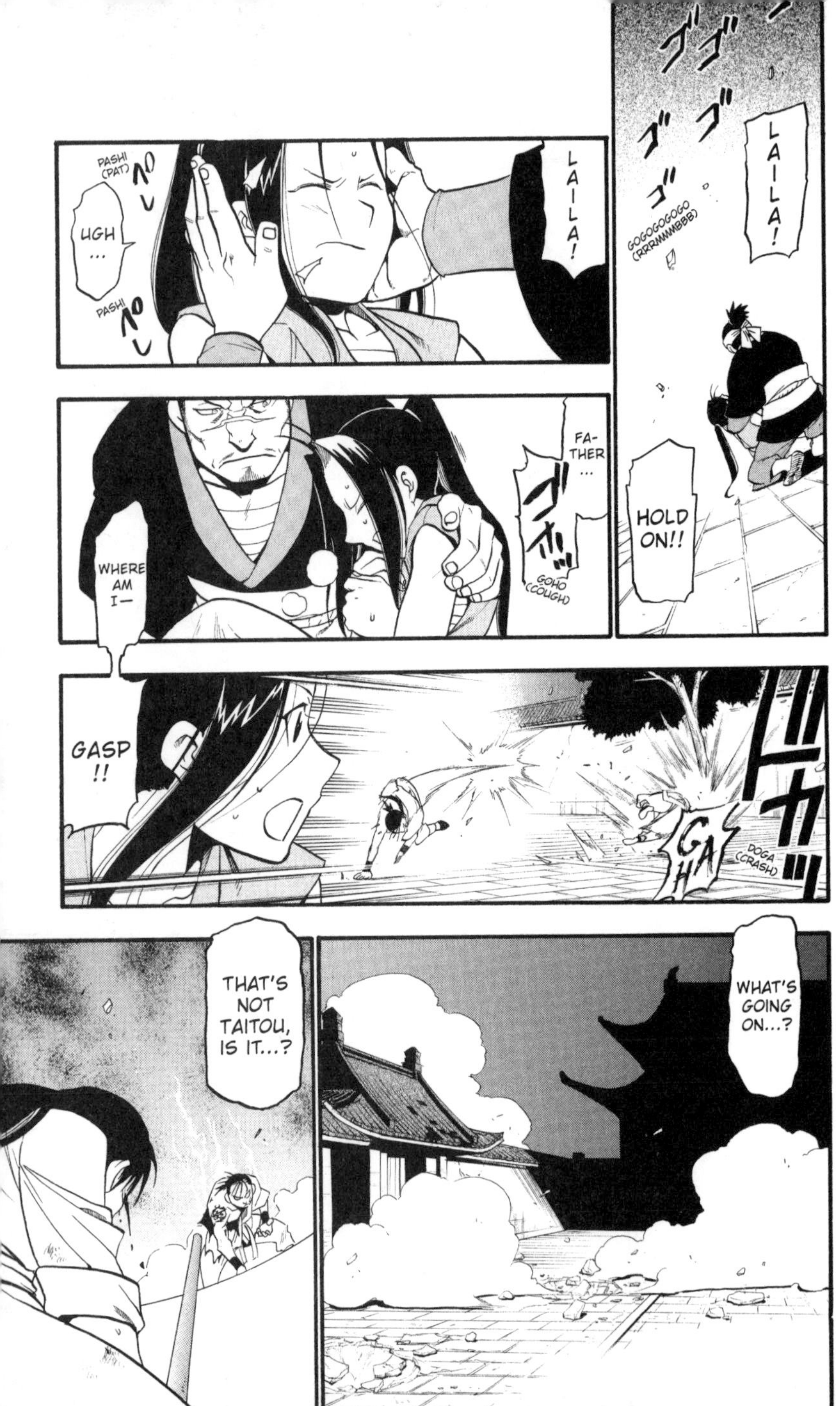
GOGOGOGOGO (RRRMMMBBB)
LAILA!
HOLD ON!!
LAILA!
PASHI (PAT)
UGH...
PASHI
FATHER...
GOHO (COUGH)
WHERE AM I—
GASP!!
DOGA (CRASH)
GAH
WHAT'S GOING ON...?
THAT'S NOT TAITOU, IS IT...?

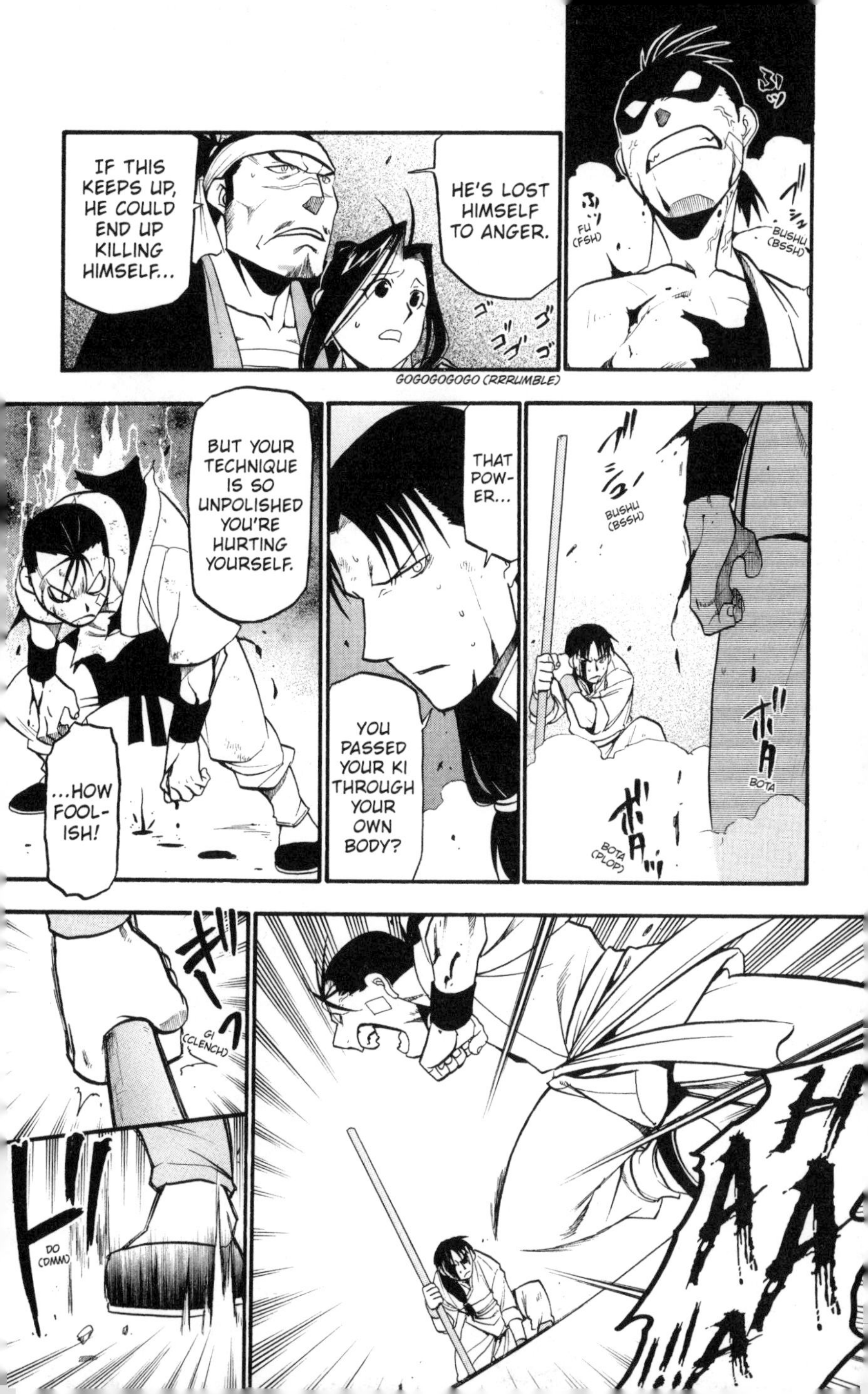
FU (FSH)
BUSHU (BSSH)
HE'S LOST HIMSELF TO ANGER.
IF THIS KEEPS UP, HE COULD END UP KILLING HIMSELF...
GOGOGOGOGO (RRRUMBLE)
BUSHU (BSSH)
BOTA
BOTA (PLOP)
THAT POW-ER...
YOU PASSED YOUR KI THROUGH YOUR OWN BODY?
BUT YOUR TECHNIQUE IS SO UNPOLISHED YOU'RE HURTING YOURSELF.
...HOW FOOL-ISH!
HAAAA!!!
GI (CLENCH)
DO (DMM)

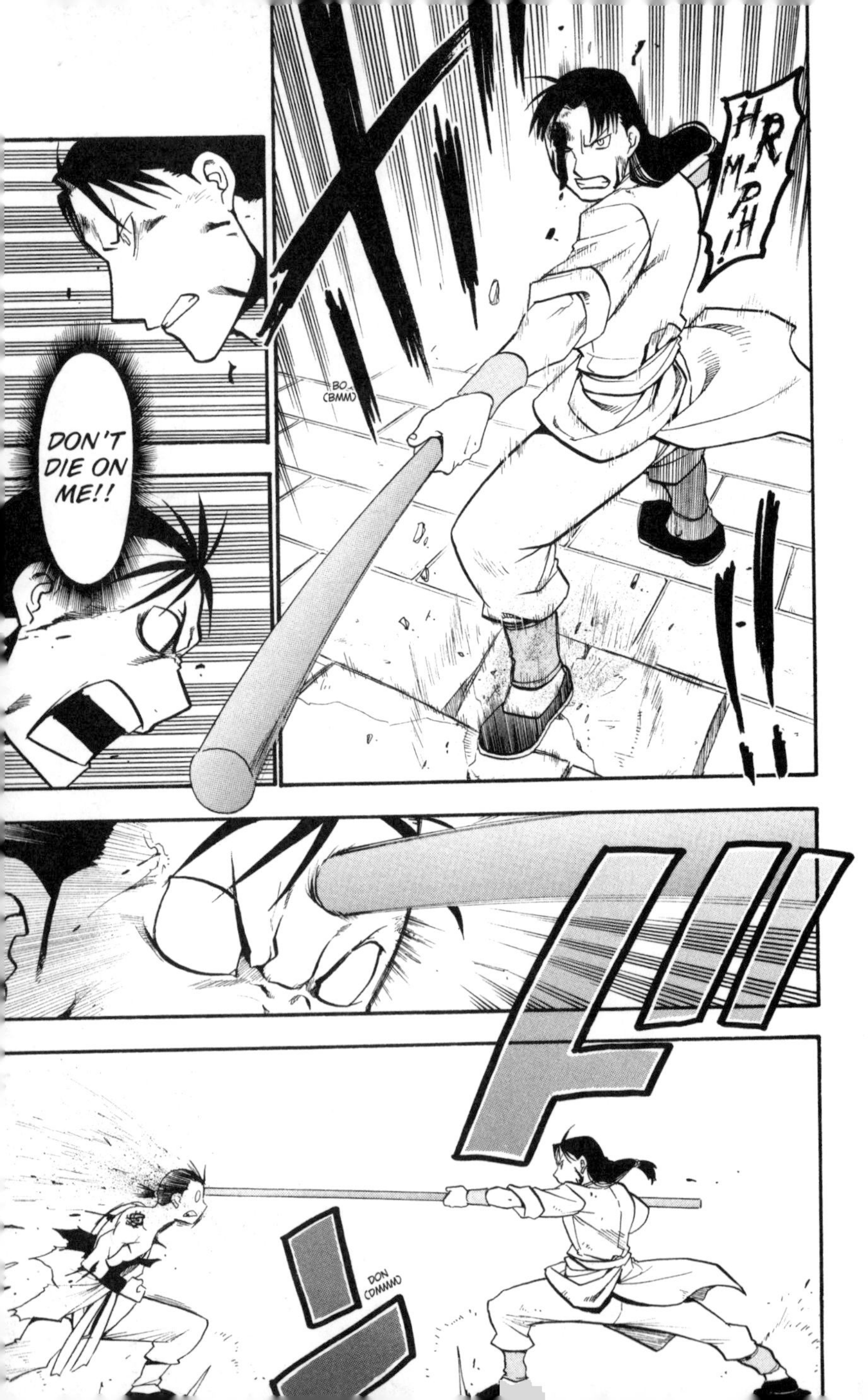
HRMPH!!
BO (BMM)
DON'T DIE ON ME!!
DON (DMMM)

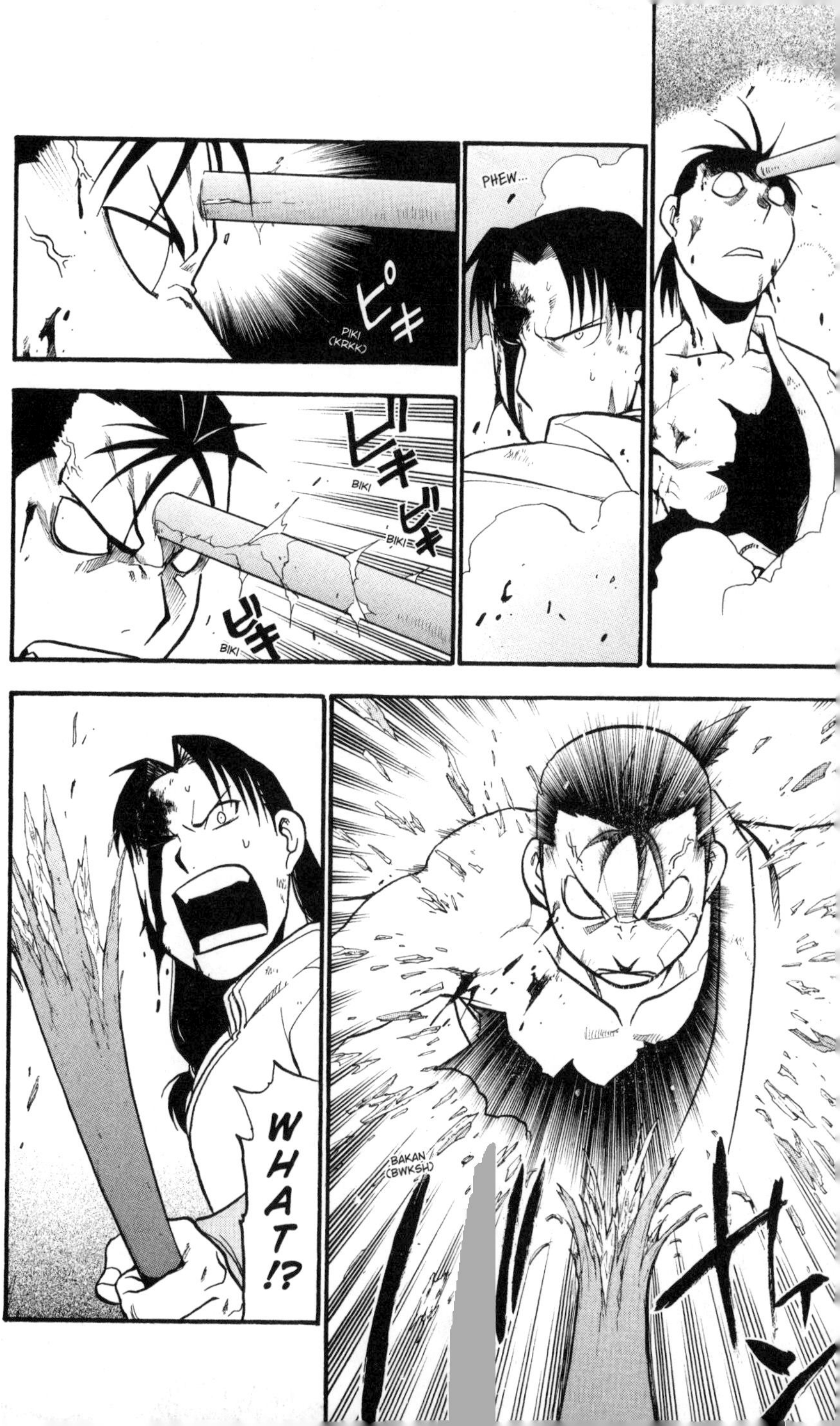
PHEW...
ピキ
PIKI (KRKK)
ビキ
BIKI
ビキ
BIKI
ビキ
BIKI
BAKAN (BWKSH)
WHAT!?

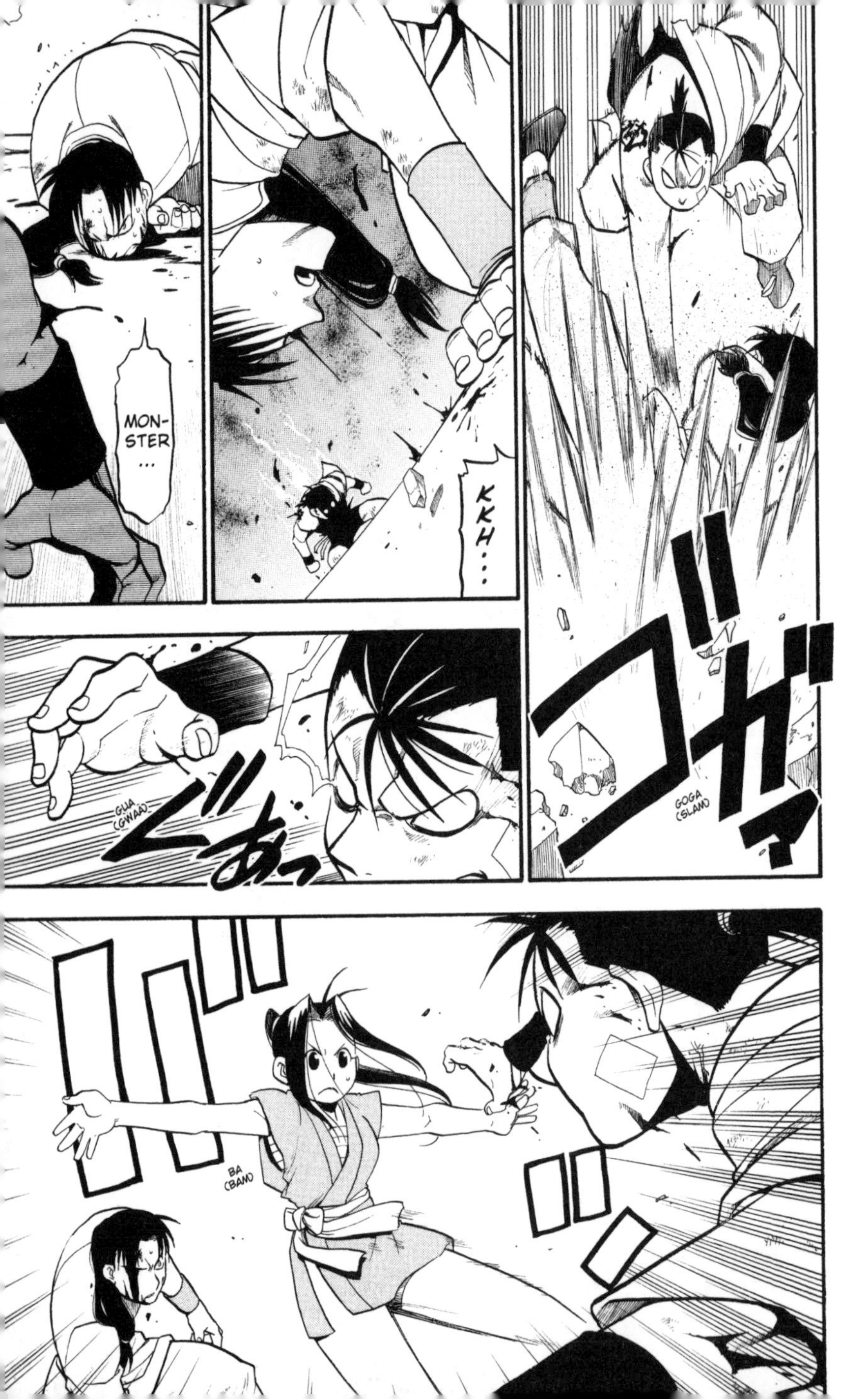
GOGA (SLAM)
KKH...
MON-STER...
GUA (GWAA)
BA (BAM)

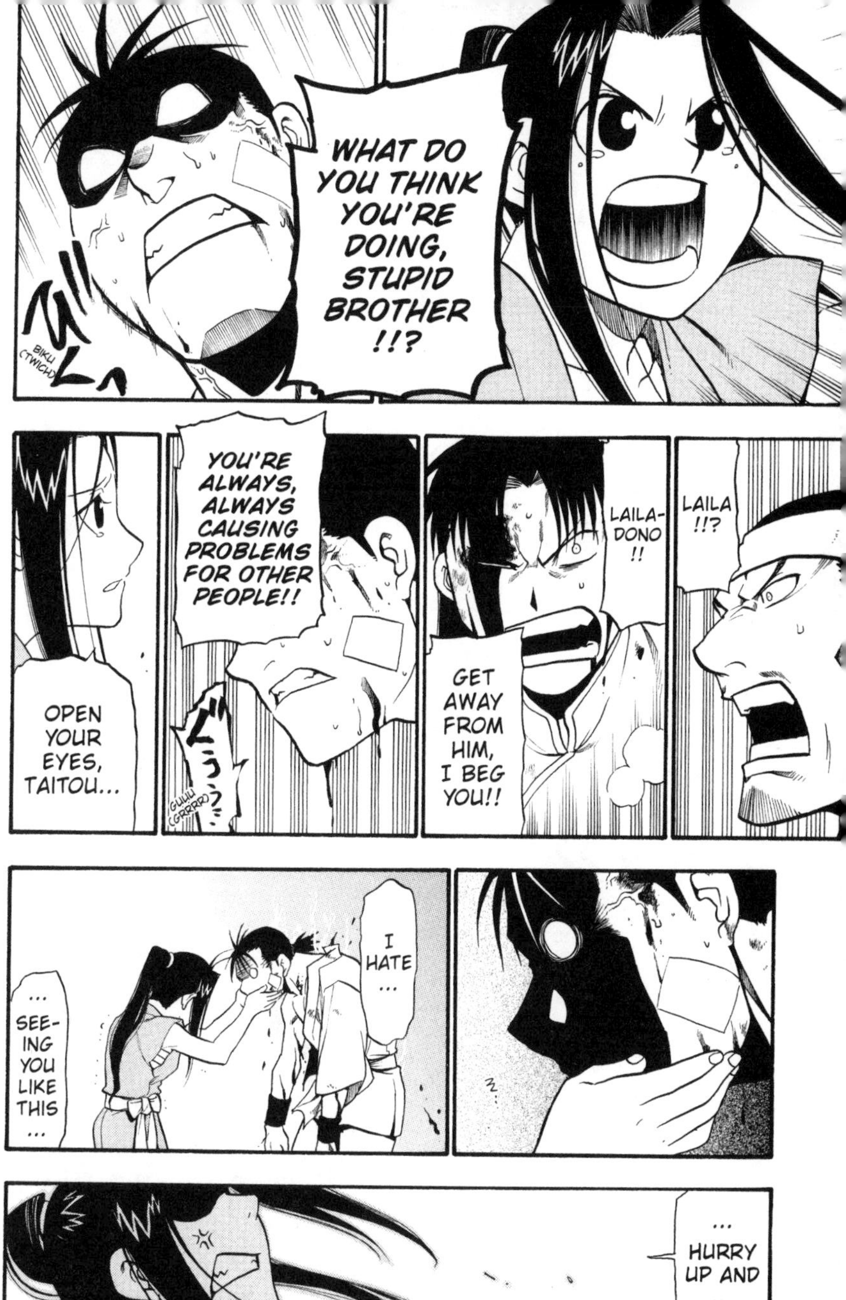
WHAT DO YOU THINK YOU'RE DOING, STUPID BROTHER !!?
BIKU (TWICH)
LAILA !!?
LAILA-DONO !!
GET AWAY FROM HIM, I BEG YOU!!
YOU'RE ALWAYS, ALWAYS CAUSING PROBLEMS FOR OTHER PEOPLE!!
GUUU (GRRRR)
OPEN YOUR EYES, TAITOU...
I HATE ...
... SEE- ING YOU LIKE THIS ...
... HURRY UP AND ...

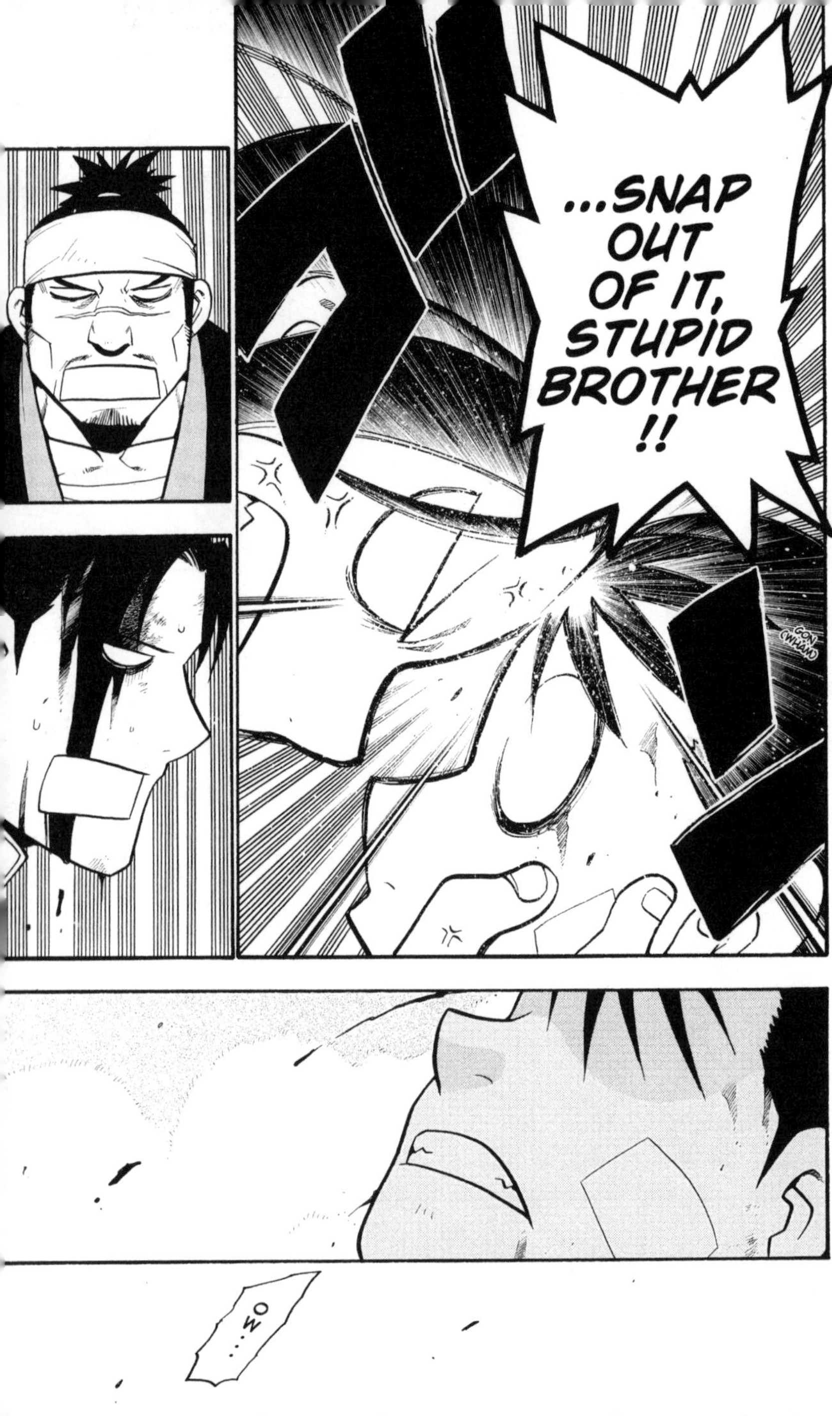
...SNAP OUT OF IT, STUPID BROTHER !!
GON (WHAM)
OW...

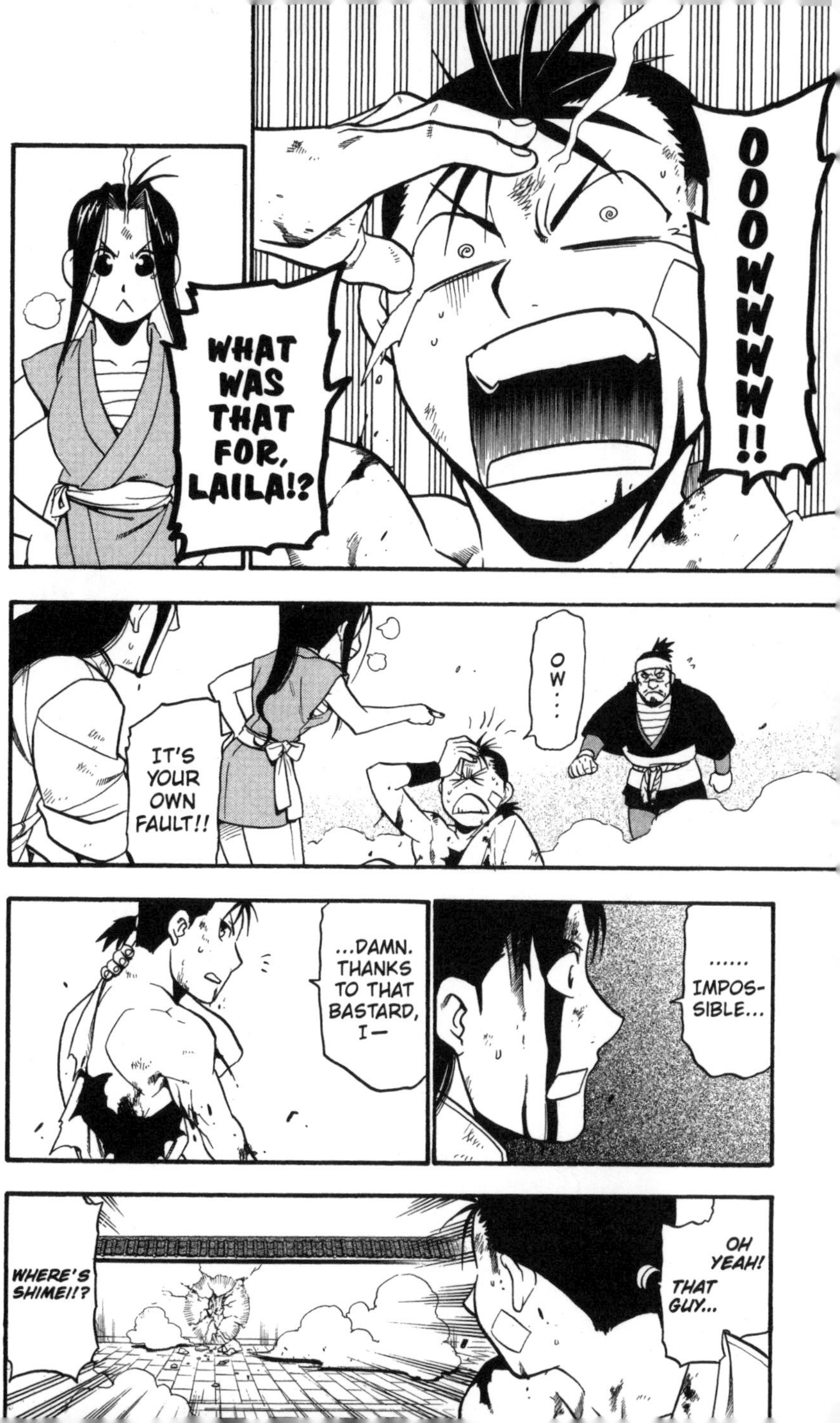
OOOWWWWW!!
WHAT WAS THAT FOR, LAILA!?
OW...
IT'S YOUR OWN FAULT!!
......IMPOSSIBLE...
...DAMN. THANKS TO THAT BASTARD, I—
OH YEAH! THAT GUY...
WHERE'S SHIME!?

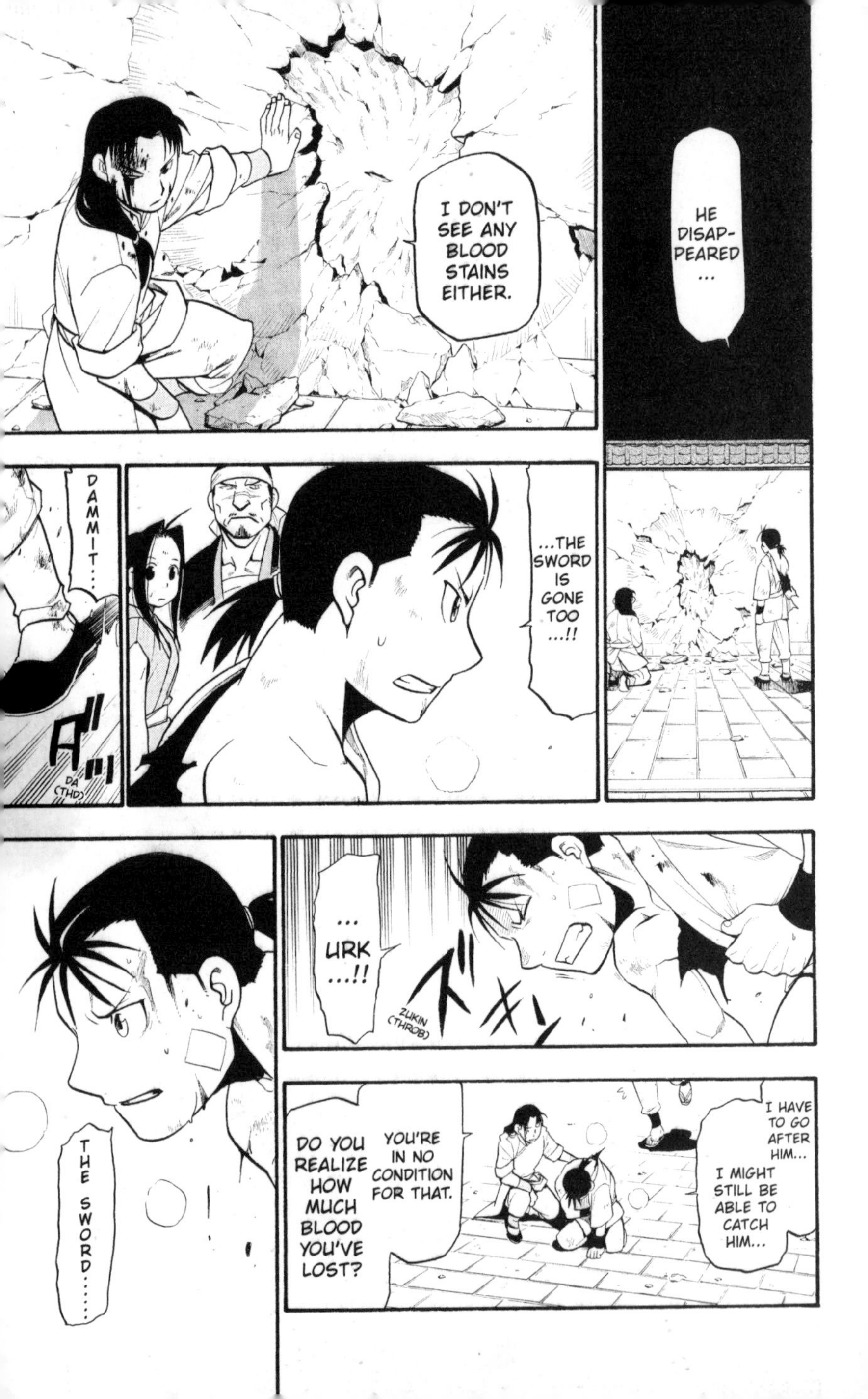
HE DISAPPEARED...
I DON'T SEE ANY BLOOD STAINS EITHER.
...THE SWORD IS GONE TOO ...!!
DAMMIT...
DA (THD)
... URK ...!!
ZUKIN (THROB)
I HAVE TO GO AFTER HIM...
I MIGHT STILL BE ABLE TO CATCH HIM...
YOU'RE IN NO CONDITION FOR THAT.
DO YOU REALIZE HOW MUCH BLOOD YOU'VE LOST?
THE SWORD......

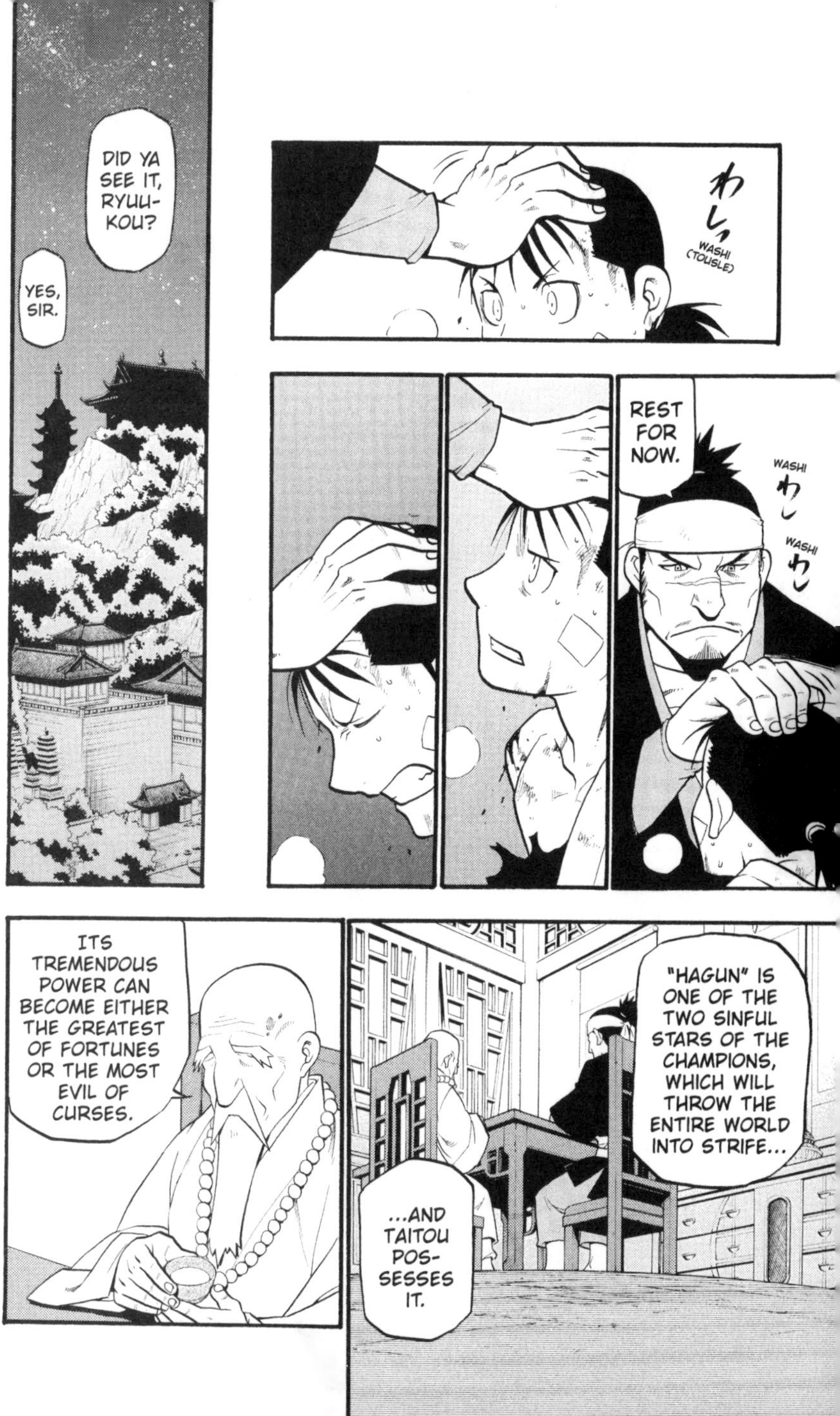
わし
WASHI (TOUSLE)
REST FOR NOW.
WASHI わし
WASHI わし
DID YA SEE IT, RYUU-KOU?
YES, SIR.
"HAGUN" IS ONE OF THE TWO SINFUL STARS OF THE CHAMPIONS, WHICH WILL THROW THE ENTIRE WORLD INTO STRIFE...
...AND TAITOU POS-SESSES IT.
ITS TREMENDOUS POWER CAN BECOME EITHER THE GREATEST OF FORTUNES OR THE MOST EVIL OF CURSES.

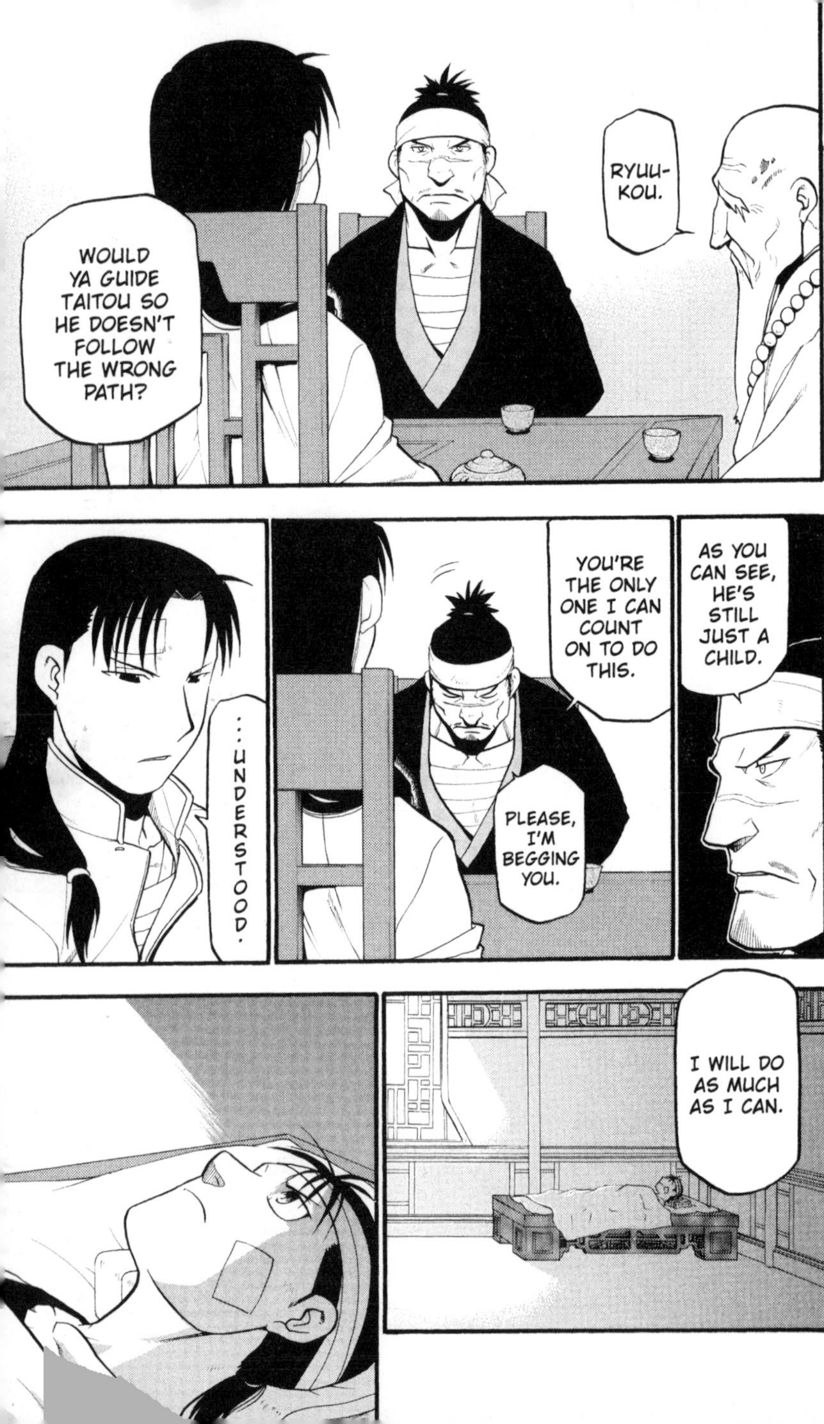
RYUU-KOU.
WOULD YA GUIDE TAITOU SO HE DOESN'T FOLLOW THE WRONG PATH?
AS YOU CAN SEE, HE'S STILL JUST A CHILD.
YOU'RE THE ONLY ONE I CAN COUNT ON TO DO THIS.
PLEASE, I'M BEGGING YOU.
...UNDERSTOOD.
I WILL DO AS MUCH AS I CAN.

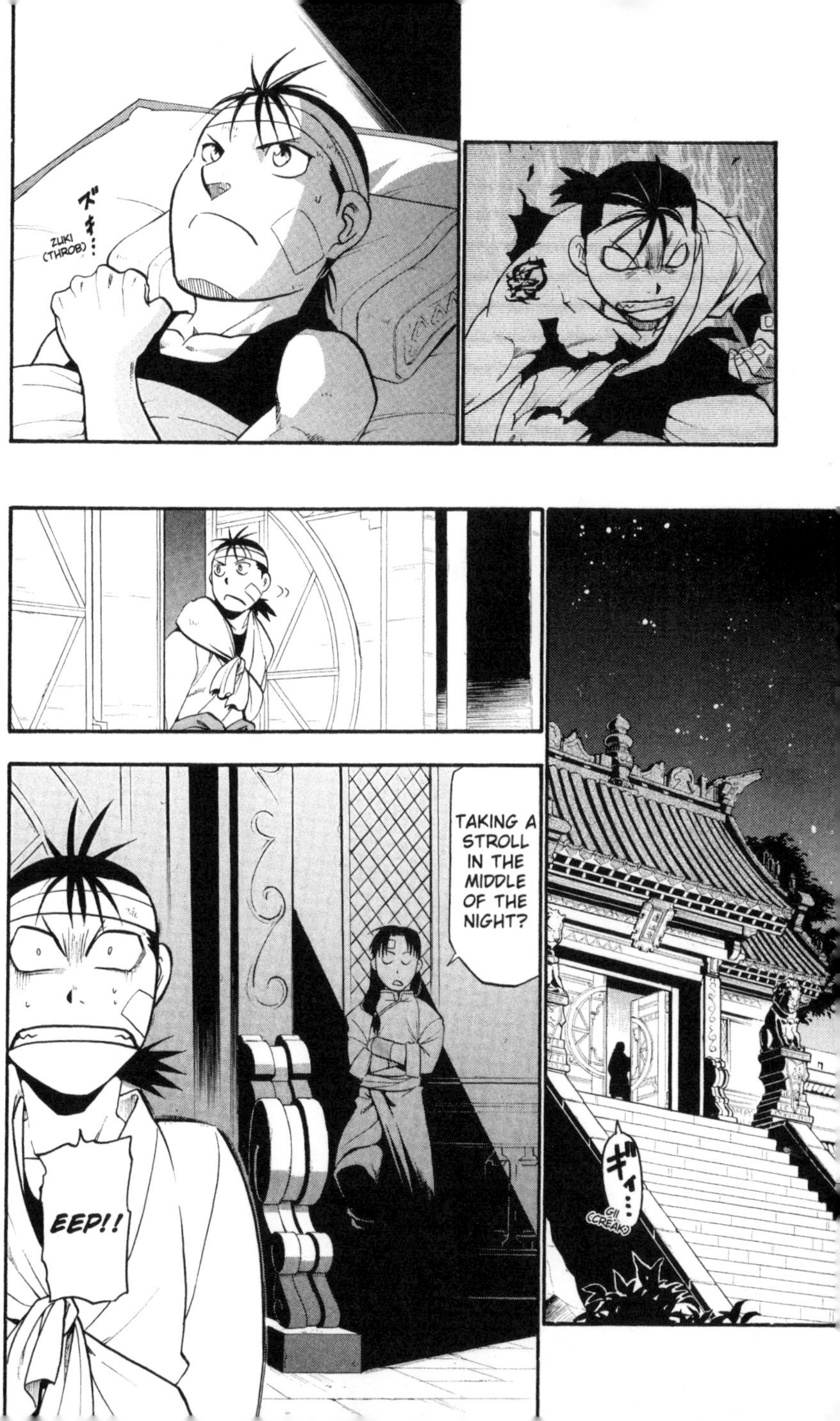
ズキ…
ZUKI (THROB)
ギィ…
GII (CREAK)
TAKING A STROLL IN THE MIDDLE OF THE NIGHT?
EEP!!

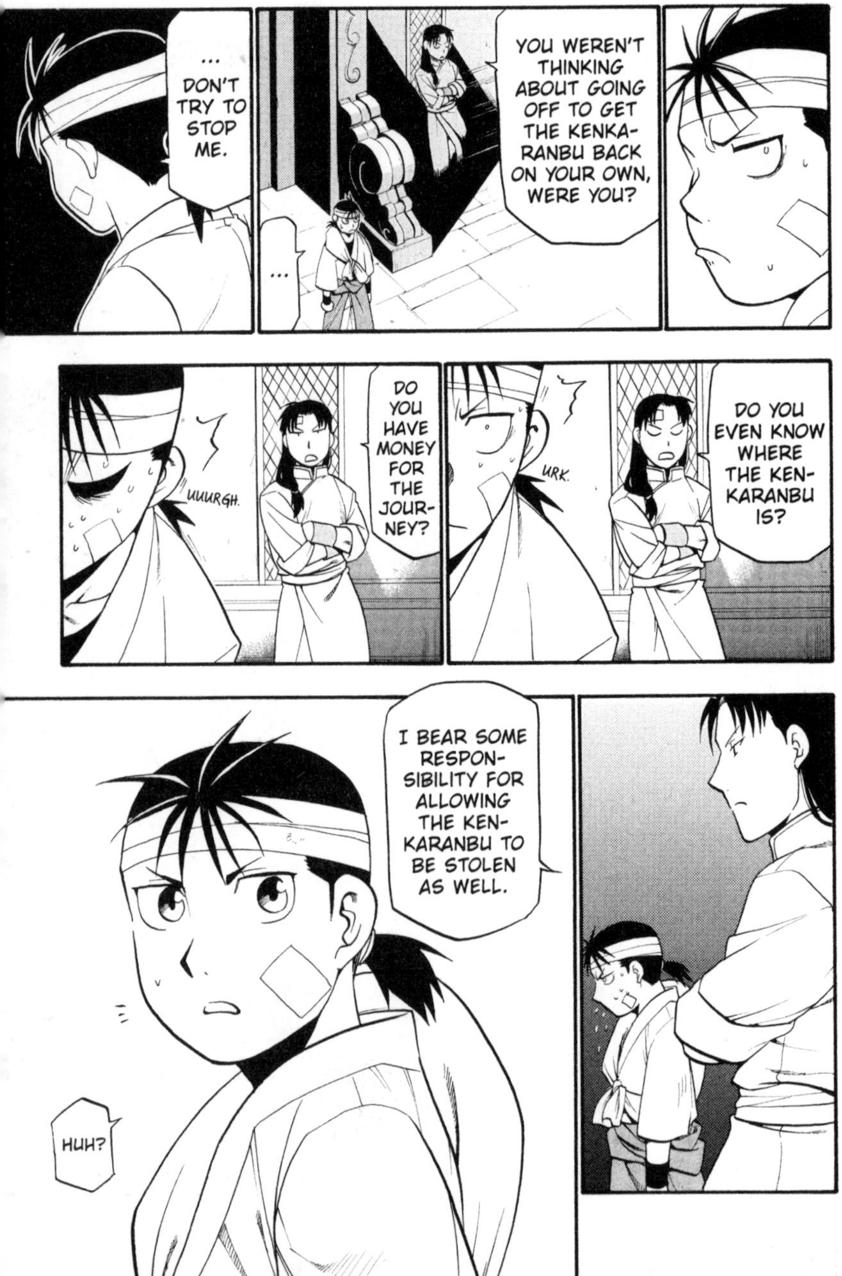

YOU WEREN'T THINKING ABOUT GOING OFF TO GET THE KENKA-RANBU BACK ON YOUR OWN, WERE YOU?
...
... DON'T TRY TO STOP ME.
DO YOU EVEN KNOW WHERE THE KEN-KARANBU IS?
URK.
DO YOU HAVE MONEY FOR THE JOURNEY?
UUURGH.
I BEAR SOME RESPONSIBILITY FOR ALLOWING THE KEN-KARANBU TO BE STOLEN AS WELL.
HUH?

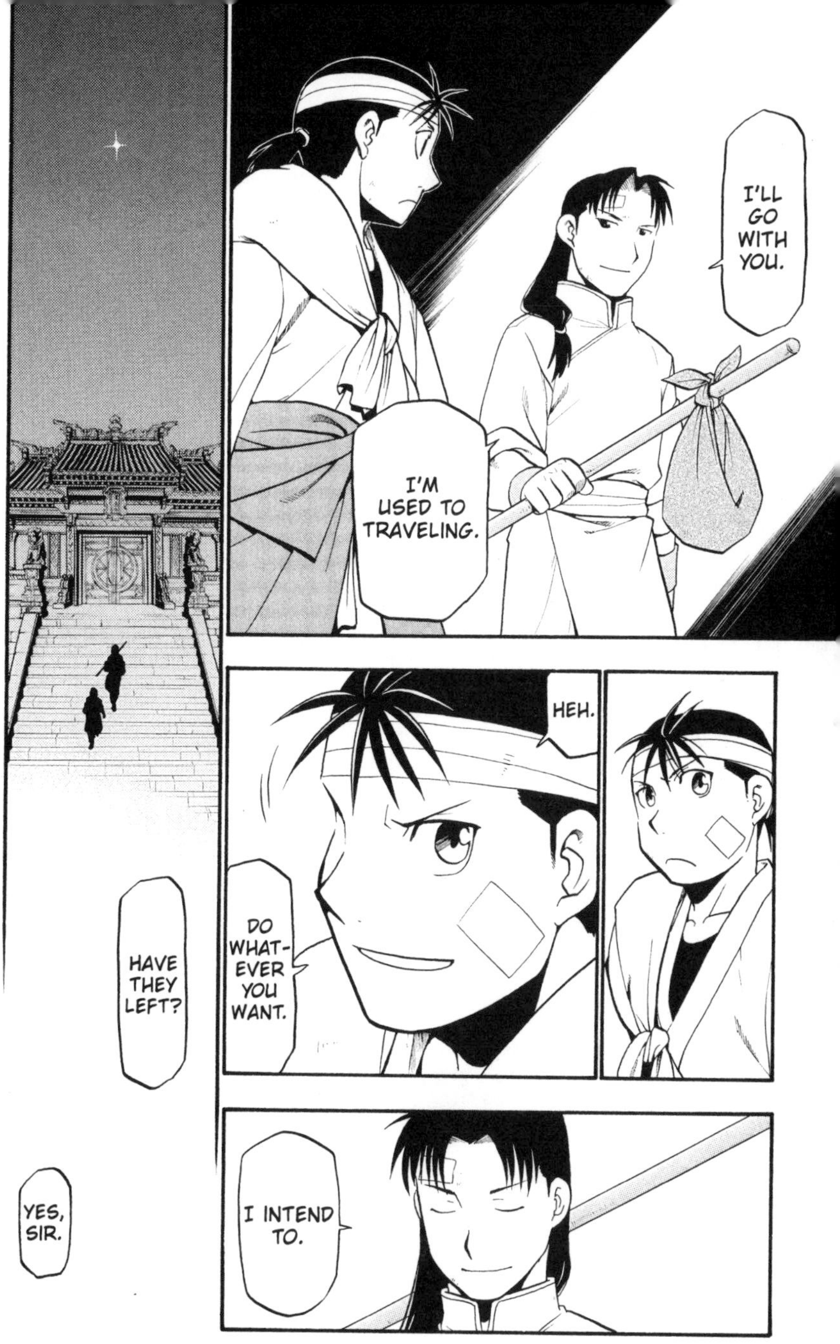
I'LL GO WITH YOU.
I'M USED TO TRAVELING.
HEH.
DO WHATEVER YOU WANT.
I INTEND TO.
HAVE THEY LEFT?
YES, SIR.

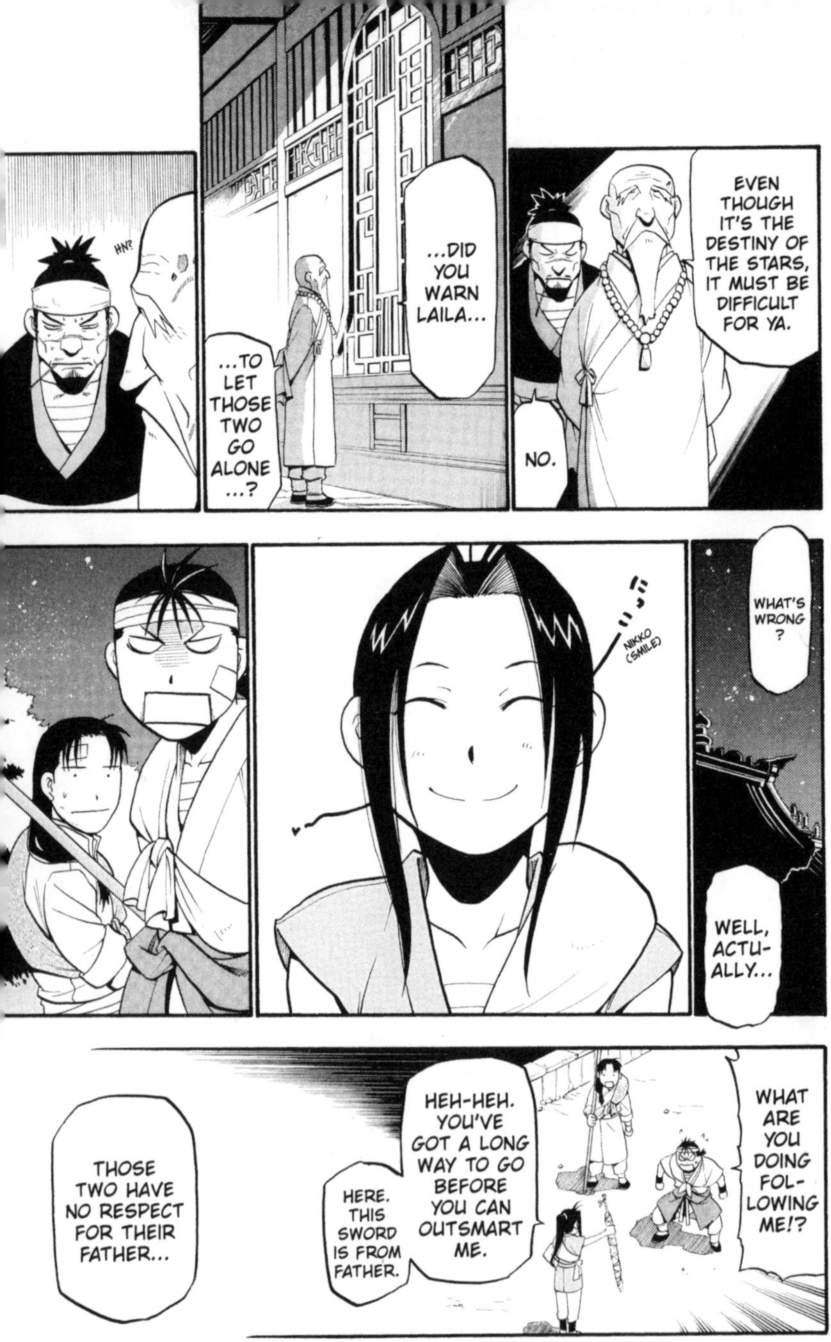
EVEN THOUGH IT'S THE DESTINY OF THE STARS, IT MUST BE DIFFICULT FOR YA.
NO.
...DID YOU WARN LAILA...
...TO LET THOSE TWO GO ALONE...?
HN?
WHAT'S WRONG?
WELL, ACTU-ALLY...
NIKKO (SMILE)
WHAT ARE YOU DOING FOL-LOWING ME!?
HEH-HEH. YOU'VE GOT A LONG WAY TO GO BEFORE YOU CAN OUTSMART ME.
HERE. THIS SWORD IS FROM FATHER.
THOSE TWO HAVE NO RESPECT FOR THEIR FATHER...

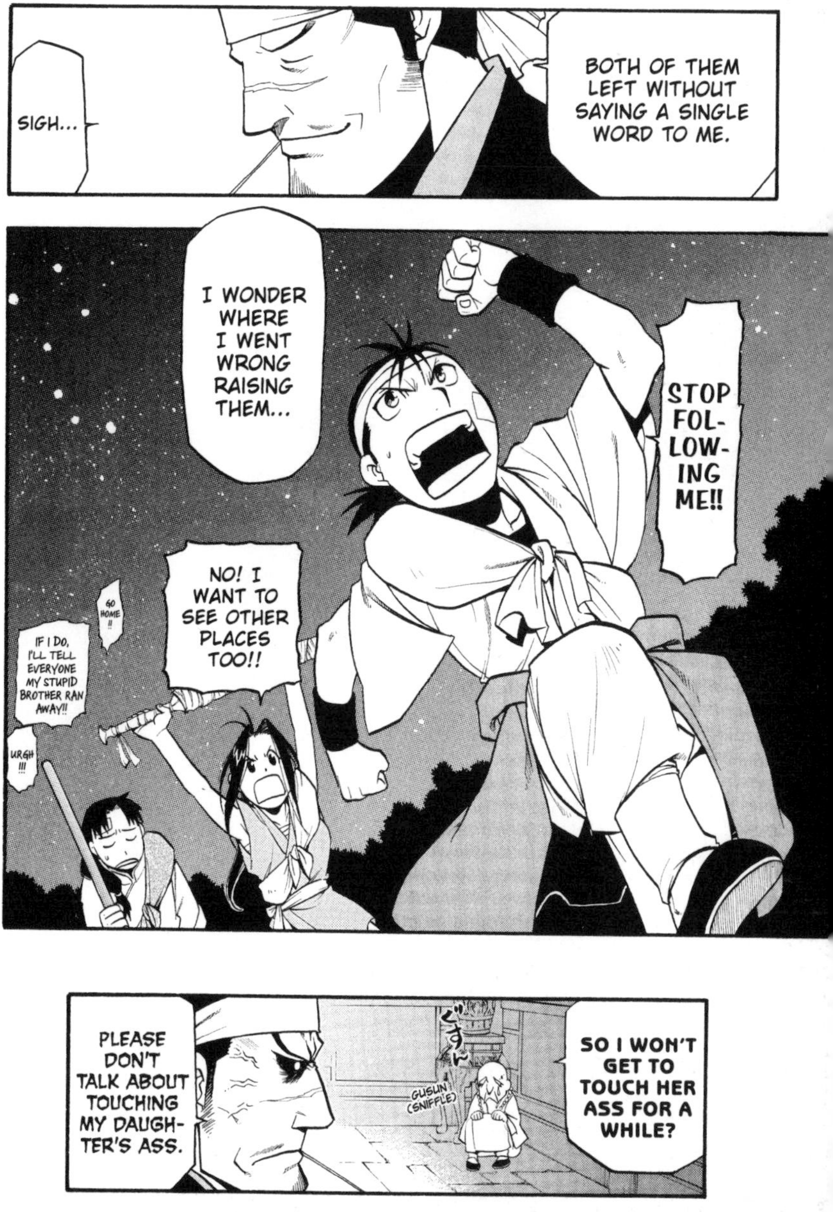
BOTH OF THEM LEFT WITHOUT SAYING A SINGLE WORD TO ME.
SIGH...
STOP FOL-LOW-ING ME!!
I WONDER WHERE I WENT WRONG RAISING THEM...
NO! I WANT TO SEE OTHER PLACES TOO!!
GO HOME!!
IF I DO, I'LL TELL EVERYONE MY STUPID BROTHER RAN AWAY!!
URGH!!!
SO I WON'T GET TO TOUCH HER ASS FOR A WHILE?
ぐすん
GUSUN (SNIFFLE)
PLEASE DON'T TALK ABOUT TOUCHING MY DAUGHTER'S ASS.

HERO TALES
獣　神　演　武

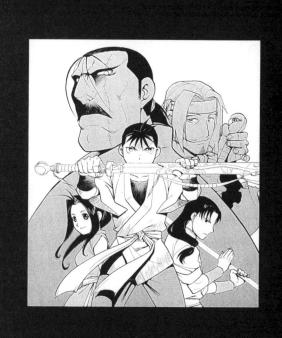

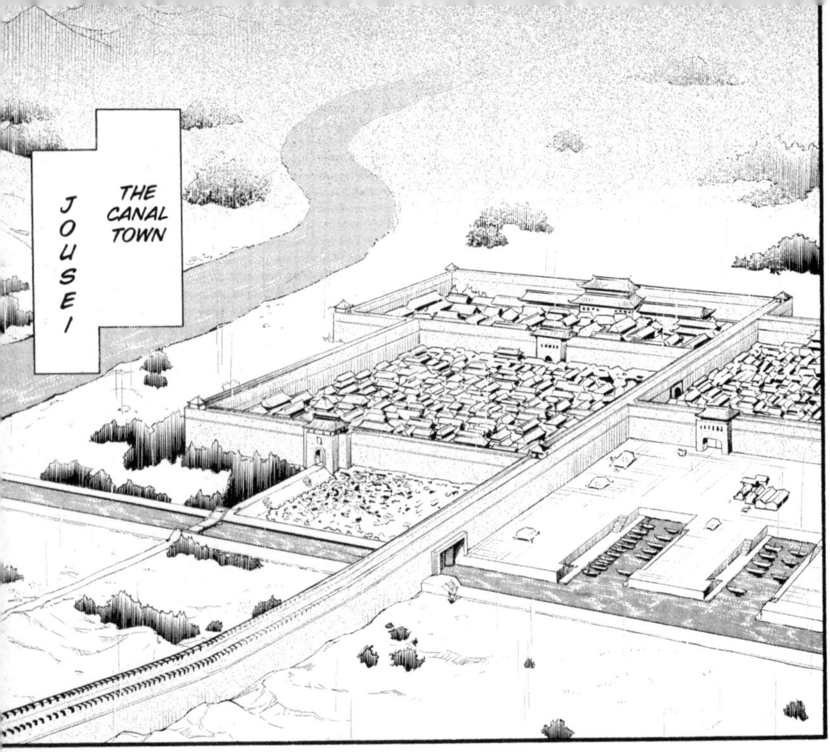
THE CANAL TOWN
JOUSEI

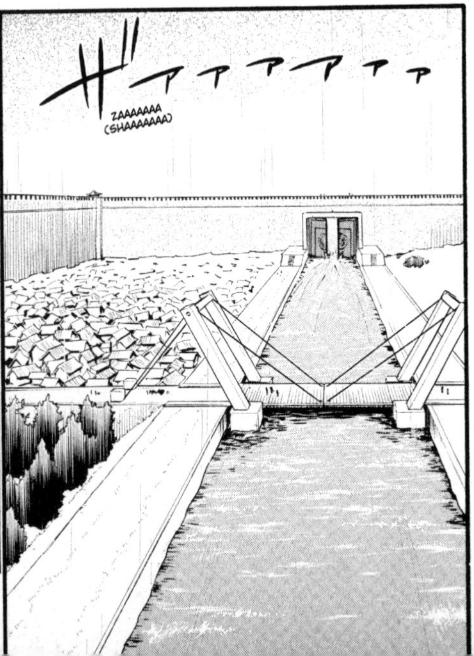
ザァァァァァァ
ZAAAAAAA
(SHAAAAAAA)

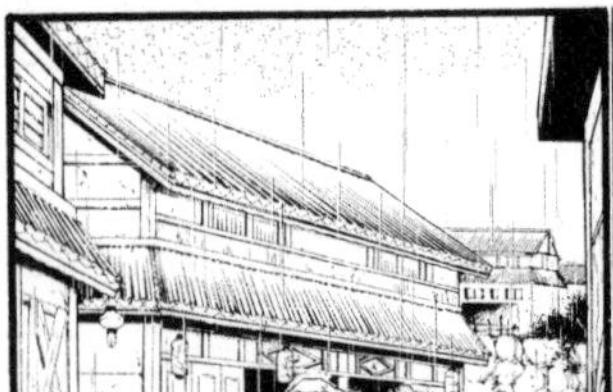

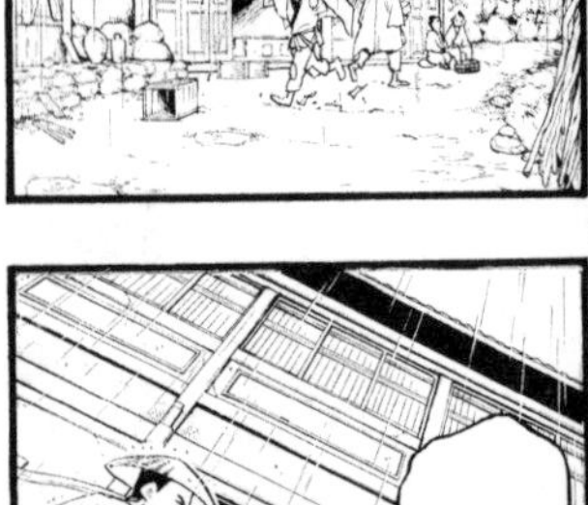
HRRR-
RNNN...

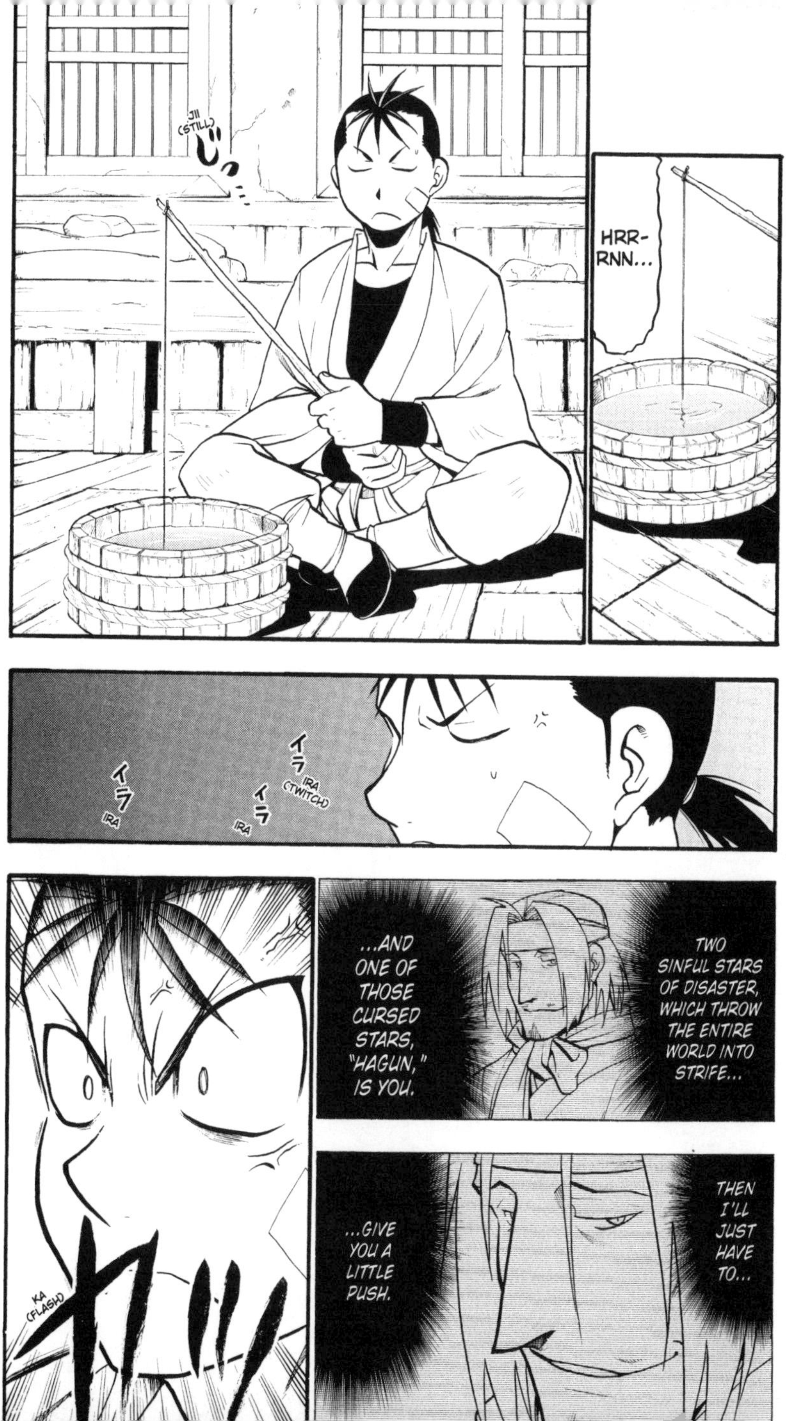
HRR-RNN...
JII (STILL)
じっ
イラ
IRA (TWITCH)
イラ
IRA
イラ
IRA
TWO SINFUL STARS OF DISASTER, WHICH THROW THE ENTIRE WORLD INTO STRIFE...
...AND ONE OF THOSE CURSED STARS, "HAGUN," IS YOU.
THEN I'LL JUST HAVE TO...
...GIVE YOU A LITTLE PUSH.
KA (FLASH)

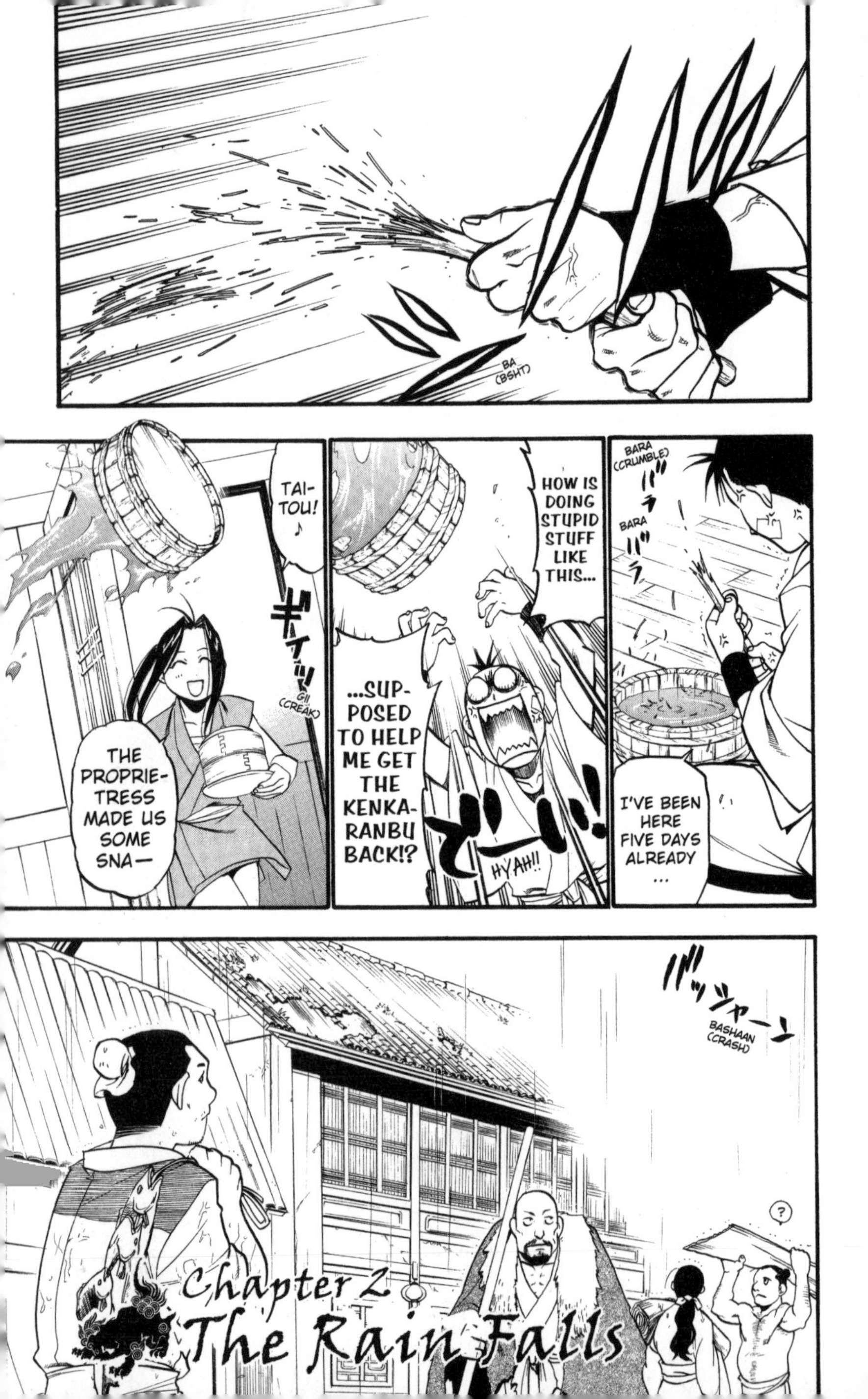
BA
(BSHT)
BARA
(CRUMBLE)
BARA
I'VE BEEN HERE FIVE DAYS ALREADY...
HOW IS DOING STUPID STUFF LIKE THIS...
...SUP-POSED TO HELP ME GET THE KENKA-RANBU BACK!?
HYAH!!
TAI-TOU! ♪
GII
(CREAK)
THE PROPRIE-TRESS MADE US SOME SNA—
BASHAAN
(CRASH)
?
Chapter 2
The Rain Falls

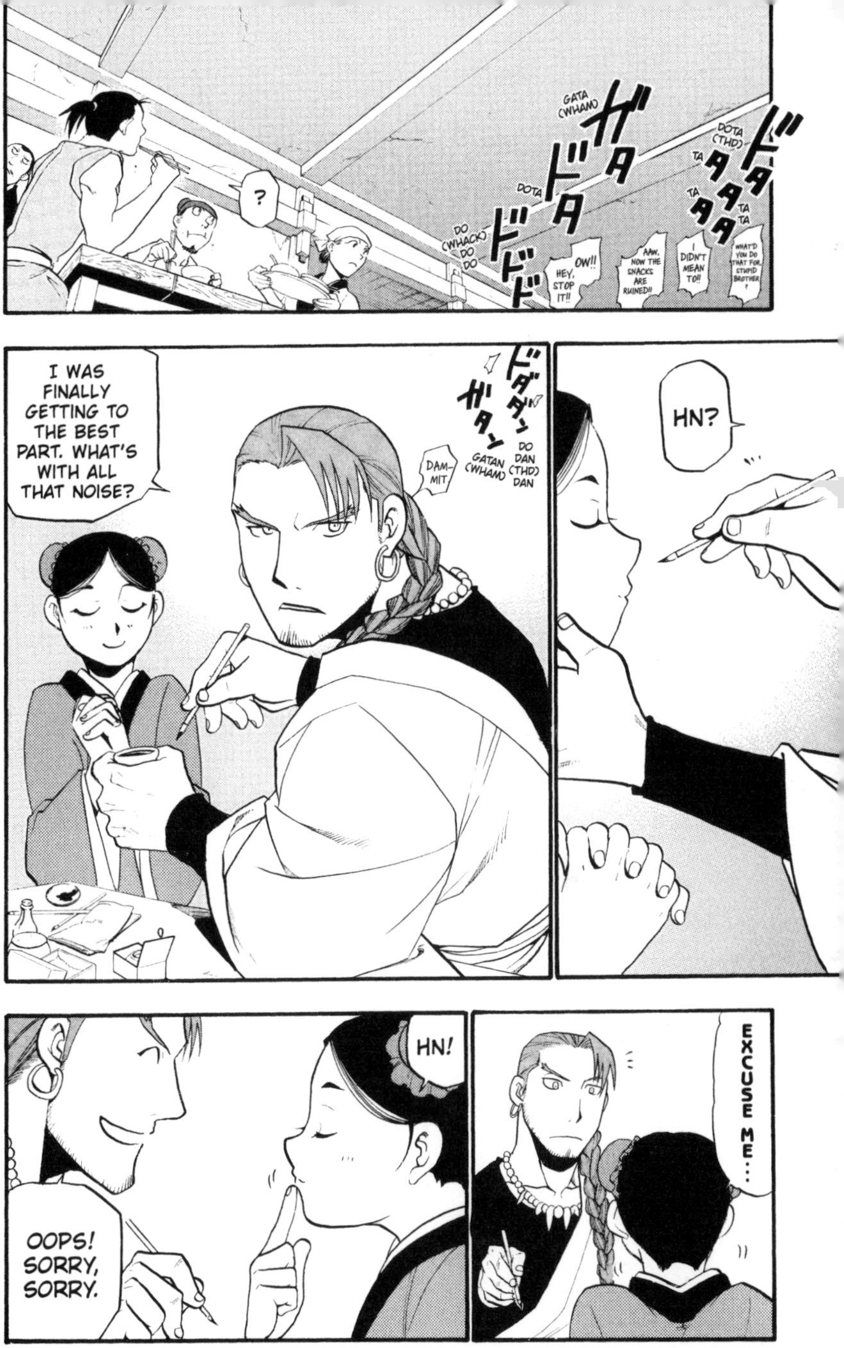
DOTA (THD)
TA
TA
TA TA
GATA (WHAM)
DOTA
DO (WHACK) DO DO
WHAT'D YOU DO THAT FOR, STUPID BROTHER?
I DIDN'T MEAN TO!!
AAW, NOW THE SNACKS ARE RUINED!!
OW!!
HEY, STOP IT!!
?
HN?
DO DAN (THD) DAN
GATAN (WHAM)
DAM-MIT.
I WAS FINALLY GETTING TO THE BEST PART. WHAT'S WITH ALL THAT NOISE?
EXCUSE ME...
HN!
OOPS! SORRY, SORRY.

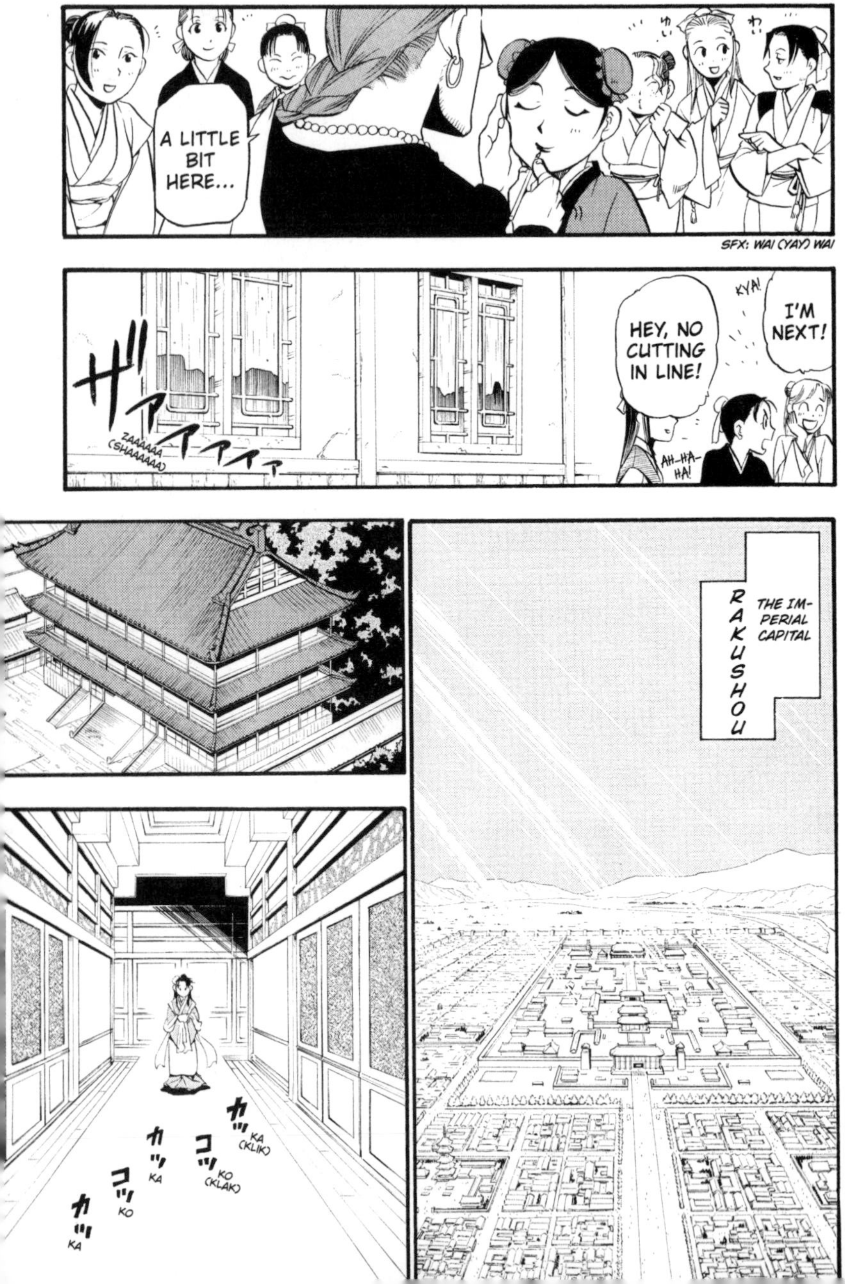
A LITTLE BIT HERE...
SFX: WAI (YAY) WAI
I'M NEXT!
KYA!
HEY, NO CUTTING IN LINE!
AH-HA-HA!
ザァァァァ
ZAAAAAA (SHAAAAAA)
RAKUSHOU
THE IMPERIAL CAPITAL
カッ
KA (KLIK)
コッ
KO (KLAK)
カッ
KA
コッ
KO
カッ
KA

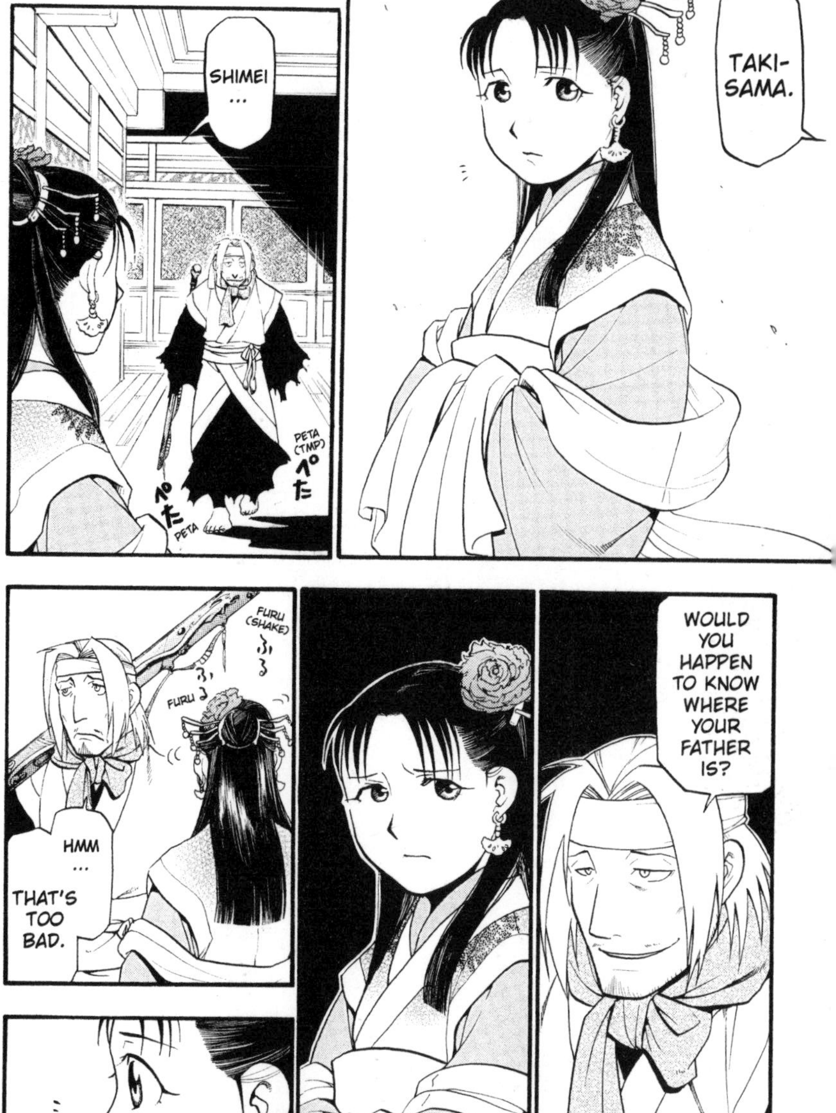
TAKI-SAMA.
SHIMEI ...
PETA (TMP)
PETA
WOULD YOU HAPPEN TO KNOW WHERE YOUR FATHER IS?
FURU (SHAKE)
FURU
HMM ... THAT'S TOO BAD.

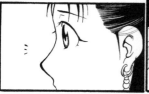

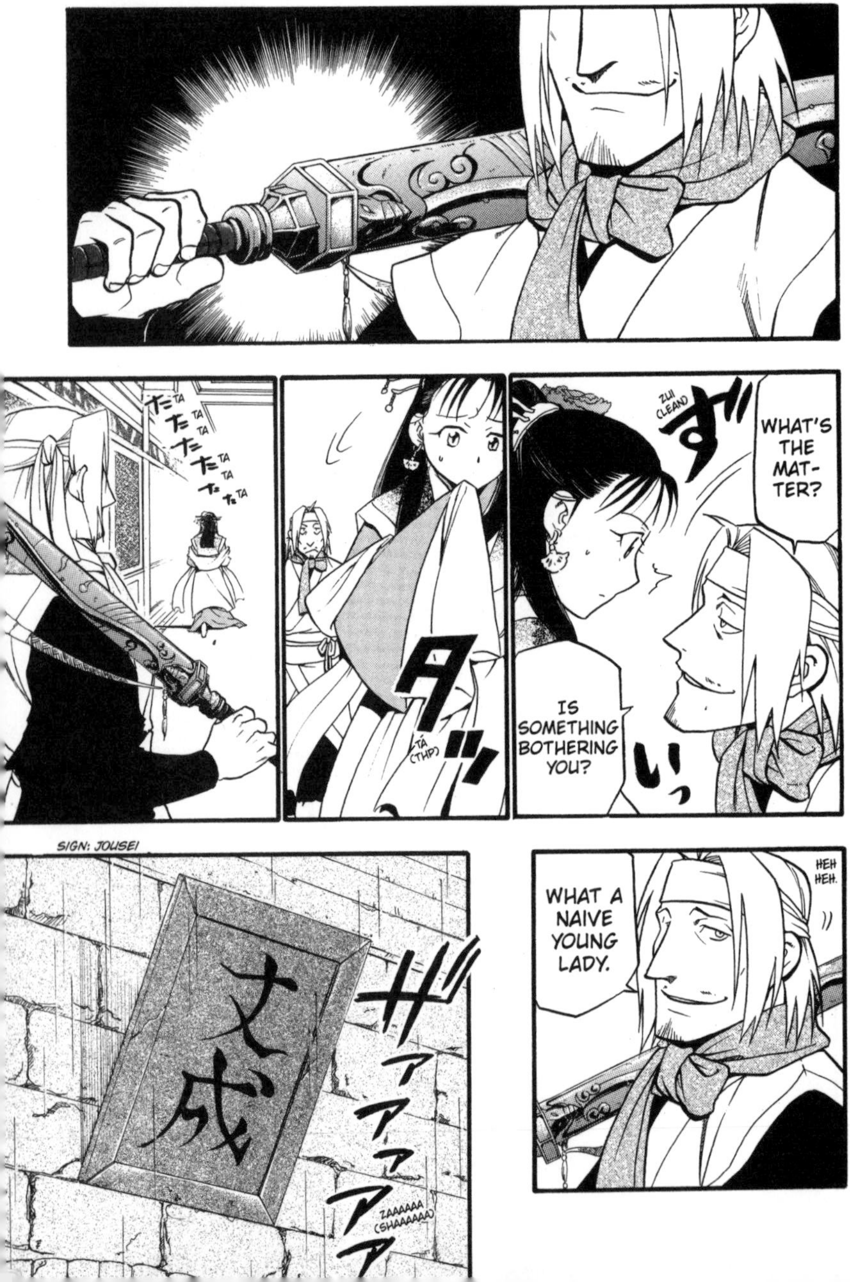
ZUI (LEAN)
WHAT'S THE MAT-TER?
IS SOMETHING BOTHERING YOU?
TA (THP)
TA TA TA TA TA TA
HEH HEH.
WHAT A NAIVE YOUNG LADY.
SIGN: JOUSEI
ZAAAAAA (SHAAAAAA)

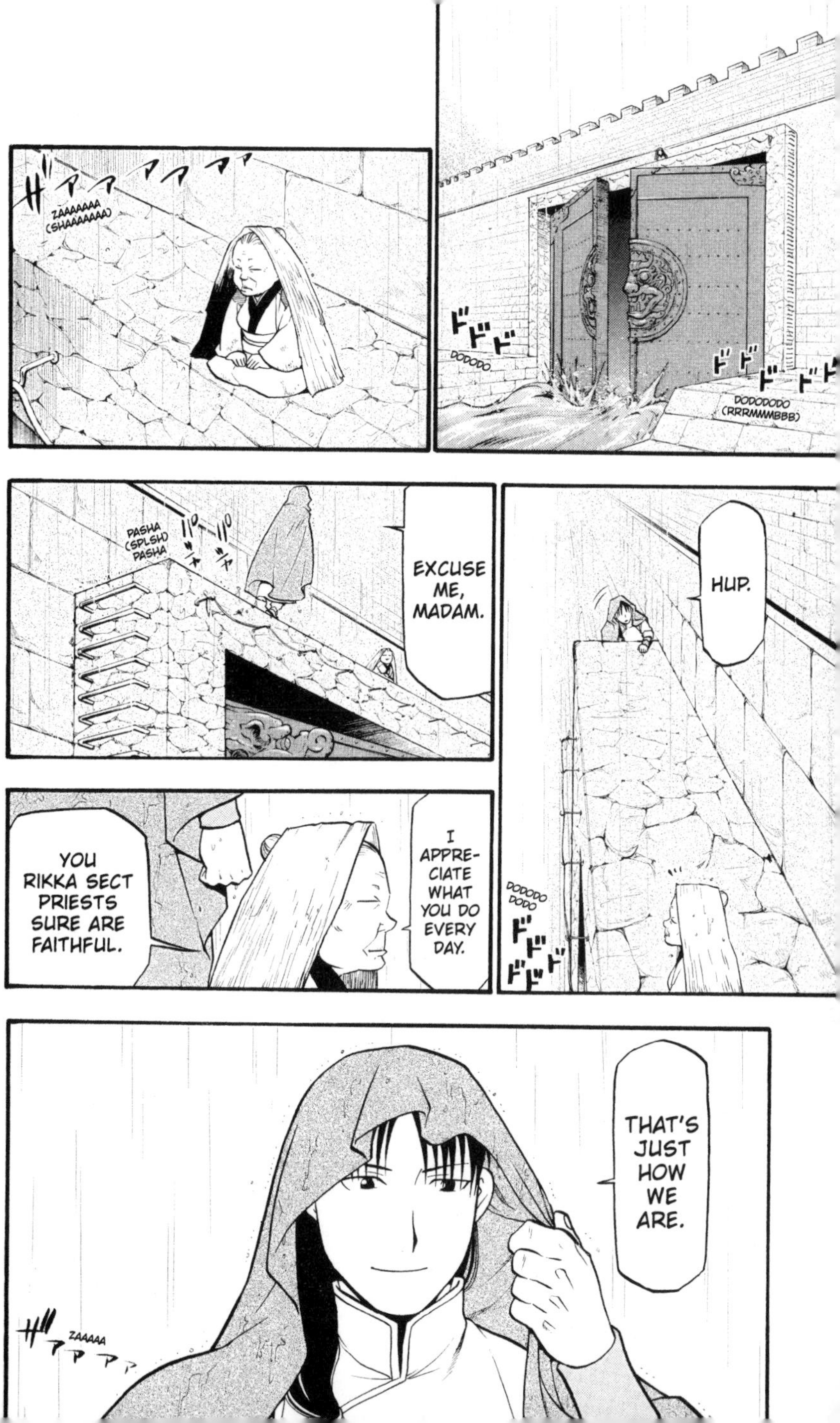
DODODO
DODODODO (RRRMMMBBB)
ZAAAAAAA (SHAAAAAAA)
HUP.
DODODO DODO
EXCUSE ME, MADAM.
PASHA (SPLSH) PASHA
I APPRECIATE WHAT YOU DO EVERY DAY.
YOU RIKKA SECT PRIESTS SURE ARE FAITHFUL.
THAT'S JUST HOW WE ARE.
ZAAAAA

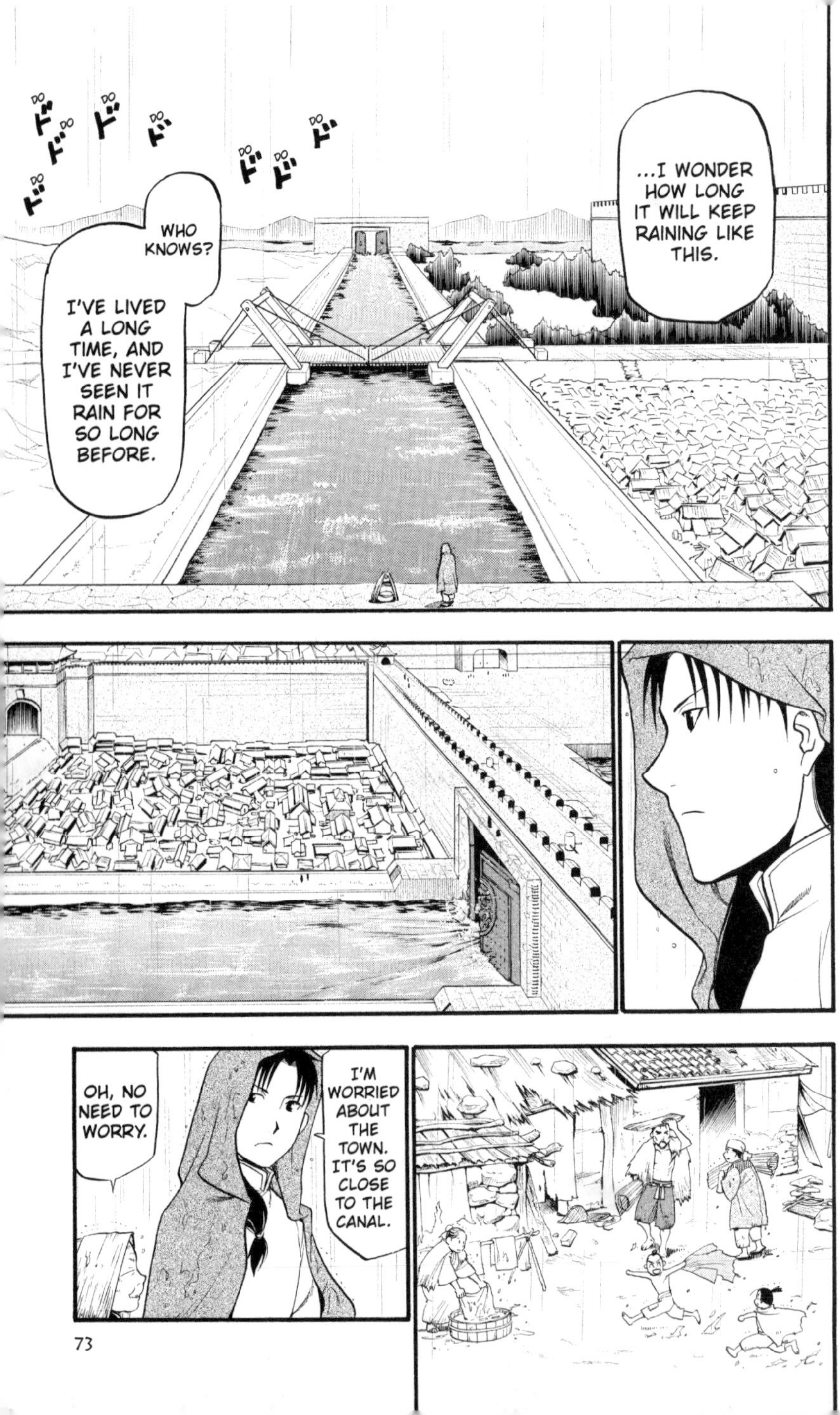
...I WONDER HOW LONG IT WILL KEEP RAINING LIKE THIS.
DO DO DO DO DO DO DO DO
ドドドドドドドド
WHO KNOWS?
I'VE LIVED A LONG TIME, AND I'VE NEVER SEEN IT RAIN FOR SO LONG BEFORE.
I'M WORRIED ABOUT THE TOWN. IT'S SO CLOSE TO THE CANAL.
OH, NO NEED TO WORRY.

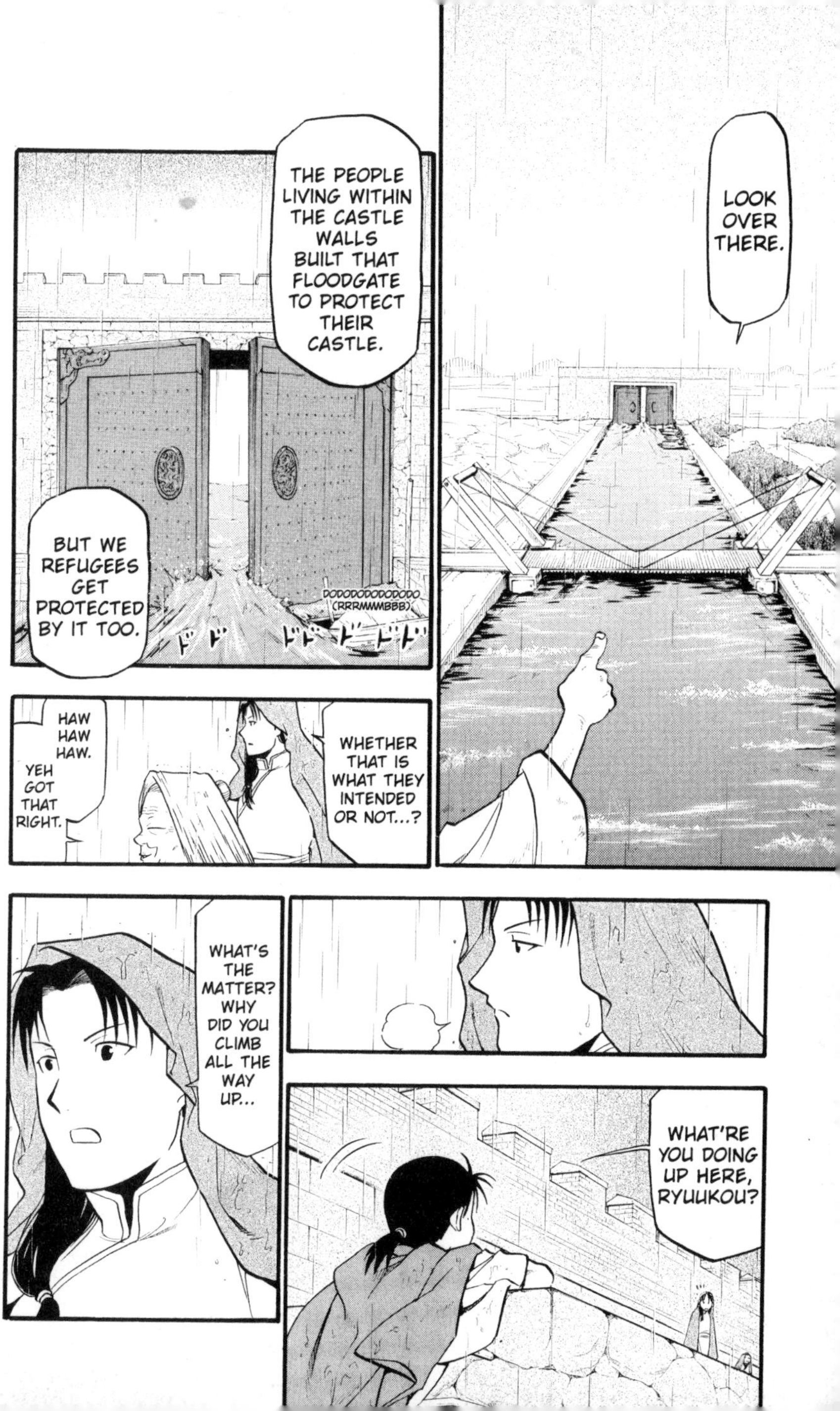
LOOK OVER THERE.
THE PEOPLE LIVING WITHIN THE CASTLE WALLS BUILT THAT FLOODGATE TO PROTECT THEIR CASTLE.
BUT WE REFUGEES GET PROTECTED BY IT TOO.
DODODODODODODO (RRRMMMBBB)
WHETHER THAT IS WHAT THEY INTENDED OR NOT...?
HAW HAW HAW. YEH GOT THAT RIGHT.
WHAT'RE YOU DOING UP HERE, RYUUKOU?
WHAT'S THE MATTER? WHY DID YOU CLIMB ALL THE WAY UP...

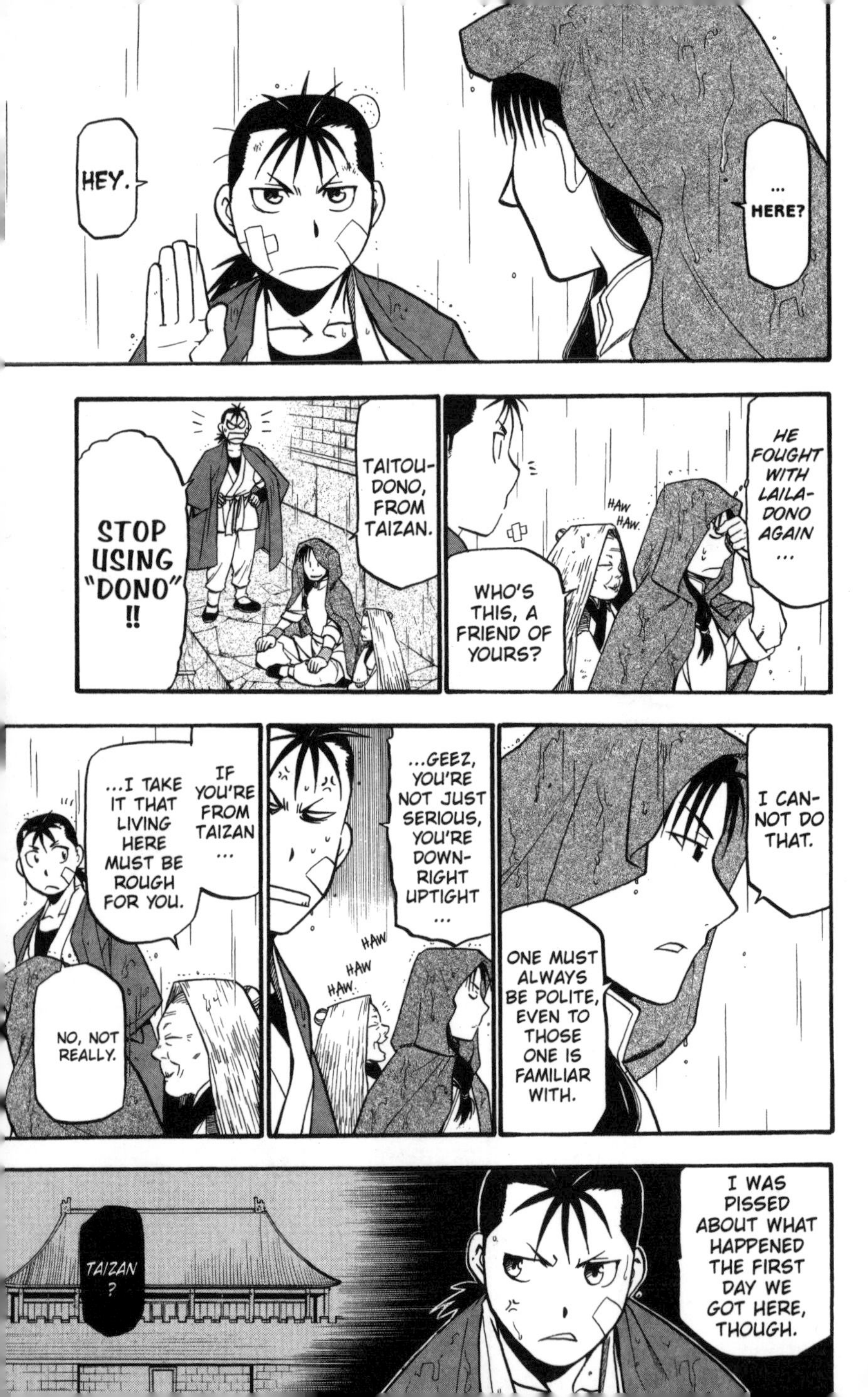

... HERE?
HEY.
HE FOUGHT WITH LAILA-DONO AGAIN ...
HAW HAW.
WHO'S THIS, A FRIEND OF YOURS?
TAITOU-DONO, FROM TAIZAN.
STOP USING "DONO" !!
I CAN-NOT DO THAT.
ONE MUST ALWAYS BE POLITE, EVEN TO THOSE ONE IS FAMILIAR WITH.
...GEEZ, YOU'RE NOT JUST SERIOUS, YOU'RE DOWN-RIGHT UPTIGHT ...
HAW HAW HAW.
IF YOU'RE FROM TAIZAN ...
...I TAKE IT THAT LIVING HERE MUST BE ROUGH FOR YOU.
NO, NOT REALLY.
I WAS PISSED ABOUT WHAT HAPPENED THE FIRST DAY WE GOT HERE, THOUGH.
TAIZAN ?

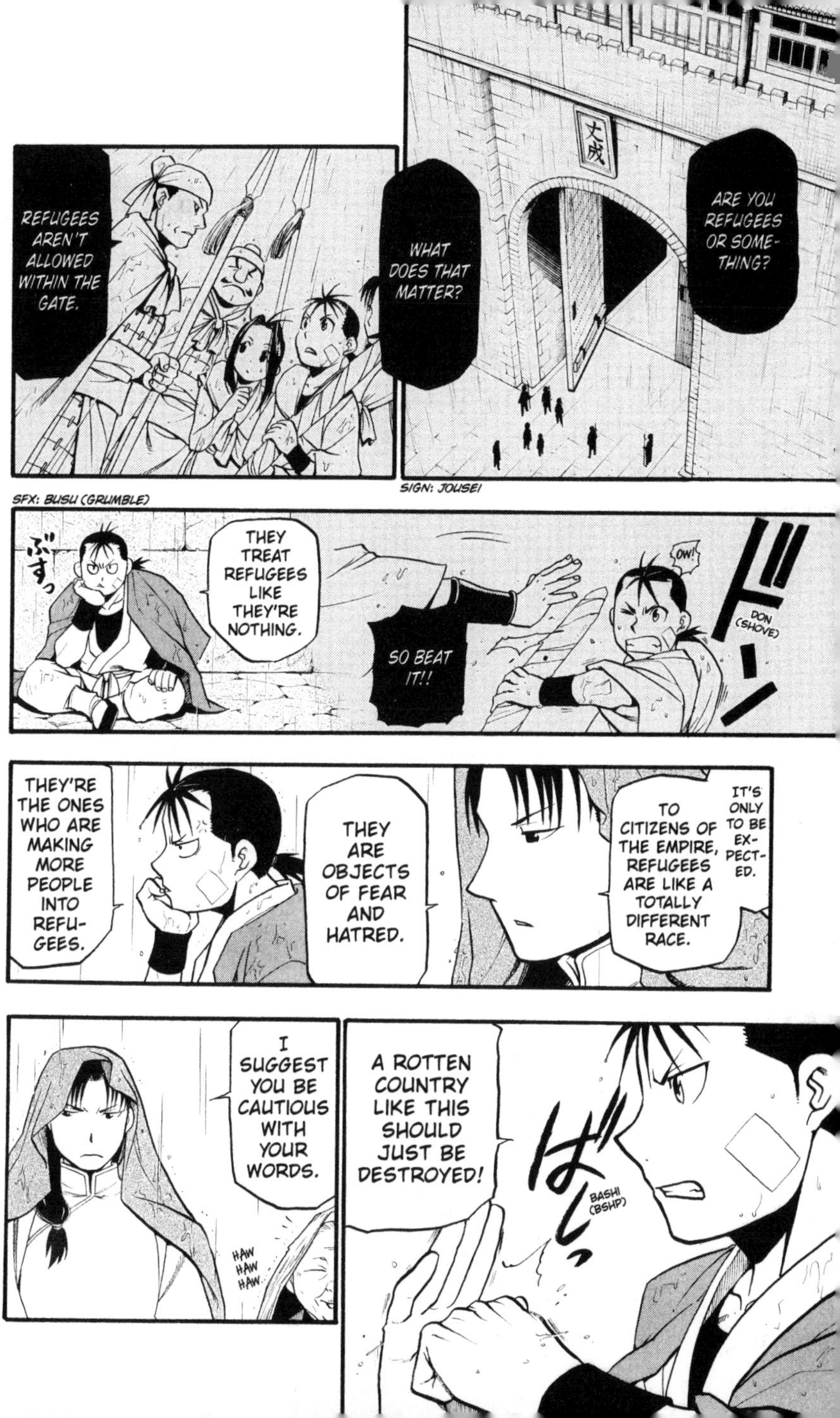
ARE YOU REFUGEES OR SOME-THING?
WHAT DOES THAT MATTER?
SIGN: JOUSEI
REFUGEES AREN'T ALLOWED WITHIN THE GATE.
SFX: BUSU (GRUMBLE)
OW!
DON (SHOVE)
SO BEAT IT!!
THEY TREAT REFUGEES LIKE THEY'RE NOTHING.
IT'S ONLY TO BE EX-PECT-ED.
TO CITIZENS OF THE EMPIRE, REFUGEES ARE LIKE A TOTALLY DIFFERENT RACE.
THEY ARE OBJECTS OF FEAR AND HATRED.
THEY'RE THE ONES WHO ARE MAKING MORE PEOPLE INTO REFU-GEES.
A ROTTEN COUNTRY LIKE THIS SHOULD JUST BE DESTROYED!
BASHI (BSHP)
I SUGGEST YOU BE CAUTIOUS WITH YOUR WORDS.
HAW HAW HAW.

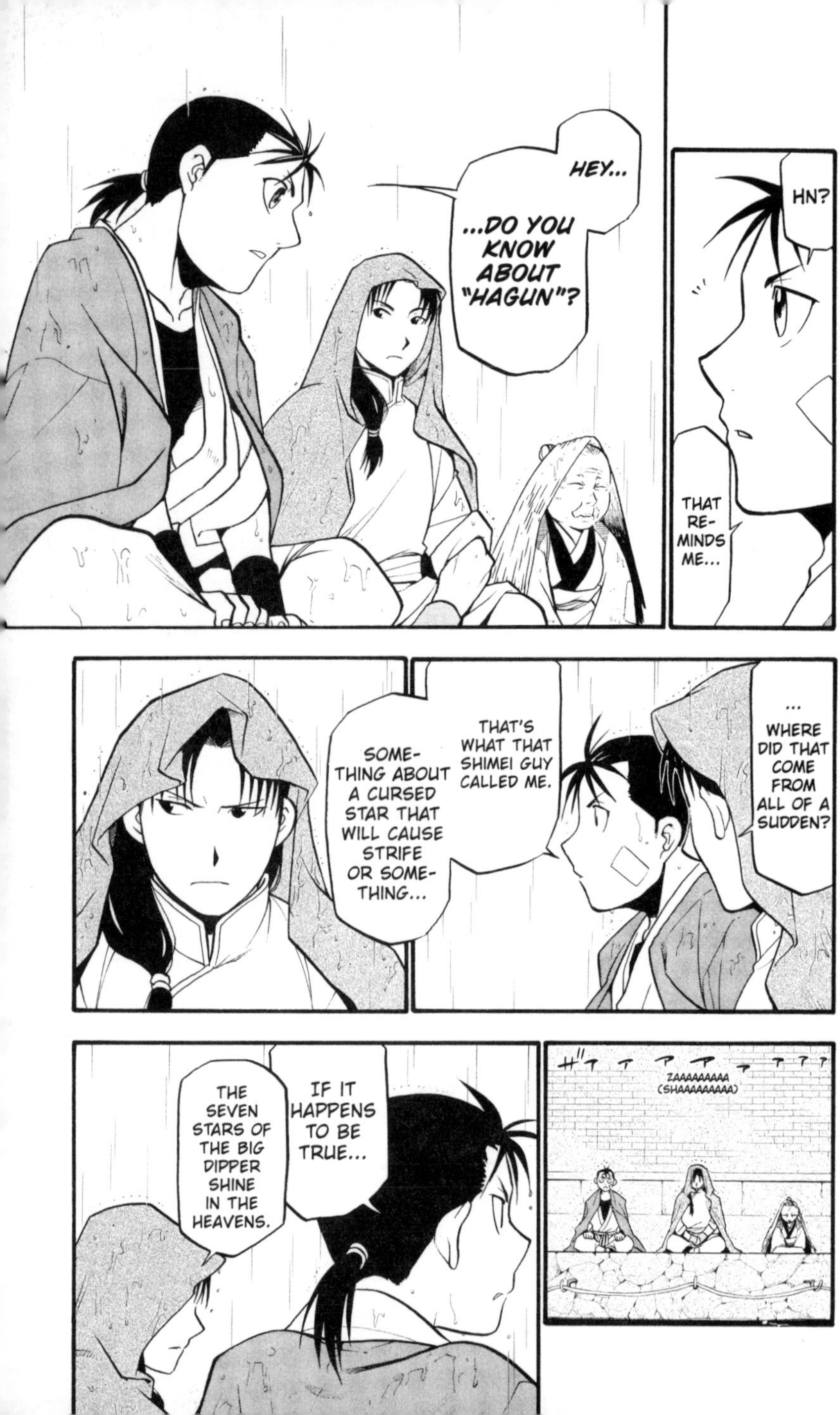
HN?
THAT RE-MINDS ME...
HEY...
...DO YOU KNOW ABOUT "HAGUN"?
... WHERE DID THAT COME FROM ALL OF A SUDDEN?
THAT'S WHAT THAT SHIMEI GUY CALLED ME.
SOME-THING ABOUT A CURSED STAR THAT WILL CAUSE STRIFE OR SOME-THING...
ZAAAAAAAAA (SHAAAAAAAAA)
IF IT HAPPENS TO BE TRUE...
THE SEVEN STARS OF THE BIG DIPPER SHINE IN THE HEAVENS.

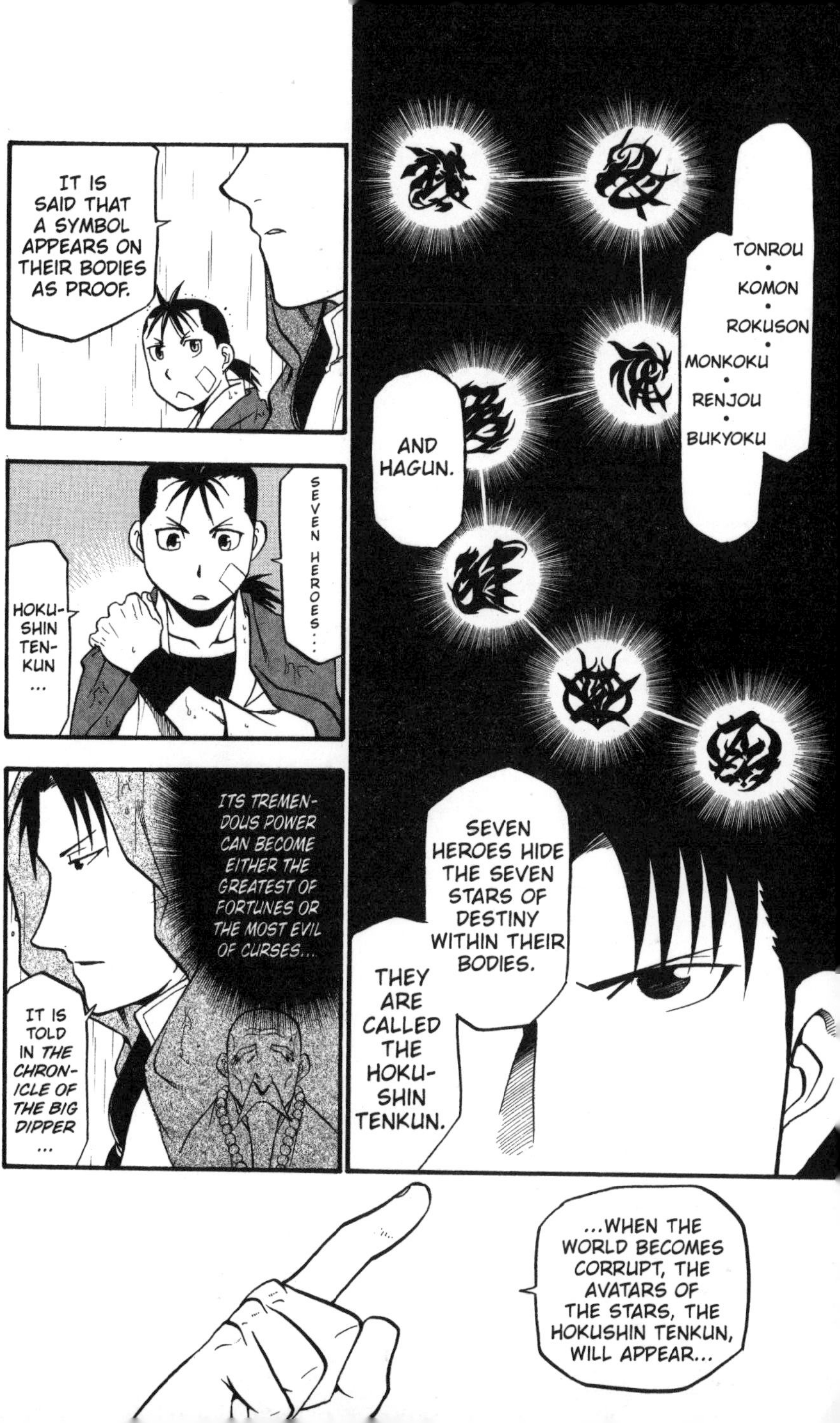
TONROU • KOMON • ROKUSON • MONKOKU • RENJOU • BUKYOKU
AND HAGUN.
SEVEN HEROES HIDE THE SEVEN STARS OF DESTINY WITHIN THEIR BODIES.
THEY ARE CALLED THE HOKUSHIN TENKUN.
IT IS SAID THAT A SYMBOL APPEARS ON THEIR BODIES AS PROOF.
SEVEN HEROES...
HOKUSHIN TENKUN...
ITS TREMENDOUS POWER CAN BECOME EITHER THE GREATEST OF FORTUNES OR THE MOST EVIL OF CURSES...
IT IS TOLD IN *THE CHRONICLE OF THE BIG DIPPER*...
...WHEN THE WORLD BECOMES CORRUPT, THE AVATARS OF THE STARS, THE HOKUSHIN TENKUN, WILL APPEAR...

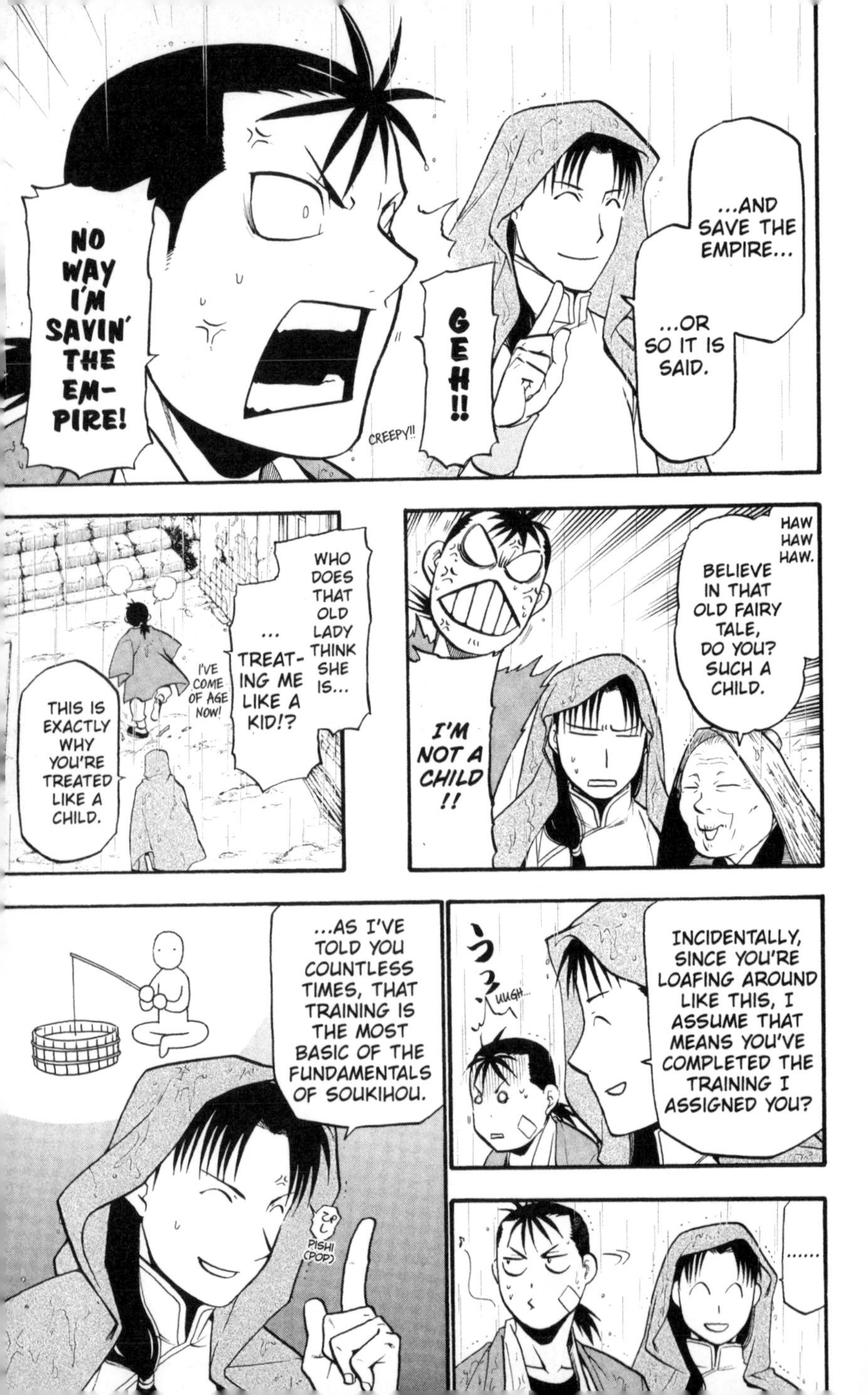

...AND SAVE THE EMPIRE...
...OR SO IT IS SAID.
GEH!!
CREEPY!!
NO WAY I'M SAVIN' THE EMPIRE!
HAW HAW HAW.
BELIEVE IN THAT OLD FAIRY TALE, DO YOU? SUCH A CHILD.
I'M NOT A CHILD!!
WHO DOES THAT OLD LADY THINK SHE IS...
...TREATING ME LIKE A KID!?
I'VE COME OF AGE NOW!
THIS IS EXACTLY WHY YOU'RE TREATED LIKE A CHILD.
INCIDENTALLY, SINCE YOU'RE LOAFING AROUND LIKE THIS, I ASSUME THAT MEANS YOU'VE COMPLETED THE TRAINING I ASSIGNED YOU?
UUGH...
......
...AS I'VE TOLD YOU COUNTLESS TIMES, THAT TRAINING IS THE MOST BASIC OF THE FUNDAMENTALS OF SOUKIHOU.
PISHI (POP)

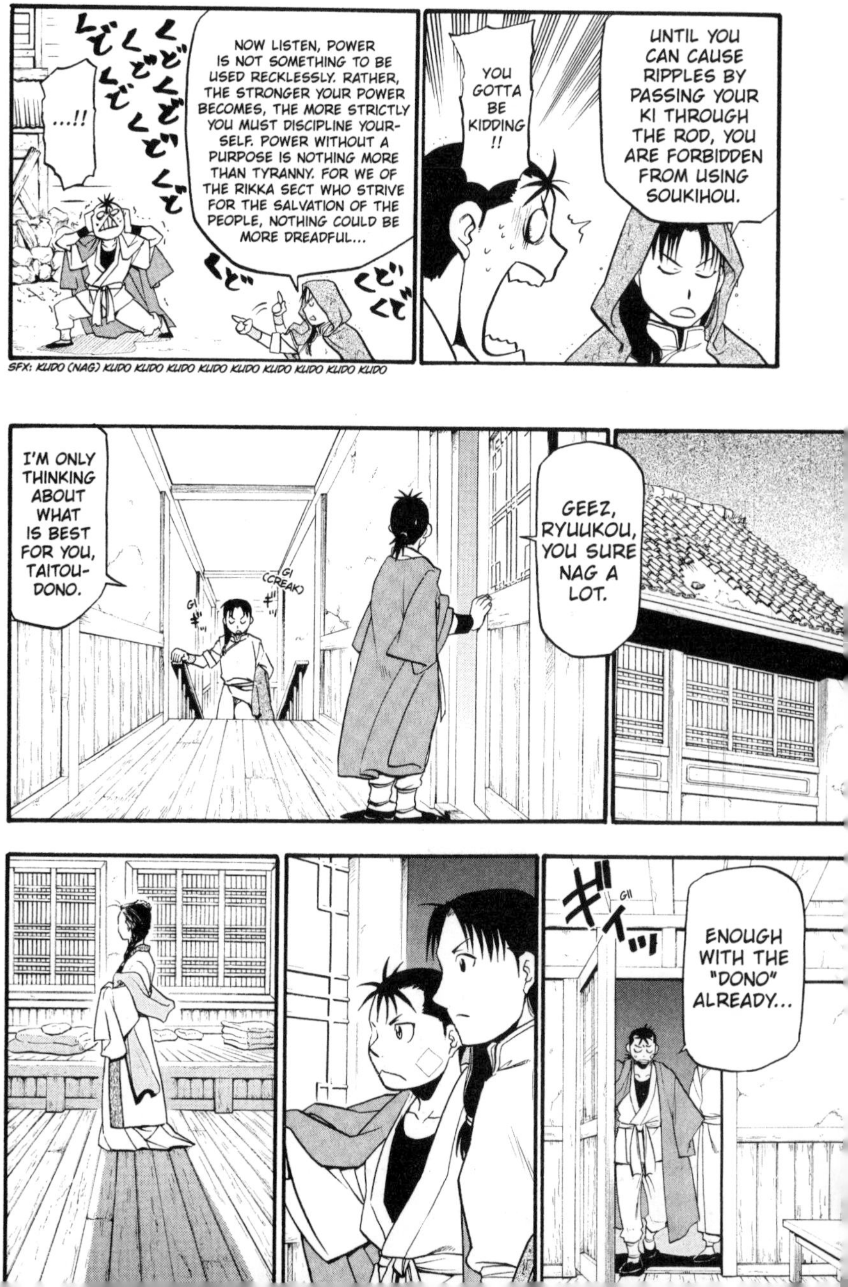
UNTIL YOU CAN CAUSE RIPPLES BY PASSING YOUR KI THROUGH THE ROD, YOU ARE FORBIDDEN FROM USING SOUKIHOU.
YOU GOTTA BE KIDDING!!
NOW LISTEN, POWER IS NOT SOMETHING TO BE USED RECKLESSLY. RATHER, THE STRONGER YOUR POWER BECOMES, THE MORE STRICTLY YOU MUST DISCIPLINE YOURSELF. POWER WITHOUT A PURPOSE IS NOTHING MORE THAN TYRANNY. FOR WE OF THE RIKKA SECT WHO STRIVE FOR THE SALVATION OF THE PEOPLE, NOTHING COULD BE MORE DREADFUL...
...!!
SFX: KUDO (NAG) KUDO KUDO KUDO KUDO KUDO KUDO KUDO KUDO KUDO
GEEZ, RYUUKOU, YOU SURE NAG A LOT.
GI (CREAK)
GI
I'M ONLY THINKING ABOUT WHAT IS BEST FOR YOU, TAITOU-DONO.
GII
ENOUGH WITH THE "DONO" ALREADY...

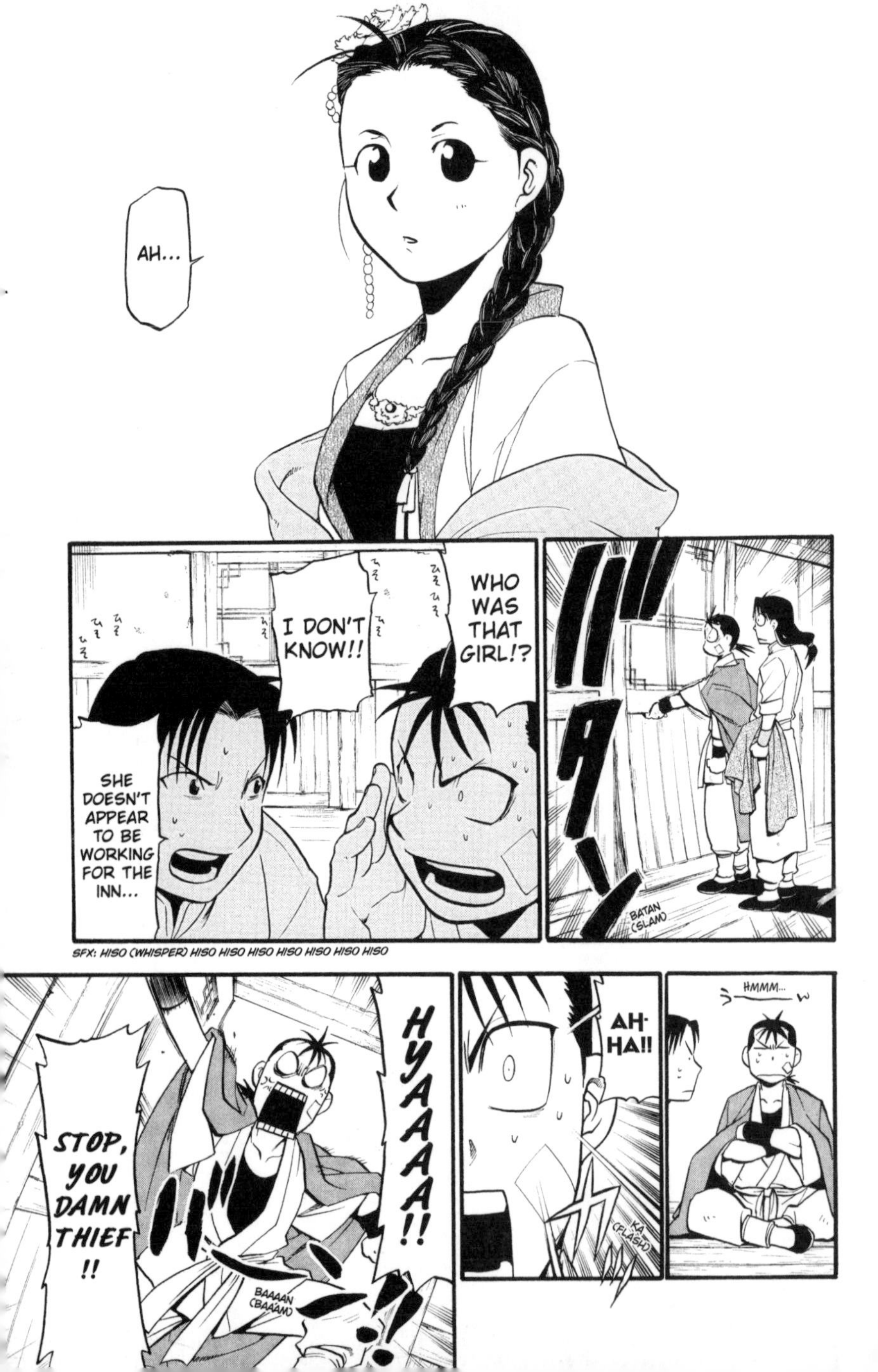
AH...
BATAN (SLAM)
WHO WAS THAT GIRL!?
I DON'T KNOW!!
SHE DOESN'T APPEAR TO BE WORKING FOR THE INN...
SFX: HISO (WHISPER) HISO HISO HISO HISO HISO HISO HISO
HMMM...
AH-HA!!
KA (FLASH)
HYAAAAA!!
STOP, YOU DAMN THIEF!!
BAAAAN (BAAAM)

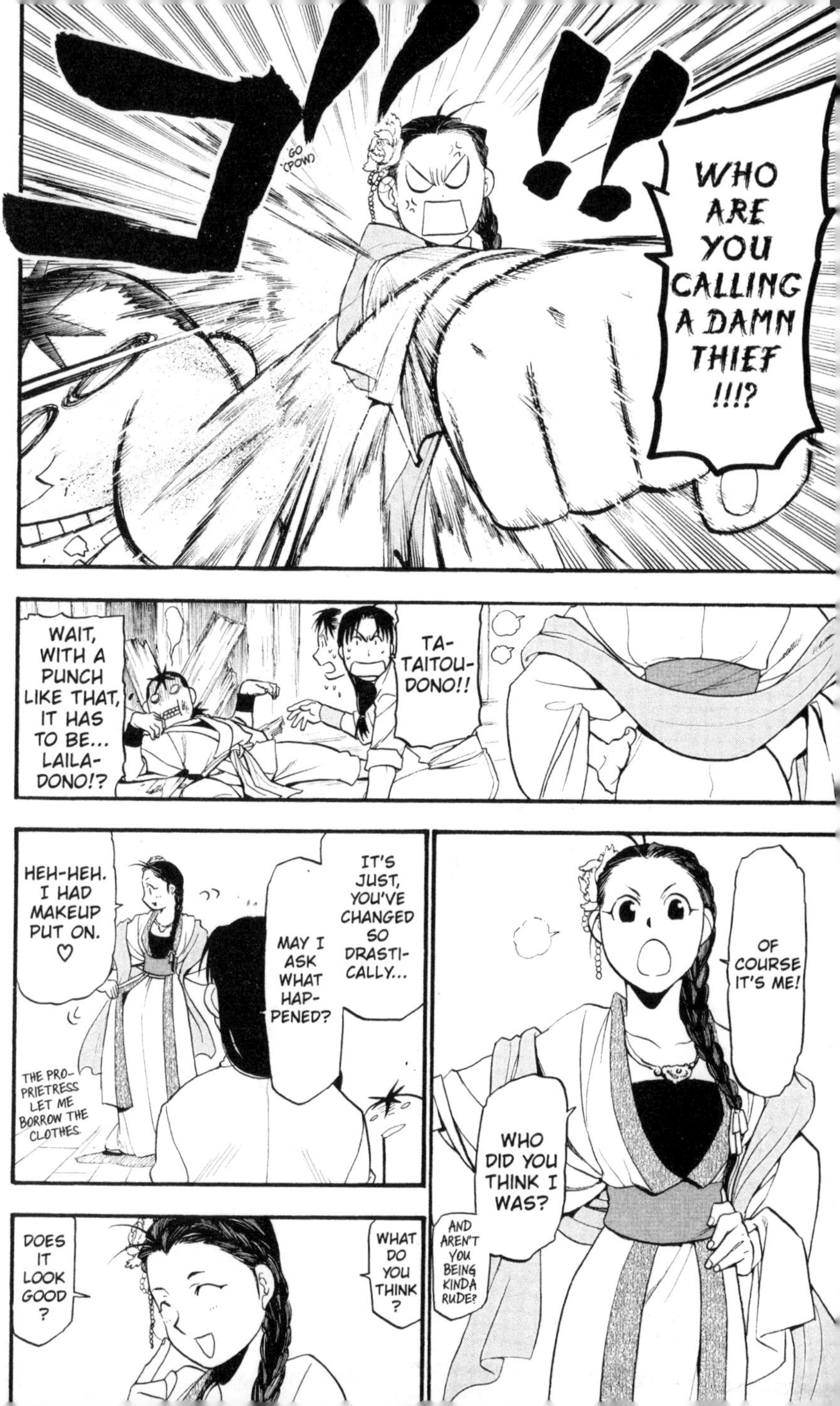
WHO ARE YOU CALLING A DAMN THIEF !!!?
GO (POW)
TA-TAITOU-DONO!!
WAIT, WITH A PUNCH LIKE THAT, IT HAS TO BE... LAILA-DONO!?
OF COURSE IT'S ME!
WHO DID YOU THINK I WAS?
AND AREN'T YOU BEING KINDA RUDE?
IT'S JUST, YOU'VE CHANGED SO DRASTI-CALLY...
MAY I ASK WHAT HAP-PENED?
HEH-HEH. I HAD MAKEUP PUT ON. ♡
THE PRO-PRIETRESS LET ME BORROW THE CLOTHES.
WHAT DO YOU THINK ?
DOES IT LOOK GOOD ?

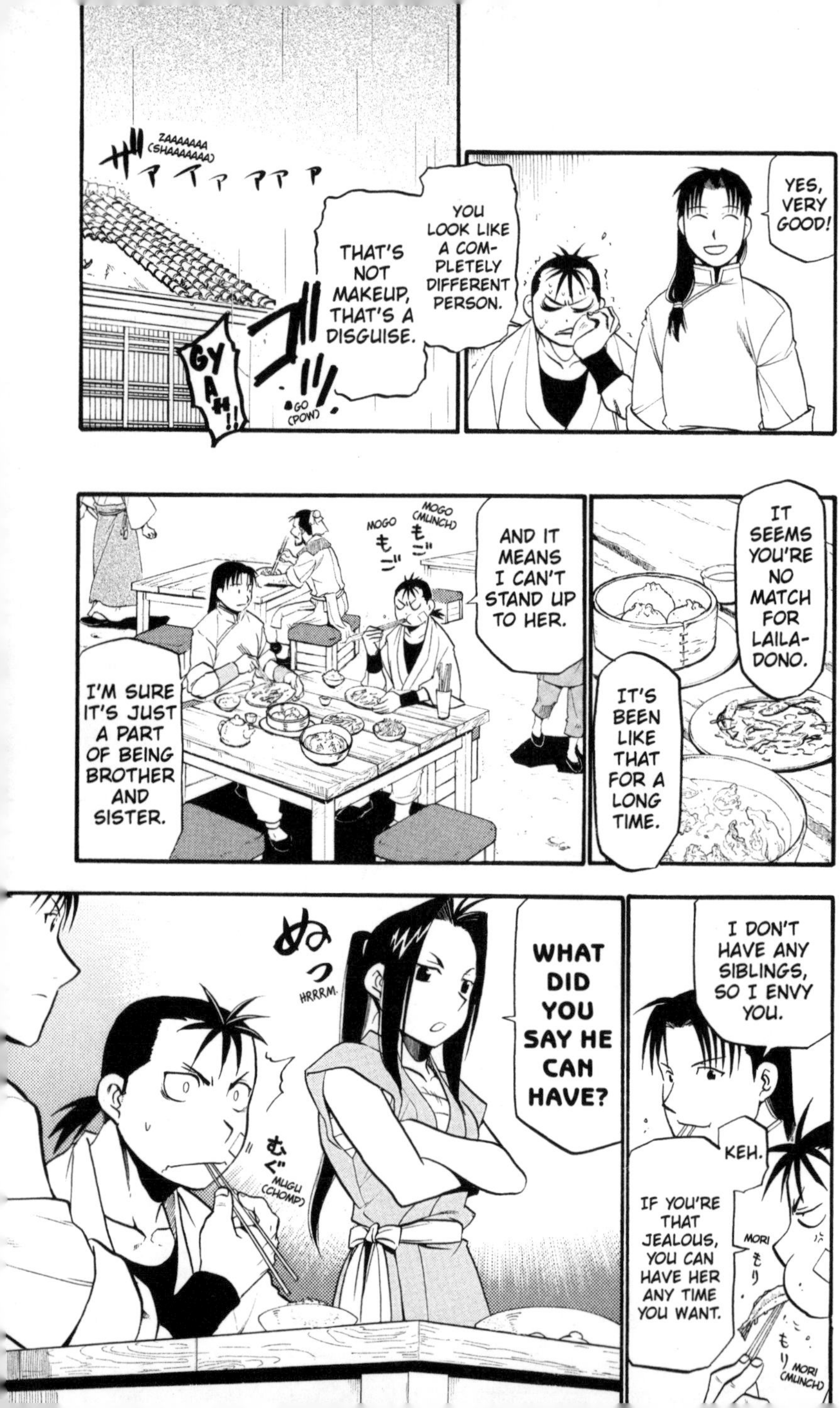
YES, VERY GOOD!
YOU LOOK LIKE A COM-PLETELY DIFFERENT PERSON.
THAT'S NOT MAKEUP, THAT'S A DISGUISE.
ZAAAAAAA (SHAAAAAAAA)
GYAH!!
GO (POW)
IT SEEMS YOU'RE NO MATCH FOR LAILA-DONO.
IT'S BEEN LIKE THAT FOR A LONG TIME.
MOGO (MUNCH)
MOGO
AND IT MEANS I CAN'T STAND UP TO HER.
I'M SURE IT'S JUST A PART OF BEING BROTHER AND SISTER.
I DON'T HAVE ANY SIBLINGS, SO I ENVY YOU.
KEH.
IF YOU'RE THAT JEALOUS, YOU CAN HAVE HER ANY TIME YOU WANT.
MORI
MORI (MUNCH)
WHAT DID YOU SAY HE CAN HAVE?
HRRRM.
MUGU (CHOMP)

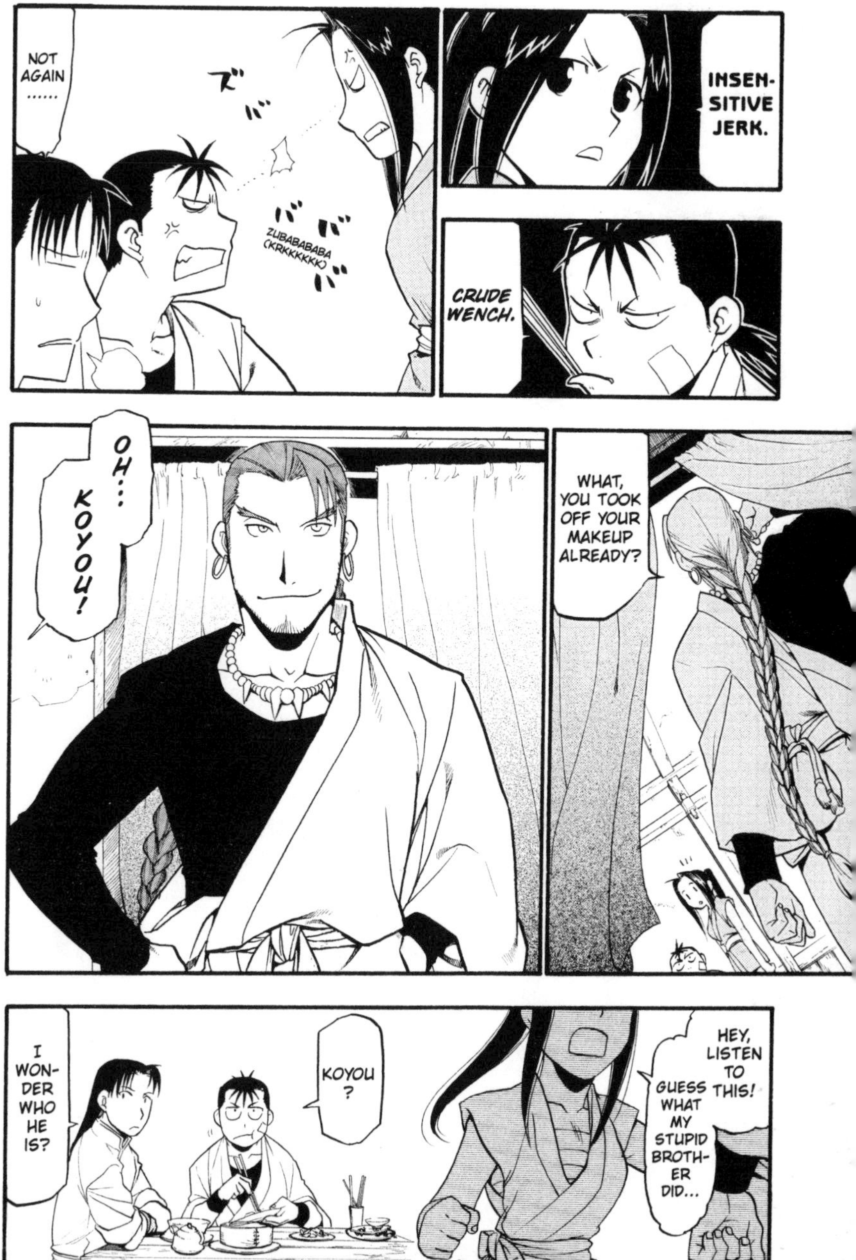
INSEN-SITIVE JERK.
CRUDE WENCH.
NOT AGAIN ......
ZUBABABABA (KRKKKKKK)
WHAT, YOU TOOK OFF YOUR MAKEUP ALREADY?
OH... KOYOU!
HEY, LISTEN TO THIS!
GUESS WHAT MY STUPID BROTH-ER DID...
KOYOU?
I WON-DER WHO HE IS?

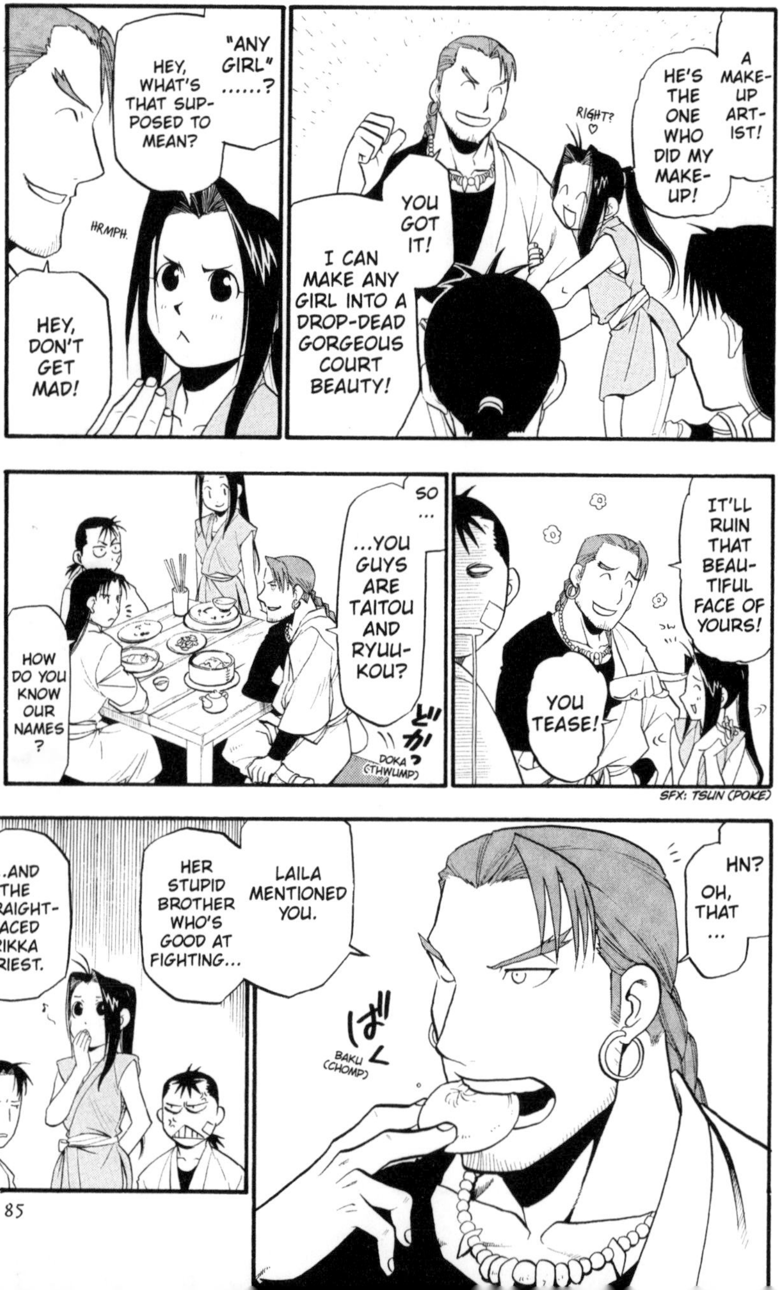
A MAKE-UP ARTIST!
HE'S THE ONE WHO DID MY MAKE-UP!
RIGHT? ♡
YOU GOT IT!
I CAN MAKE ANY GIRL INTO A DROP-DEAD GORGEOUS COURT BEAUTY!
"ANY GIRL" ......?
HEY, WHAT'S THAT SUPPOSED TO MEAN?
HRMPH.
HEY, DON'T GET MAD!
IT'LL RUIN THAT BEAUTIFUL FACE OF YOURS!
YOU TEASE!
SFX: TSUN (POKE)
SO ...
...YOU GUYS ARE TAITOU AND RYUUKOU?
DOKA (THWUMP)
HOW DO YOU KNOW OUR NAMES?
HN?
OH, THAT ...
BAKU (CHOMP)
LAILA MENTIONED YOU.
HER STUPID BROTHER WHO'S GOOD AT FIGHTING...
...AND THE STRAIGHT-LACED RIKKA PRIEST.

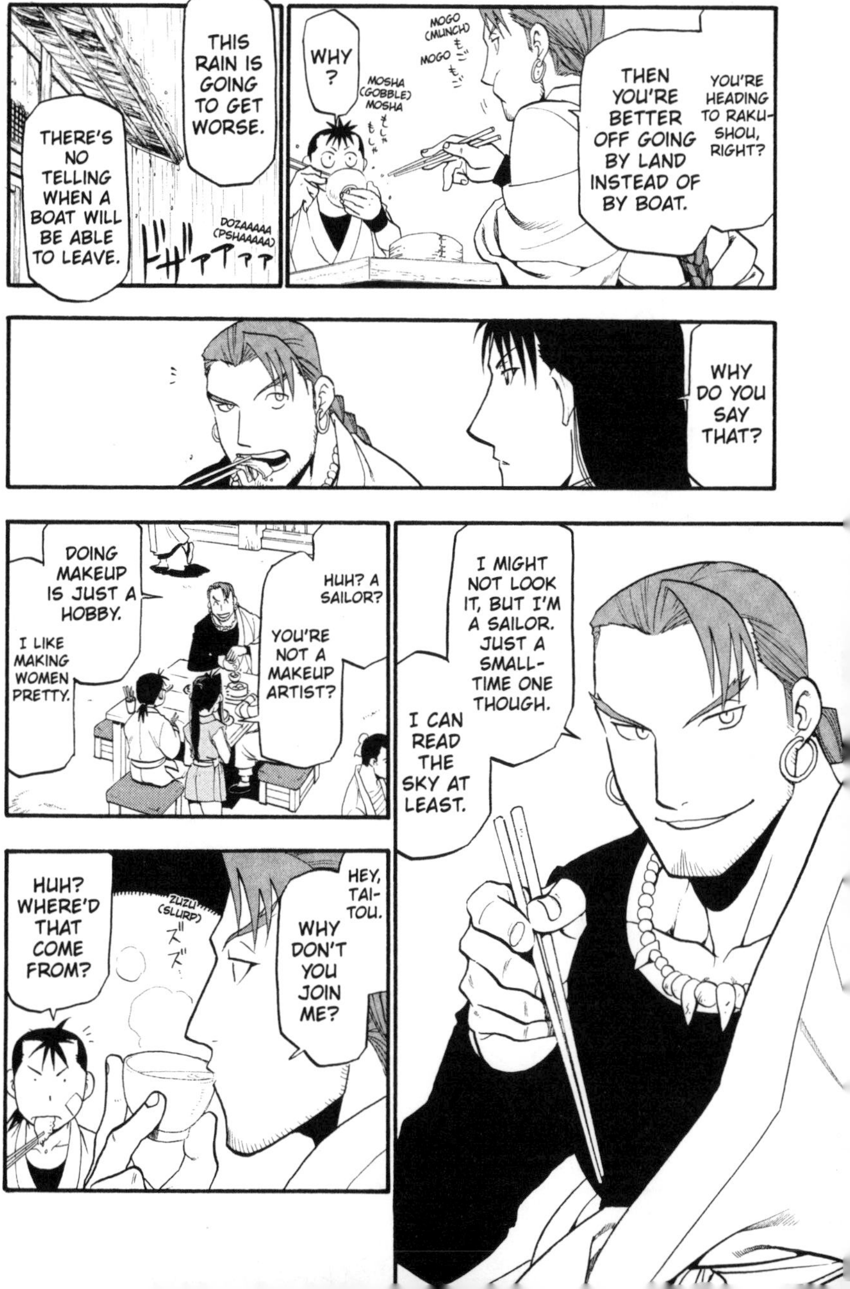
YOU'RE HEADING TO RAKU-SHOU, RIGHT?
THEN YOU'RE BETTER OFF GOING BY LAND INSTEAD OF BY BOAT.
MOGO (MUNCH) MOGO
MOSHA (GOBBLE) MOSHA
WHY?
THIS RAIN IS GOING TO GET WORSE.
THERE'S NO TELLING WHEN A BOAT WILL BE ABLE TO LEAVE.
DOZAAAAA (PSHAAAAA)
WHY DO YOU SAY THAT?
I MIGHT NOT LOOK IT, BUT I'M A SAILOR. JUST A SMALL-TIME ONE THOUGH.
I CAN READ THE SKY AT LEAST.
HUH? A SAILOR?
YOU'RE NOT A MAKEUP ARTIST?
DOING MAKEUP IS JUST A HOBBY.
I LIKE MAKING WOMEN PRETTY.
HEY, TAI-TOU.
WHY DON'T YOU JOIN ME?
ZUZU (SLURP)
HUH? WHERE'D THAT COME FROM?

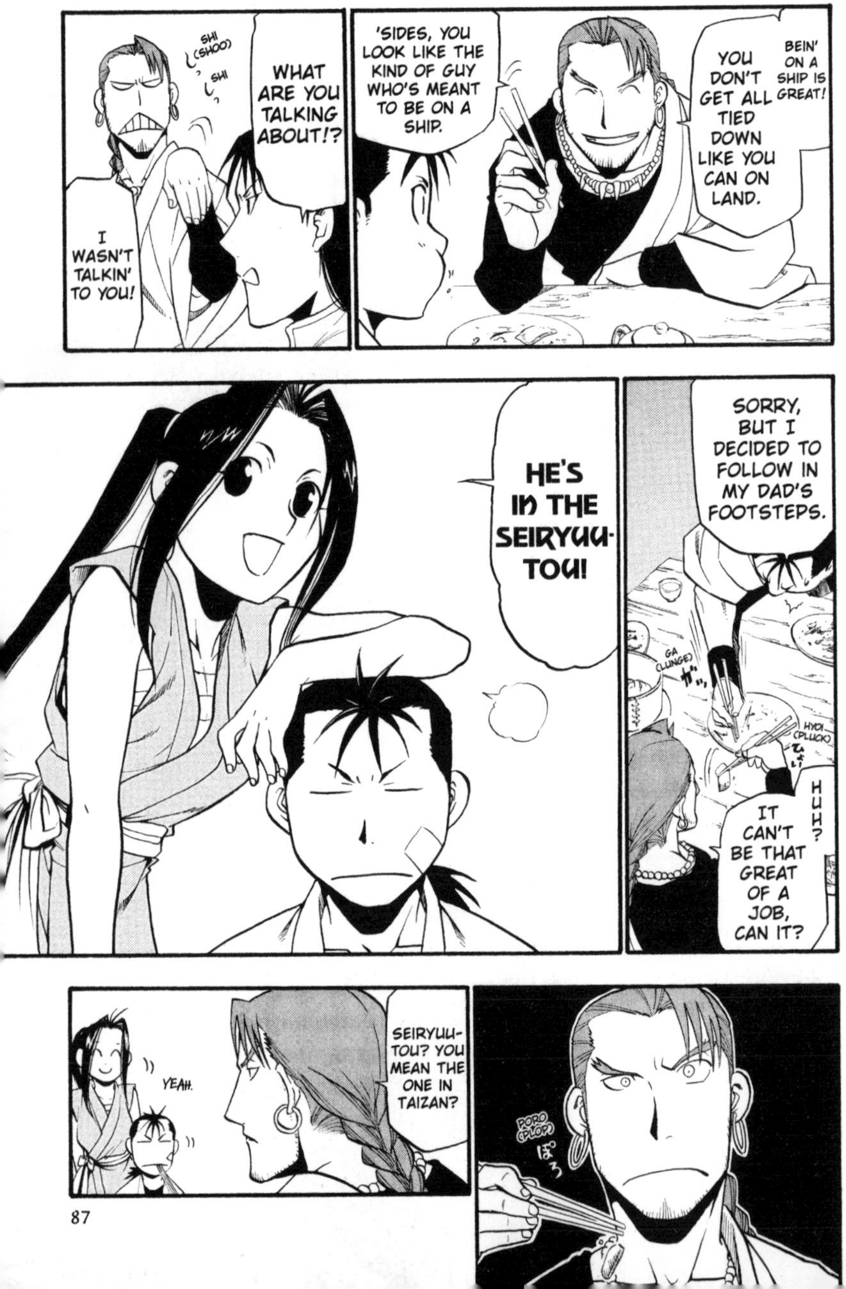
BEIN' ON A SHIP IS GREAT!
YOU DON'T GET ALL TIED DOWN LIKE YOU CAN ON LAND.
'SIDES, YOU LOOK LIKE THE KIND OF GUY WHO'S MEANT TO BE ON A SHIP.
WHAT ARE YOU TALKING ABOUT!?
SHI (SHOO) SHI
I WASN'T TALKIN' TO YOU!
SORRY, BUT I DECIDED TO FOLLOW IN MY DAD'S FOOTSTEPS.
GA (LUNGE)
HYOI (PLUCK)
HUH?
IT CAN'T BE THAT GREAT OF A JOB, CAN IT?
HE'S IN THE SEIRYUU-TOU!
PORO (PLOP)
SEIRYUU-TOU? YOU MEAN THE ONE IN TAIZAN?
YEAH.

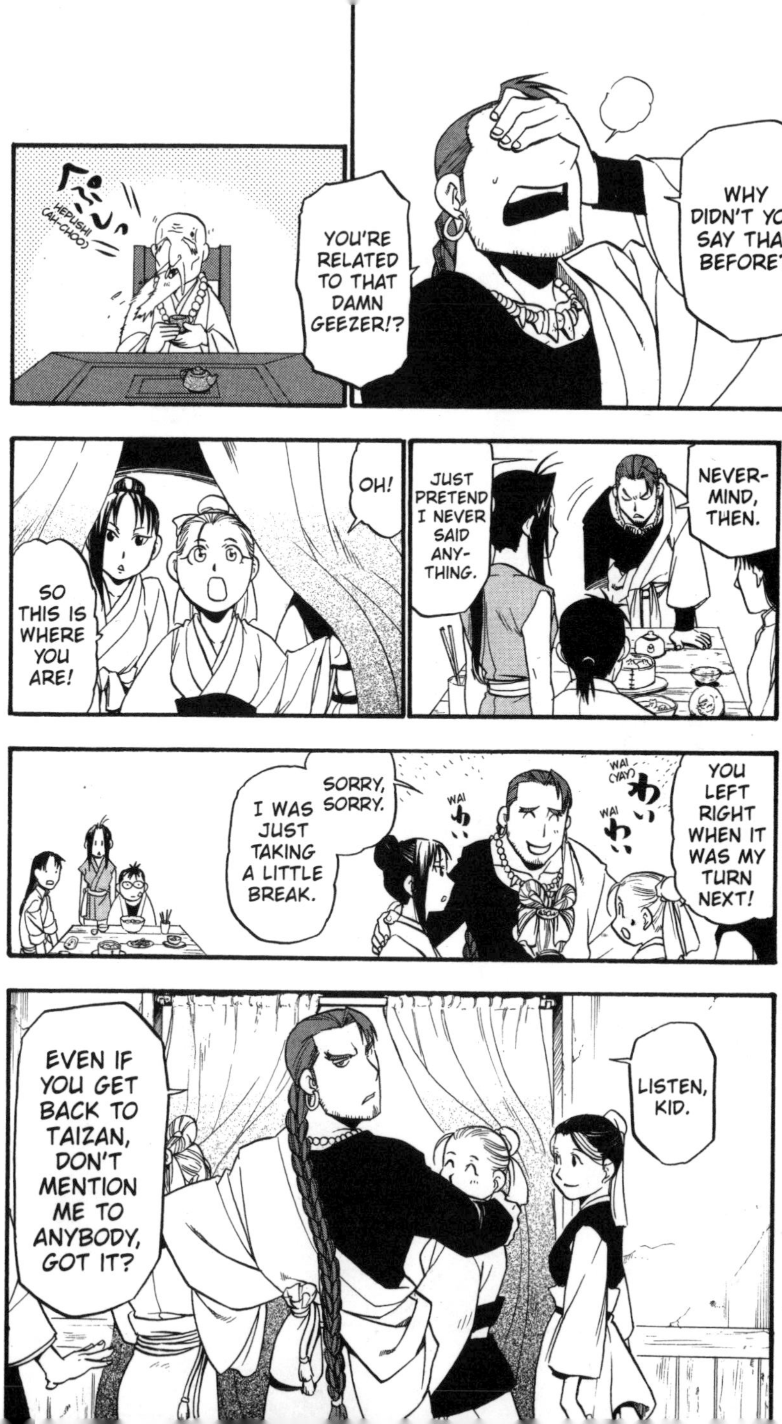
WHY DIDN'T YOU SAY THAT BEFORE?
YOU'RE RELATED TO THAT DAMN GEEZER!?
HEPUSHI (AH-CHOO)
NEVER-MIND, THEN.
JUST PRETEND I NEVER SAID ANYTHING.
OH!
SO THIS IS WHERE YOU ARE!
YOU LEFT RIGHT WHEN IT WAS MY TURN NEXT!
WAI (YAY)
WAI
WAI
SORRY, SORRY.
I WAS JUST TAKING A LITTLE BREAK.
LISTEN, KID.
EVEN IF YOU GET BACK TO TAIZAN, DON'T MENTION ME TO ANYBODY, GOT IT?

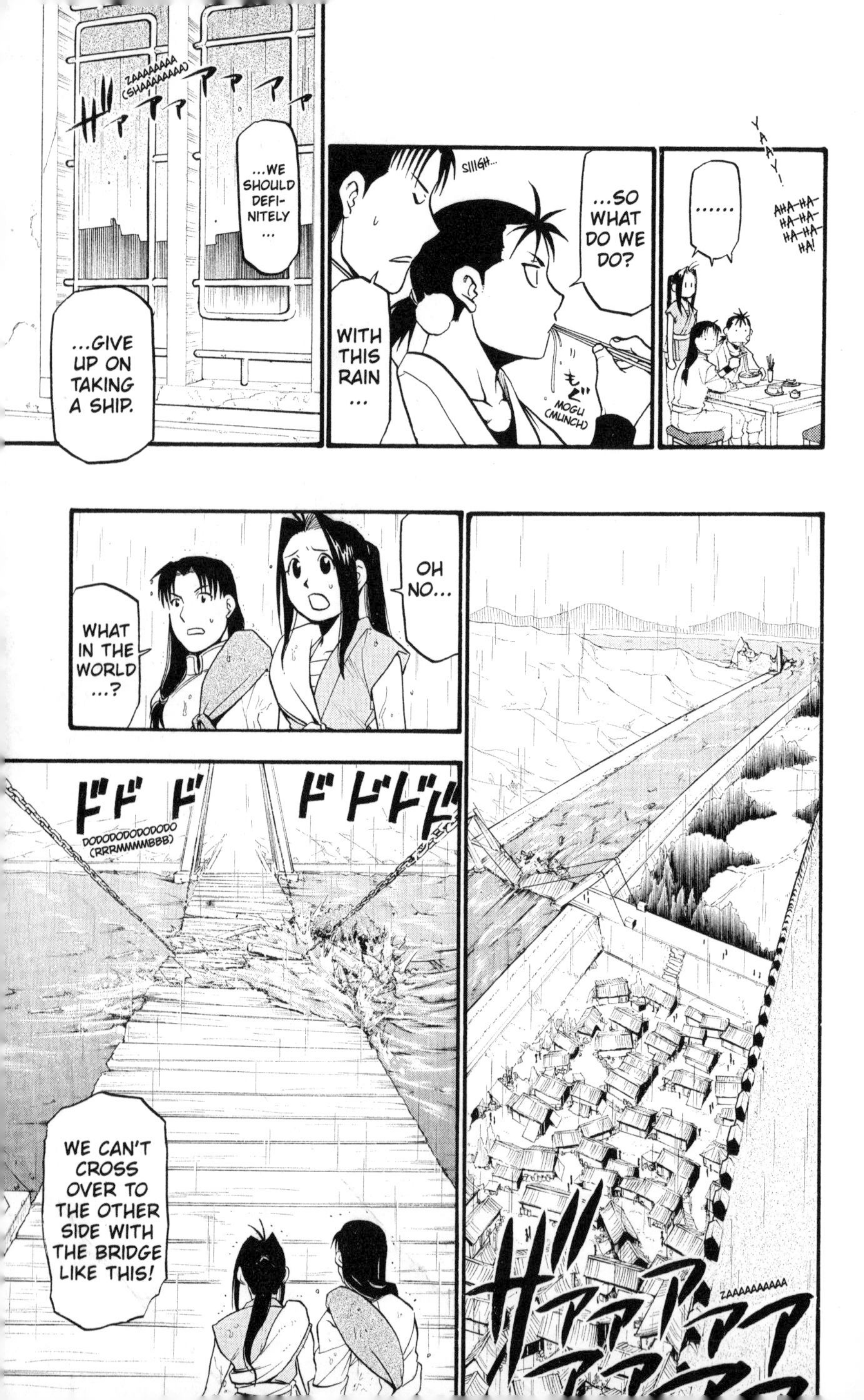

YAAAY!
AHA-HA-HA-HA-HA-HA-HA!
......
SIIIGH...
...SO WHAT DO WE DO?
WITH THIS RAIN...
もぐ
MOGU (MUNCH)
ZAAAAAAAA (SHAAAAAAAA)
...WE SHOULD DEFINITELY...
...GIVE UP ON TAKING A SHIP.
ZAAAAAAAAA
OH NO...
WHAT IN THE WORLD...?
DODODODODODODO (RRRMMMMBBB)
WE CAN'T CROSS OVER TO THE OTHER SIDE WITH THE BRIDGE LIKE THIS!

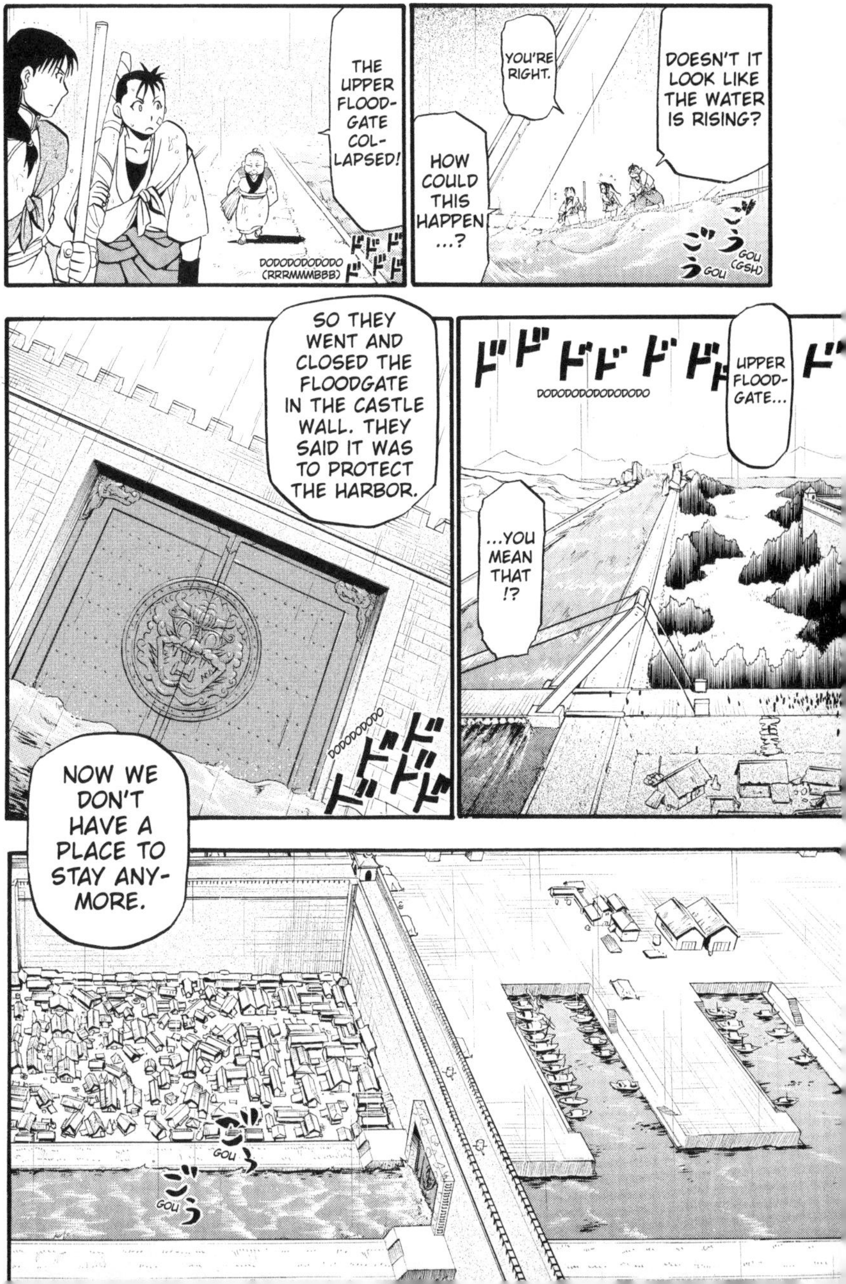
DOESN'T IT LOOK LIKE THE WATER IS RISING?
YOU'RE RIGHT.
HOW COULD THIS HAPPEN ...?
GOU (GSH)
GOU
THE UPPER FLOOD-GATE COL-LAPSED!
DODODODODODO (RRRMMMBBB)
UPPER FLOOD-GATE...
DODODODODODODODO
...YOU MEAN THAT !?
SO THEY WENT AND CLOSED THE FLOODGATE IN THE CASTLE WALL. THEY SAID IT WAS TO PROTECT THE HARBOR.
DODODODODO
NOW WE DON'T HAVE A PLACE TO STAY ANY-MORE.
GOU
GOU

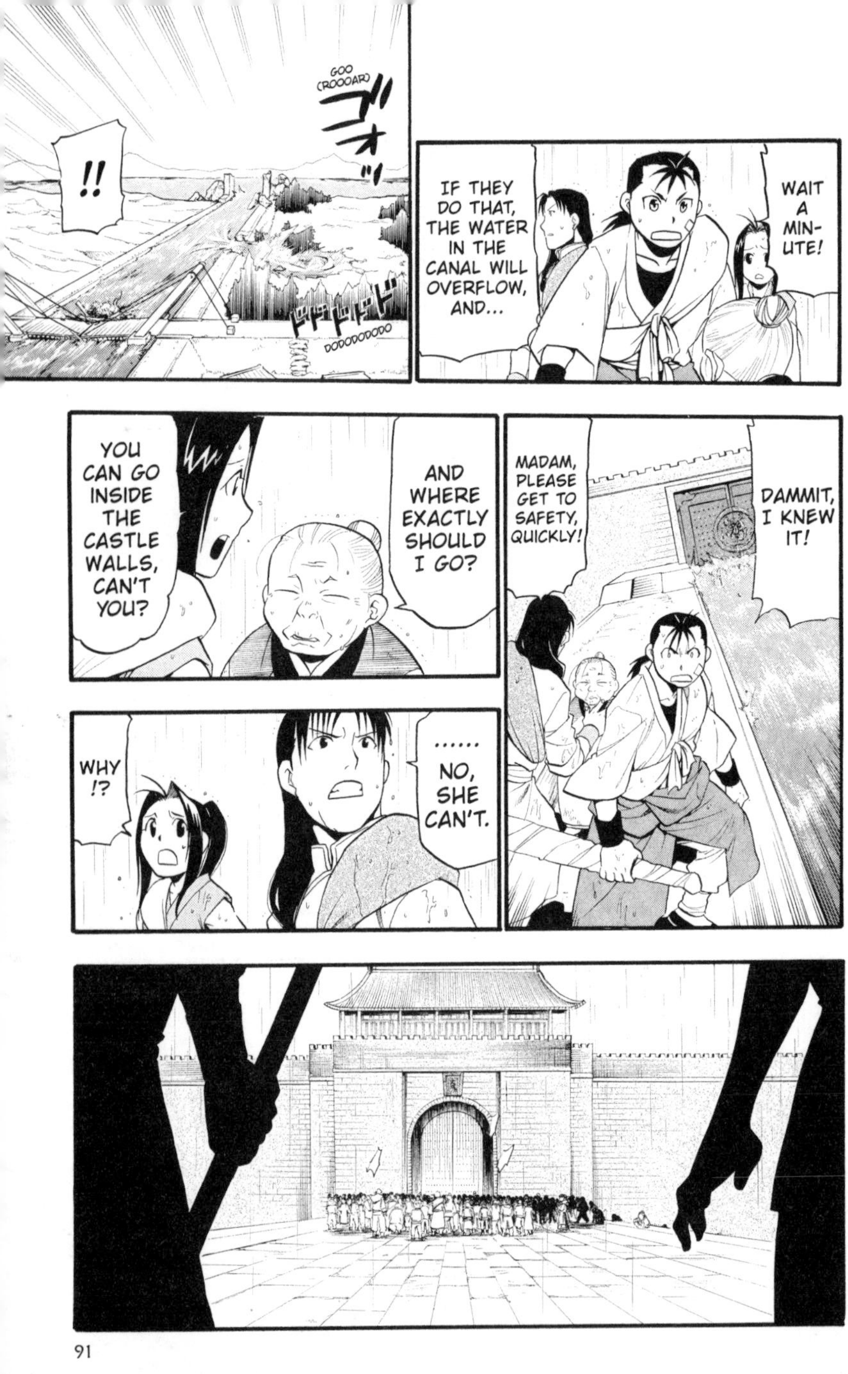
WAIT A MIN-UTE!
IF THEY DO THAT, THE WATER IN THE CANAL WILL OVERFLOW, AND...
GOO (ROOOAR)
ゴオォッ
!!
ドドドドド
DODODODODO
DAMMIT, I KNEW IT!
MADAM, PLEASE GET TO SAFETY, QUICKLY!
AND WHERE EXACTLY SHOULD I GO?
YOU CAN GO INSIDE THE CASTLE WALLS, CAN'T YOU?
......
NO, SHE CAN'T.
WHY!?

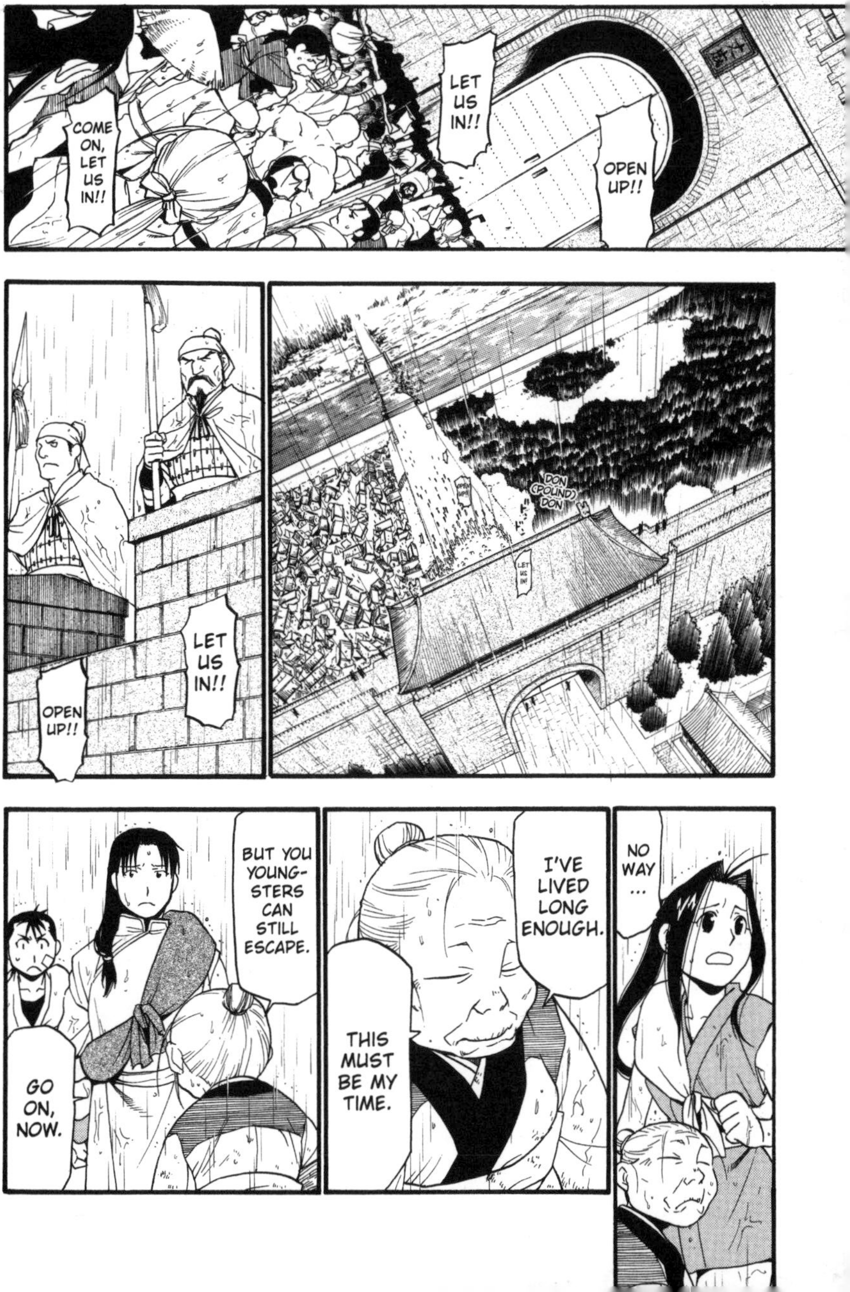
OPEN UP!!
LET US IN!!
COME ON, LET US IN!!
OPEN UP!!
DON (POUND) DON
LET US IN!
LET US IN!!
OPEN UP!!
NO WAY ...
I'VE LIVED LONG ENOUGH.
THIS MUST BE MY TIME.
BUT YOU YOUNGSTERS CAN STILL ESCAPE.
GO ON, NOW.

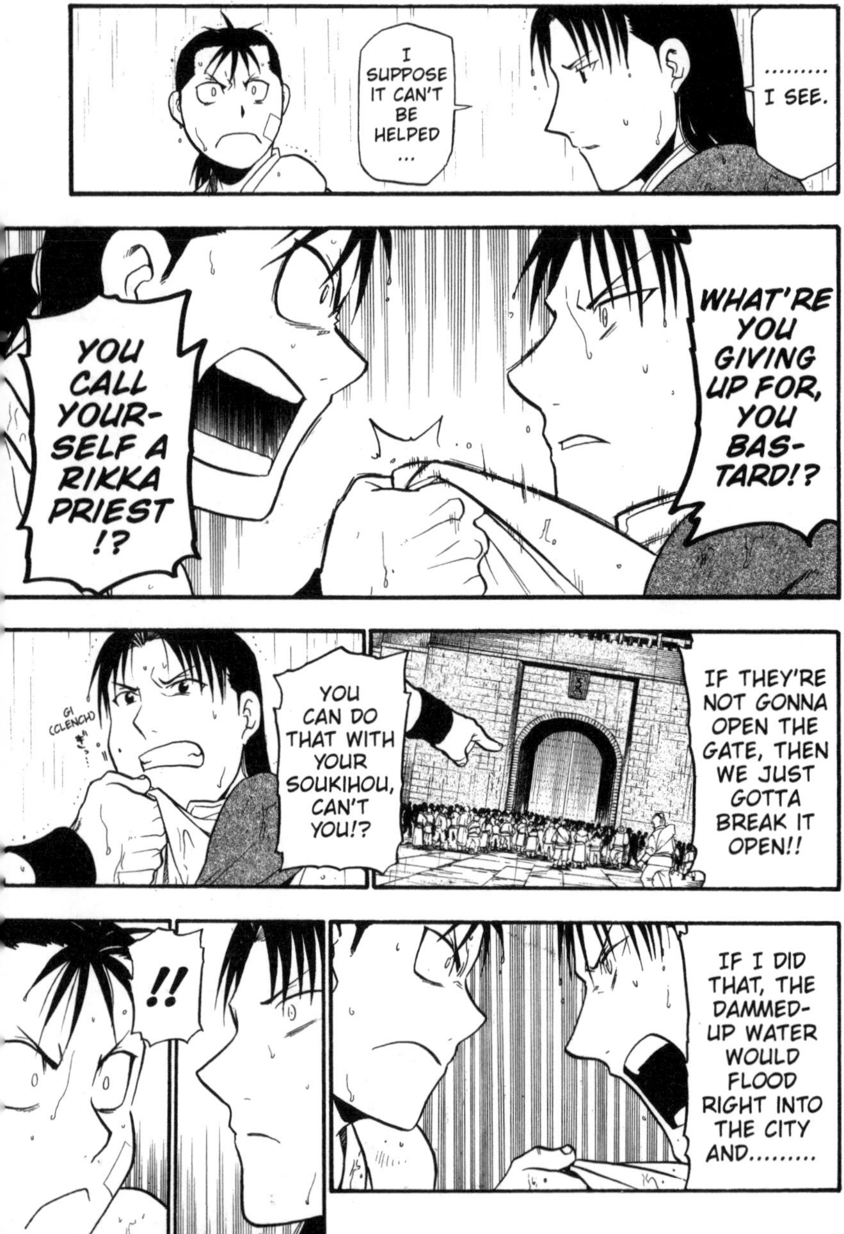

.... I SEE.
I SUPPOSE IT CAN'T BE HELPED ...
WHAT'RE YOU GIVING UP FOR, YOU BASTARD!?
YOU CALL YOURSELF A RIKKA PRIEST!?
IF THEY'RE NOT GONNA OPEN THE GATE, THEN WE JUST GOTTA BREAK IT OPEN!!
YOU CAN DO THAT WITH YOUR SOUKIHOU, CAN'T YOU!?
GI (CLENCH)
IF I DID THAT, THE DAMMED-UP WATER WOULD FLOOD RIGHT INTO THE CITY AND.........
!!

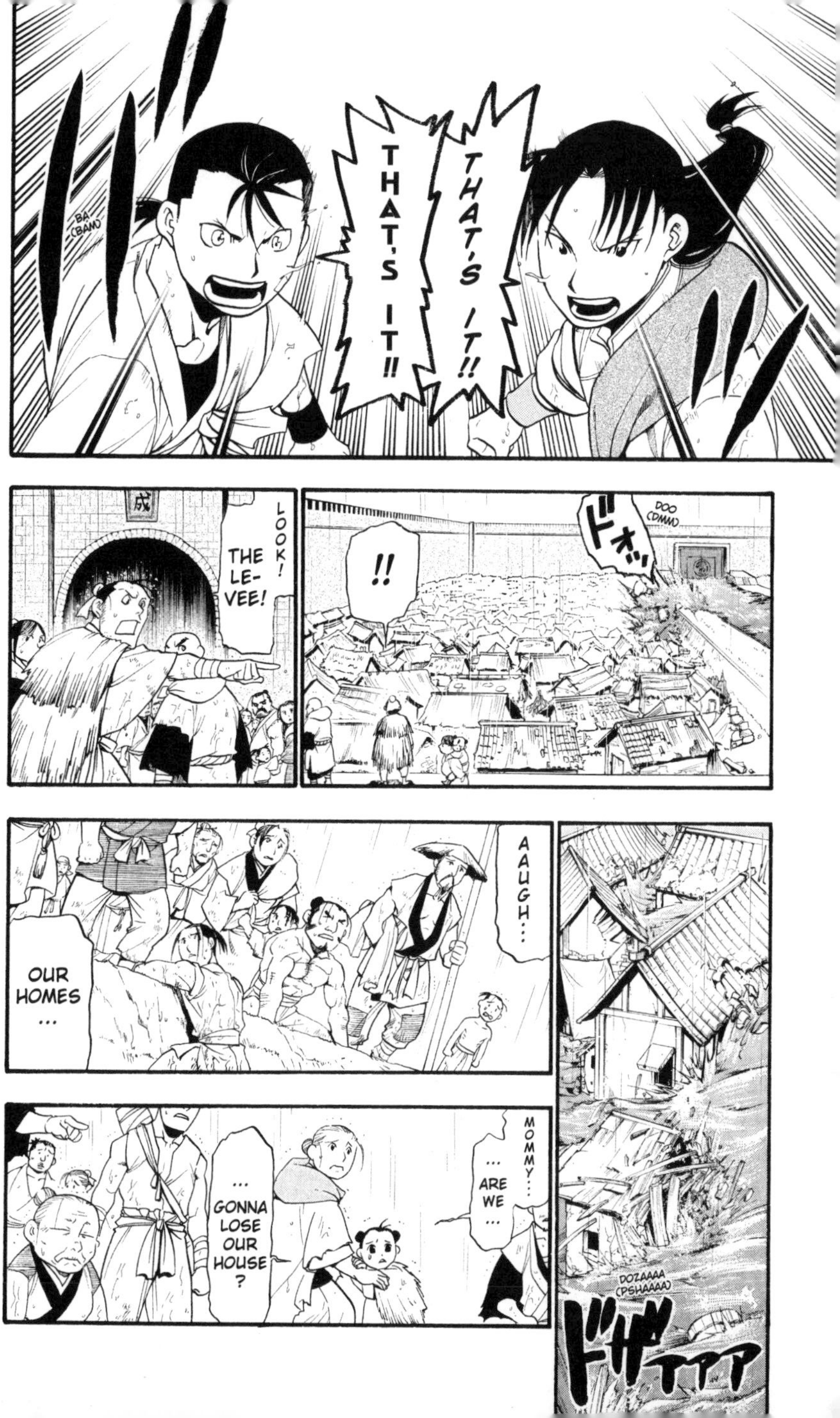
THAT'S IT!!
THAT'S IT!!
BA (BAM)
DOO (DMM)
!!
LOOK! THE LEVEE!
DOZAAAA (PSHAAAA)
AAUGH...
OUR HOMES...
MOMMY... ...ARE WE...
...GONNA LOSE OUR HOUSE?

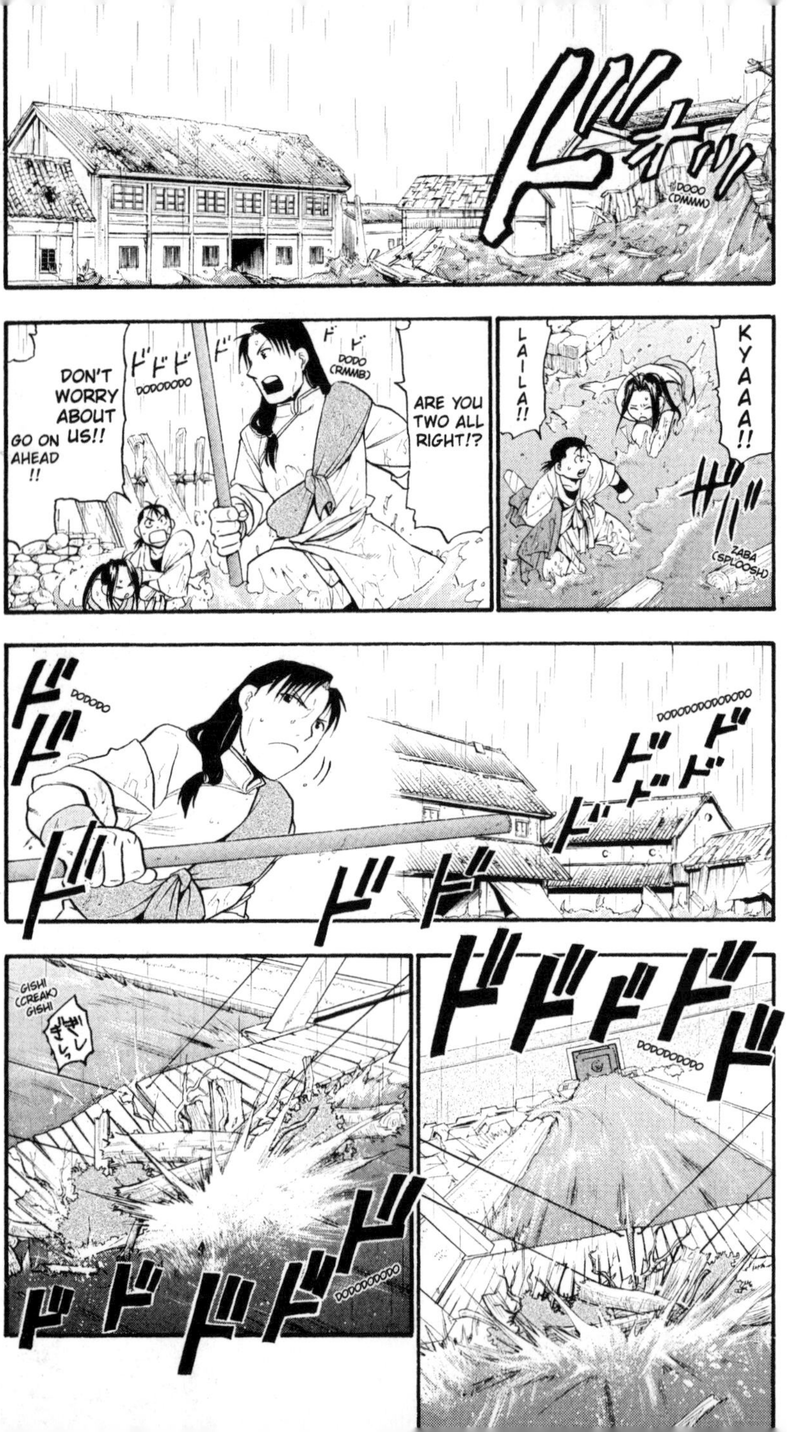
DOOO (DMMM)
KYAAAA!!
LAILA!!
ZABA (SPLOOSH)
ARE YOU TWO ALL RIGHT!?
DODO (RMMB)
DODODODO
DON'T WORRY ABOUT US!!
GO ON AHEAD!!
DODODODODODODO
DODODO
DODODODODO
GISHI (CREAK) GISHI
DODODODODO

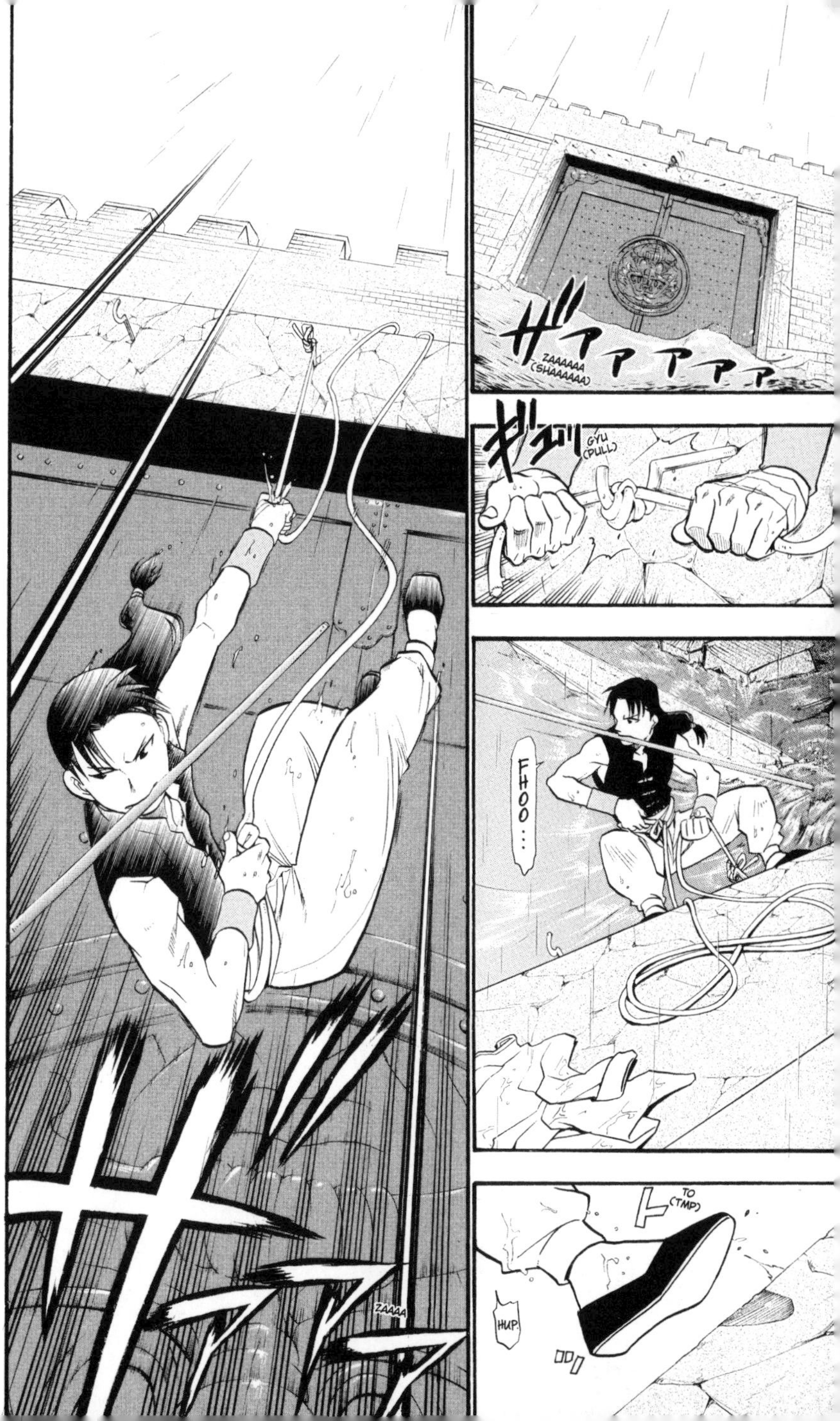
ZAAAAAA
(SHAAAAAA)
GYU
(PULL)
FHOO...
TO
(TMP)
HUP.
ZAAAA

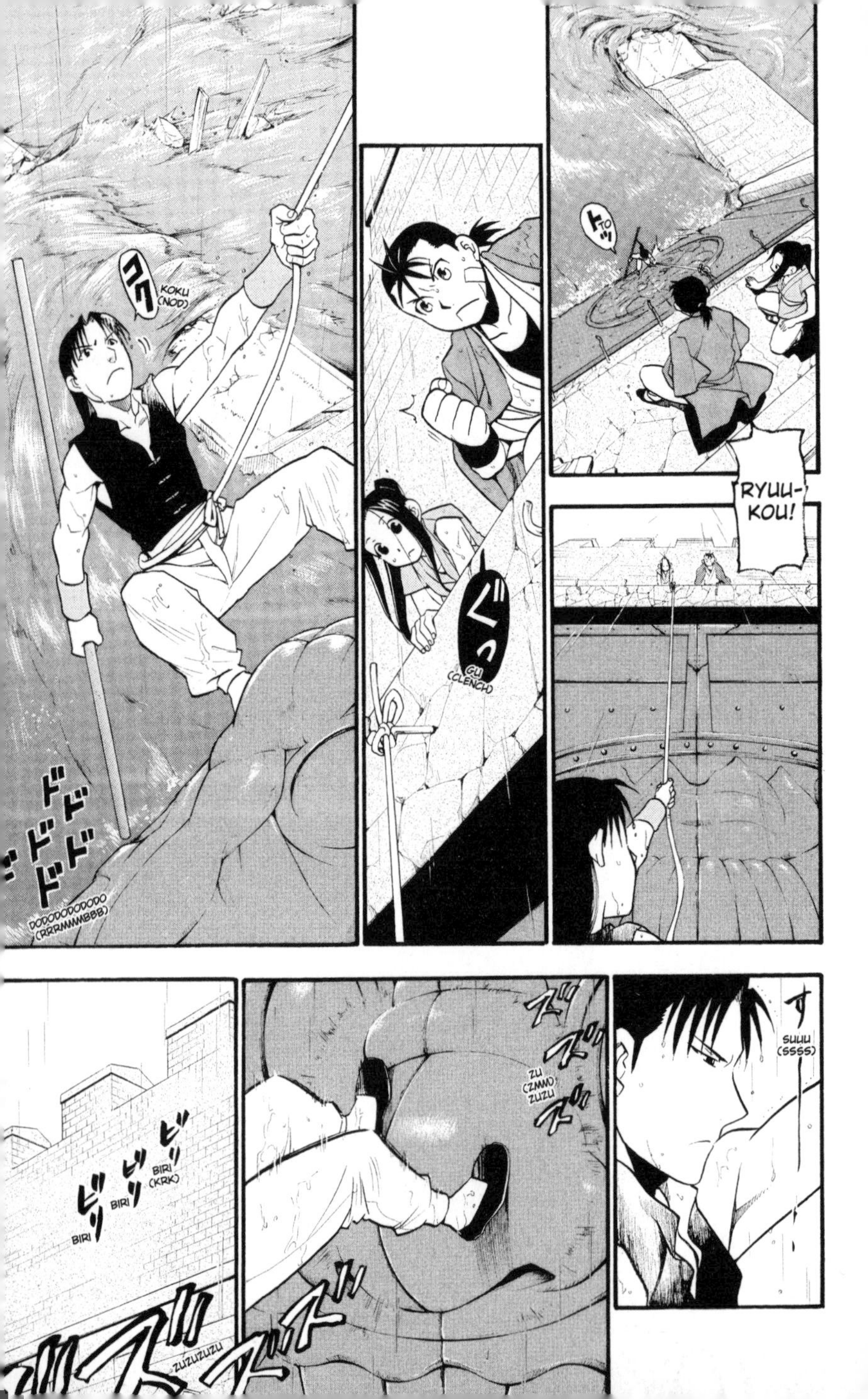

トッ
TO
RYUU-KOU!
ぐっ
GU (CLENCH)
コク
KOKU (NOD)
ドドドドドド
DODODODODO (RRRMMMBBB)
す
SUUU (SSSS)
ズッ
ZU (ZMM) ZUZU
ビリ
BIRI (KRK)
BIRI
BIRI
ZUZUZUZU

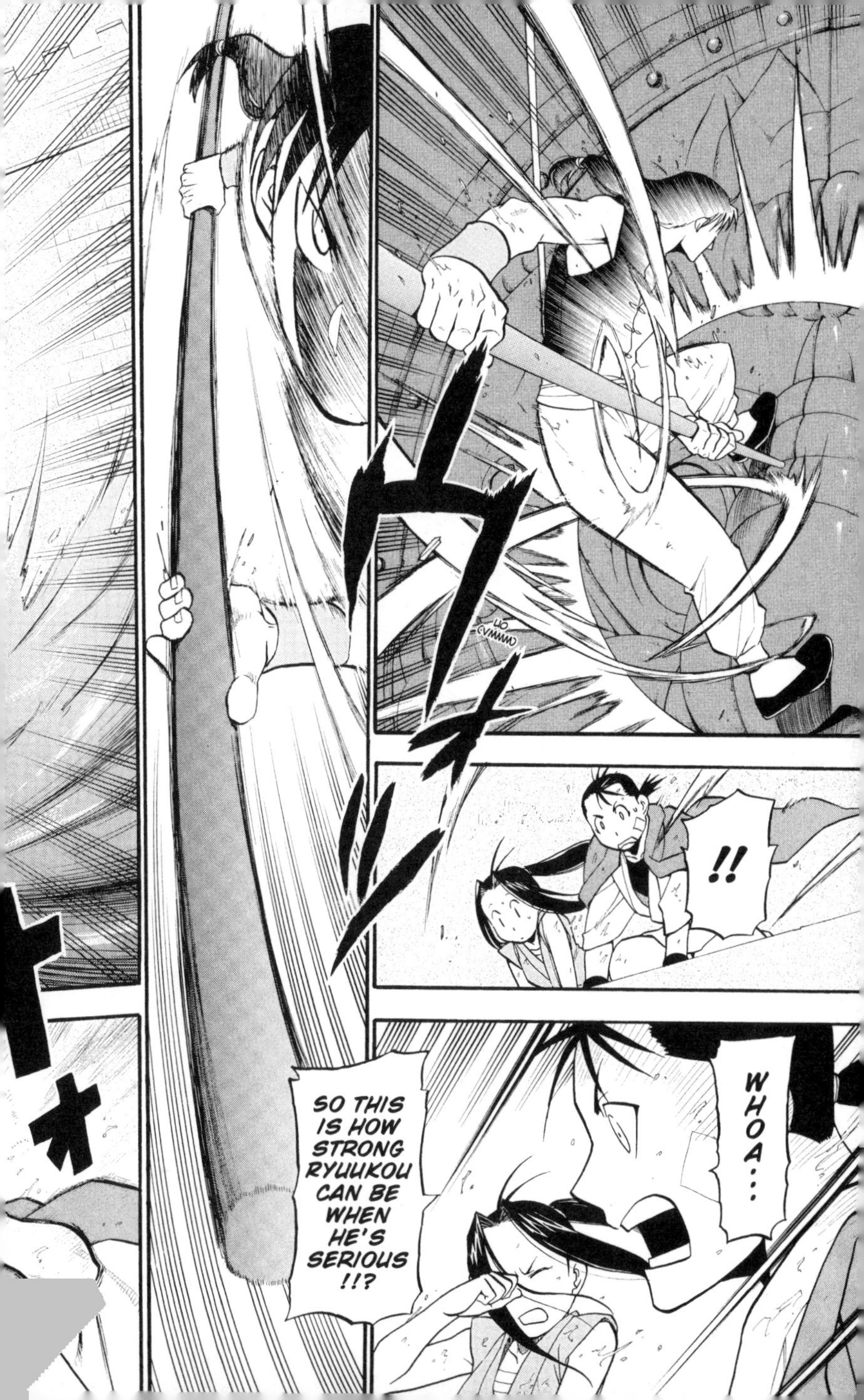
(VMMM)
!!
WHOA...
SO THIS IS HOW STRONG RYUUKOU CAN BE WHEN HE'S SERIOUS !!?

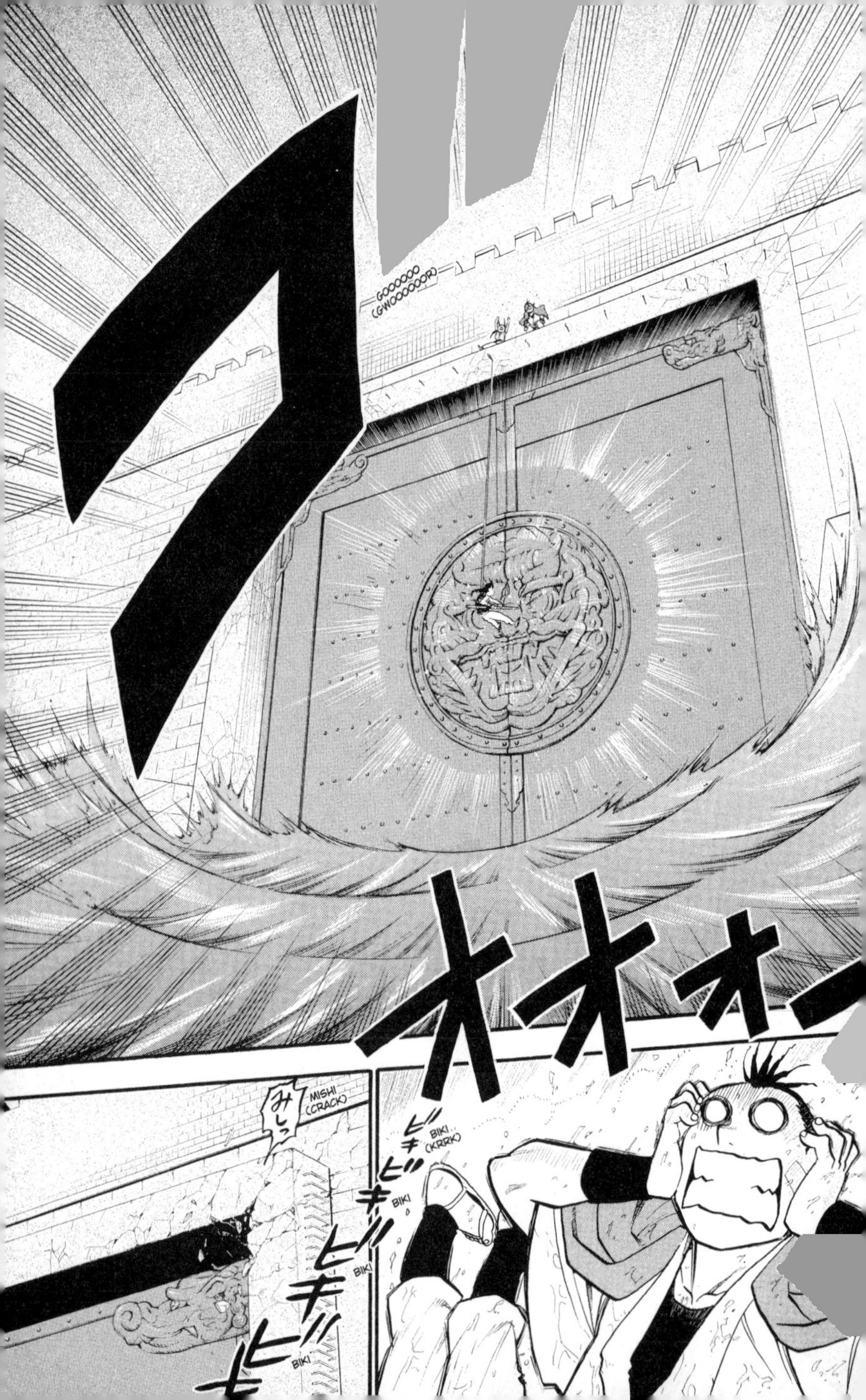
GOOOOOO
(GWOOOOOOR)
ビキ
BIKI
(KRRK)
ビキッ
BIKI
ビキッ
BIKI
ビキッ
BIKI
みしっ
MISHI
(CRACK)

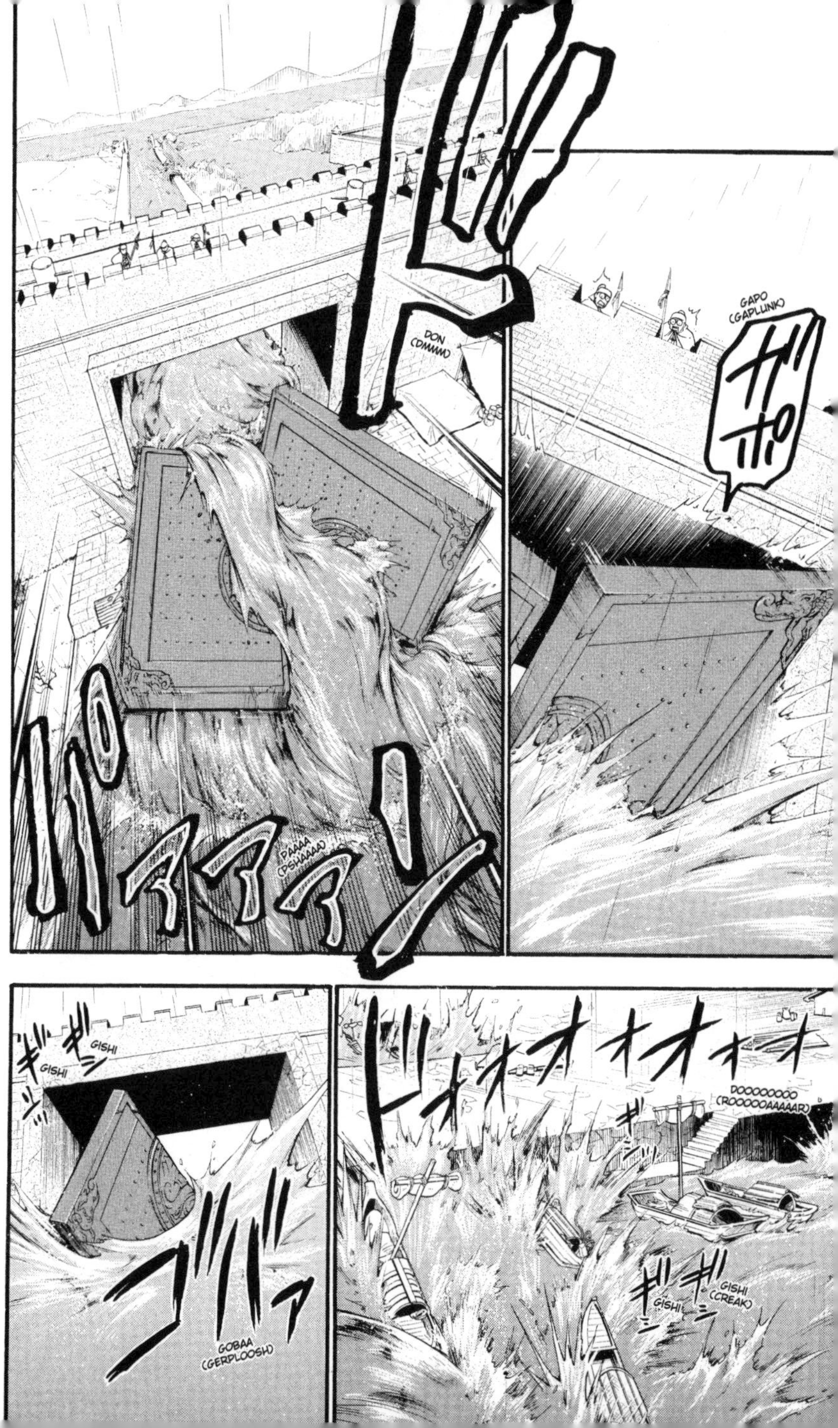
GAPO (GAPLUNK)
DON (DMMM)
PAAAA (PSHAAAA)
DOOOOOOOOO (ROOOOOAAAAAR)
GISHI (CREAK)
GISHI
GISHI
GISHI
GOBAA (GERPLOOSH)

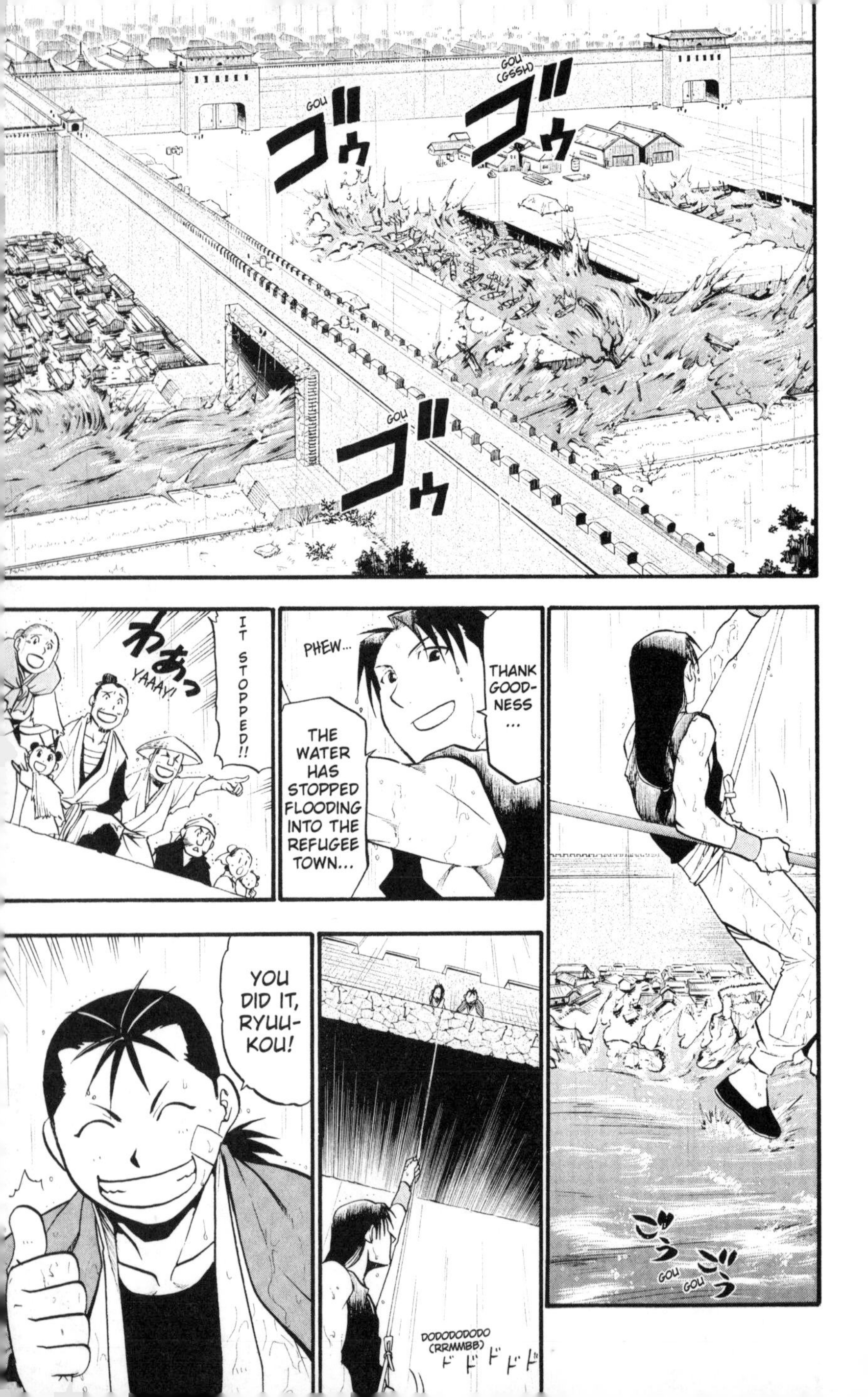
GOU (GSSH)
ゴウ
GOU
ゴウ
GOU
ゴウ
ごう ごう
GOU GOU
THANK GOODNESS...
PHEW...
THE WATER HAS STOPPED FLOODING INTO THE REFUGEE TOWN...
IT STOPPED!!
わあっ
YAAAY!
DODODODODO (RRMMBB)
ドドドドド
YOU DID IT, RYUUKOU!

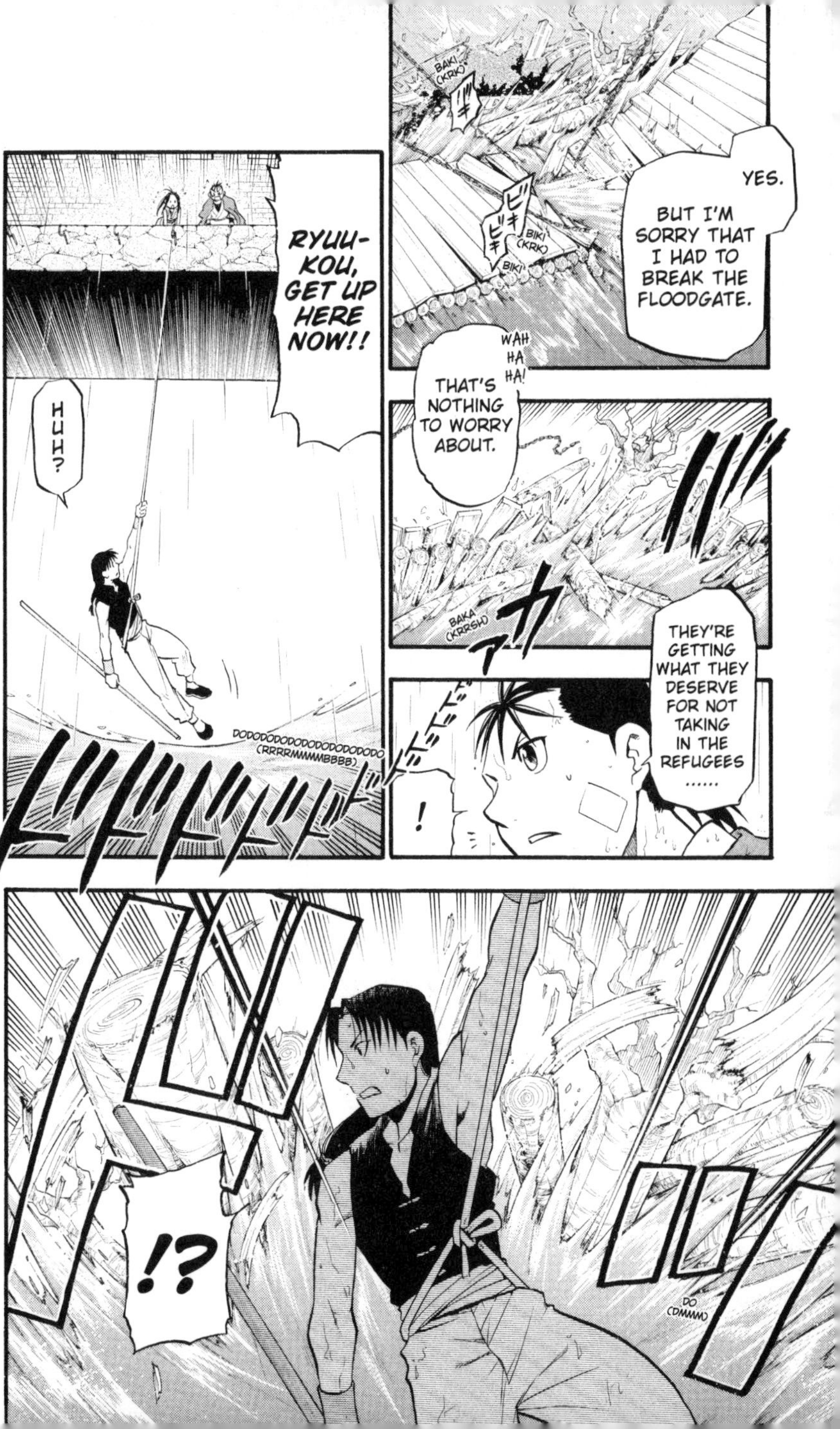
BAKI (KRK)
BIKI (KRK)
BIKI
YES.
BUT I'M SORRY THAT I HAD TO BREAK THE FLOODGATE.
WAH HA HA!
THAT'S NOTHING TO WORRY ABOUT.
BAKA (KRRSH)
THEY'RE GETTING WHAT THEY DESERVE FOR NOT TAKING IN THE REFUGEES ......
!
RYUU-KOU, GET UP HERE NOW!!
HUH?
DODODODODODODODODODODO (RRRRMMMMBBBB)
!?
DO (DMMM)

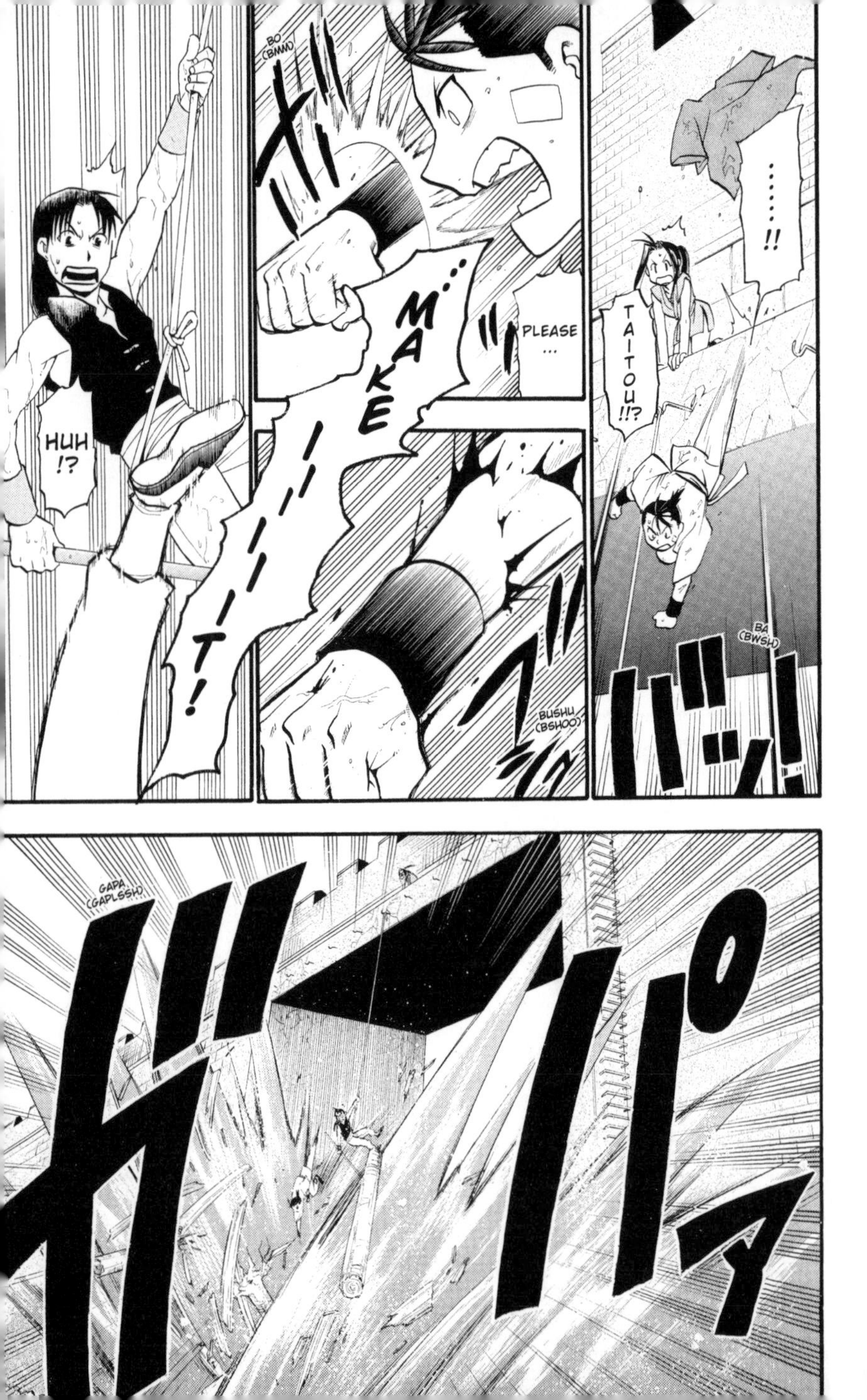
......!!
TAITOU!!?
BA (BWSH)
PLEASE ...
BO (BMM)
...MAKE ------IT!
BUSHU (BSHOO)
HUH!?
GAPA (GAPLSSH)

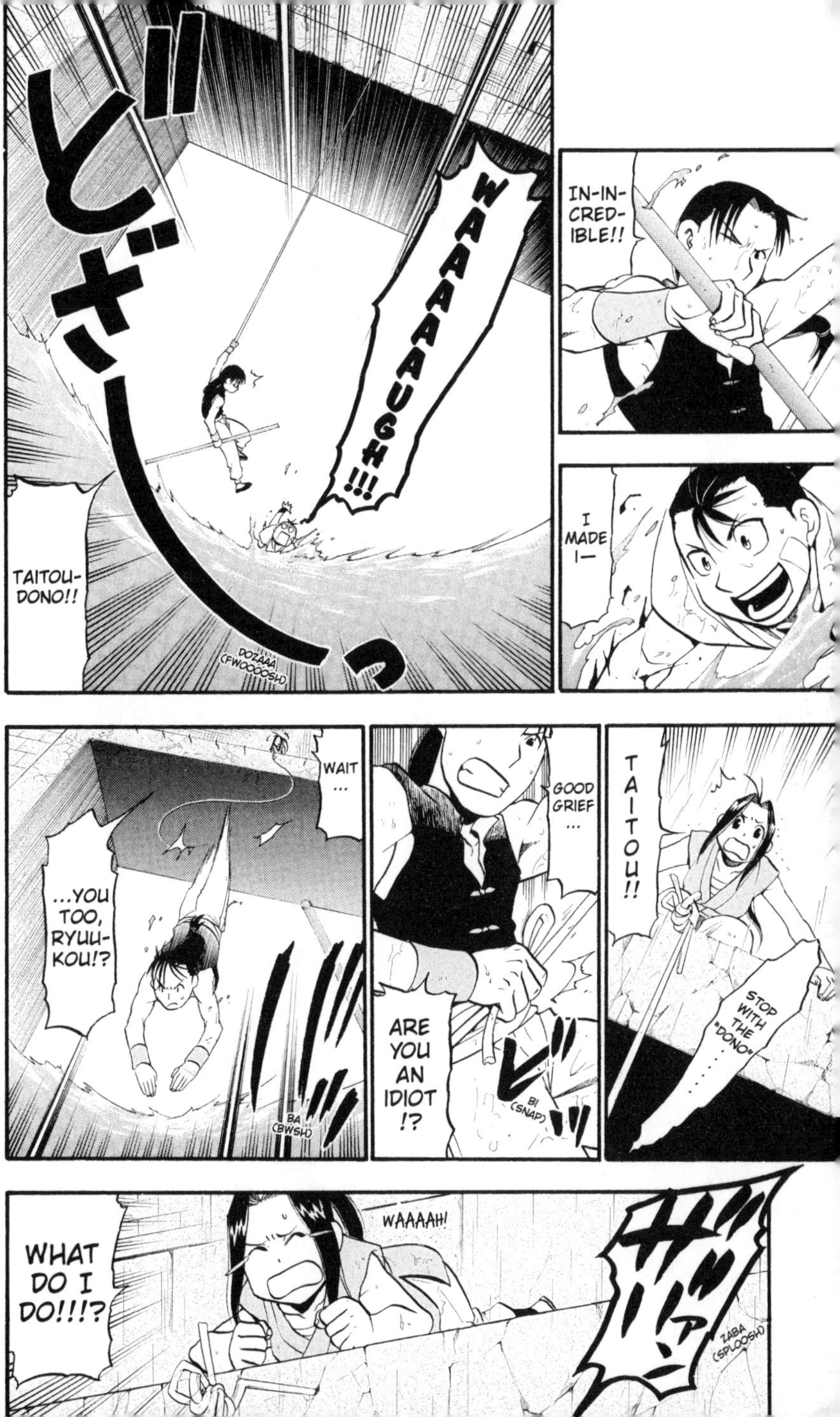
IN-IN-CRED-IBLE!!
I MADE I—
WAAAAAAAUGH!!!
TAITOU-DONO!!
DOZAAA (FWOOOOSH)
TAITOU!!
STOP WITH THE "DONO"......
GOOD GRIEF...
ARE YOU AN IDIOT!?
BI (SNAP)
WAIT...
...YOU TOO, RYUUKOU!?
BA (BWSH)
WAAAAH!
WHAT DO I DO!!!?
ZABA (SPLOOSH)

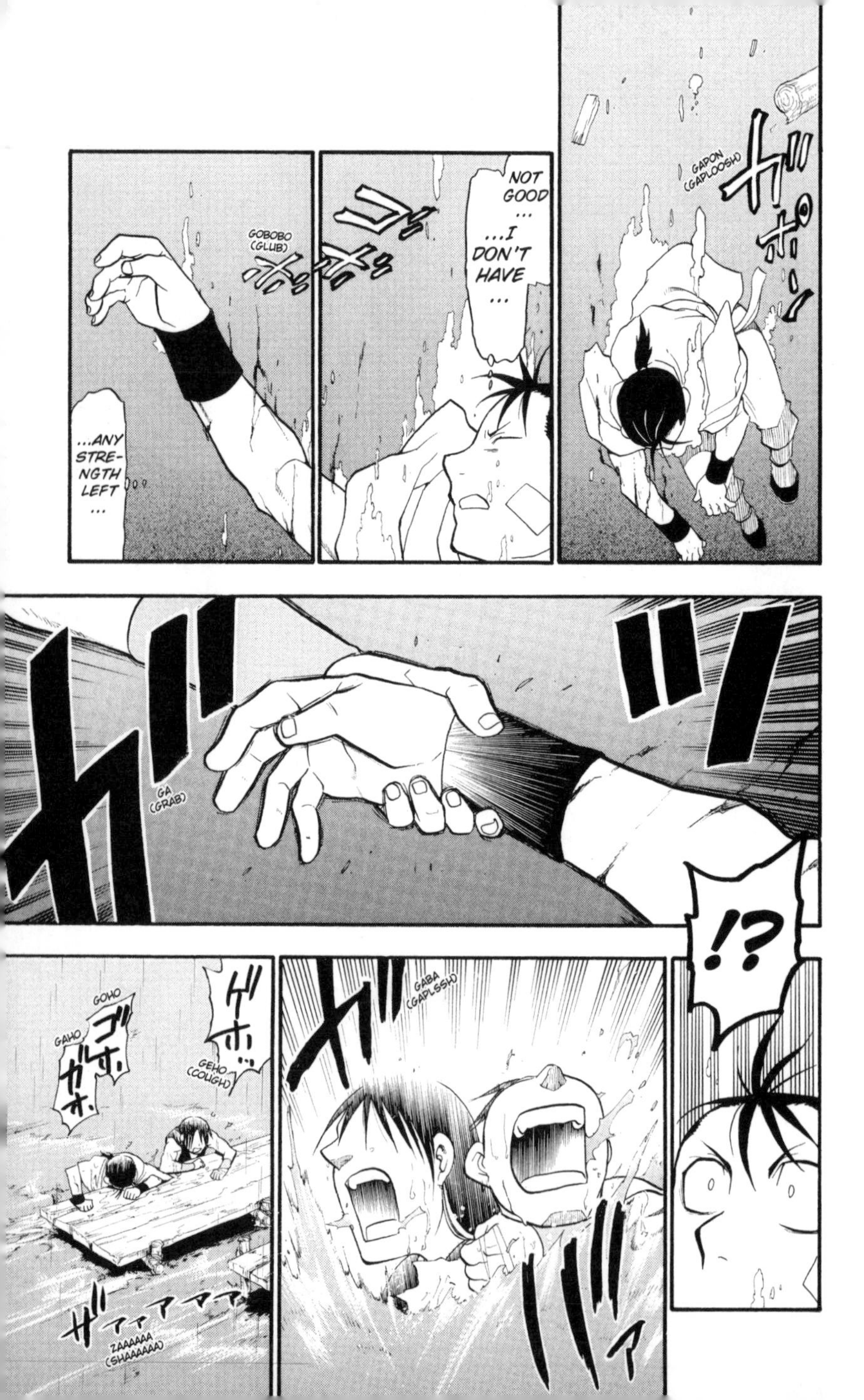
GAPON (GAPLOOSH)
NOT GOOD...
...I DON'T HAVE...
GOBOBO (GLUB)
...ANY STRENGTH LEFT...
GA (GRAB)
!?
GABA (GAPLSSH)
GEHO (COUGH)
GOHO
GAHO
ZAAAAAA (SHAAAAAA)

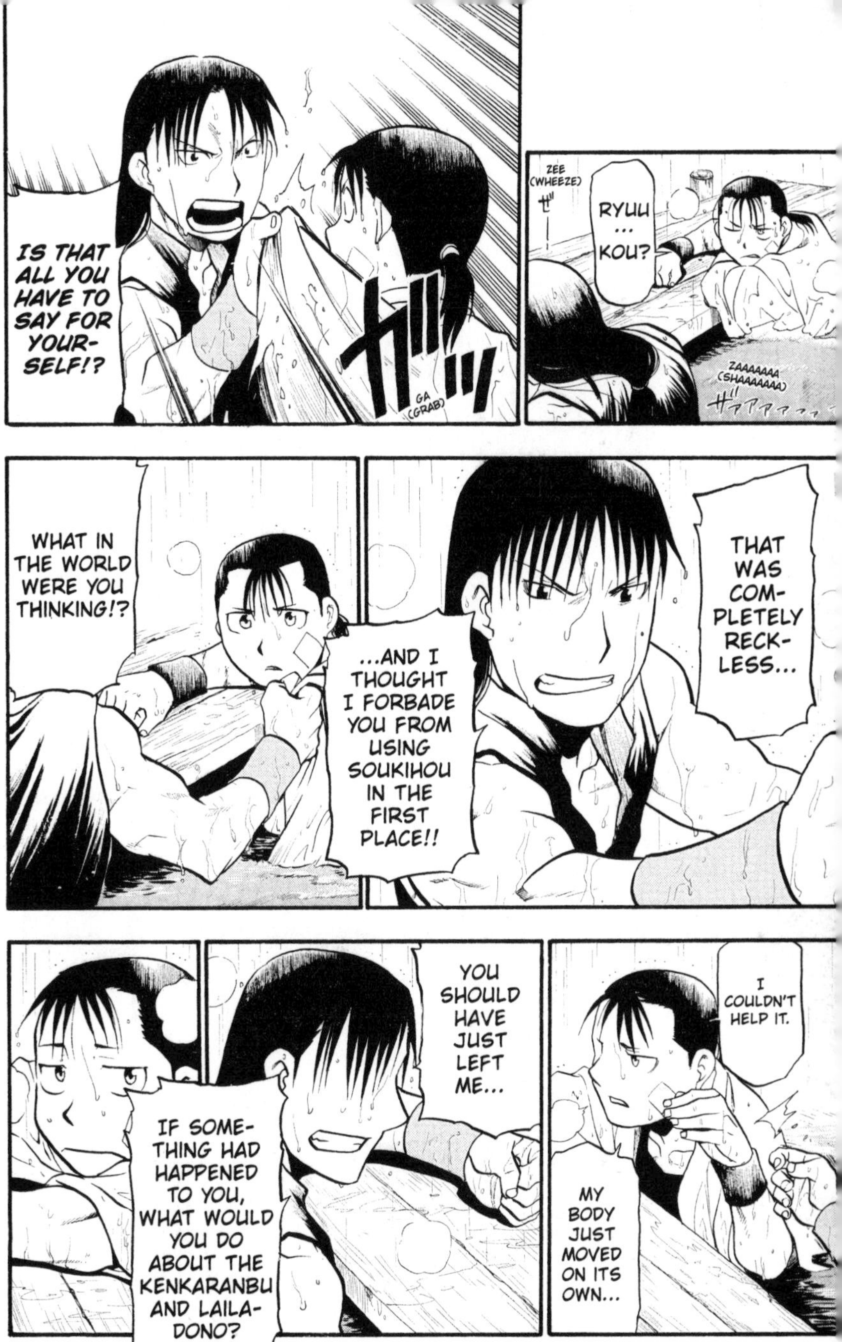
ZEE (WHEEZE)
ゼ
RYUU... KOU?
ZAAAAAAA (SHAAAAAAA)
ザァァァァァァ
IS THAT ALL YOU HAVE TO SAY FOR YOURSELF!?
GA (GRAB)
THAT WAS COMPLETELY RECKLESS...
...AND I THOUGHT I FORBADE YOU FROM USING SOUKIHOU IN THE FIRST PLACE!!
WHAT IN THE WORLD WERE YOU THINKING!?
I COULDN'T HELP IT.
MY BODY JUST MOVED ON ITS OWN...
YOU SHOULD HAVE JUST LEFT ME...
IF SOMETHING HAD HAPPENED TO YOU, WHAT WOULD YOU DO ABOUT THE KENKARANBU AND LAILA-DONO?

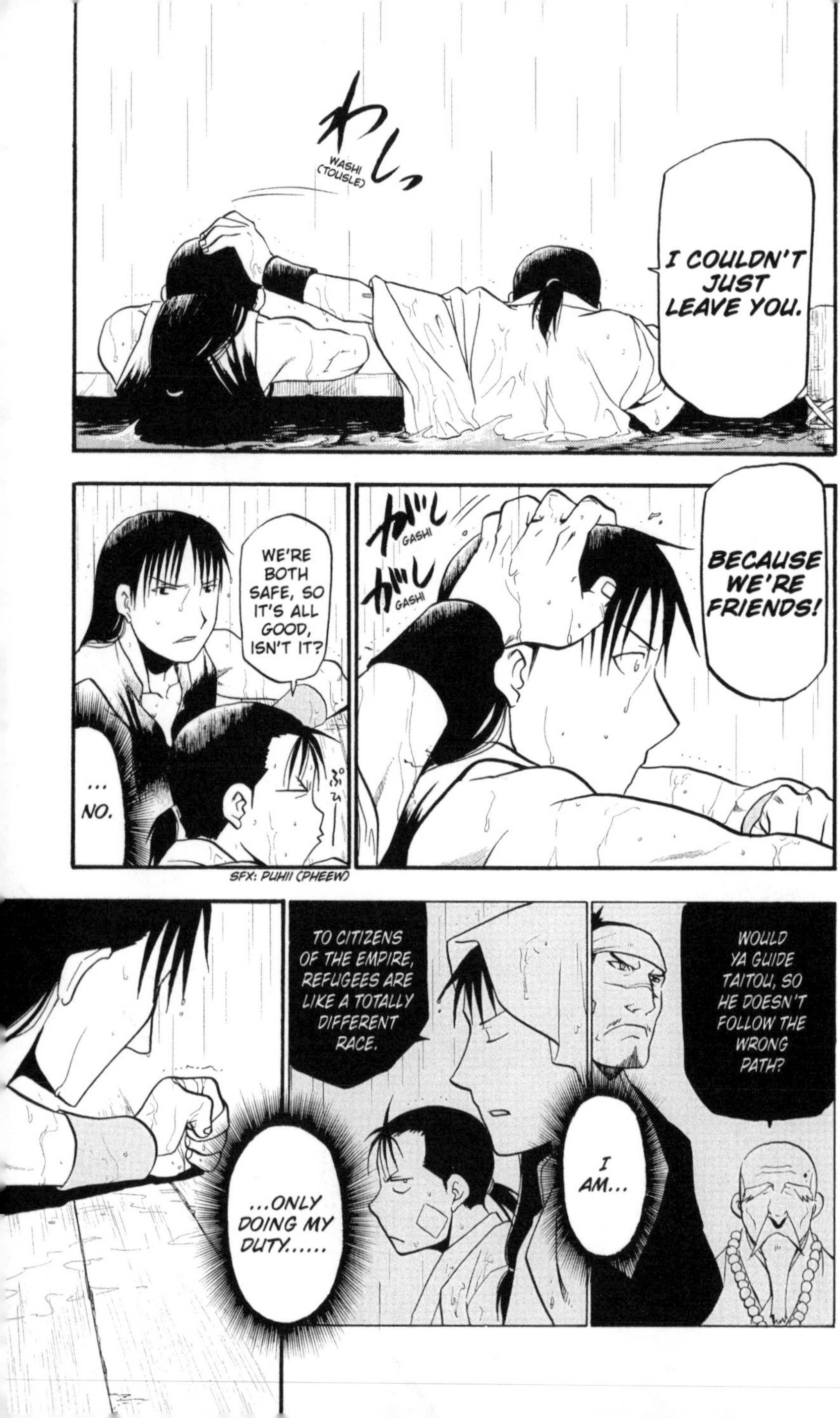
I COULDN'T JUST LEAVE YOU.
WASHI (TOUSLE)
BECAUSE WE'RE FRIENDS!
GASHI
GASHI
WE'RE BOTH SAFE, SO IT'S ALL GOOD, ISN'T IT?
... NO.
SFX: PUHII (PHEEW)
WOULD YA GUIDE TAITOU, SO HE DOESN'T FOLLOW THE WRONG PATH?
I AM...
TO CITIZENS OF THE EMPIRE, REFUGEES ARE LIKE A TOTALLY DIFFERENT RACE.
...ONLY DOING MY DUTY......

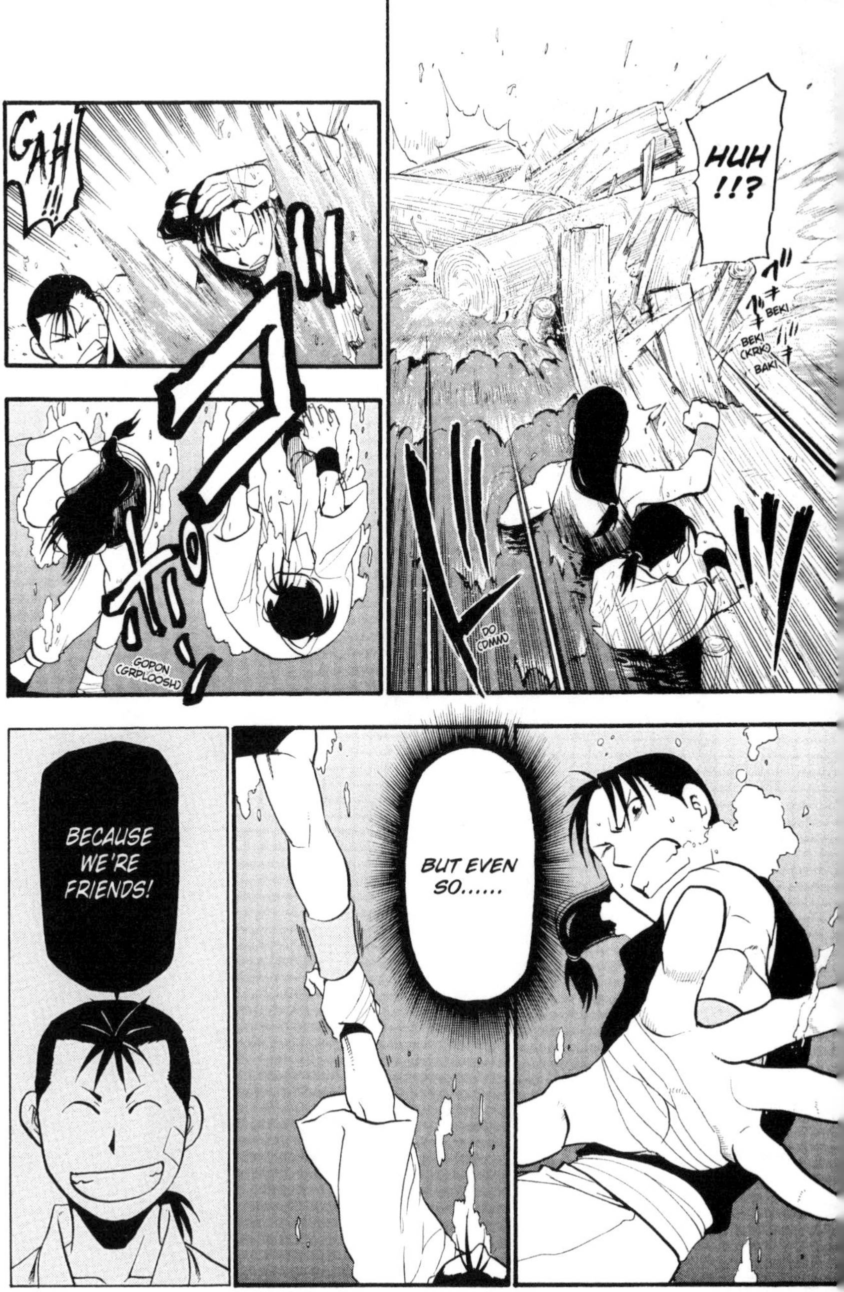
HUH !!?
BEKI
BEKI (KRK)
BAKI
DO (DMM)
GAH!!!
GOPON (GRPLOOSH)
BUT EVEN SO......
BECAUSE WE'RE FRIENDS!

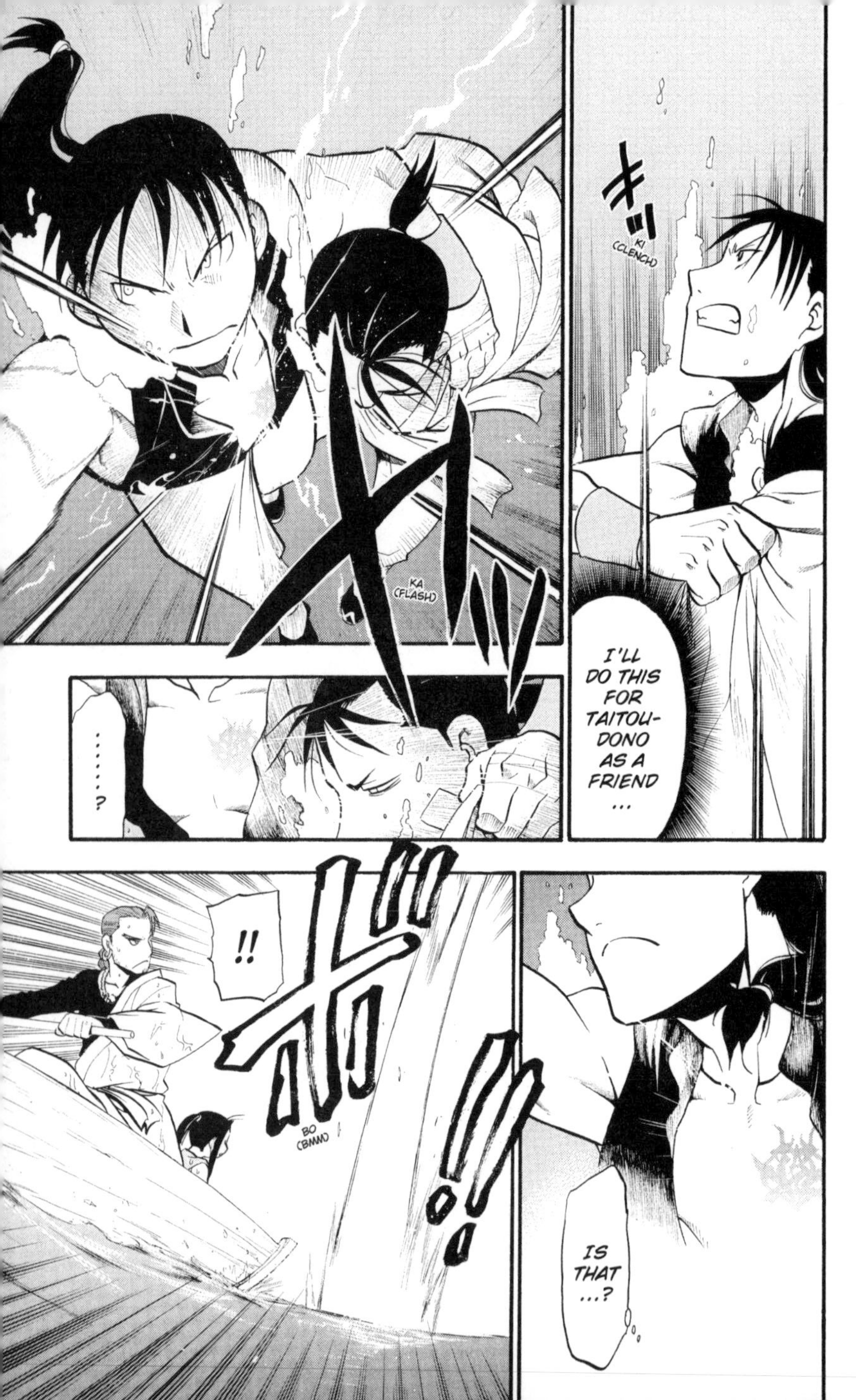
KI (CLENCH)
I'LL DO THIS FOR TAITOU-DONO AS A FRIEND ...
KA (FLASH)
......?
IS THAT ...?
!!
BO (BMM)

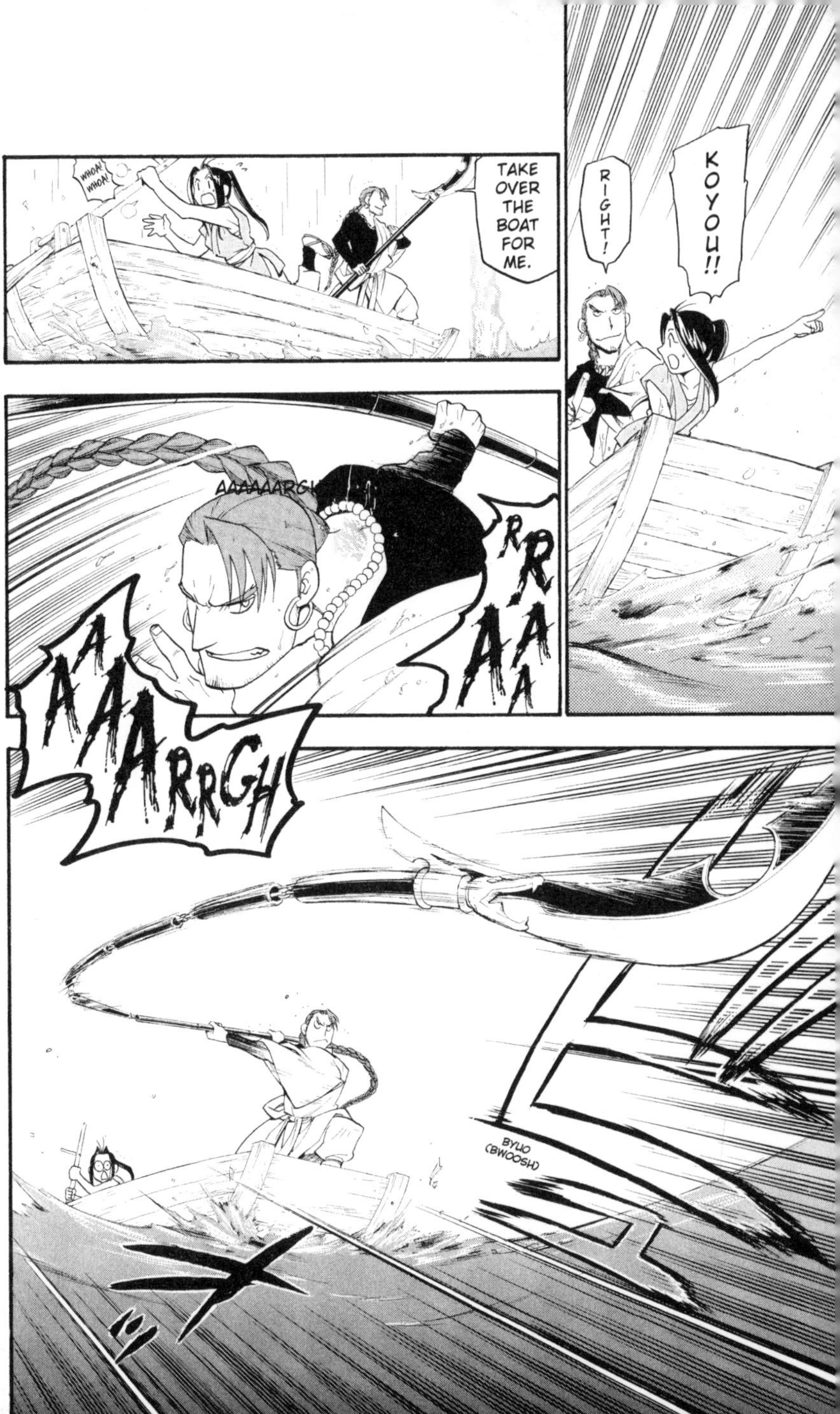
KOYOU!!
RIGHT!
TAKE OVER THE BOAT FOR ME.
WHOA! WHOA!
AAAAARGH
RRAAAA
AAAARRGH
BYUO (BWOOSH)

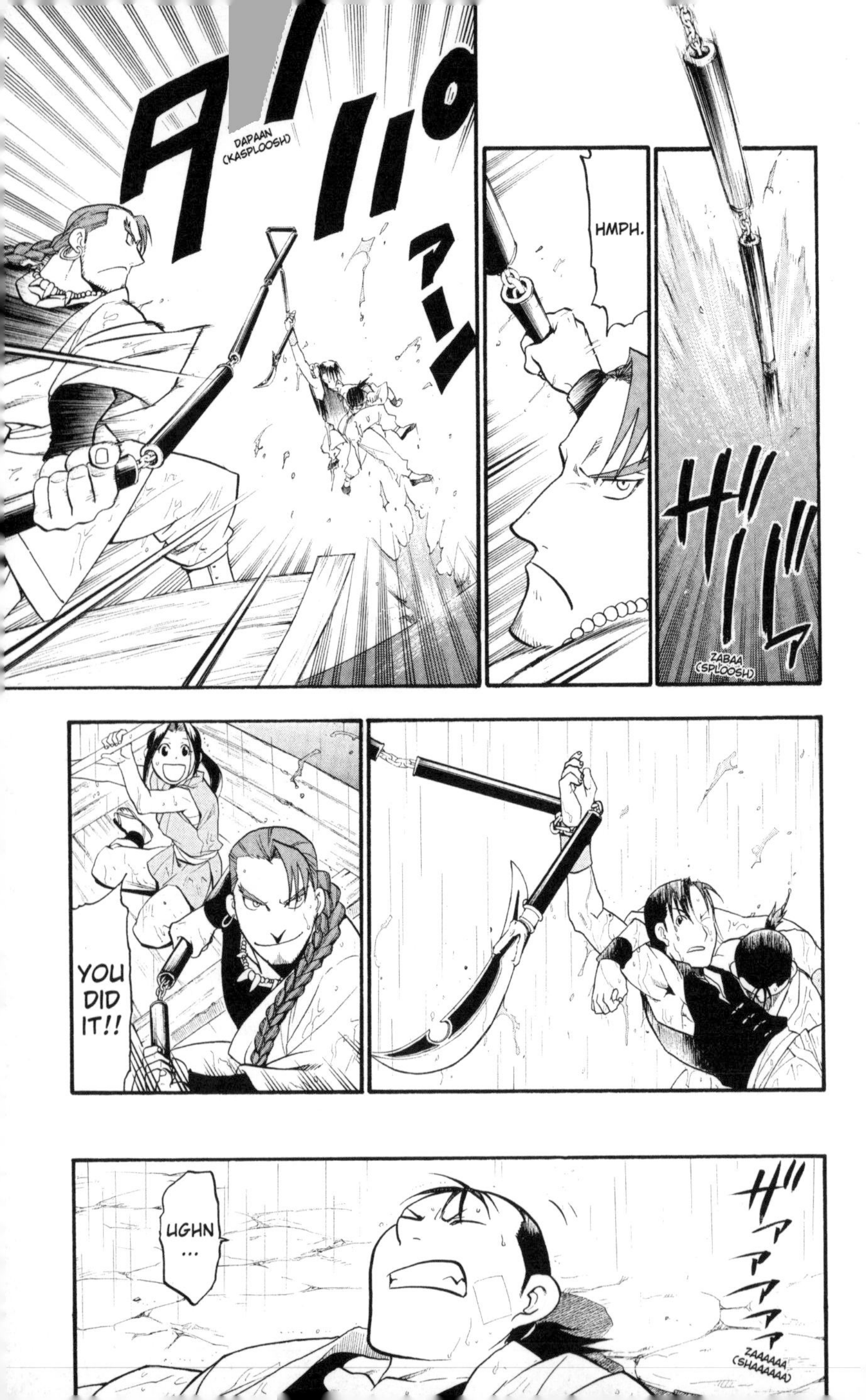
ZABAA (SPLOOSH)
HMPH.
DAPAAN (KASPLOOSH)
YOU DID IT!!
UGHN...
ZAAAAAA (SHAAAAAA)

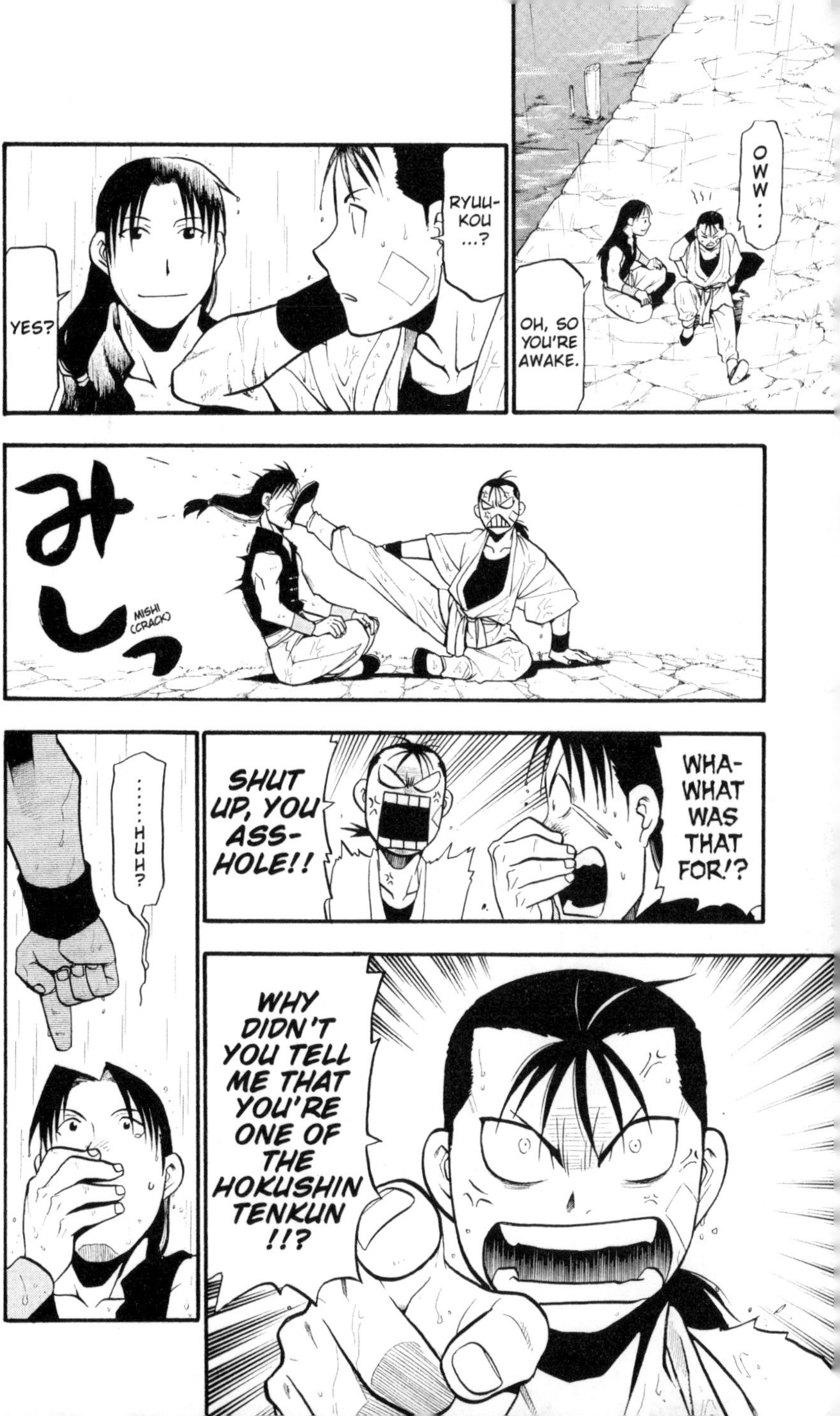
OWW...
OH, SO YOU'RE AWAKE.
RYUU-KOU ...?
YES?
みしっ
MISHI (CRACK)
WHA-WHAT WAS THAT FOR!?
SHUT UP, YOU ASS-HOLE!!
WHY DIDN'T YOU TELL ME THAT YOU'RE ONE OF THE HOKUSHIN TENKUN !!?
......HUH?

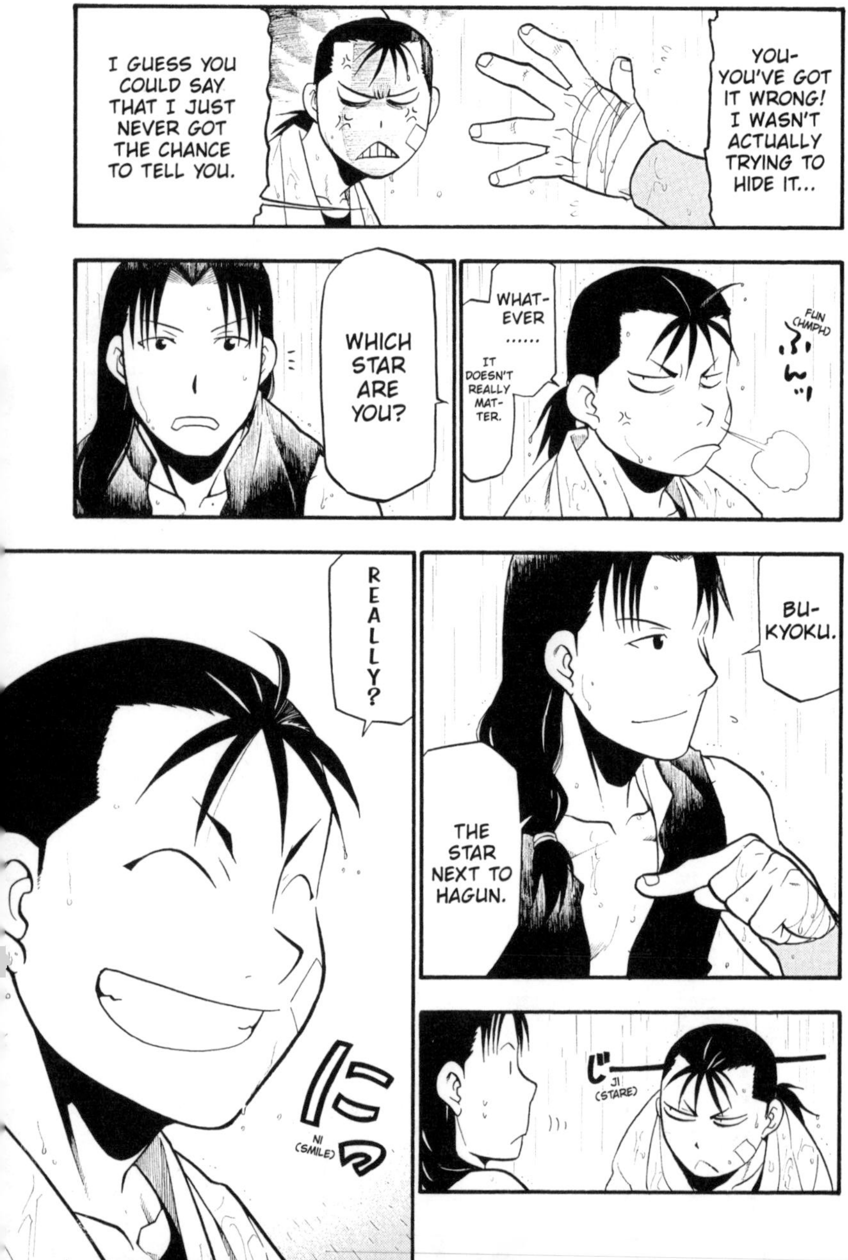
YOU-YOU'VE GOT IT WRONG! I WASN'T ACTUALLY TRYING TO HIDE IT...
I GUESS YOU COULD SAY THAT I JUST NEVER GOT THE CHANCE TO TELL YOU.
FUN (HMPH)
WHAT-EVER ......
IT DOESN'T REALLY MAT-TER.
WHICH STAR ARE YOU?
BU-KYOKU.
THE STAR NEXT TO HAGUN.
JI (STARE)
REALLY?
NI (SMILE)

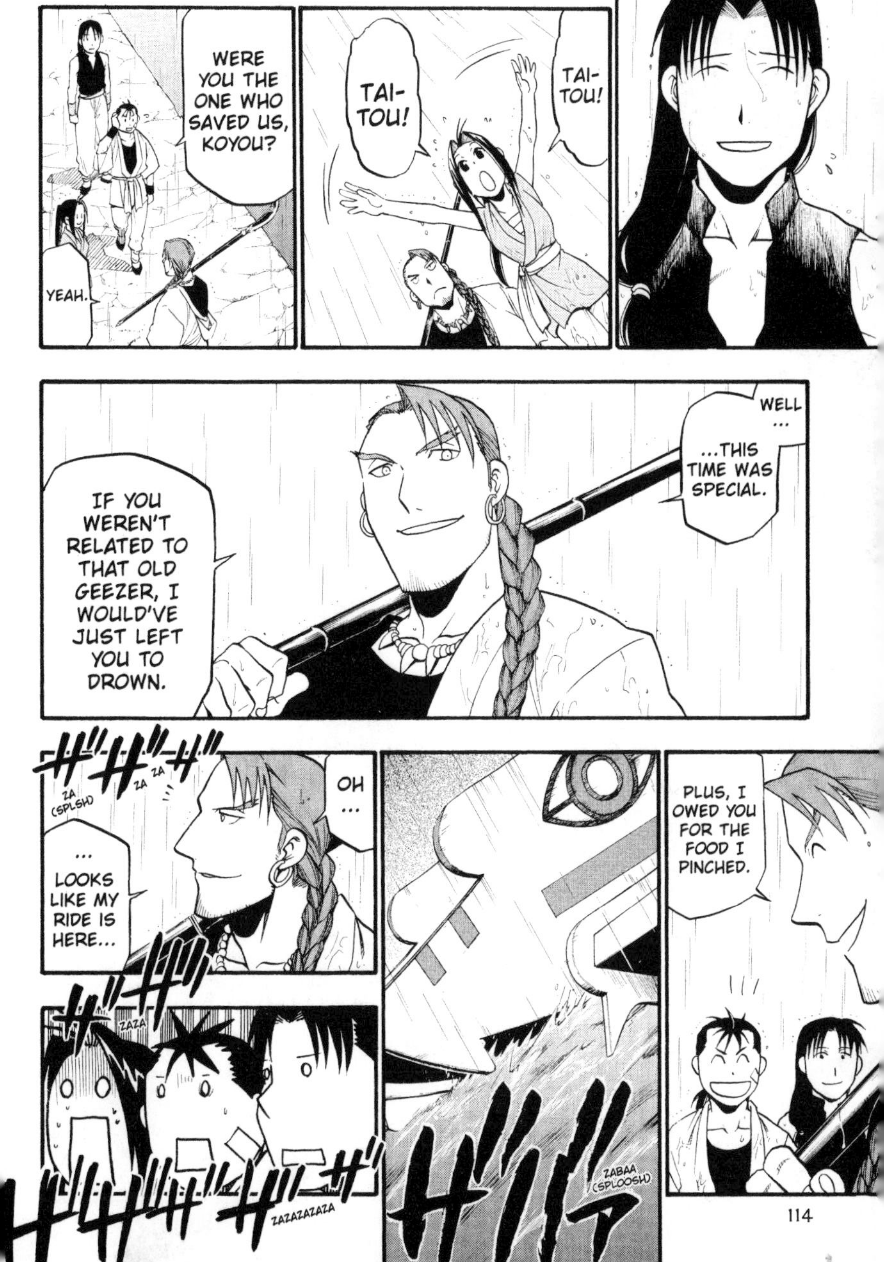
TAI-TOU!
TAI-TOU!
WERE YOU THE ONE WHO SAVED US, KOYOU?
YEAH.
WELL ...
...THIS TIME WAS SPECIAL.
IF YOU WEREN'T RELATED TO THAT OLD GEEZER, I WOULD'VE JUST LEFT YOU TO DROWN.
PLUS, I OWED YOU FOR THE FOOD I PINCHED.
ZABAA (SPLOOSH)
ZA (SPLSH)
ZA ZA
OH ...
... LOOKS LIKE MY RIDE IS HERE...
ZAZA
ZAZAZAZAZA

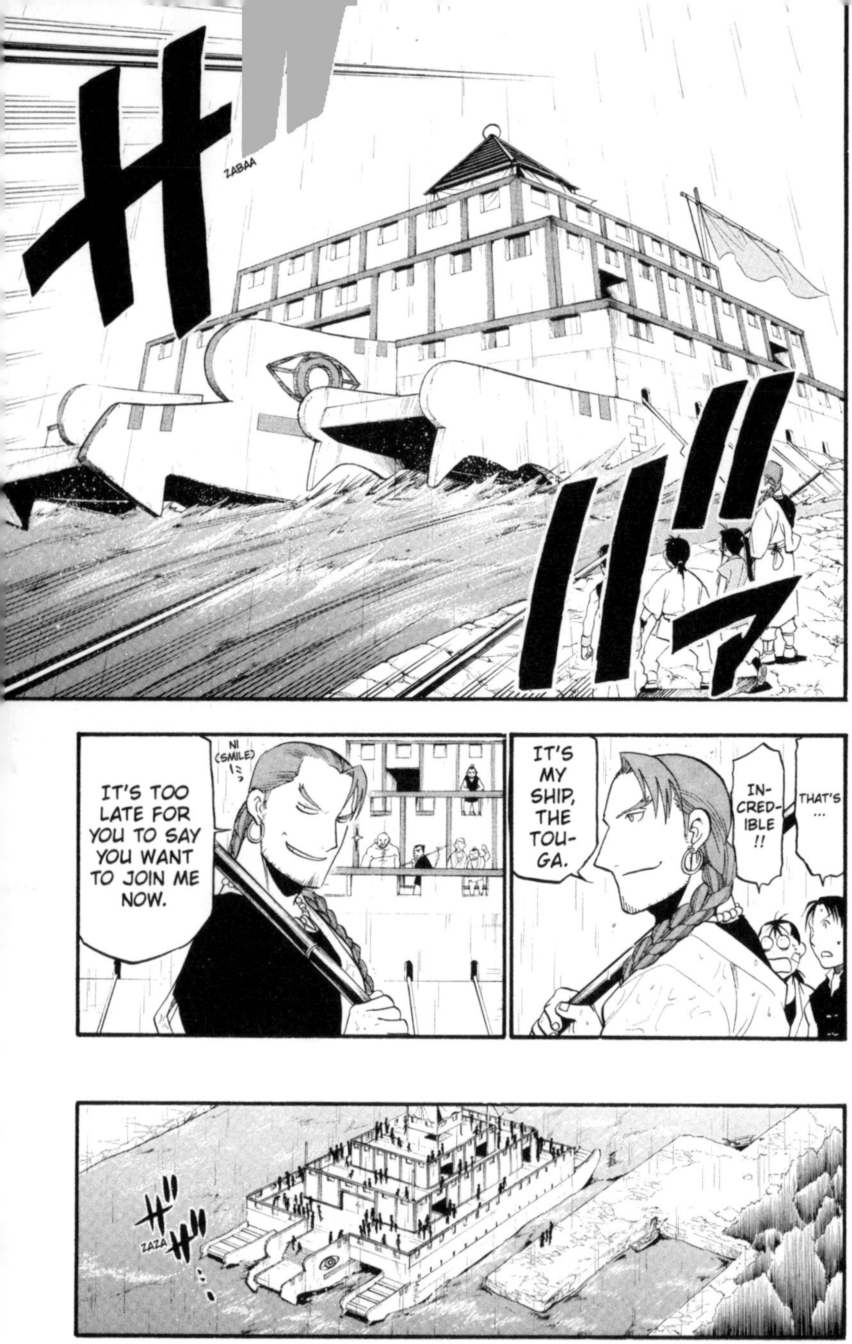
ZABAA
THAT'S ...
INCREDIBLE!!
IT'S MY SHIP, THE TOUGA.
NI (SMILE)
IT'S TOO LATE FOR YOU TO SAY YOU WANT TO JOIN ME NOW.
ZAZA

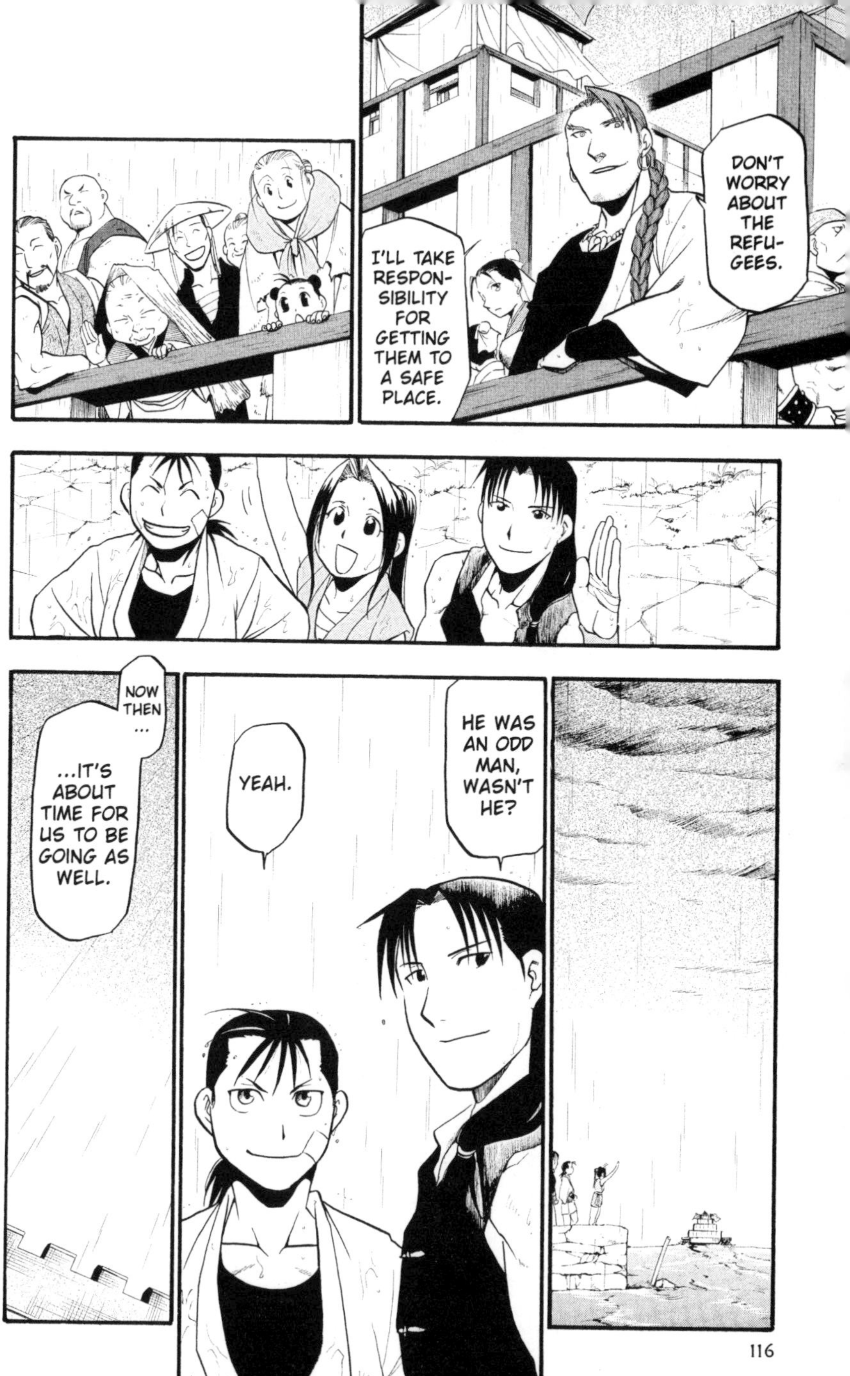
DON'T WORRY ABOUT THE REFUGEES.
I'LL TAKE RESPONSIBILITY FOR GETTING THEM TO A SAFE PLACE.
HE WAS AN ODD MAN, WASN'T HE?
YEAH.
NOW THEN ...
...IT'S ABOUT TIME FOR US TO BE GOING AS WELL.

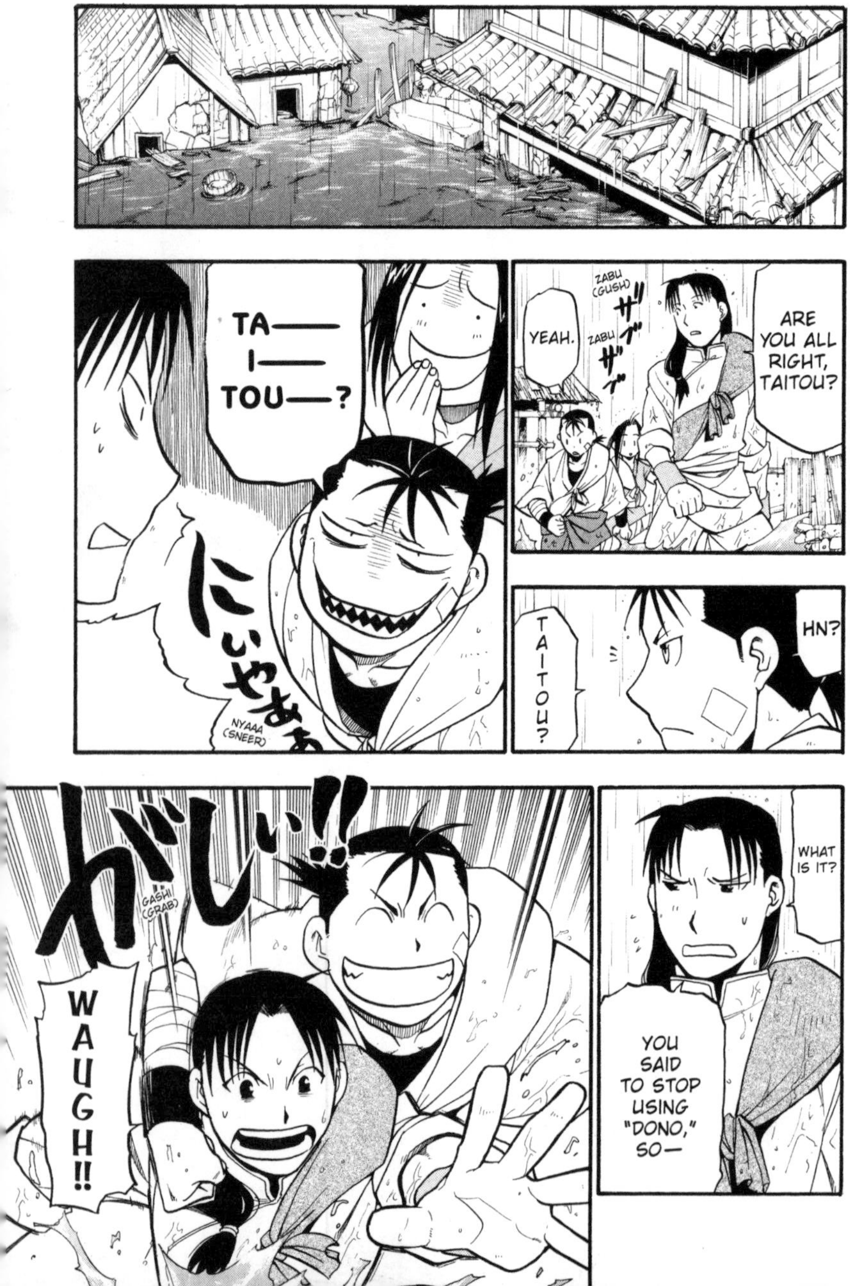
ARE YOU ALL RIGHT, TAITOU?
ザブザブ
ZABU (GUSH) ZABU
YEAH.
HN?
TAITOU?
TA—— I—— TOU——?
にいやぁぁ
NYAAA (SNEER)
WHAT IS IT?
YOU SAID TO STOP USING "DONO," SO—
がしぃ!!
GASHI (GRAB)
WAUGH!!

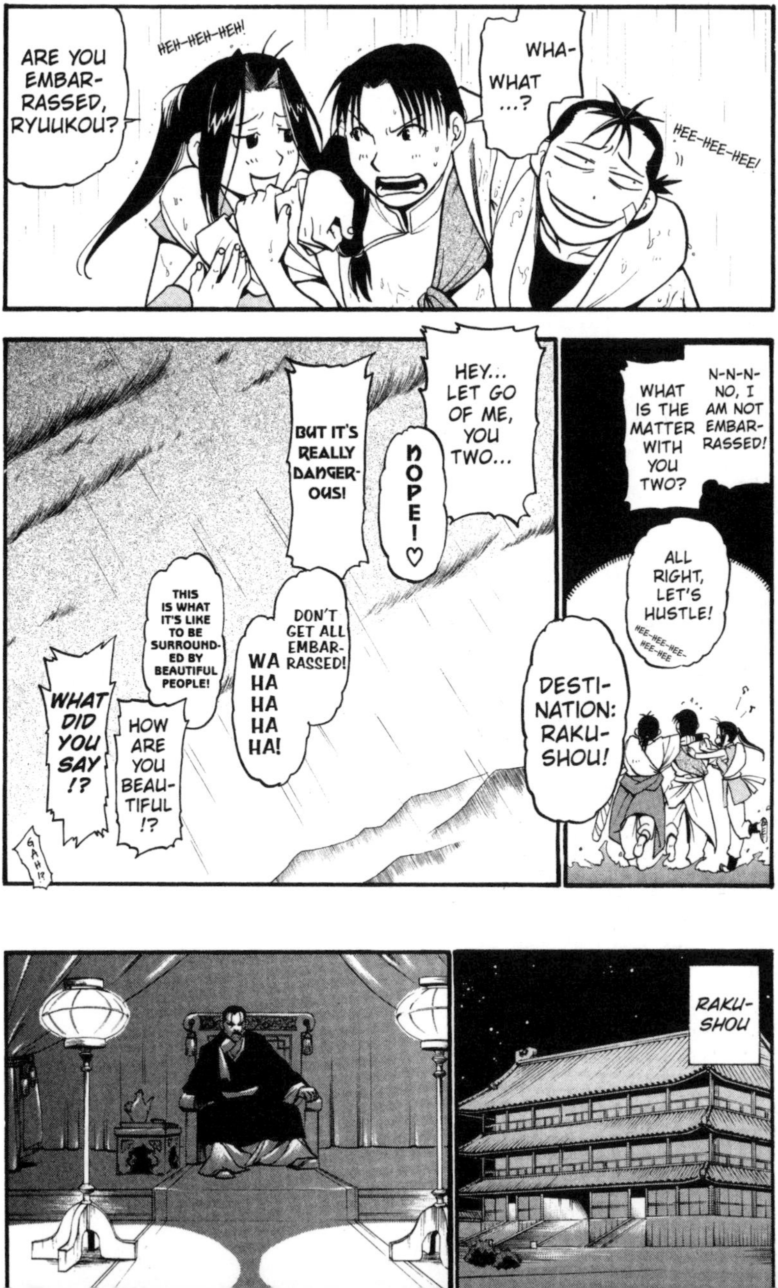
WHA- WHAT ...?
HEE-HEE-HEE!
HEH-HEH-HEH!
ARE YOU EMBAR-RASSED, RYUUKOU?
N-N-N-NO, I AM NOT EMBAR-RASSED!
WHAT IS THE MATTER WITH YOU TWO?
ALL RIGHT, LET'S HUSTLE!
HEE-HEE-HEE-HEE-HEE
DESTI-NATION: RAKU-SHOU!
HEY... LET GO OF ME, YOU TWO...
NOPE! ♡
BUT IT'S REALLY DANGER-OUS!
DON'T GET ALL EMBAR-RASSED!
WA HA HA HA HA!
THIS IS WHAT IT'S LIKE TO BE SURROUND-ED BY BEAUTIFUL PEOPLE!
HOW ARE YOU BEAU-TIFUL !?
WHAT DID YOU SAY !?
GAH!?
RAKU-SHOU

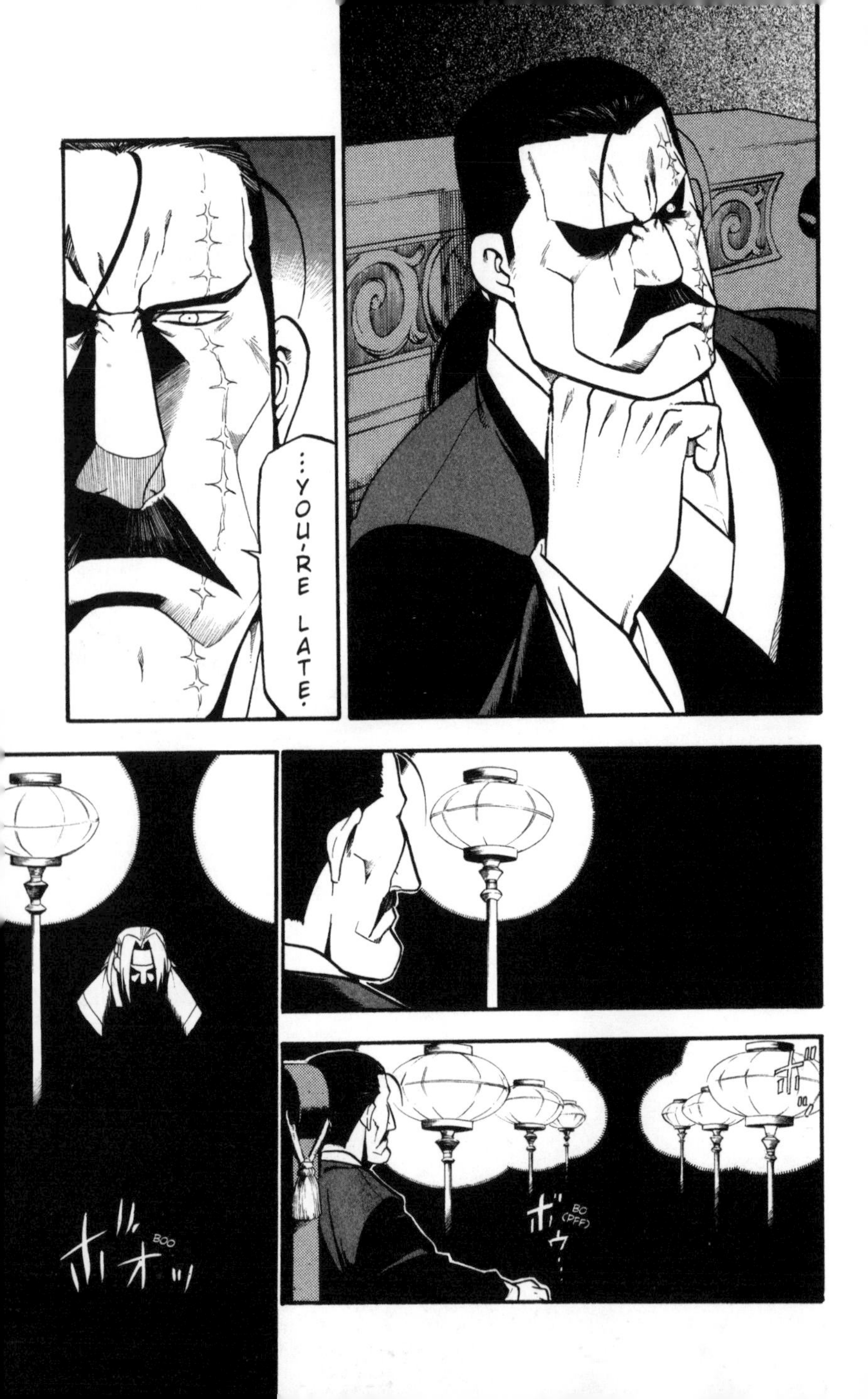
...YOU'RE LATE.
BO (PFF)
BOO

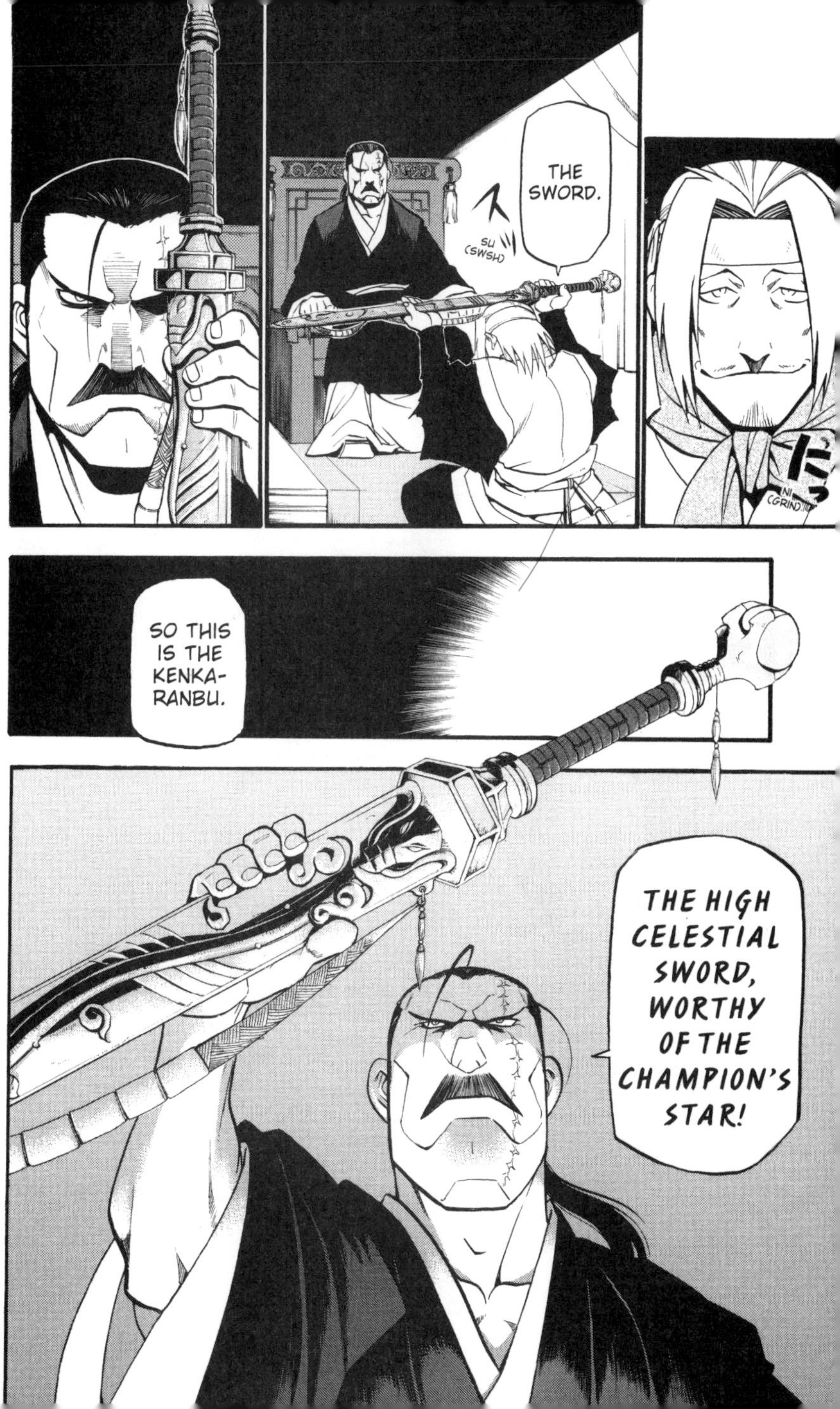
NI (GRIND)
THE SWORD.
SU (SWSH)
SO THIS IS THE KENKA-RANBU.
THE HIGH CELESTIAL SWORD, WORTHY OF THE CHAMPION'S STAR!

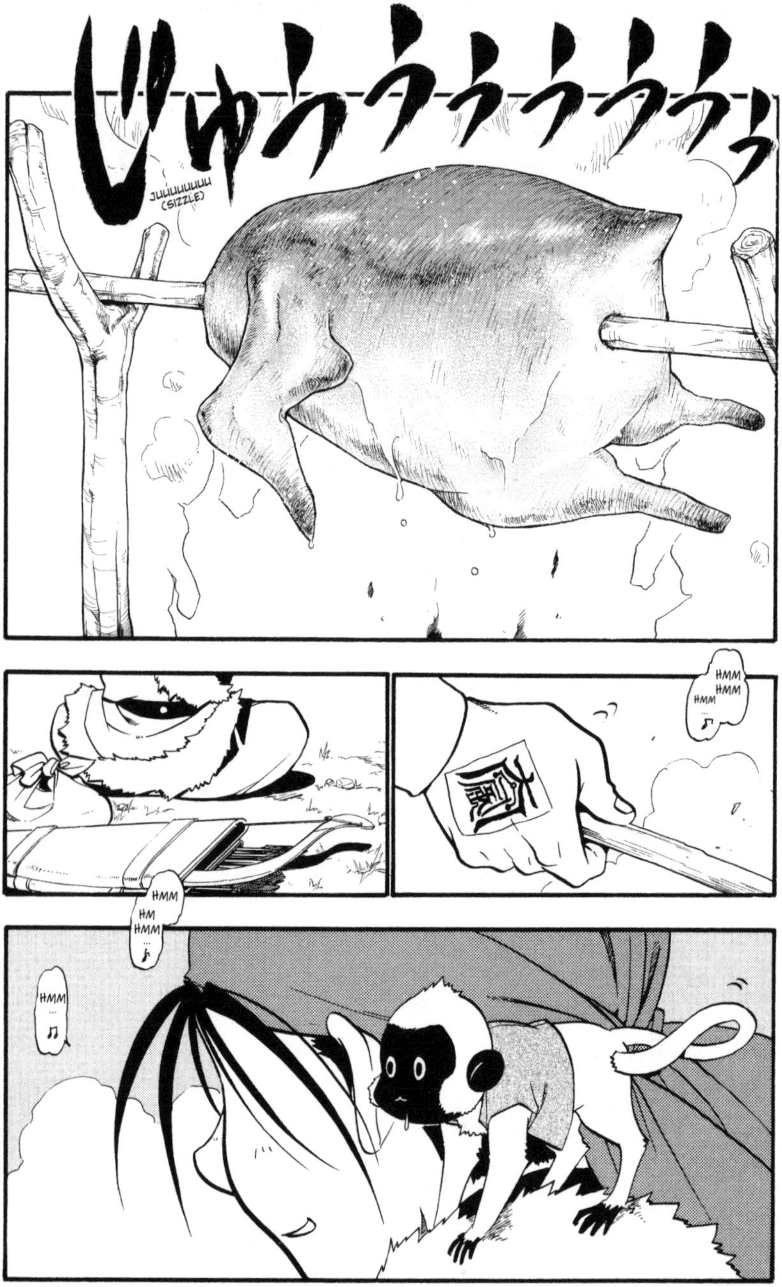

じゅううううううぅ
JUUUUUUUUU (SIZZLE)
HMM HMM HMM... ♪
HMM HM HMM... ♪
HMM... ♪

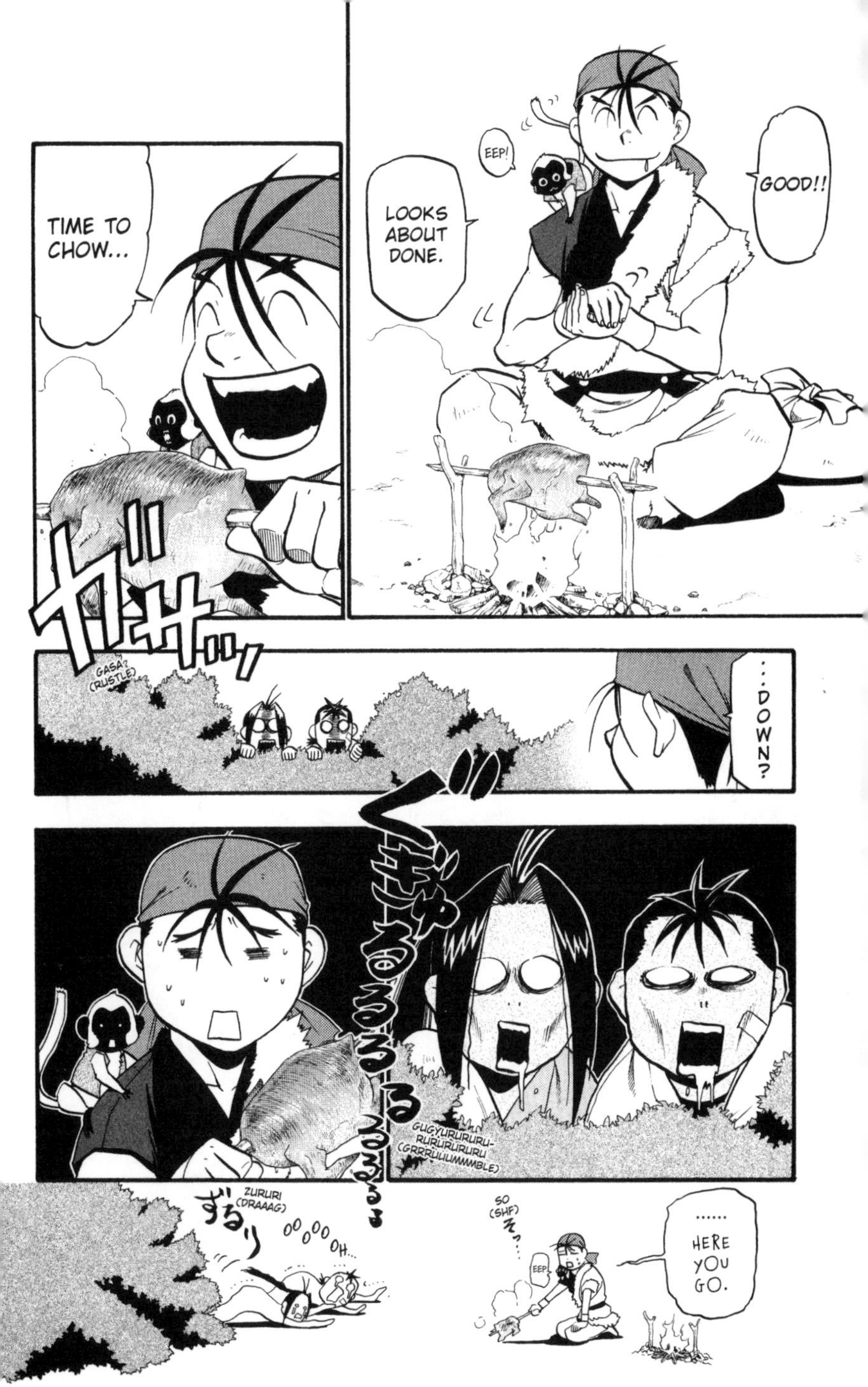
GOOD!!
EEP!
LOOKS ABOUT DONE.
TIME TO CHOW...
GASA (RUSTLE)
...DOWN?
GUGYURURURU-RURURURURU (GRRRUUUMMMBLE)
......HERE YOU GO.
SO (SHF)
EEP
ZURURI (DRAAAG)
OOOOOOH...

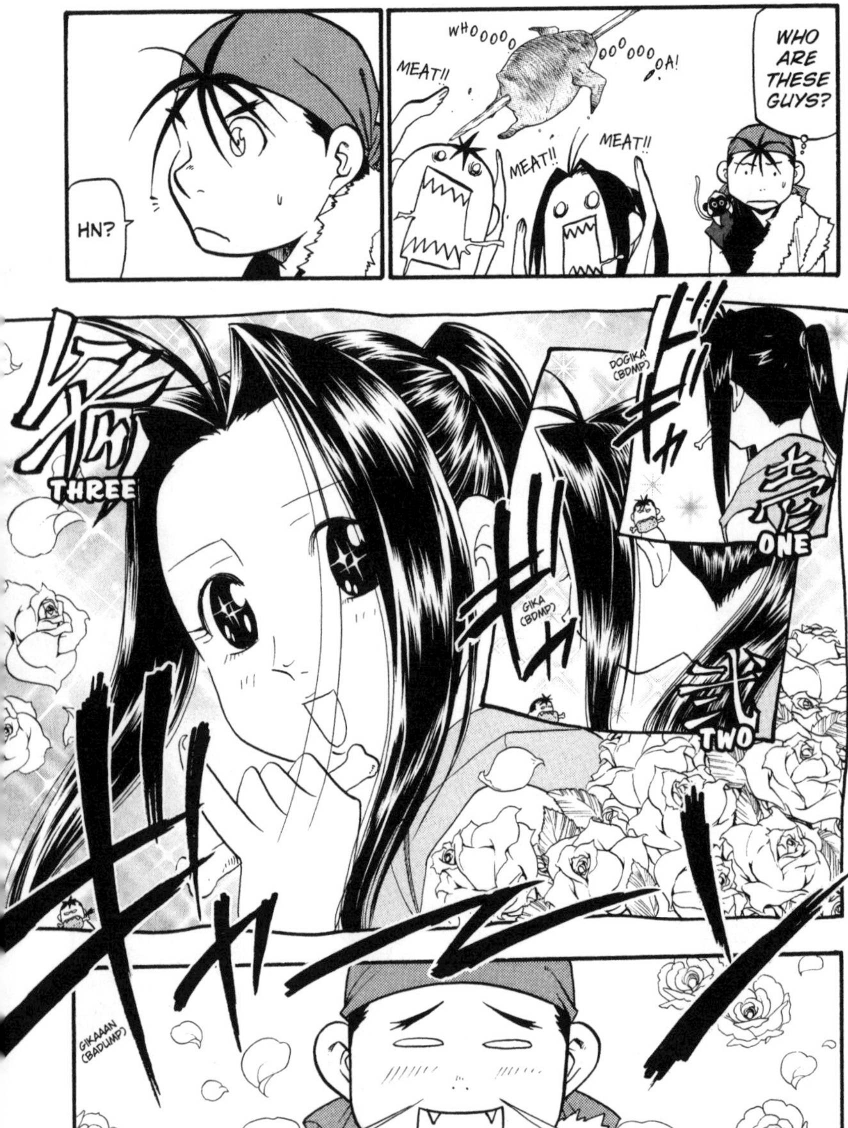
WHO ARE THESE GUYS?
MEAT!!
WHOOOOO OOOOOOOA!
MEAT!!
MEAT!!
HN?
DOGIKA (BDMP)
ONE
GIKA (BDMP)
TWO
THREE
GIKAAAN (BADUMP)

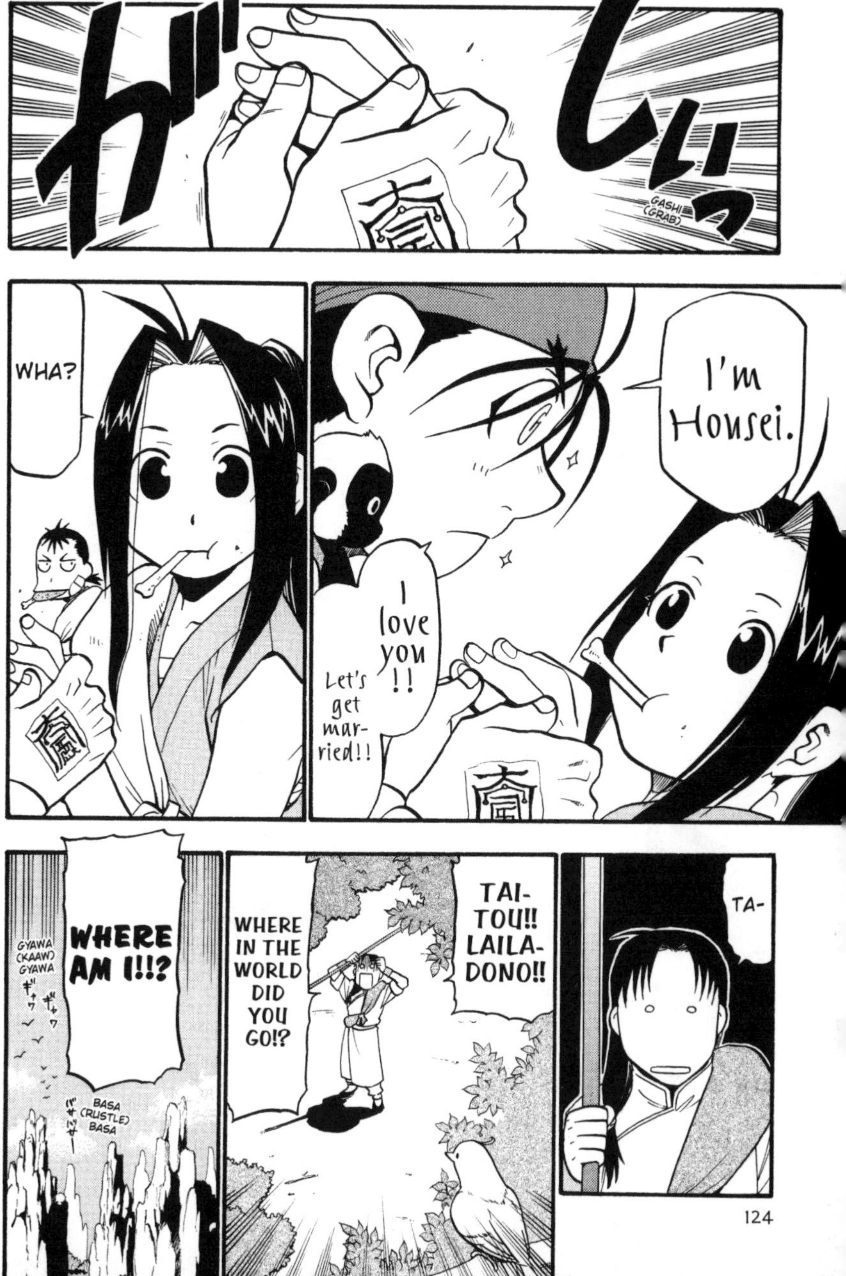
GASHI (GRAB)
I'm Housei.
I love you!!
Let's get married!!
WHA?
TA-
TAI-TOU!! LAILA-DONO!!
WHERE IN THE WORLD DID YOU GO!?
WHERE AM I!!?
GYAWA (KAAW) GYAWA
BASA (RUSTLE) BASA

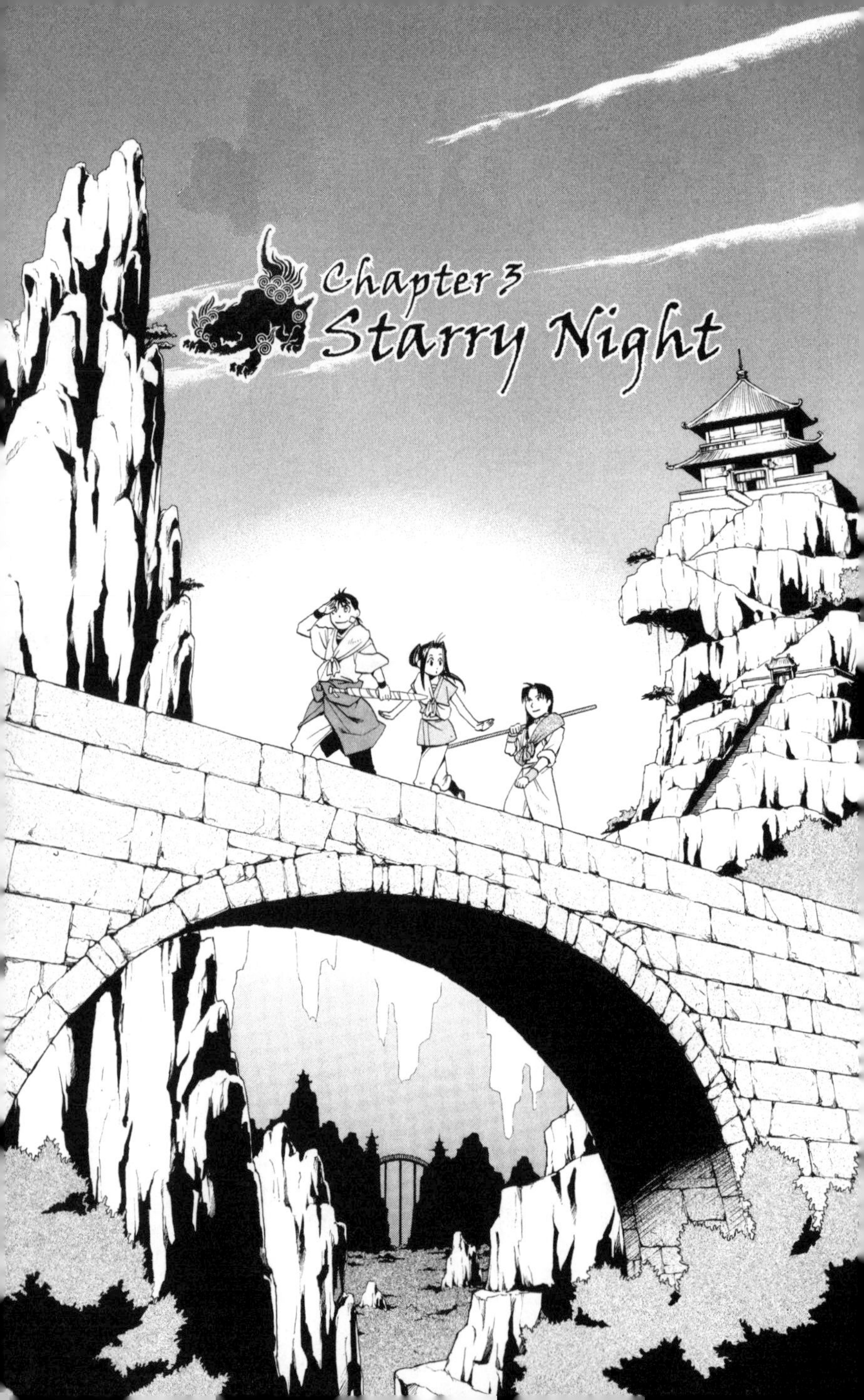
Chapter 3
Starry Night

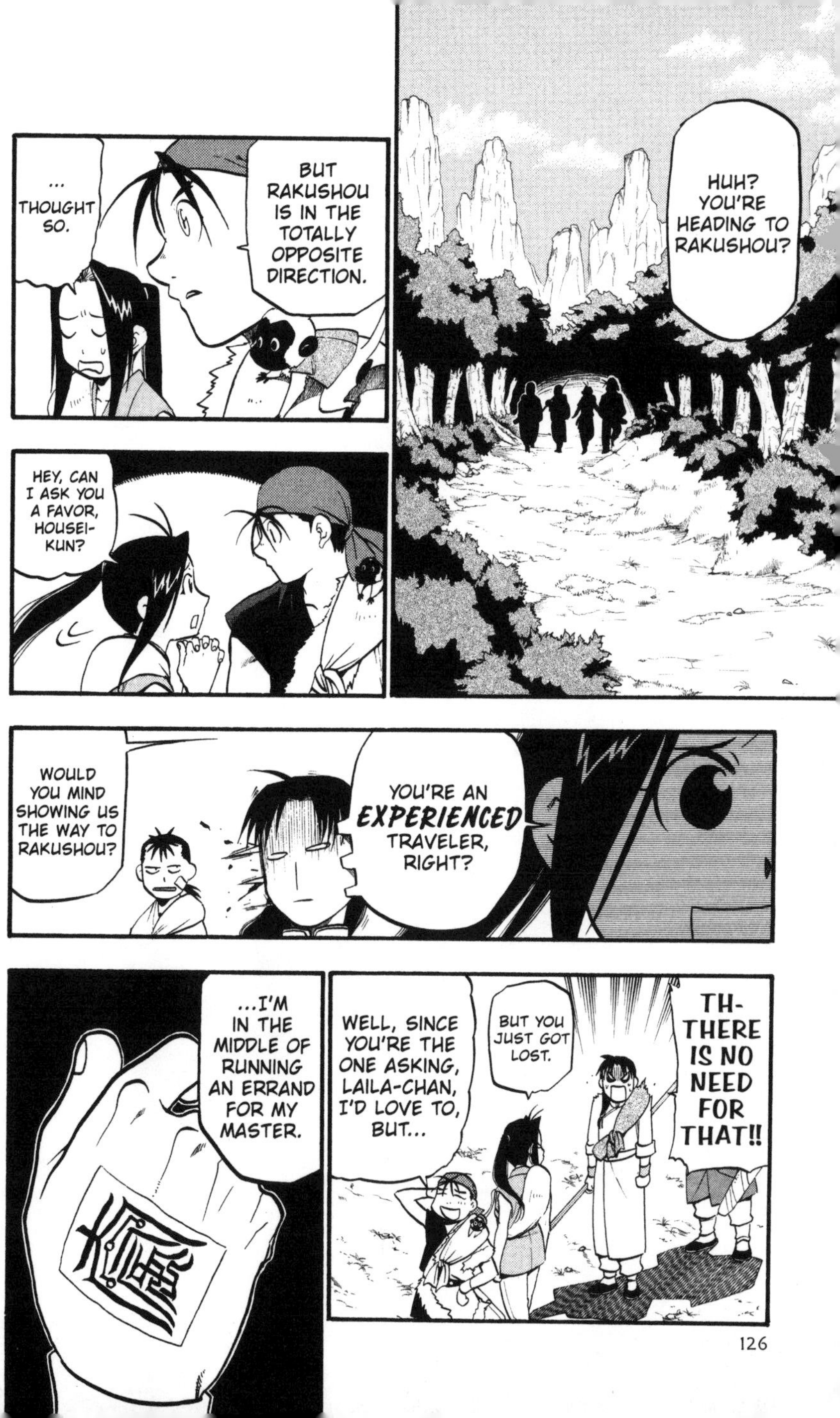
HUH? YOU'RE HEADING TO RAKUSHOU?
BUT RAKUSHOU IS IN THE TOTALLY OPPOSITE DIRECTION.
... THOUGHT SO.
HEY, CAN I ASK YOU A FAVOR, HOUSEI-KUN?
YOU'RE AN EXPERIENCED TRAVELER, RIGHT?
WOULD YOU MIND SHOWING US THE WAY TO RAKUSHOU?
TH-THERE IS NO NEED FOR THAT!!
BUT YOU JUST GOT LOST.
WELL, SINCE YOU'RE THE ONE ASKING, LAILA-CHAN, I'D LOVE TO, BUT...
...I'M IN THE MIDDLE OF RUNNING AN ERRAND FOR MY MASTER.

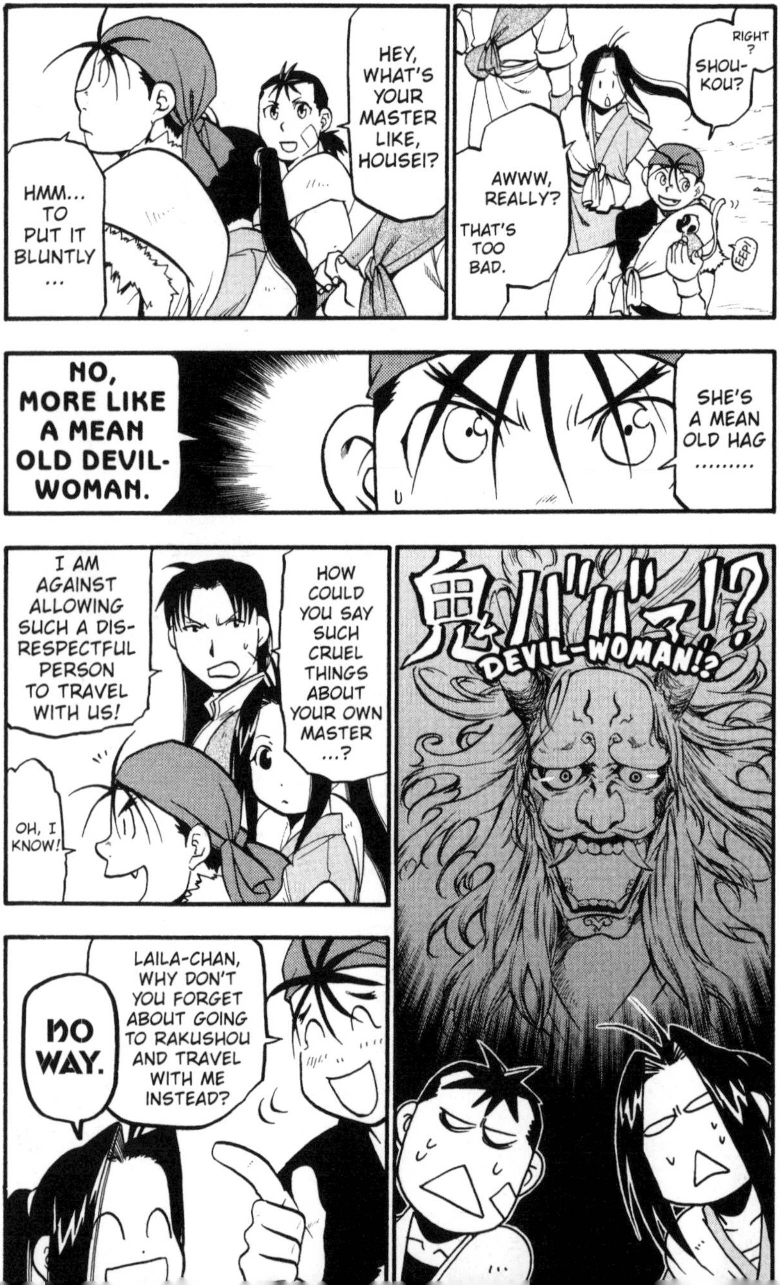
RIGHT? SHOU-KOU?
AWWW, REALLY?
THAT'S TOO BAD.
EEP!
HEY, WHAT'S YOUR MASTER LIKE, HOUSEI?
HMM... TO PUT IT BLUNTLY ...
SHE'S A MEAN OLD HAG ....
NO, MORE LIKE A MEAN OLD DEVIL-WOMAN.
鬼ババァ!?
DEVIL-WOMAN!?
...
HOW COULD YOU SAY SUCH CRUEL THINGS ABOUT YOUR OWN MASTER ...?
I AM AGAINST ALLOWING SUCH A DIS-RESPECTFUL PERSON TO TRAVEL WITH US!
OH, I KNOW!
LAILA-CHAN, WHY DON'T YOU FORGET ABOUT GOING TO RAKUSHOU AND TRAVEL WITH ME INSTEAD?
NO WAY.

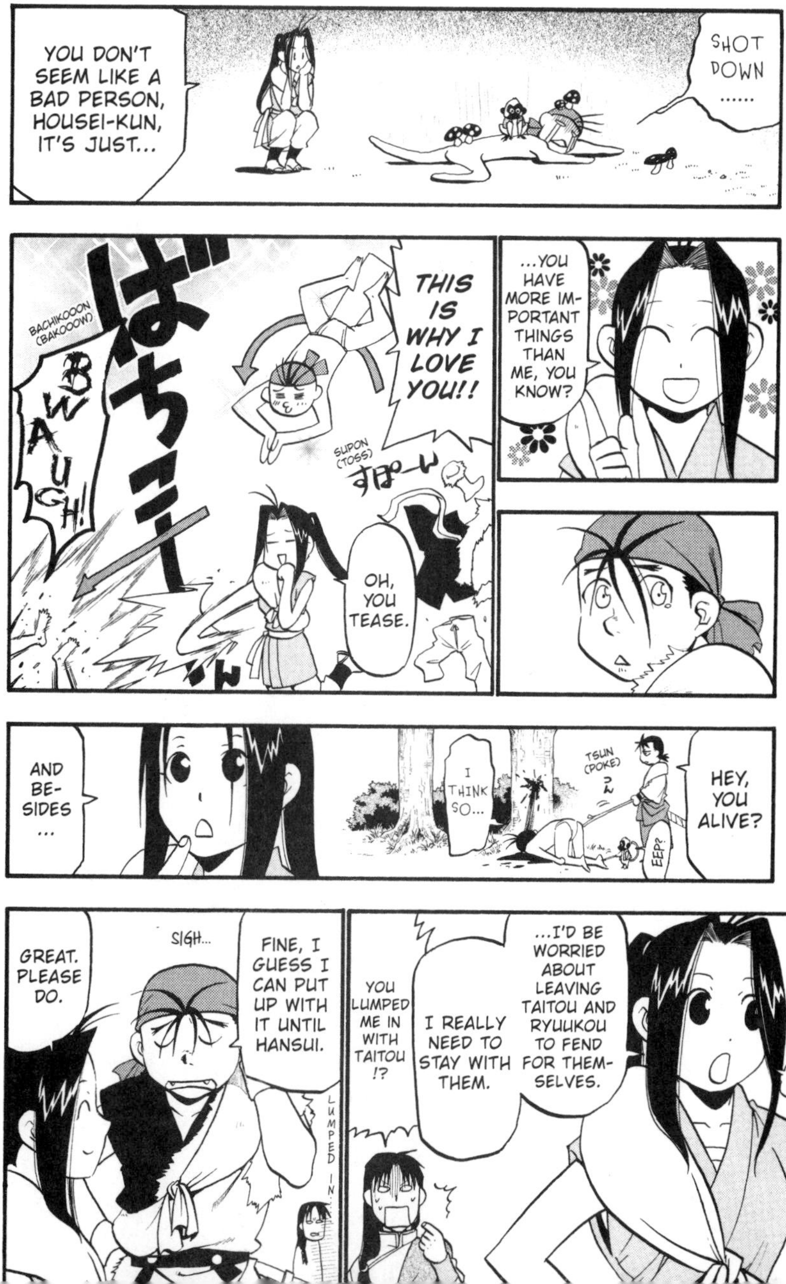
SHOT DOWN ......
YOU DON'T SEEM LIKE A BAD PERSON, HOUSEI-KUN, IT'S JUST...
...YOU HAVE MORE IMPORTANT THINGS THAN ME, YOU KNOW?
THIS IS WHY I LOVE YOU!!
SUPON (TOSS)
すぽーん
OH, YOU TEASE.
BACHIKOOON (BAKOOOW)
ばちこーん
BWAUGH!
HEY, YOU ALIVE?
TSUN (POKE)
つん
EEP?
I THINK SO...
AND BESIDES...
...I'D BE WORRIED ABOUT LEAVING TAITOU AND RYUUKOU TO FEND FOR THEMSELVES.
I REALLY NEED TO STAY WITH THEM.
YOU LUMPED ME IN WITH TAITOU!?
LUMPED IN...
FINE, I GUESS I CAN PUT UP WITH IT UNTIL HANSUI.
SIGH...
GREAT. PLEASE DO.

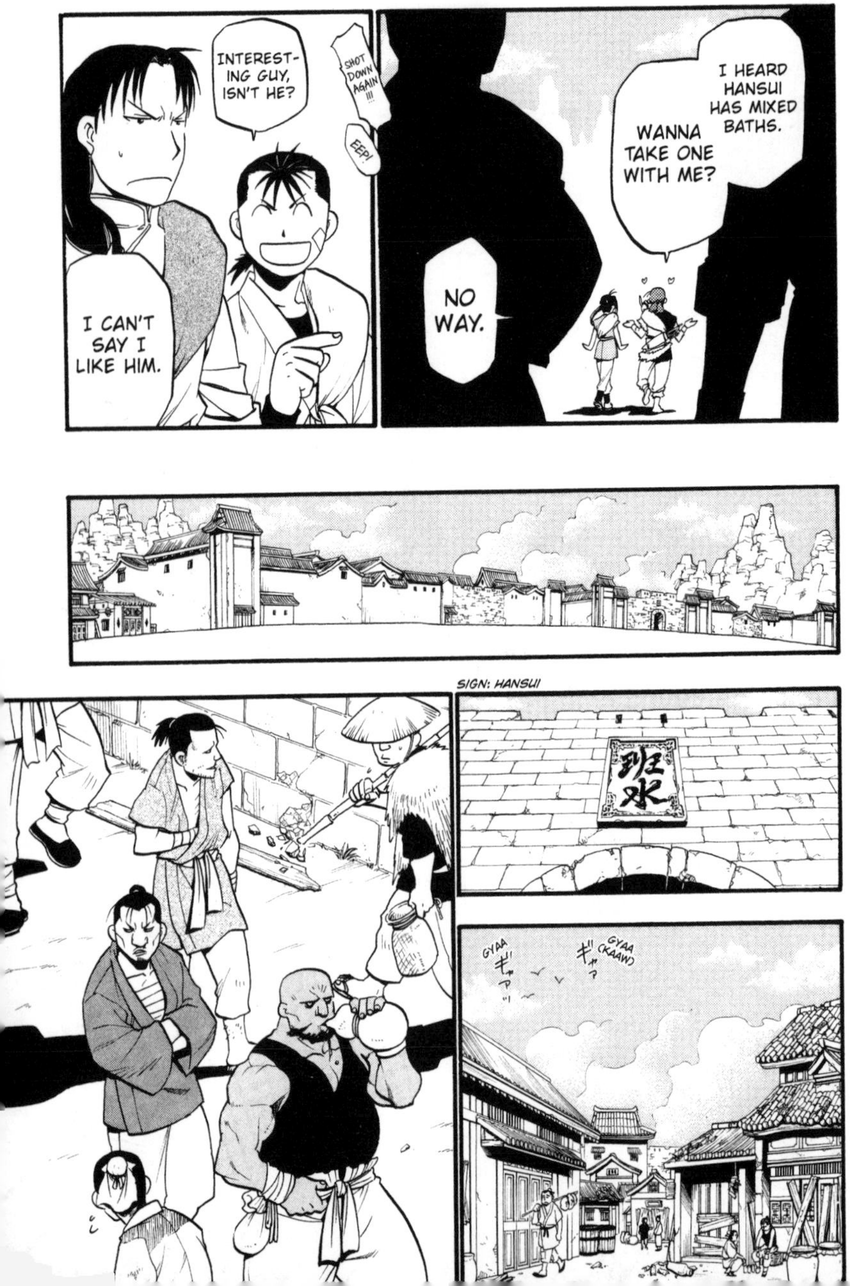
I HEARD HANSUI HAS MIXED BATHS.
WANNA TAKE ONE WITH ME?
NO WAY.
SHOT DOWN AGAIN!!!
INTERESTING GUY, ISN'T HE?
EEP!
I CAN'T SAY I LIKE HIM.
SIGN: HANSUI
班水
GYAA (KAAW)
ギャ
GYAA
ギャァッ

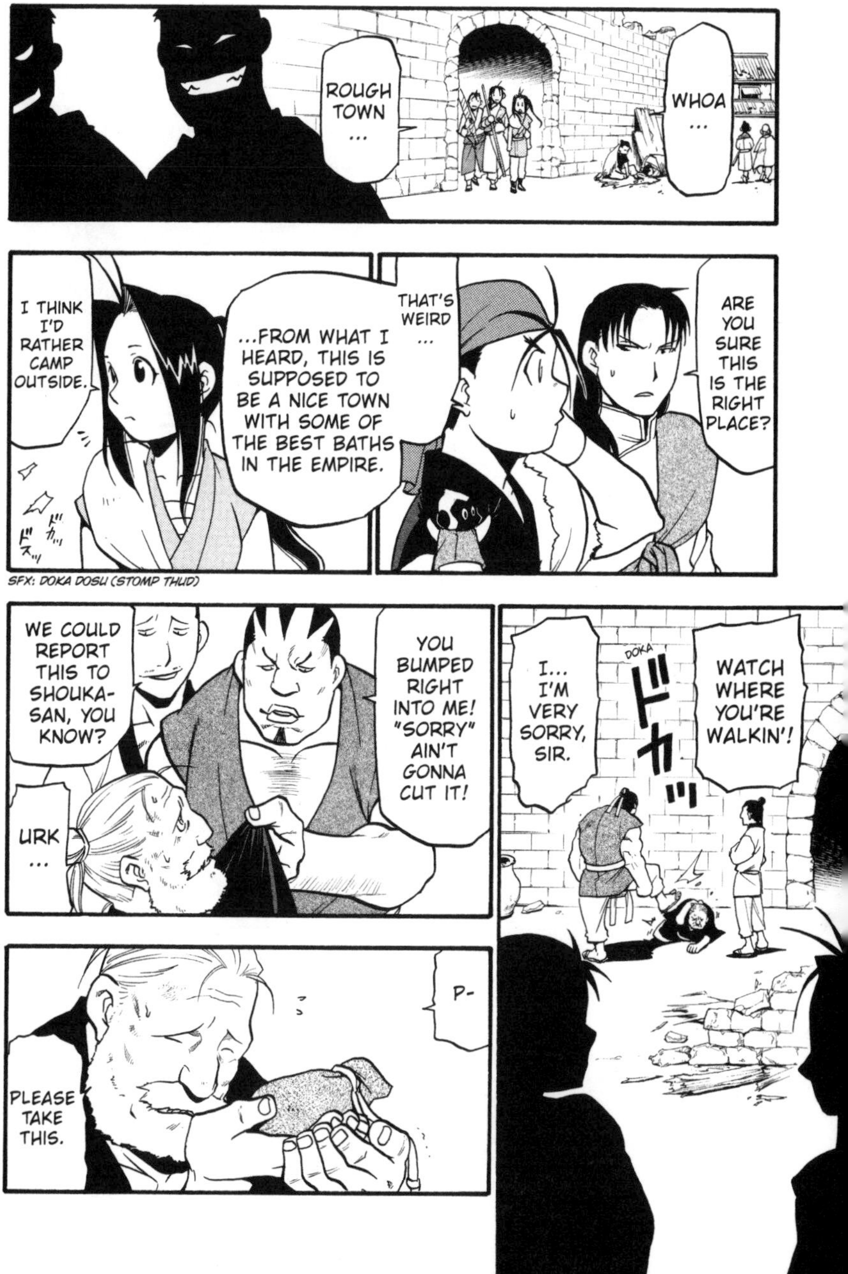
WHOA ...
ROUGH TOWN ...
ARE YOU SURE THIS IS THE RIGHT PLACE?
THAT'S WEIRD ...
...FROM WHAT I HEARD, THIS IS SUPPOSED TO BE A NICE TOWN WITH SOME OF THE BEST BATHS IN THE EMPIRE.
I THINK I'D RATHER CAMP OUTSIDE.
SFX: DOKA DOSU (STOMP THUD)
WATCH WHERE YOU'RE WALKIN'!
DOKA
I... I'M VERY SORRY, SIR.
YOU BUMPED RIGHT INTO ME! "SORRY" AIN'T GONNA CUT IT!
WE COULD REPORT THIS TO SHOUKA-SAN, YOU KNOW?
URK ...
P-
PLEASE TAKE THIS.

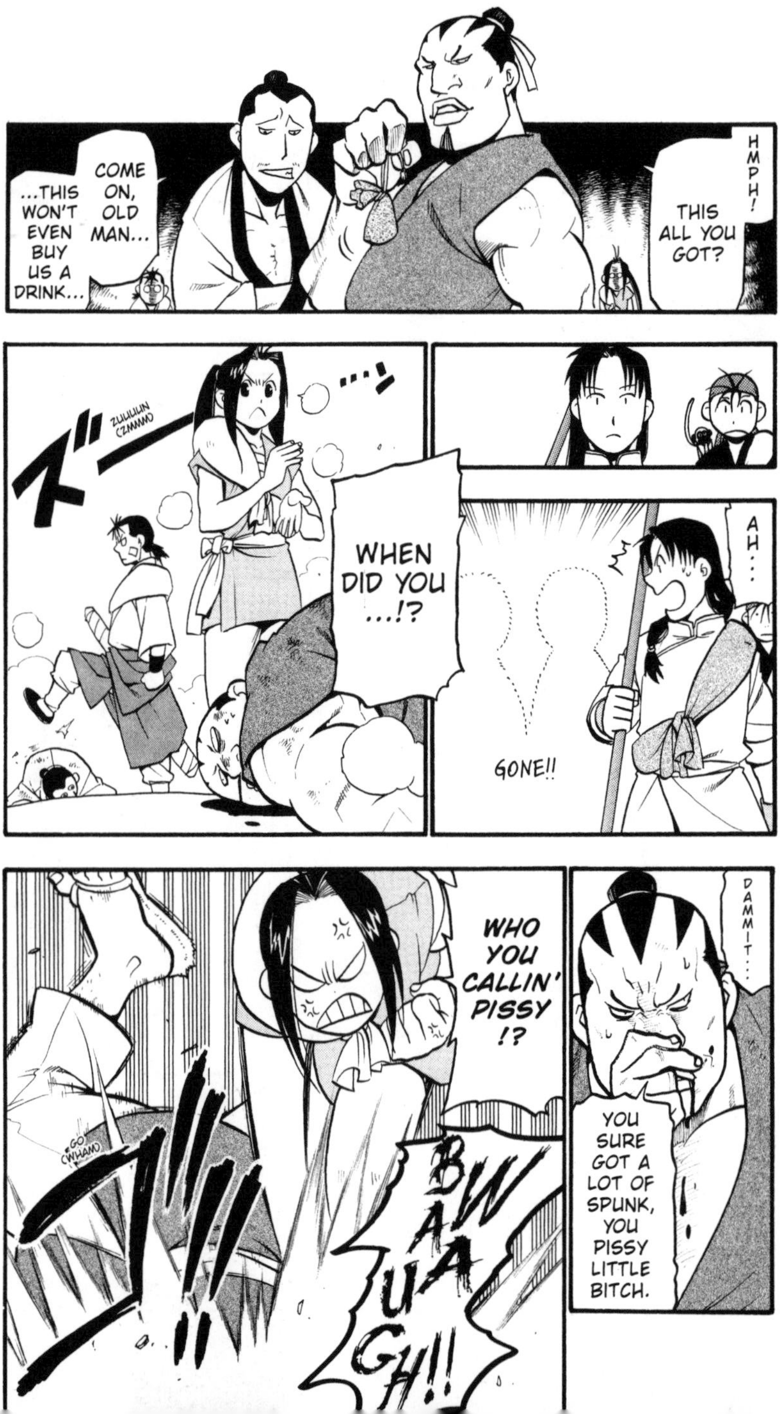
HMPH!
THIS ALL YOU GOT?
COME ON, OLD MAN...
...THIS WON'T EVEN BUY US A DRINK...
AH...
GONE!!
...!
ZUUUUN (ZMMM)
WHEN DID YOU ...!?
DAMMIT...
YOU SURE GOT A LOT OF SPUNK, YOU PISSY LITTLE BITCH.
WHO YOU CALLIN' PISSY !?
GO (WHAM)
BWAAUAGH!!

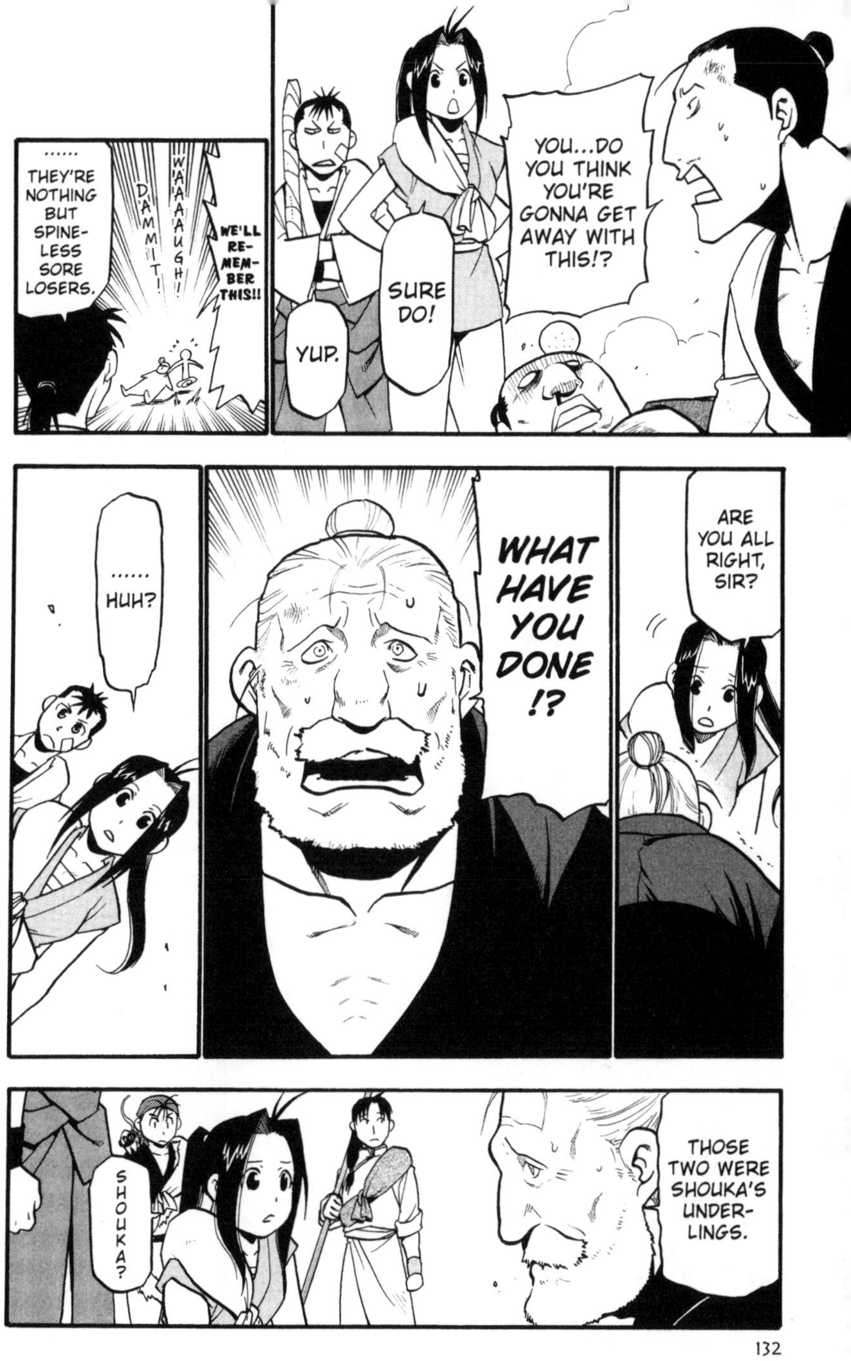
YOU...DO YOU THINK YOU'RE GONNA GET AWAY WITH THIS!?
SURE DO!
YUP.
WE'LL RE-MEM-BER THIS!!
WAAAAAUGH!
DAMMIT!
...... THEY'RE NOTHING BUT SPINE-LESS SORE LOSERS.
ARE YOU ALL RIGHT, SIR?
WHAT HAVE YOU DONE!?
...... HUH?
THOSE TWO WERE SHOUKA'S UNDER-LINGS.
SHOUKA?

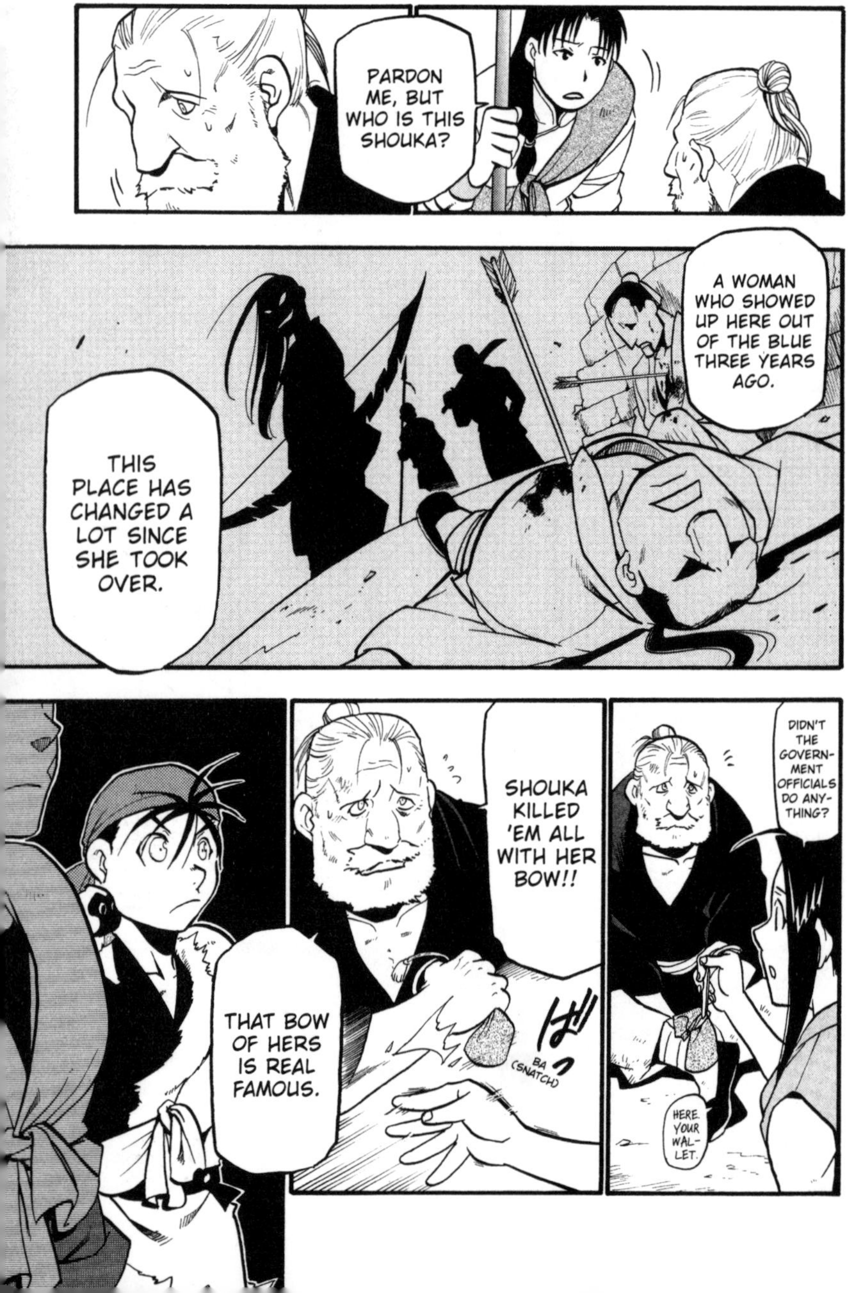
PARDON ME, BUT WHO IS THIS SHOUKA?
A WOMAN WHO SHOWED UP HERE OUT OF THE BLUE THREE YEARS AGO.
THIS PLACE HAS CHANGED A LOT SINCE SHE TOOK OVER.
DIDN'T THE GOVERNMENT OFFICIALS DO ANYTHING?
HERE. YOUR WALLET.
SHOUKA KILLED 'EM ALL WITH HER BOW!!
ばっ
BA (SNATCH)
THAT BOW OF HERS IS REAL FAMOUS.

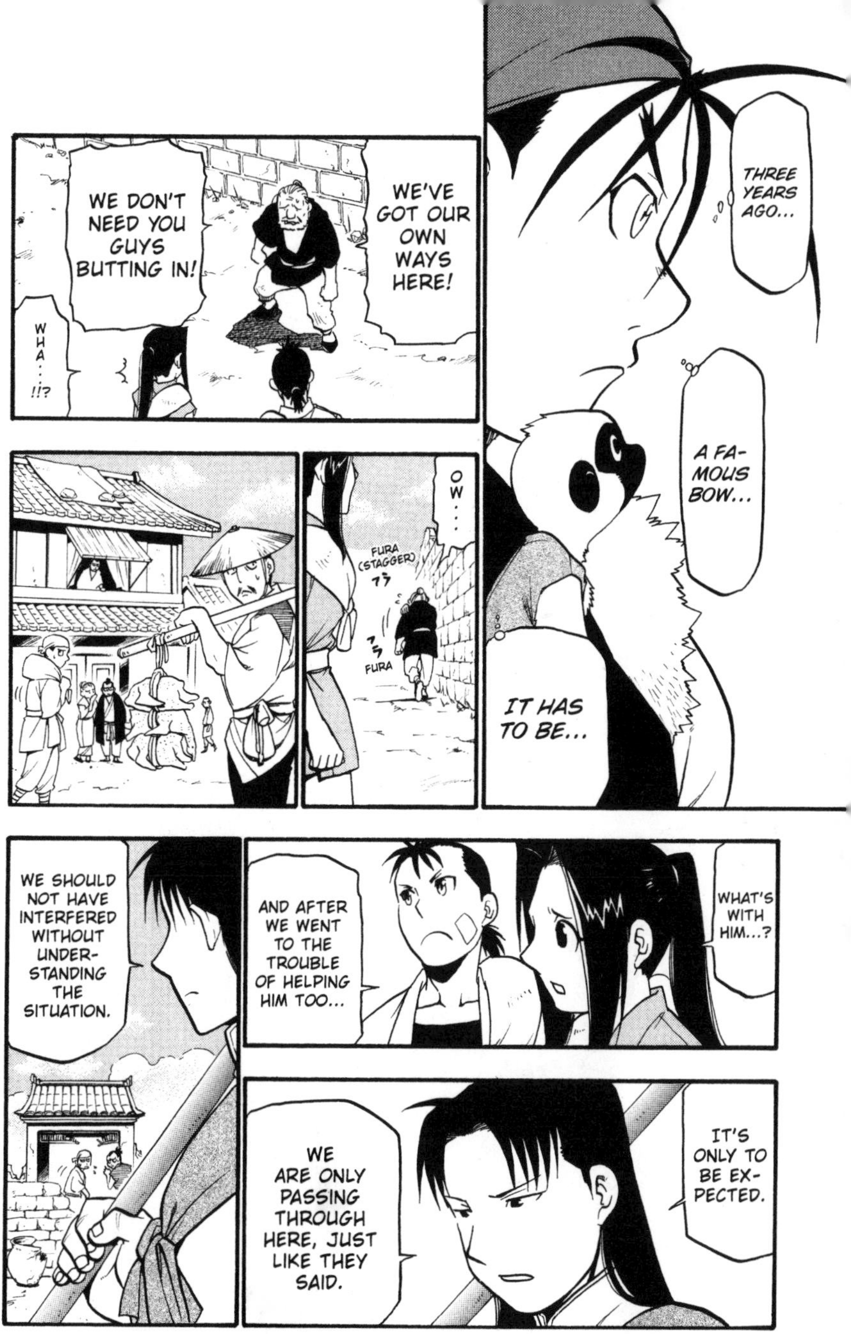

THREE YEARS AGO...
A FA-MOUS BOW...
IT HAS TO BE...
WE'VE GOT OUR OWN WAYS HERE!
WE DON'T NEED YOU GUYS BUTTING IN!
WHA...!!?
OW...
FURA (STAGGER)
FURA
WHAT'S WITH HIM...?
AND AFTER WE WENT TO THE TROUBLE OF HELPING HIM TOO...
IT'S ONLY TO BE EX-PECTED.
WE ARE ONLY PASSING THROUGH HERE, JUST LIKE THEY SAID.
WE SHOULD NOT HAVE INTERFERED WITHOUT UNDER-STANDING THE SITUATION.

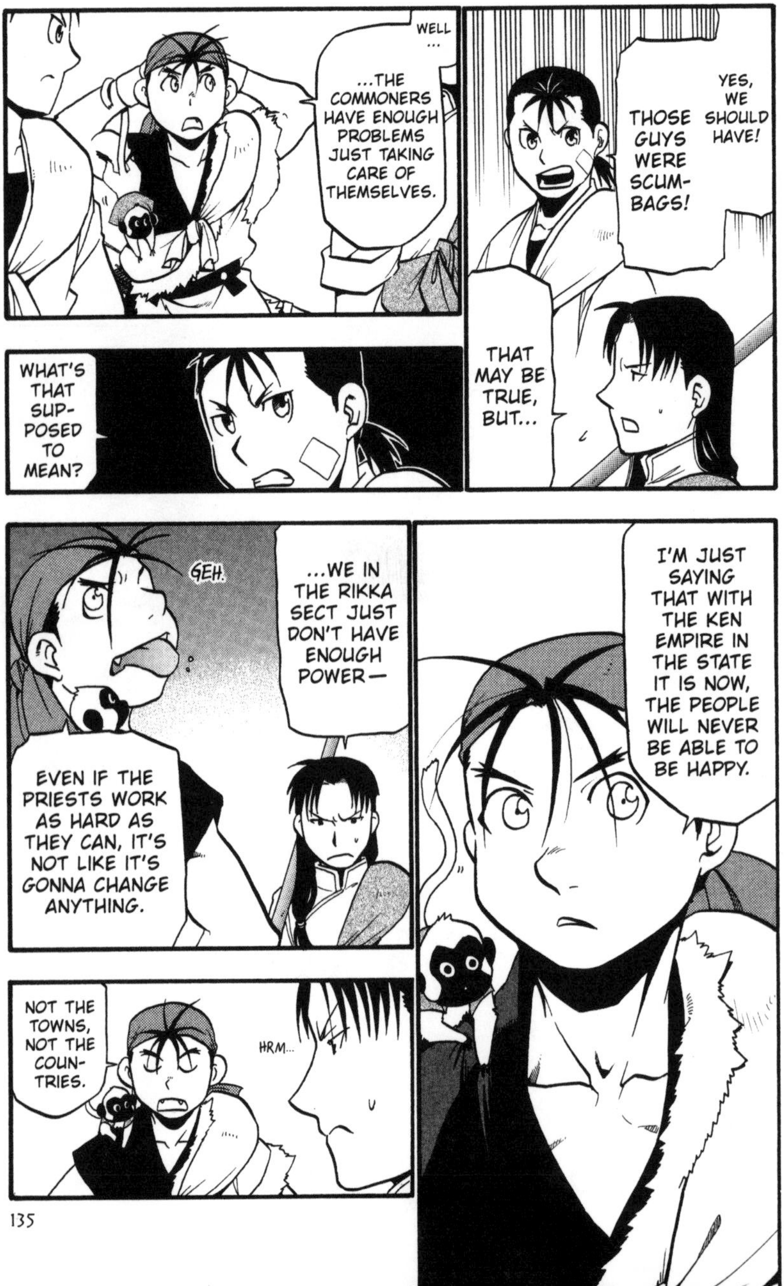
YES, WE SHOULD HAVE!
THOSE GUYS WERE SCUM-BAGS!
THAT MAY BE TRUE, BUT...
WELL ...
...THE COMMONERS HAVE ENOUGH PROBLEMS JUST TAKING CARE OF THEMSELVES.
WHAT'S THAT SUP-POSED TO MEAN?
I'M JUST SAYING THAT WITH THE KEN EMPIRE IN THE STATE IT IS NOW, THE PEOPLE WILL NEVER BE ABLE TO BE HAPPY.
...WE IN THE RIKKA SECT JUST DON'T HAVE ENOUGH POWER—
GEH.
EVEN IF THE PRIESTS WORK AS HARD AS THEY CAN, IT'S NOT LIKE IT'S GONNA CHANGE ANYTHING.
HRM...
NOT THE TOWNS, NOT THE COUN-TRIES.

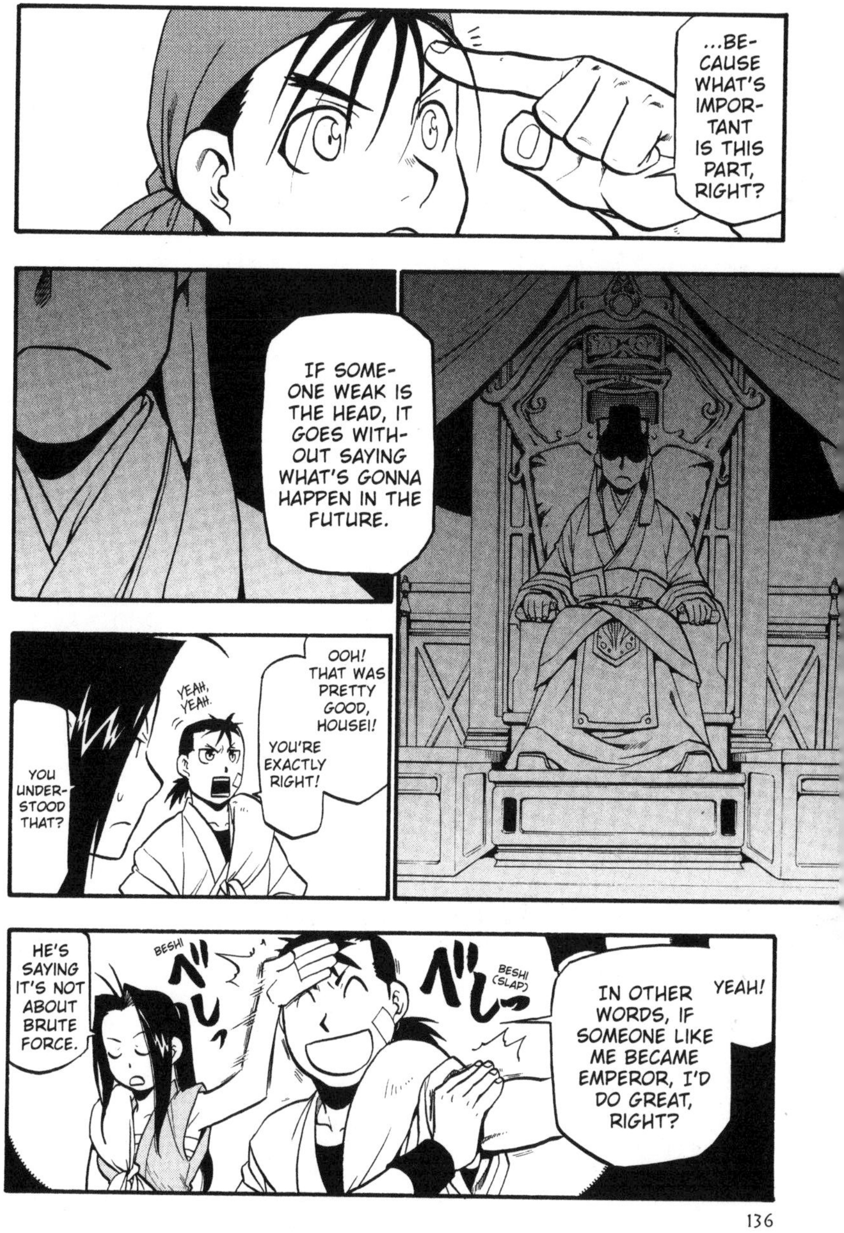
...BE-CAUSE WHAT'S IMPOR-TANT IS THIS PART, RIGHT?
IF SOME-ONE WEAK IS THE HEAD, IT GOES WITH-OUT SAYING WHAT'S GONNA HAPPEN IN THE FUTURE.
OOH! THAT WAS PRETTY GOOD, HOUSEI!
YOU'RE EXACTLY RIGHT!
YEAH, YEAH.
YOU UNDER-STOOD THAT?
YEAH!
IN OTHER WORDS, IF SOMEONE LIKE ME BECAME EMPEROR, I'D DO GREAT, RIGHT?
BESHI (SLAP)
べしっ
BESHI
べしっ
HE'S SAYING IT'S NOT ABOUT BRUTE FORCE.

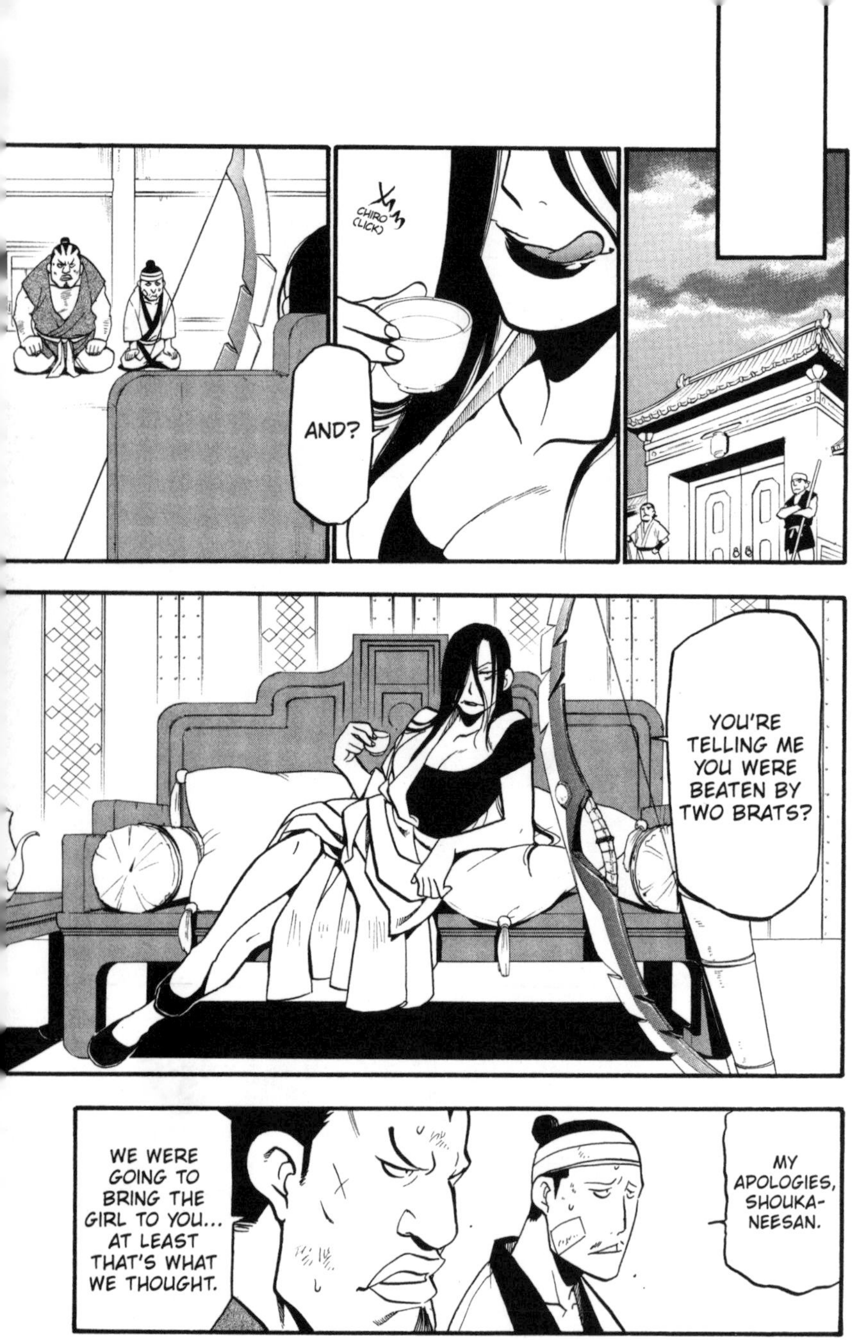
CHIRO
(CLICK)
AND?
YOU'RE TELLING ME YOU WERE BEATEN BY TWO BRATS?
MY APOLOGIES, SHOUKA-NEESAN.
WE WERE GOING TO BRING THE GIRL TO YOU... AT LEAST THAT'S WHAT WE THOUGHT.

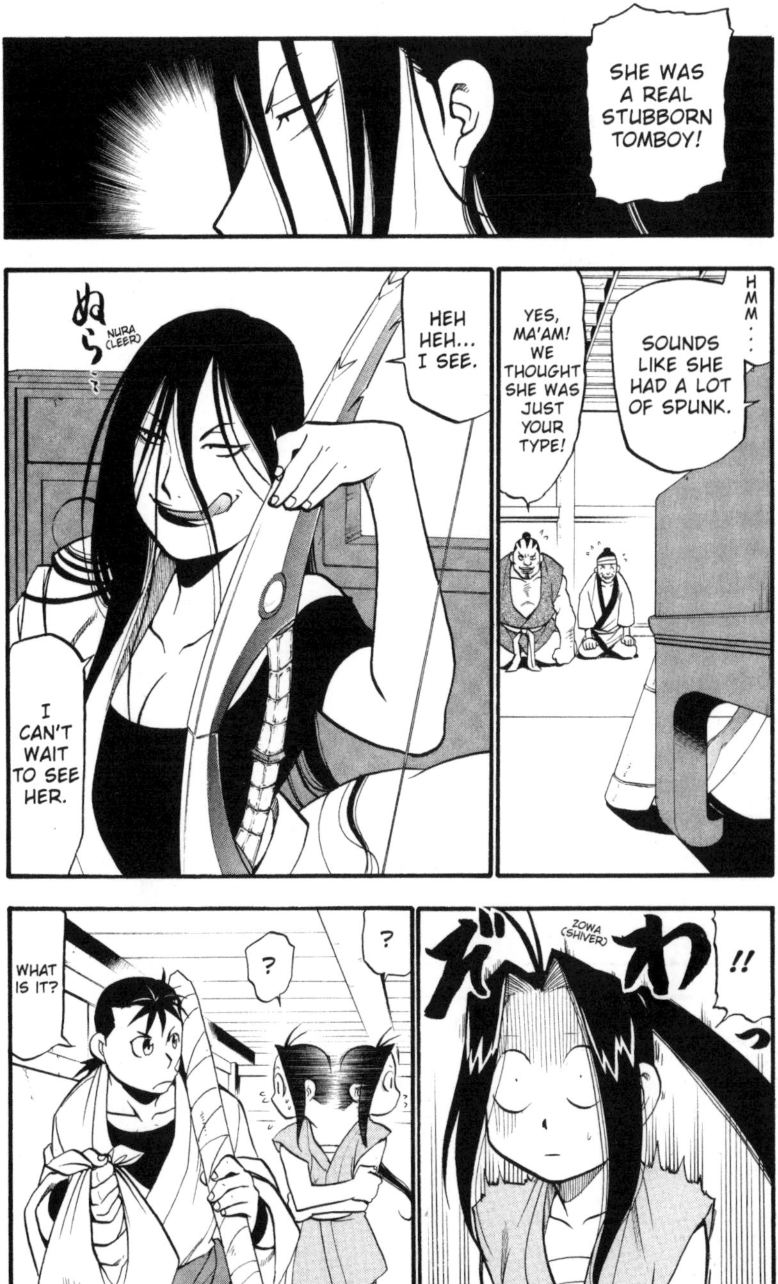
SHE WAS A REAL STUBBORN TOMBOY!
HMM...
SOUNDS LIKE SHE HAD A LOT OF SPUNK.
YES, MA'AM! WE THOUGHT SHE WAS JUST YOUR TYPE!
HEH HEH... I SEE.
ぬら
NURA (LEER)
I CAN'T WAIT TO SEE HER.
ぞわっ
ZOWA (SHIVER)
!!
?
?
WHAT IS IT?

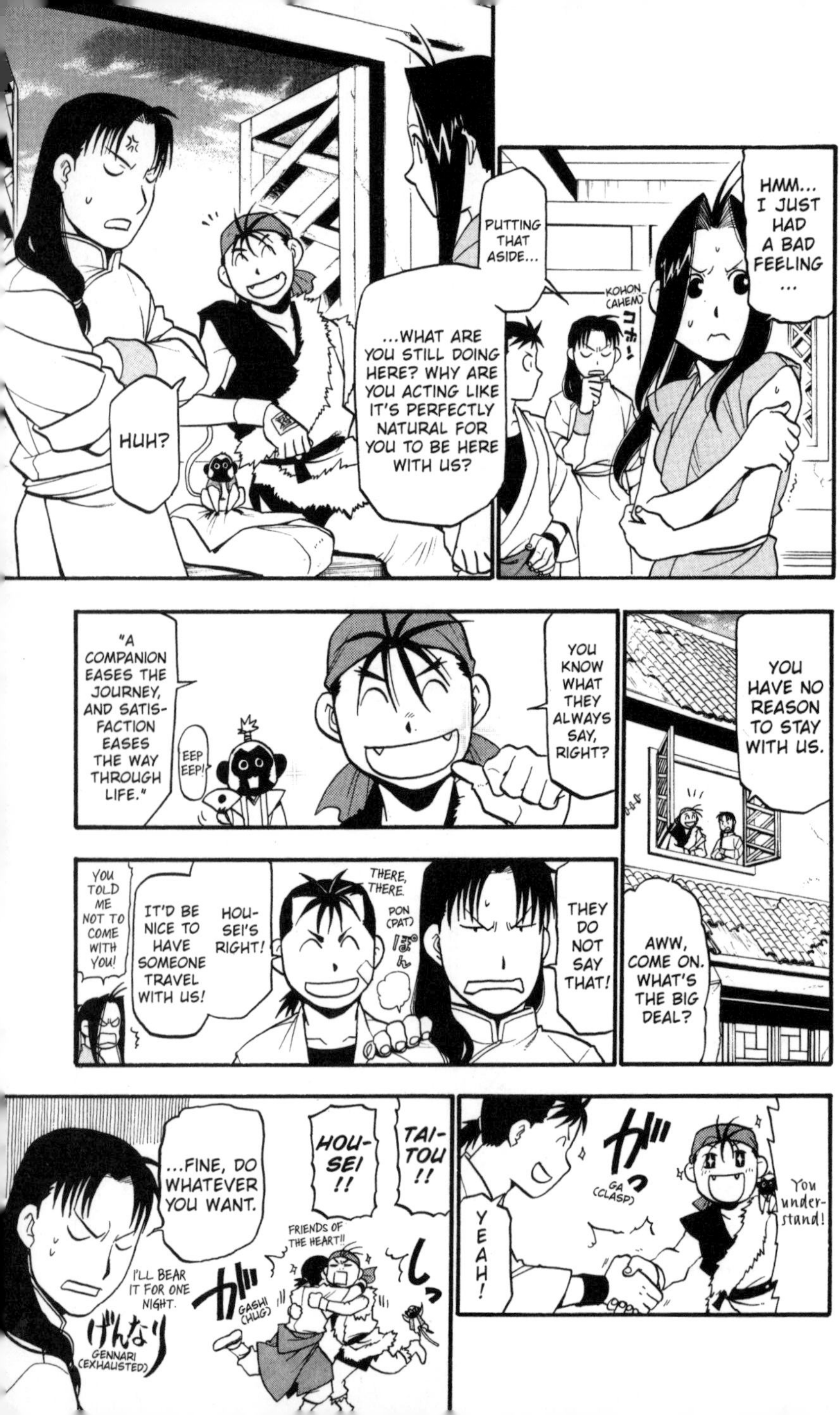

HMM... I JUST HAD A BAD FEELING ...
KOHON (AHEM)
PUTTING THAT ASIDE...
...WHAT ARE YOU STILL DOING HERE? WHY ARE YOU ACTING LIKE IT'S PERFECTLY NATURAL FOR YOU TO BE HERE WITH US?
HUH?
YOU HAVE NO REASON TO STAY WITH US.
AWW, COME ON. WHAT'S THE BIG DEAL?
YOU KNOW WHAT THEY ALWAYS SAY, RIGHT?
EEP EEP!
"A COMPANION EASES THE JOURNEY, AND SATISFACTION EASES THE WAY THROUGH LIFE."
THEY DO NOT SAY THAT!
THERE, THERE.
PON (PAT)
HOU-SEI'S RIGHT!
IT'D BE NICE TO HAVE SOMEONE TRAVEL WITH US!
YOU TOLD ME NOT TO COME WITH YOU!
You understand!
GA (CLASP)
YEAH!
TAI-TOU!!
HOU-SEI!!
...FINE, DO WHATEVER YOU WANT.
FRIENDS OF THE HEART!!
GASHI (HUG)
I'LL BEAR IT FOR ONE NIGHT.
げんなり
GENNARI (EXHAUSTED)

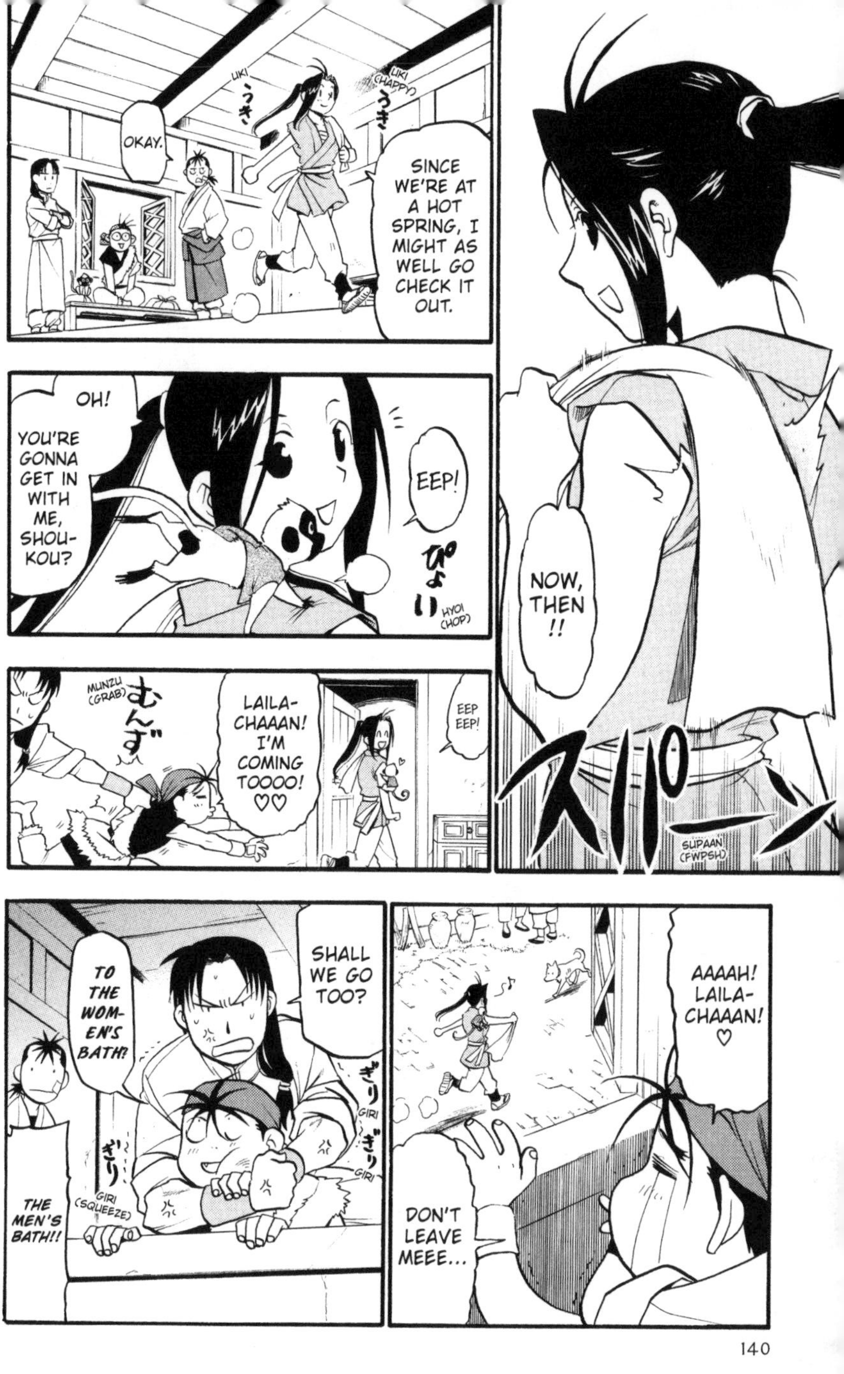
NOW, THEN!!
スパーン
SUPAAN (FWPSH)
うき
UKI (HAPPY)
SINCE WE'RE AT A HOT SPRING, I MIGHT AS WELL GO CHECK IT OUT.
うき
UKI
OKAY.
EEP!
ぴょい
HYOI (HOP)
OH!
YOU'RE GONNA GET IN WITH ME, SHOUKOU?
EEP EEP!
LAILA-CHAAAN! I'M COMING TOOOO! ♡♡
むんず
MUNZU (GRAB)
AAAAH! LAILA-CHAAAN! ♡
DON'T LEAVE MEEE...
SHALL WE GO TOO?
TO THE WOMEN'S BATH!?
ぎり
GIRI
ぎり
GIRI
ぎり
GIRI (SQUEEZE)
THE MEN'S BATH!!

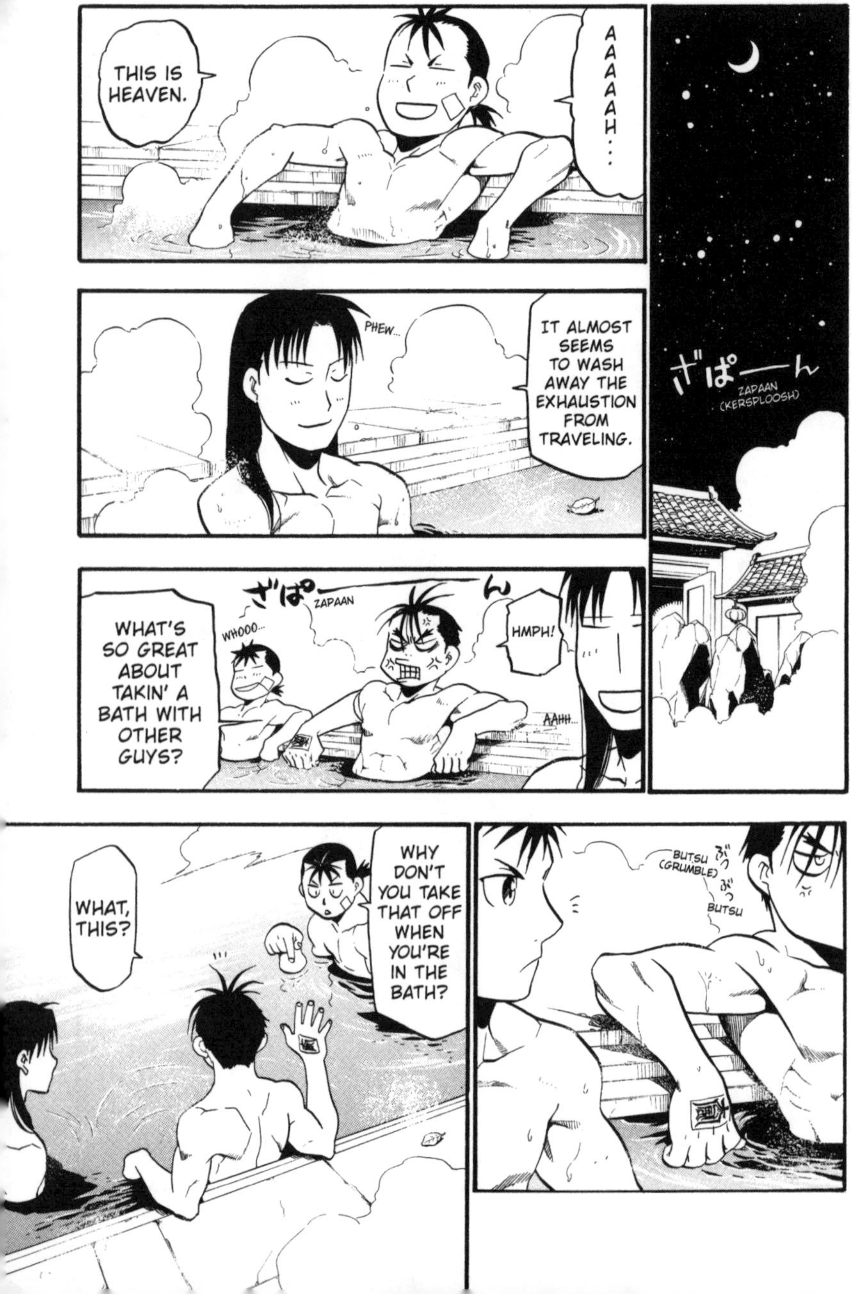
ざぱーーん
ZAPAAN (KERSPLOOSH)
AAAAAAH...
THIS IS HEAVEN.
IT ALMOST SEEMS TO WASH AWAY THE EXHAUSTION FROM TRAVELING.
PHEW...
HMPH!
AAHH...
ざぱーーーーーーーん
ZAPAAN
WHOOO...
WHAT'S SO GREAT ABOUT TAKIN' A BATH WITH OTHER GUYS?
ぶつ
BUTSU (GRUMBLE)
ぶつ
BUTSU
WHY DON'T YOU TAKE THAT OFF WHEN YOU'RE IN THE BATH?
WHAT, THIS?

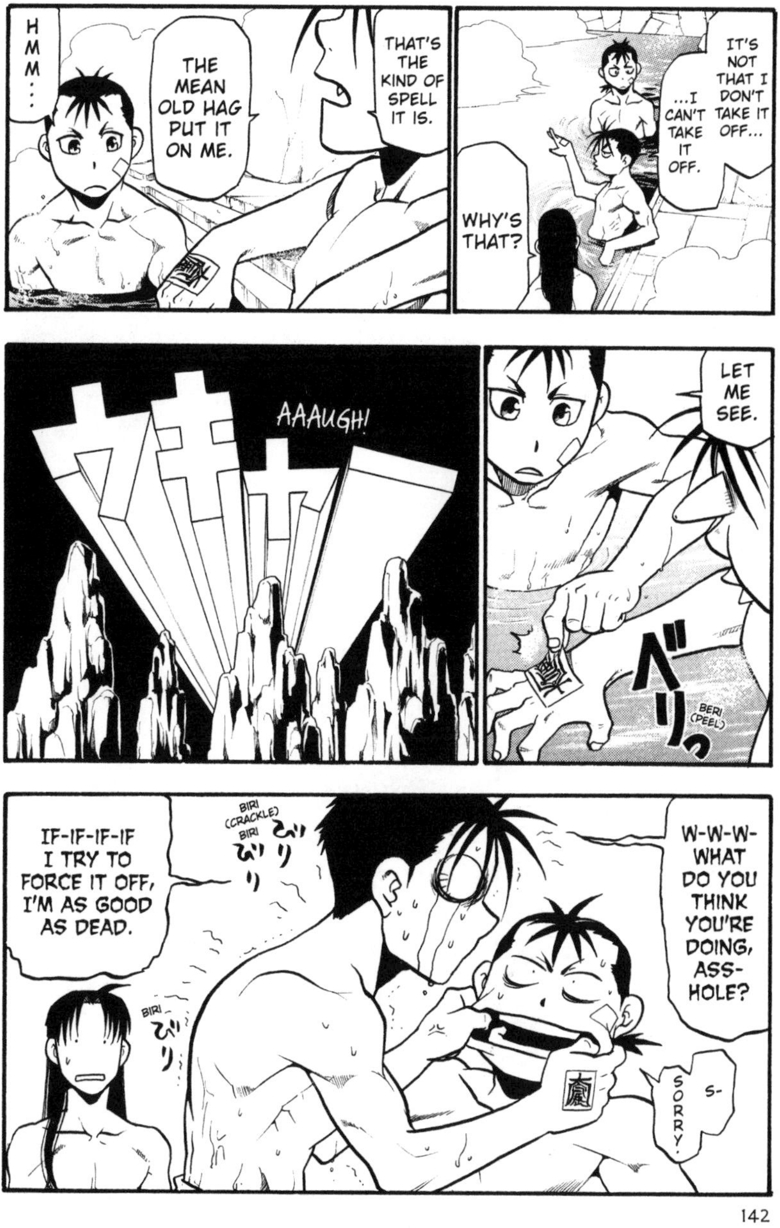
IT'S NOT THAT I DON'T TAKE IT OFF...
...I CAN'T TAKE IT OFF.
WHY'S THAT?
THAT'S THE KIND OF SPELL IT IS.
THE MEAN OLD HAG PUT IT ON ME.
HMM...
LET ME SEE.
BERI (PEEL)
AAAUGH!
W-W-W-WHAT DO YOU THINK YOU'RE DOING, ASS-HOLE?
S-SORRY.
BIRI (CRACKLE) BIRI
IF-IF-IF-IF I TRY TO FORCE IT OFF, I'M AS GOOD AS DEAD.
BIRI

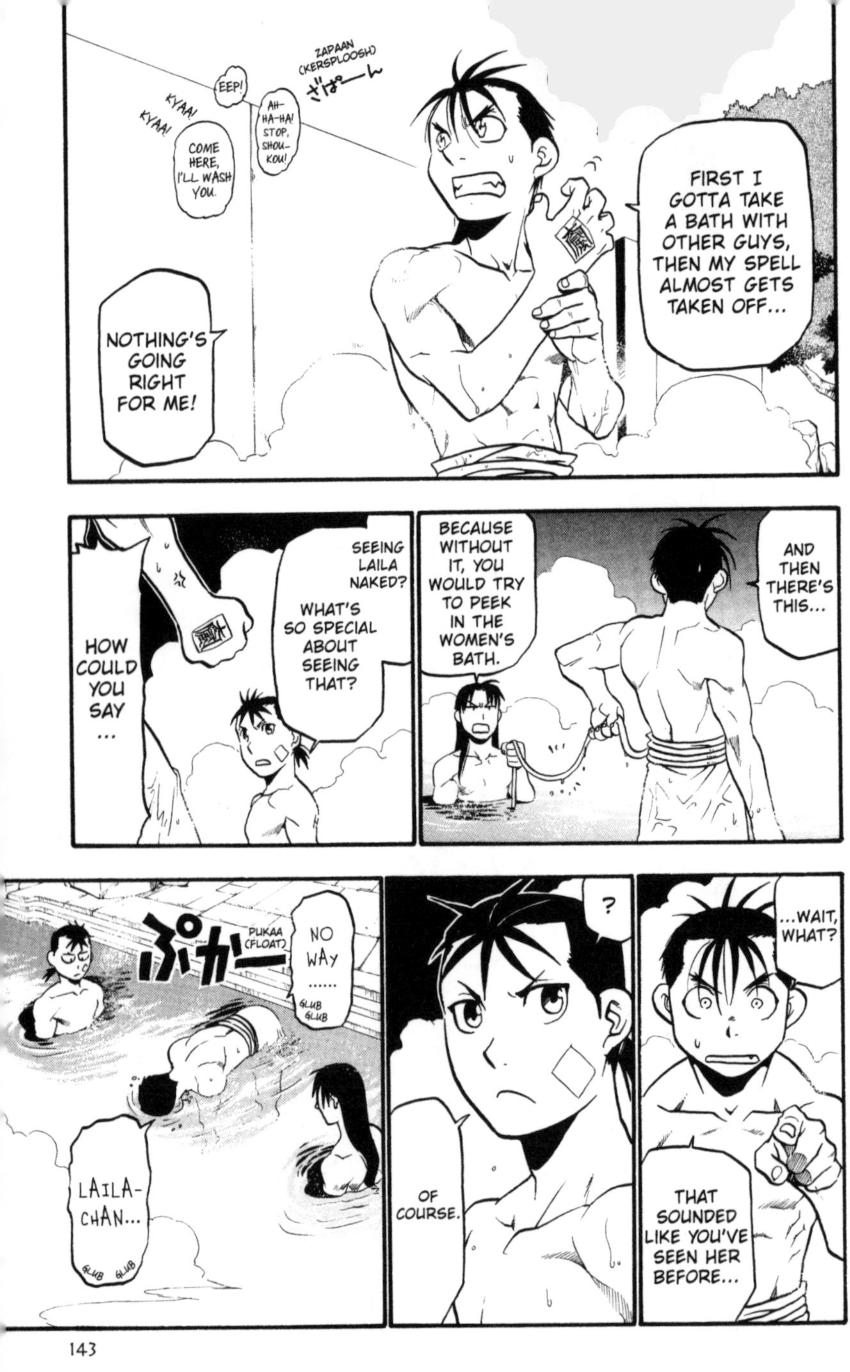
FIRST I GOTTA TAKE A BATH WITH OTHER GUYS, THEN MY SPELL ALMOST GETS TAKEN OFF...
ZAPAAN (KERSPLOOSH)
ざぱーん
EEP!
AH-HA-HA! STOP, SHOUKOU!
KYAA! KYAA!
COME HERE, I'LL WASH YOU.
NOTHING'S GOING RIGHT FOR ME!
AND THEN THERE'S THIS...
BECAUSE WITHOUT IT, YOU WOULD TRY TO PEEK IN THE WOMEN'S BATH.
SEEING LAILA NAKED?
WHAT'S SO SPECIAL ABOUT SEEING THAT?
HOW COULD YOU SAY ...
...WAIT, WHAT?
THAT SOUNDED LIKE YOU'VE SEEN HER BEFORE...
?
OF COURSE.
NO WAY ......
GLUB GLUB
PUKAA (FLOAT)
ぷカー
LAILA-CHAN...
GLUB GLUB

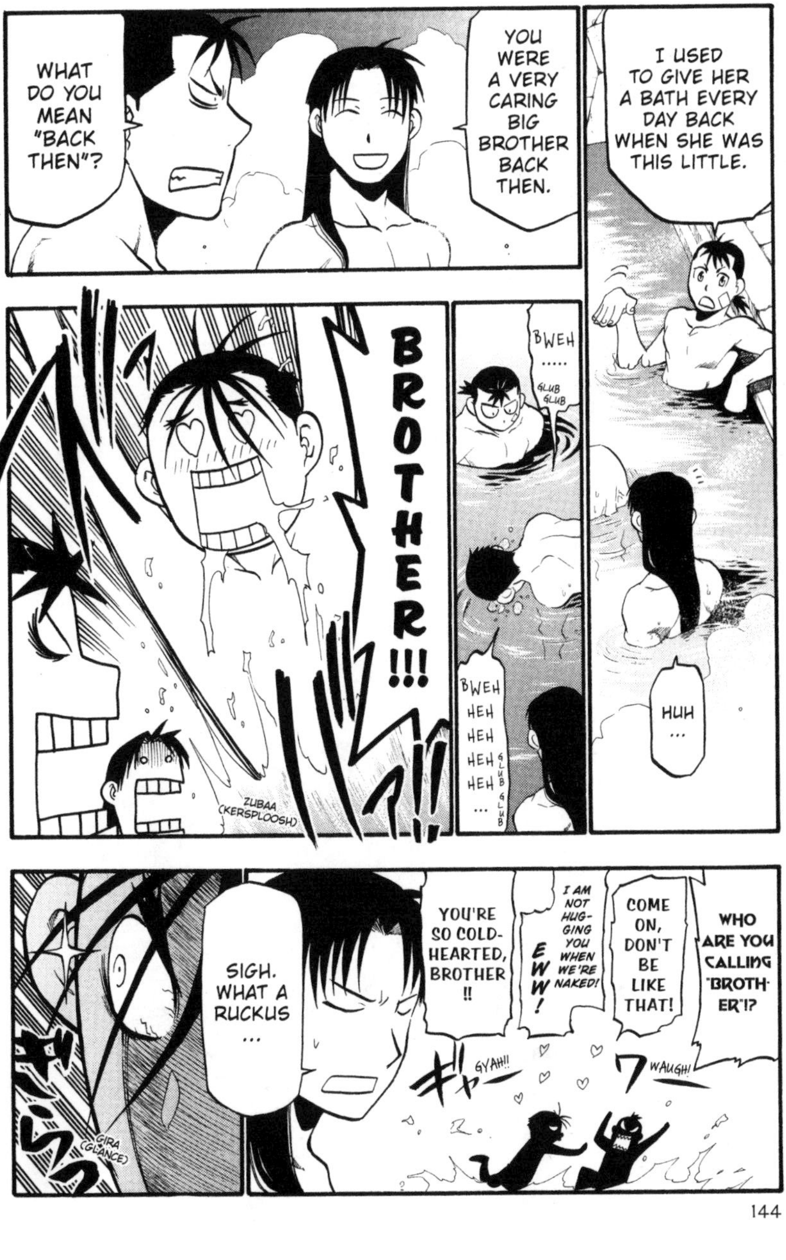
I USED TO GIVE HER A BATH EVERY DAY BACK WHEN SHE WAS THIS LITTLE.
HUH ...
YOU WERE A VERY CARING BIG BROTHER BACK THEN.
WHAT DO YOU MEAN "BACK THEN"?
BWEH .....
GLUB GLUB
BWEH HEH HEH HEH HEH ...
GLUB GLUB
BROTHER!!!
ZUBAA (KERSPLOOSH)
WHO ARE YOU CALLING "BROTHER"!?
COME ON, DON'T BE LIKE THAT!
I AM NOT HUGGING YOU WHEN WE'RE NAKED!
EWW!
YOU'RE SO COLD-HEARTED, BROTHER !!
WAUGH!
GYAH!!
SIGH. WHAT A RUCKUS ...
GIRA (GLANCE)

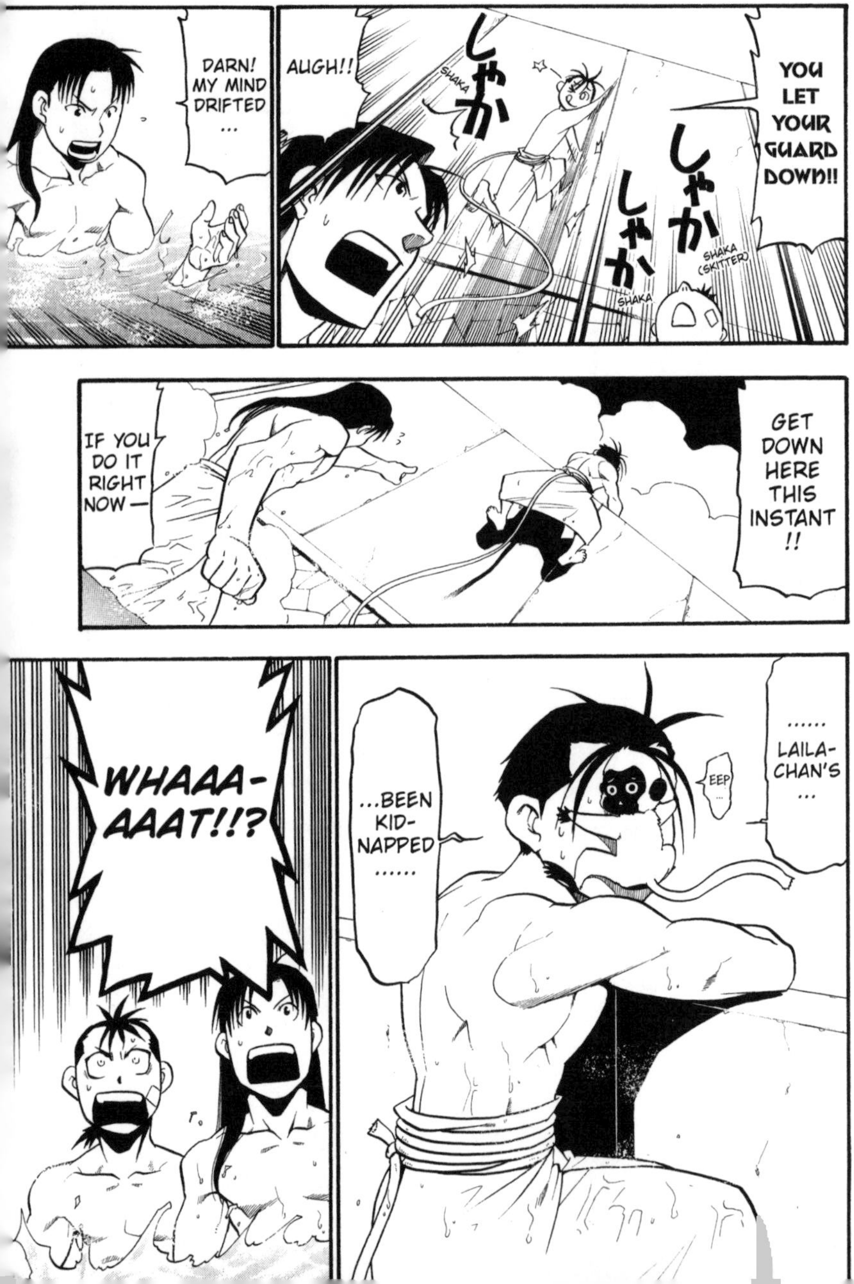
YOU LET YOUR GUARD DOWN!!
しゃか しゃか
SHAKA (SKITTER)
SHAKA
しゃか
SHAKA
AUGH!!
DARN! MY MIND DRIFTED ...
GET DOWN HERE THIS INSTANT !!
IF YOU DO IT RIGHT NOW—
...... LAILA-CHAN'S ...
EEP ...
...BEEN KID-NAPPED ......
WHAAA-AAAT!!?

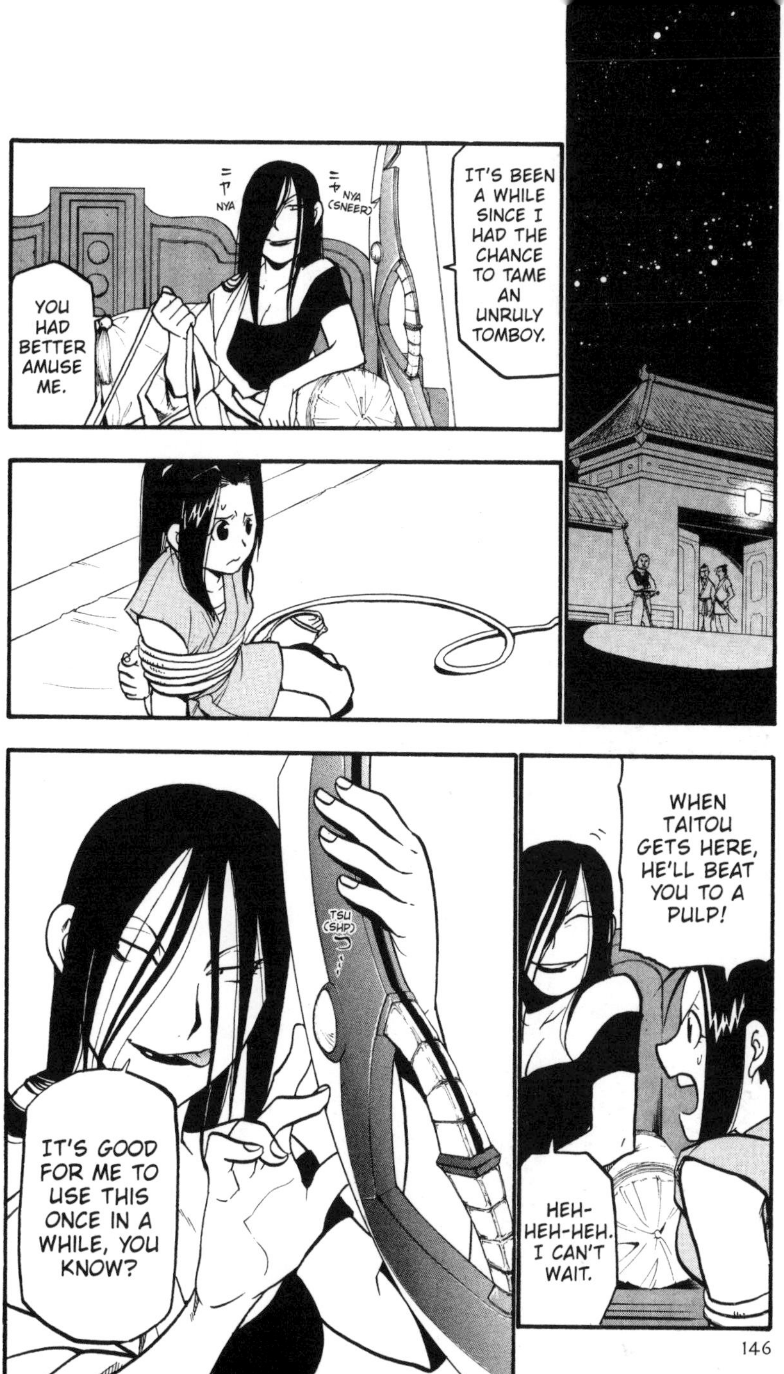
IT'S BEEN A WHILE SINCE I HAD THE CHANCE TO TAME AN UNRULY TOMBOY.
ニヤ NYA (SNEER)
ニヤ NYA
YOU HAD BETTER AMUSE ME.
WHEN TAITOU GETS HERE, HE'LL BEAT YOU TO A PULP!
HEH-HEH-HEH. I CAN'T WAIT.
TSU (SHP)
IT'S GOOD FOR ME TO USE THIS ONCE IN A WHILE, YOU KNOW?

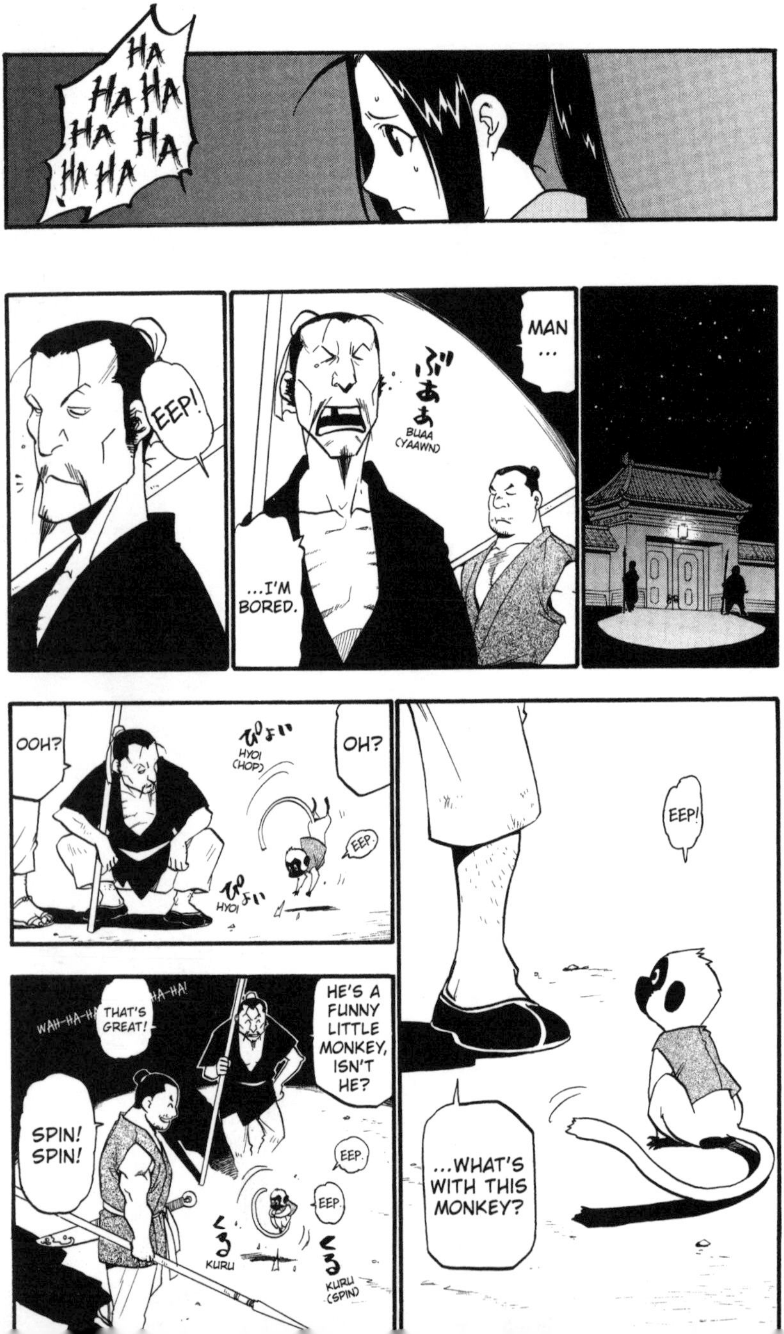
HA HA HA HA HA HA HA HA
MAN ...
ぶあぁ
BUAA (YAAWN)
...I'M BORED.
EEP!
EEP!
...WHAT'S WITH THIS MONKEY?
OH?
ぴょい
HYOI (HOP)
EEP.
OOH?
ぴょい
HYOI
HE'S A FUNNY LITTLE MONKEY, ISN'T HE?
HA-HA!
THAT'S GREAT!
WAH-HA-HA
SPIN! SPIN!
EEP.
EEP.
くる
KURU (SPIN)
くる
KURU

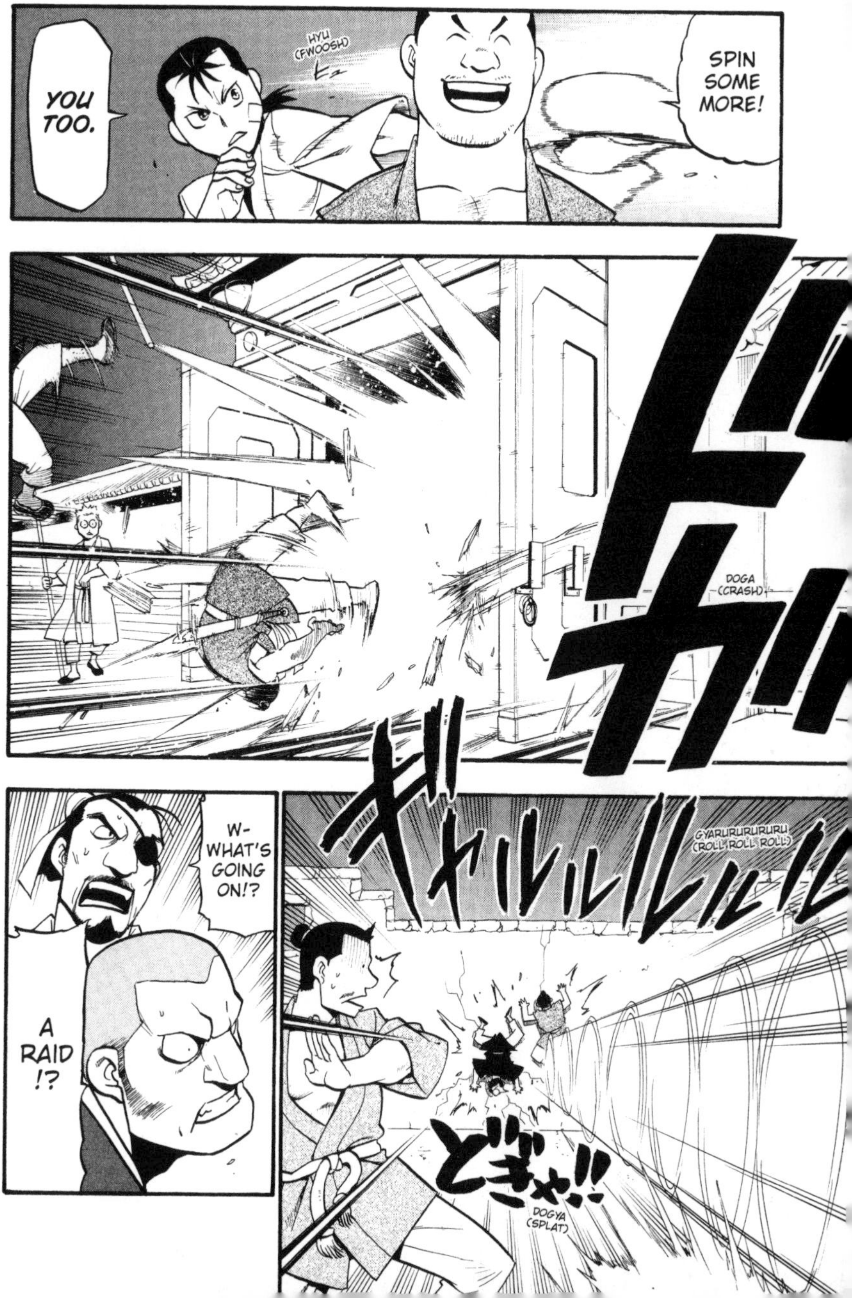
SPIN SOME MORE!
HYU (FWOOSH)
YOU TOO.
DOGA (CRASH)
GYARURURURURU (ROLL ROLL ROLL)
DOGYA (SPLAT)
W- WHAT'S GOING ON!?
A RAID !?

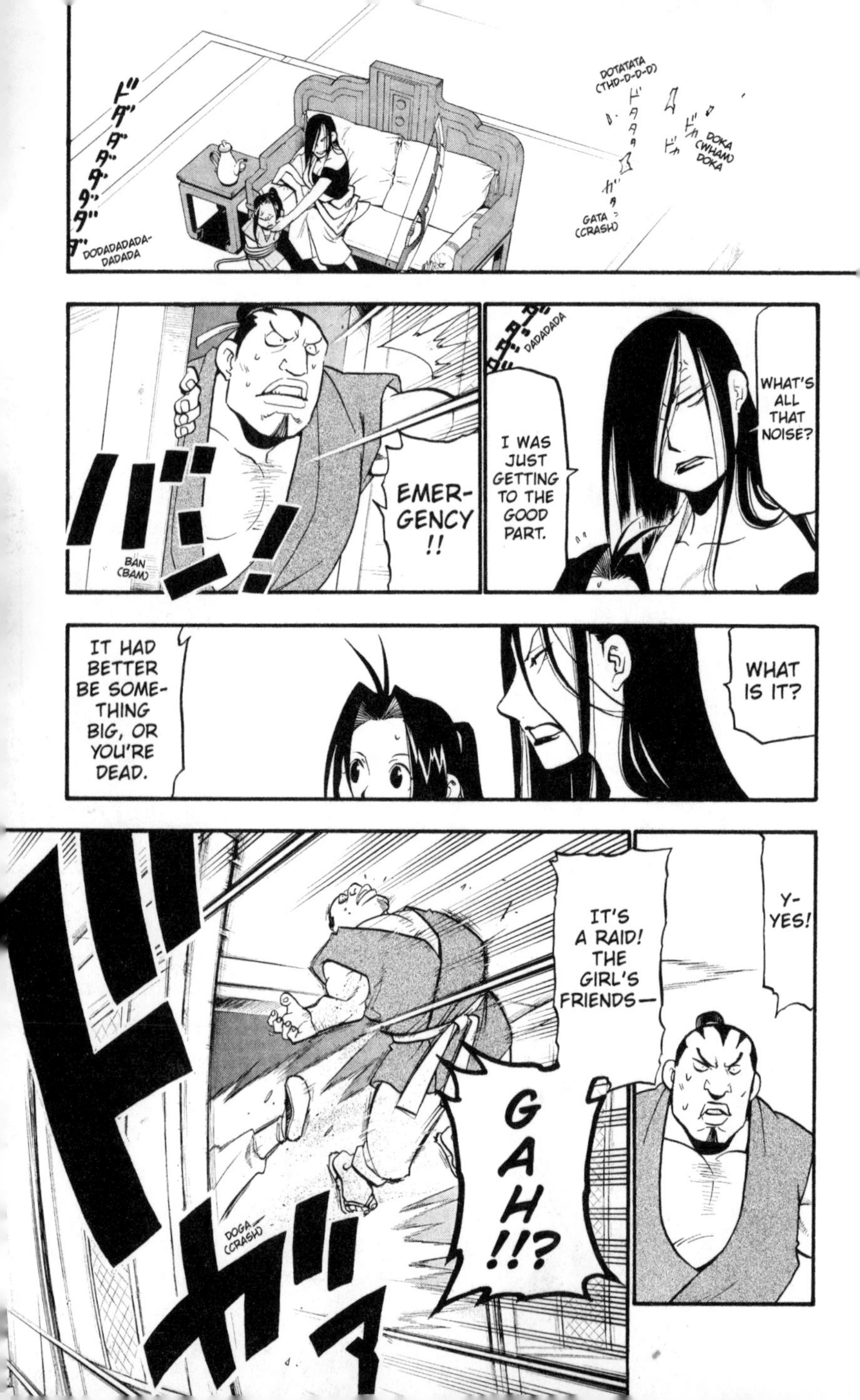
DOTATATA (THD-D-D-D)
DOKA (WHAM) DOKA
GATA (CRASH)
DODADADADA-DADADA
WHAT'S ALL THAT NOISE?
I WAS JUST GETTING TO THE GOOD PART.
DADADADA
EMER-GENCY!!
BAN (BAM)
WHAT IS IT?
IT HAD BETTER BE SOME-THING BIG, OR YOU'RE DEAD.
Y-YES!
IT'S A RAID! THE GIRL'S FRIENDS—
GAH!!?
DOGA (CRASH)

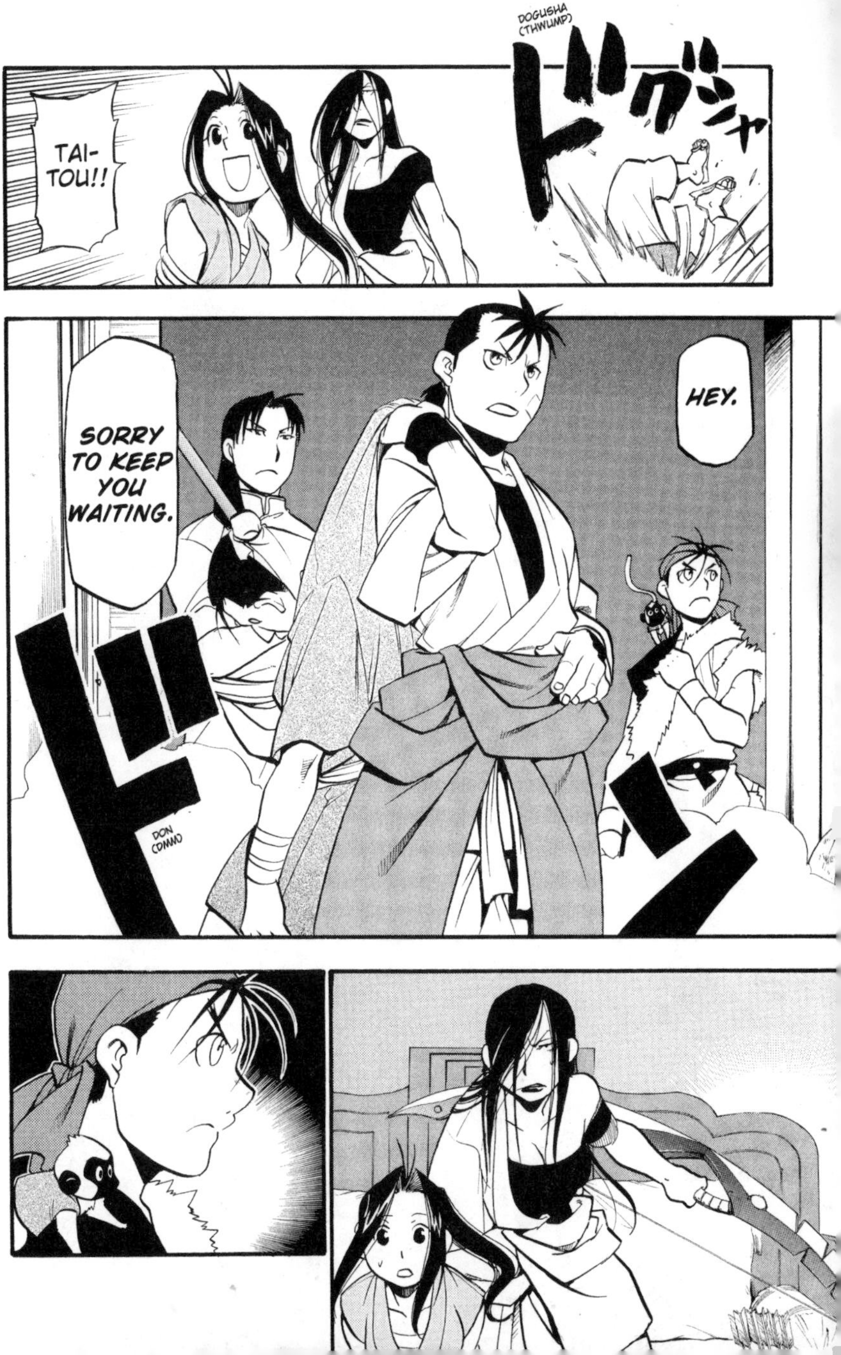
DOGUSHA (THWUMP)
TAI-TOU!!
HEY.
SORRY TO KEEP YOU WAITING.
DON (DMM)

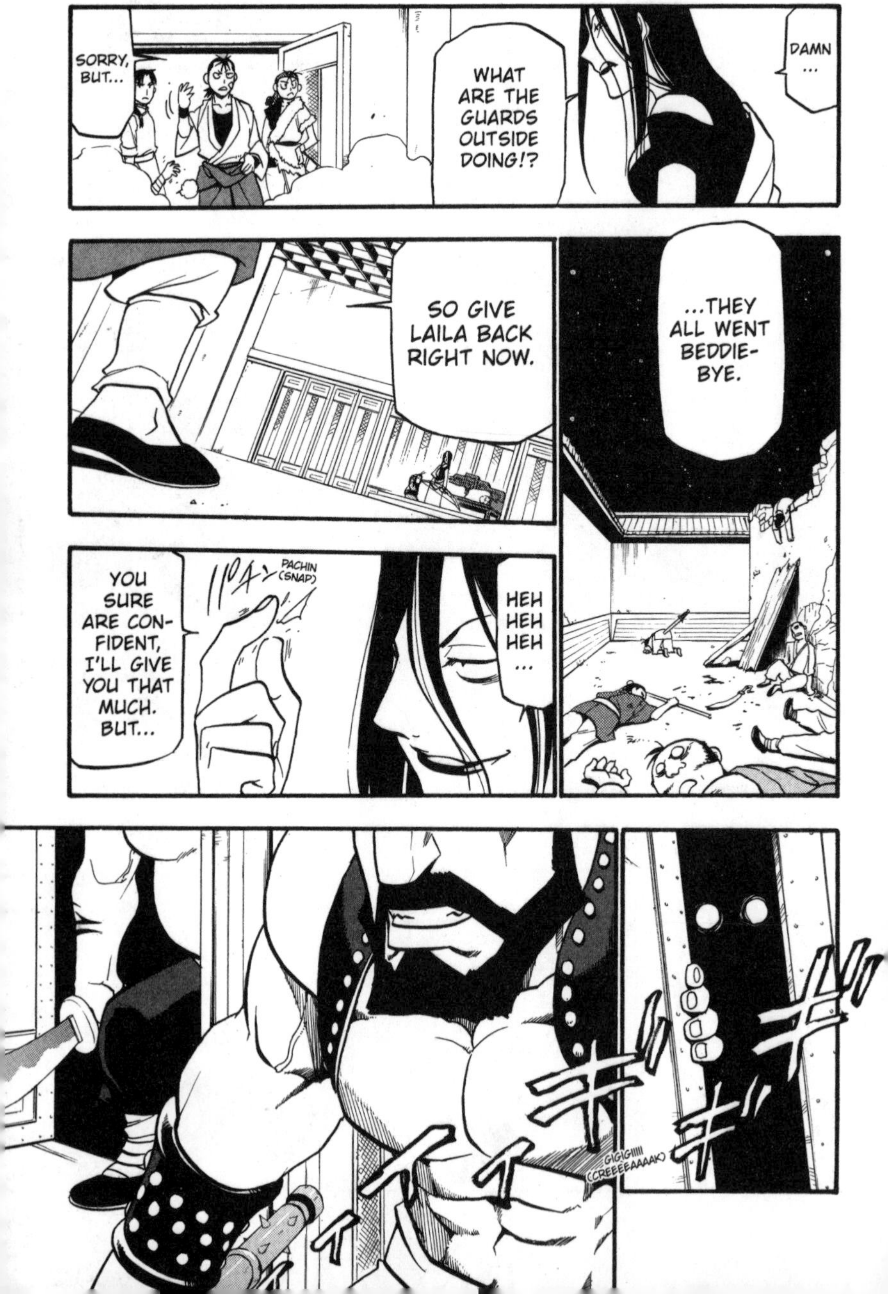
DAMN...
WHAT ARE THE GUARDS OUTSIDE DOING!?
SORRY, BUT...
...THEY ALL WENT BEDDIE-BYE.
SO GIVE LAILA BACK RIGHT NOW.
HEH HEH HEH...
PACHIN (SNAP)
YOU SURE ARE CONFIDENT, I'LL GIVE YOU THAT MUCH. BUT...
GIGIGIIII (CREEEEAAAAK)

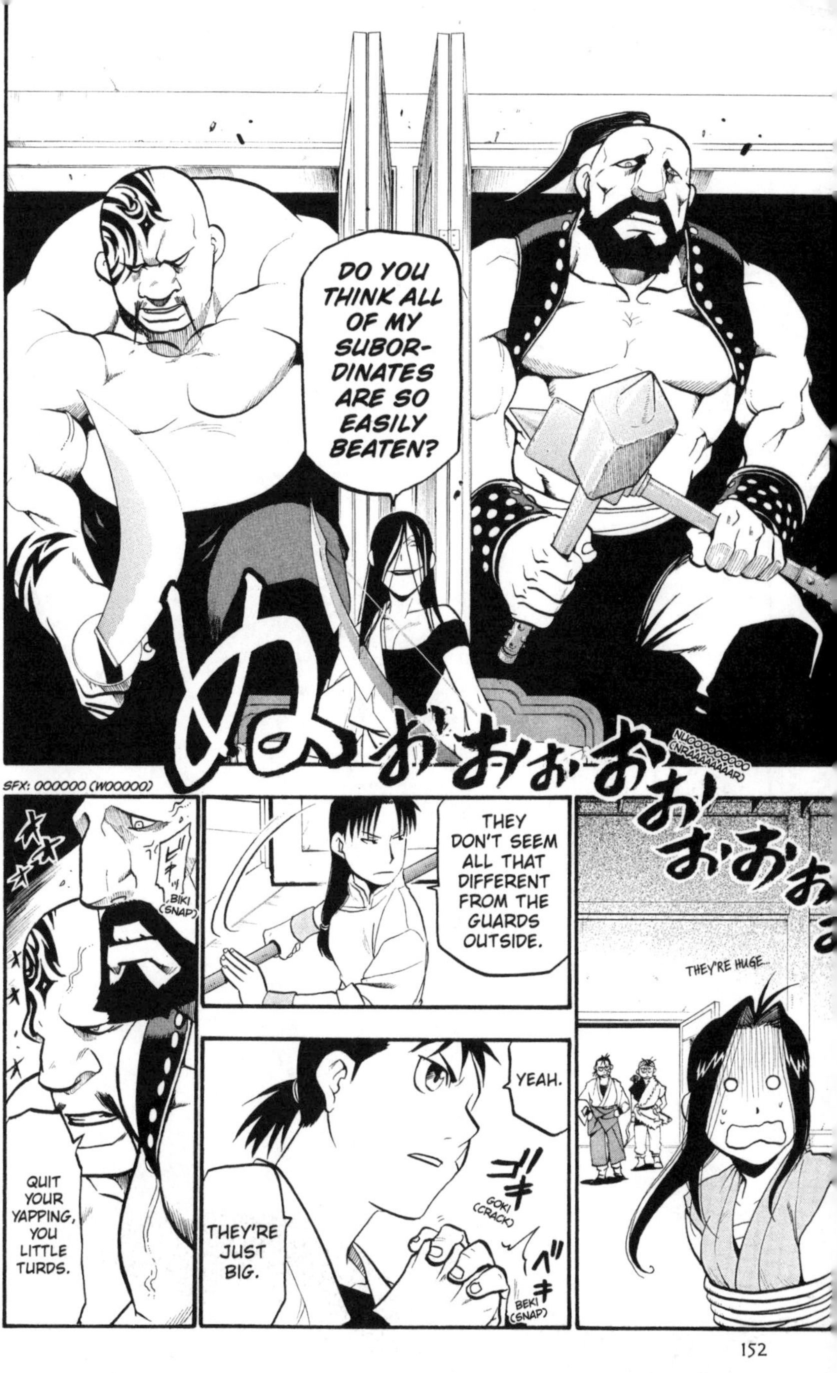

DO YOU THINK ALL OF MY SUBOR-DINATES ARE SO EASILY BEATEN?
NUOOOOOOOOOO (NRAAAAAAAAR)
SFX: OOOOOO (WOOOOO)
THEY'RE HUGE...
THEY DON'T SEEM ALL THAT DIFFERENT FROM THE GUARDS OUTSIDE.
YEAH.
THEY'RE JUST BIG.
GOKI (CRACK)
BEKI (SNAP)
BIKI (SNAP)
QUIT YOUR YAPPING, YOU LITTLE TURDS.

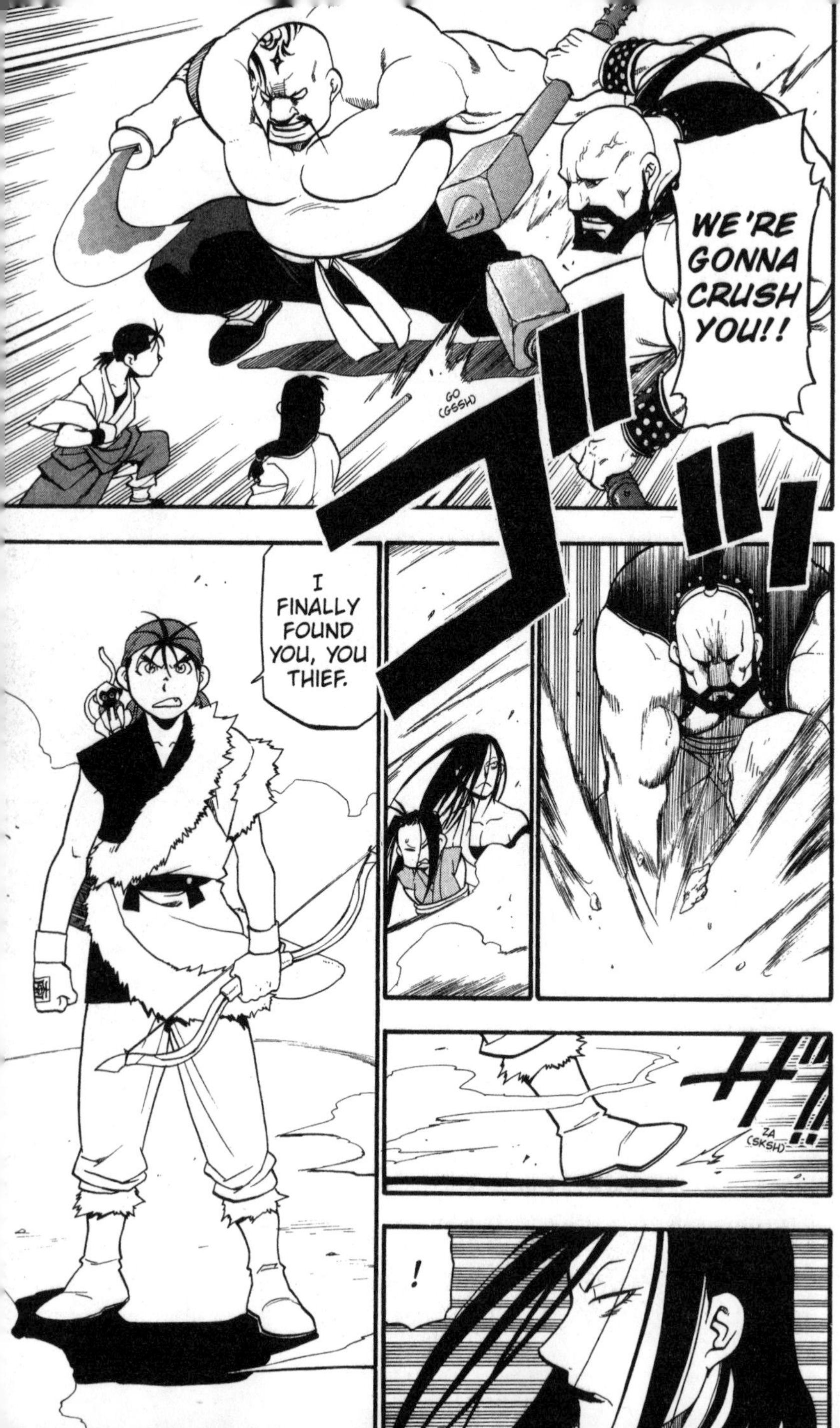

WE'RE GONNA CRUSH YOU!!
GO (GSSH)
ZA (SKSH)
!
I FINALLY FOUND YOU, YOU THIEF.

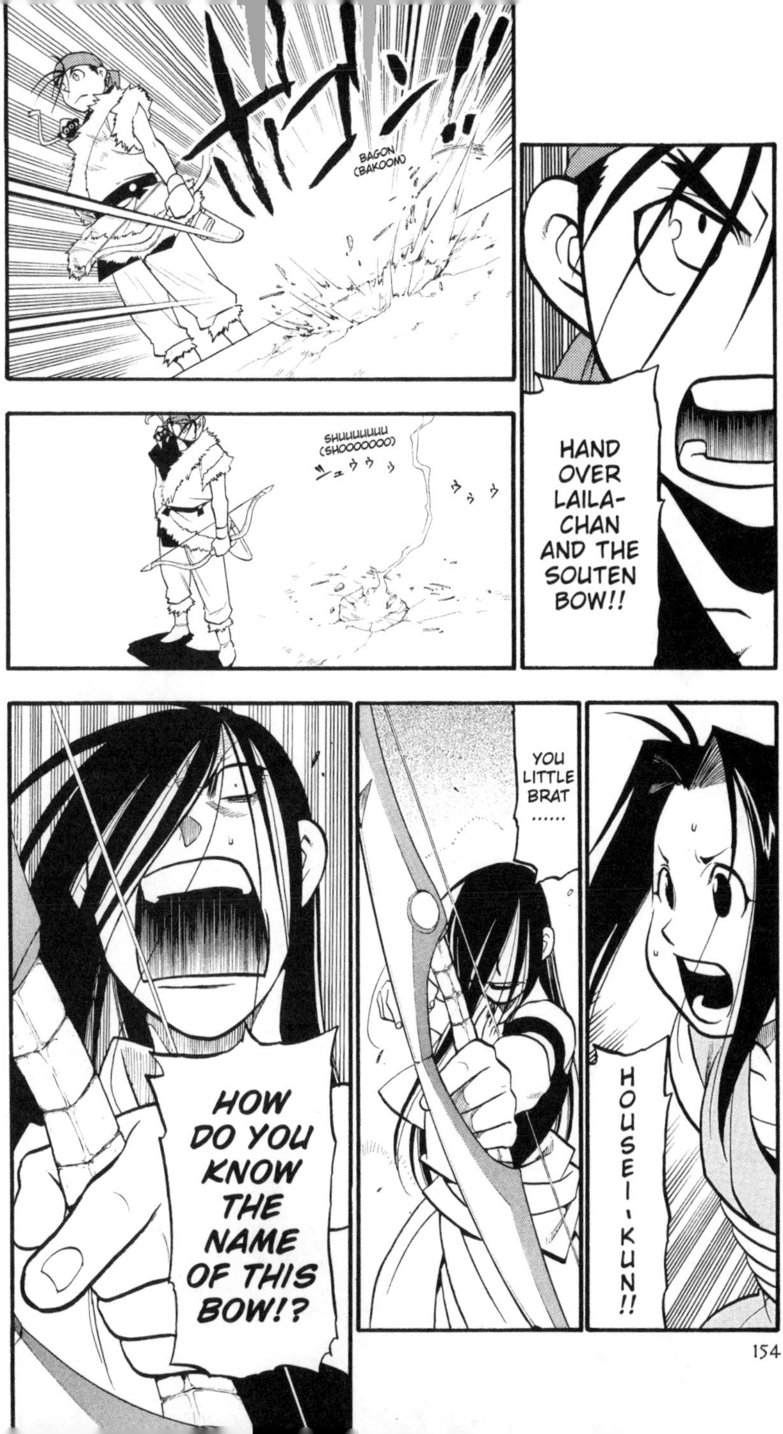
HAND OVER LAILA-CHAN AND THE SOUTEN BOW!!
BAGON (BAKOOM)
SHUUUUUUU (SHOOOOOOO)
HOUSEI-KUN!!
YOU LITTLE BRAT......
HOW DO YOU KNOW THE NAME OF THIS BOW!?

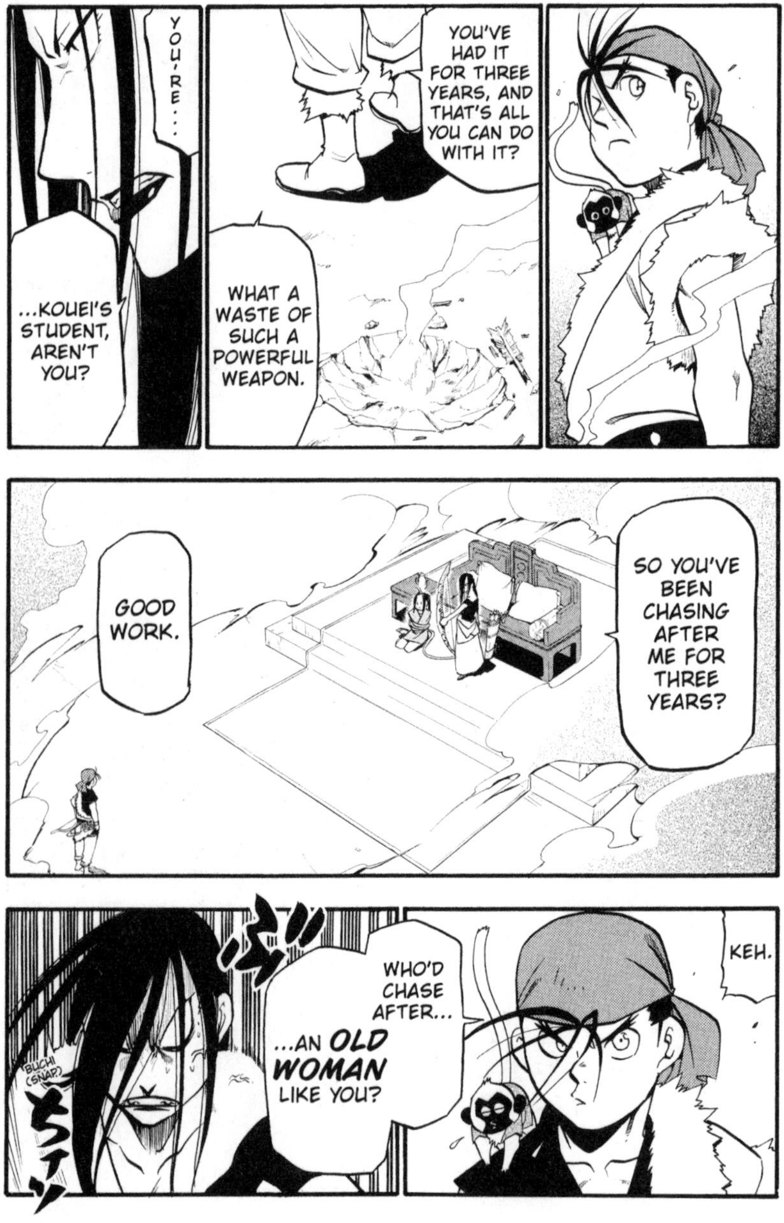
YOU'VE HAD IT FOR THREE YEARS, AND THAT'S ALL YOU CAN DO WITH IT?
WHAT A WASTE OF SUCH A POWERFUL WEAPON.
YOU-RE...
...KOUEI'S STUDENT, AREN'T YOU?
SO YOU'VE BEEN CHASING AFTER ME FOR THREE YEARS?
GOOD WORK.
KEH.
WHO'D CHASE AFTER...
...AN **OLD WOMAN** LIKE YOU?
BUCHI (SNAP)

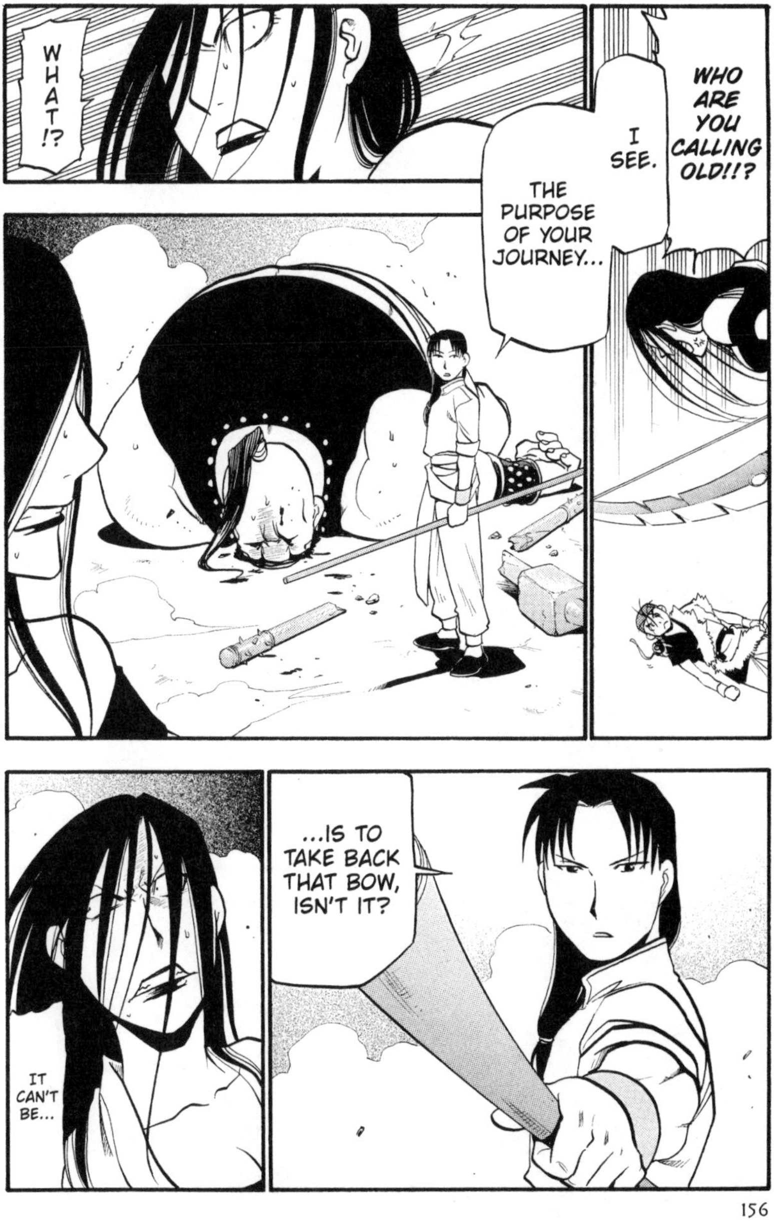

WHO ARE YOU CALLING OLD!!?
I SEE.
WHAT!?
THE PURPOSE OF YOUR JOURNEY...
...IS TO TAKE BACK THAT BOW, ISN'T IT?
IT CAN'T BE...

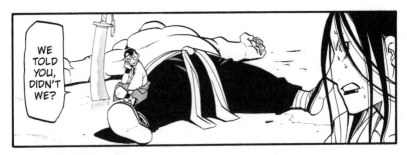

WE TOLD YOU, DIDN'T WE?

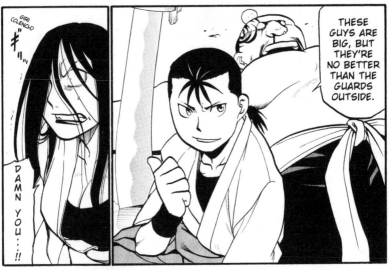

GIRI (CLENCH)

DAMN YOU...!!

THESE GUYS ARE BIG, BUT THEY'RE NO BETTER THAN THE GUARDS OUTSIDE.

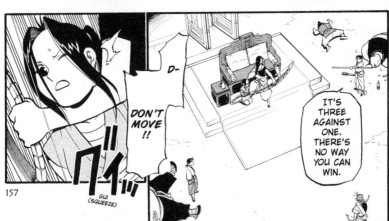

D-DON'T MOVE!!

GUI (SQUEEZE)

IT'S THREE AGAINST ONE. THERE'S NO WAY YOU CAN WIN.

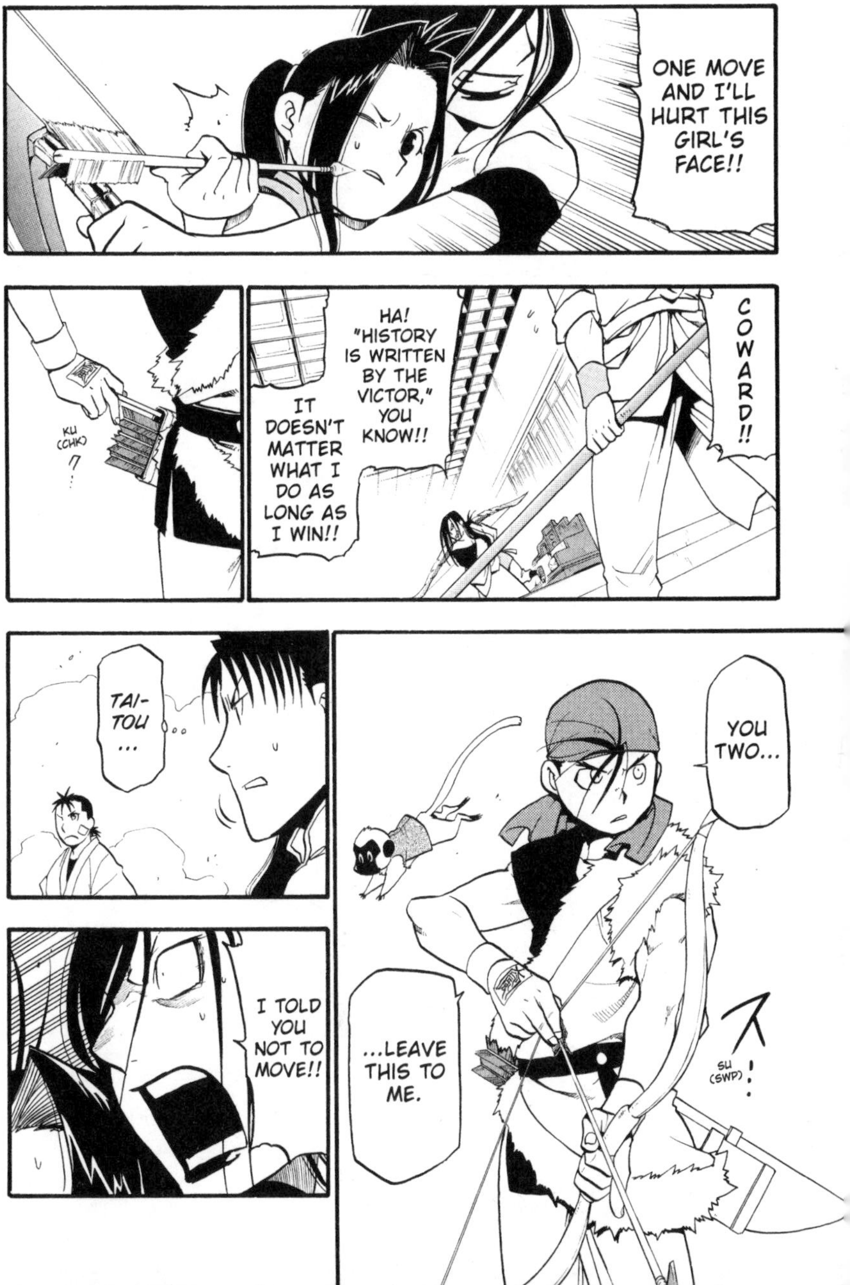
ONE MOVE AND I'LL HURT THIS GIRL'S FACE!!
COWARD!!
HA! "HISTORY IS WRITTEN BY THE VICTOR," YOU KNOW!!
IT DOESN'T MATTER WHAT I DO AS LONG AS I WIN!!
KU (CHK)
YOU TWO...
SU (SWP)
...LEAVE THIS TO ME.
TAI-TOU...
I TOLD YOU NOT TO MOVE!!

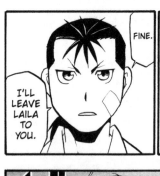

FINE.

I'LL LEAVE LAILA TO YOU.

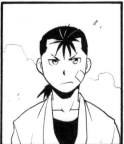

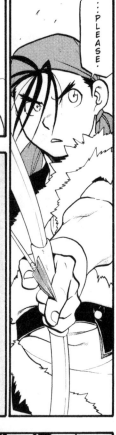

...PLEASE.

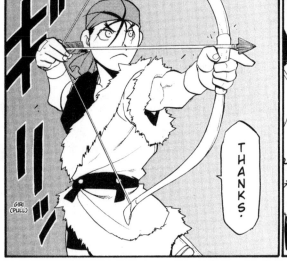

GIRI
(PULL)

THANKS.

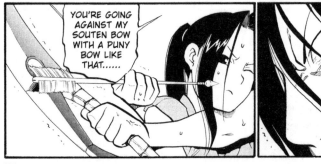

YOU'RE GOING AGAINST MY SOUTEN BOW WITH A PUNY BOW LIKE THAT......

A PUNY BOW LIKE THAT...

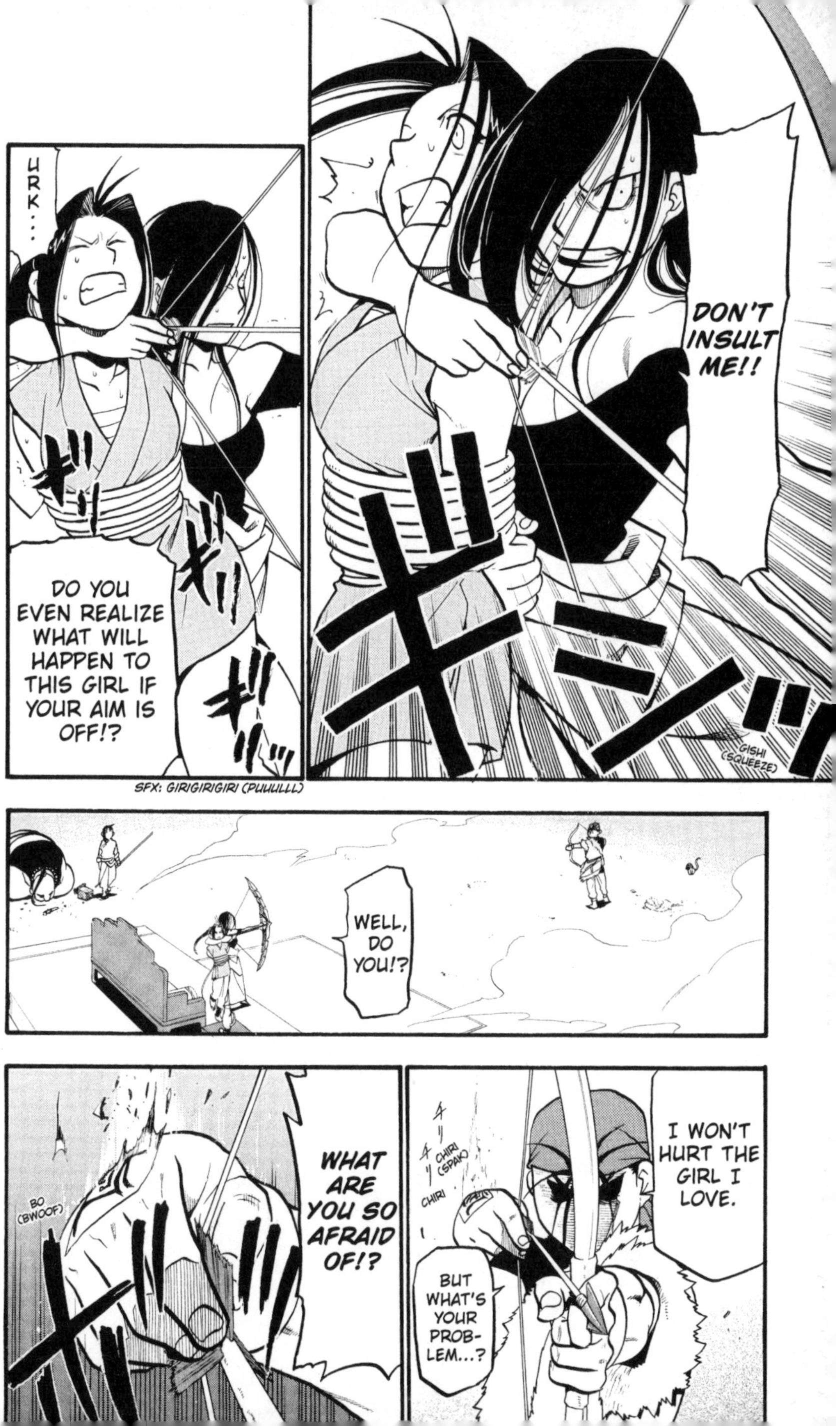
DON'T INSULT ME!!
GISHI (SQUEEZE)
URK...
DO YOU EVEN REALIZE WHAT WILL HAPPEN TO THIS GIRL IF YOUR AIM IS OFF!?
SFX: GIRIGIRIGIRI (PUUULLL)
WELL, DO YOU!?
I WON'T HURT THE GIRL I LOVE.
CHIRI (SPAK)
CHIRI
BUT WHAT'S YOUR PROB-LEM...?
WHAT ARE YOU SO AFRAID OF!?
BO (BWOOF)

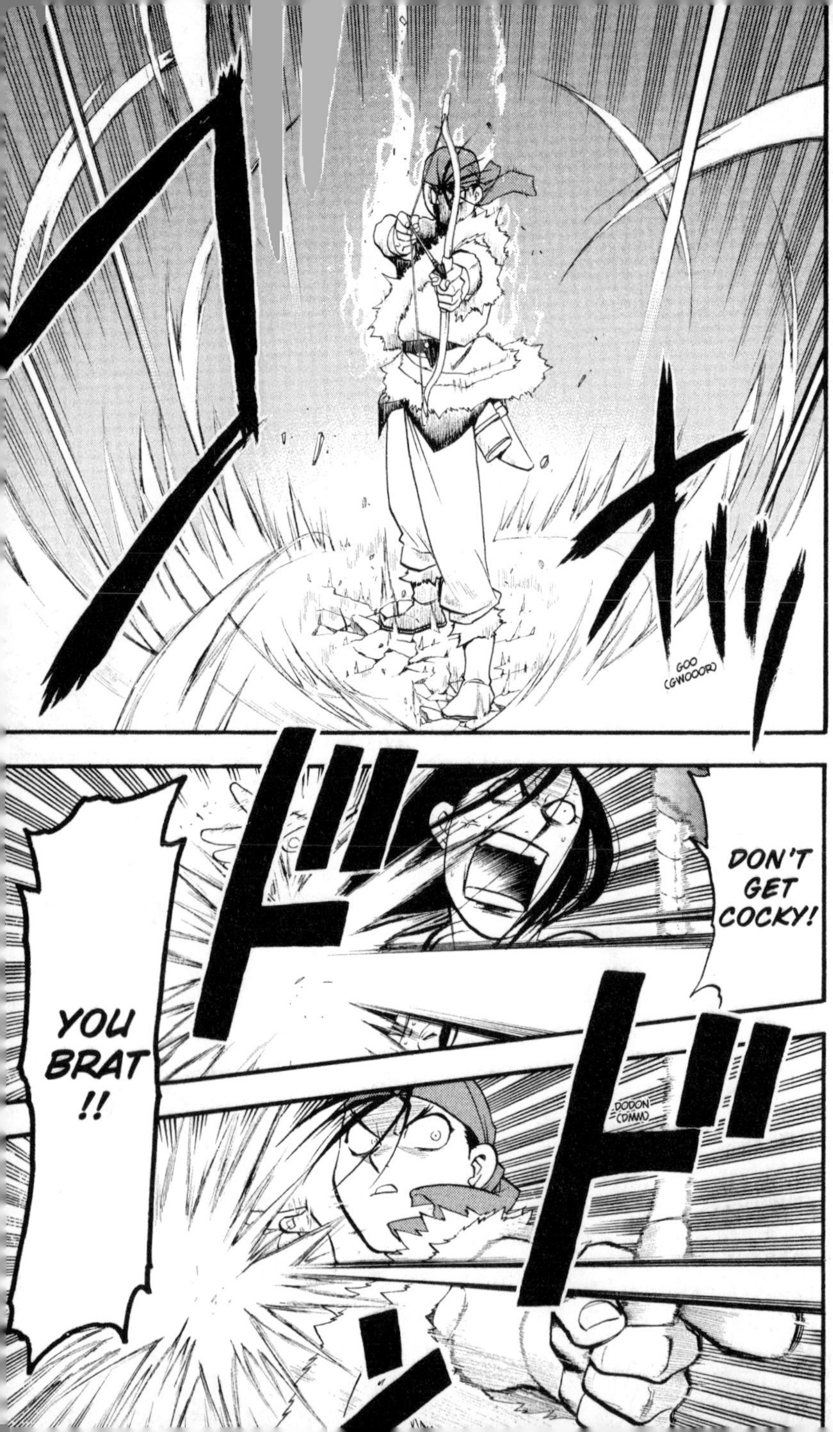
GOO
(GWOOOR)
DON'T GET COCKY!
YOU BRAT !!
DODON
(DMM)

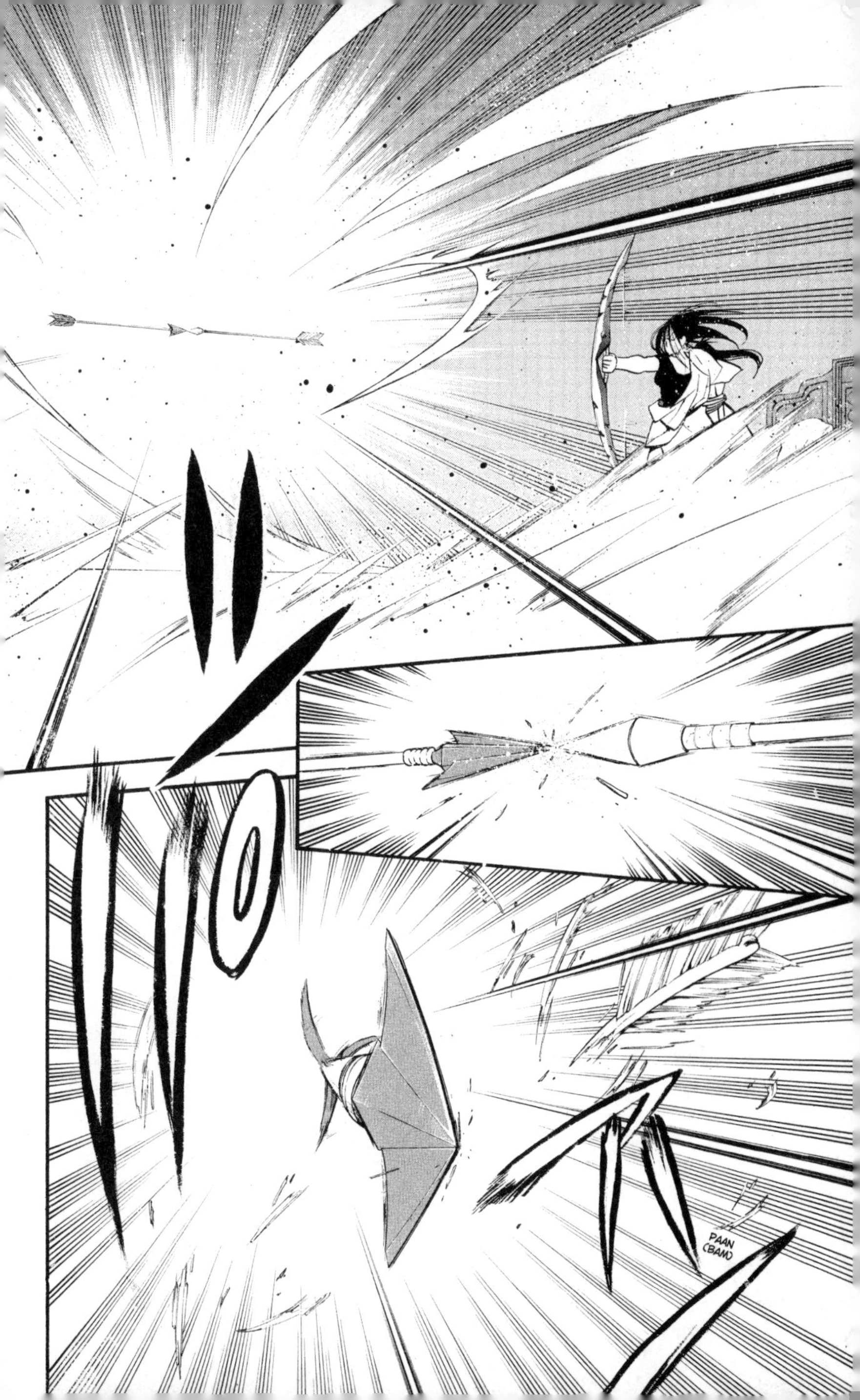
PAAN
(BAM)

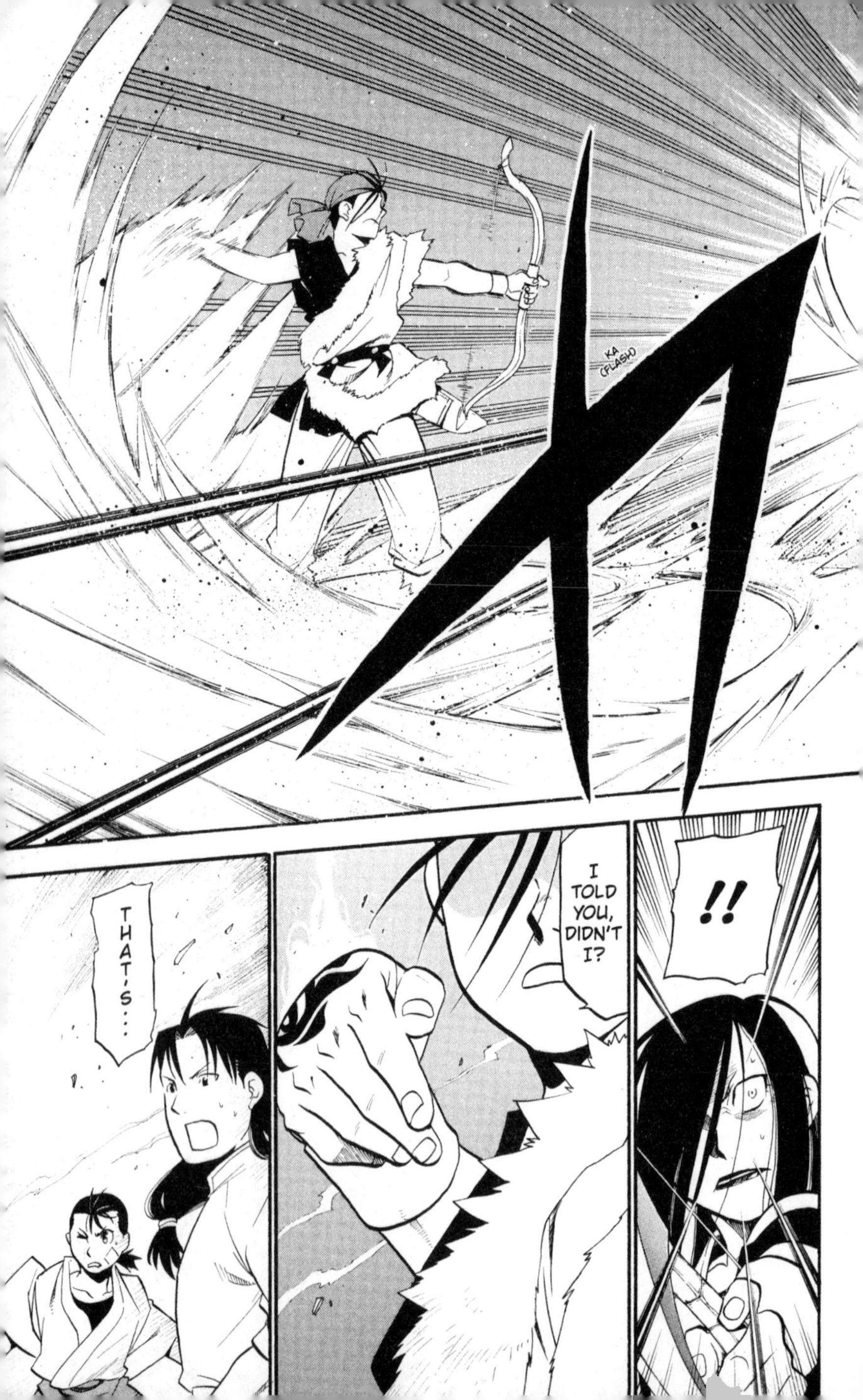
KA (FLASH)
!!
I TOLD YOU, DIDN'T I?
THAT'S...

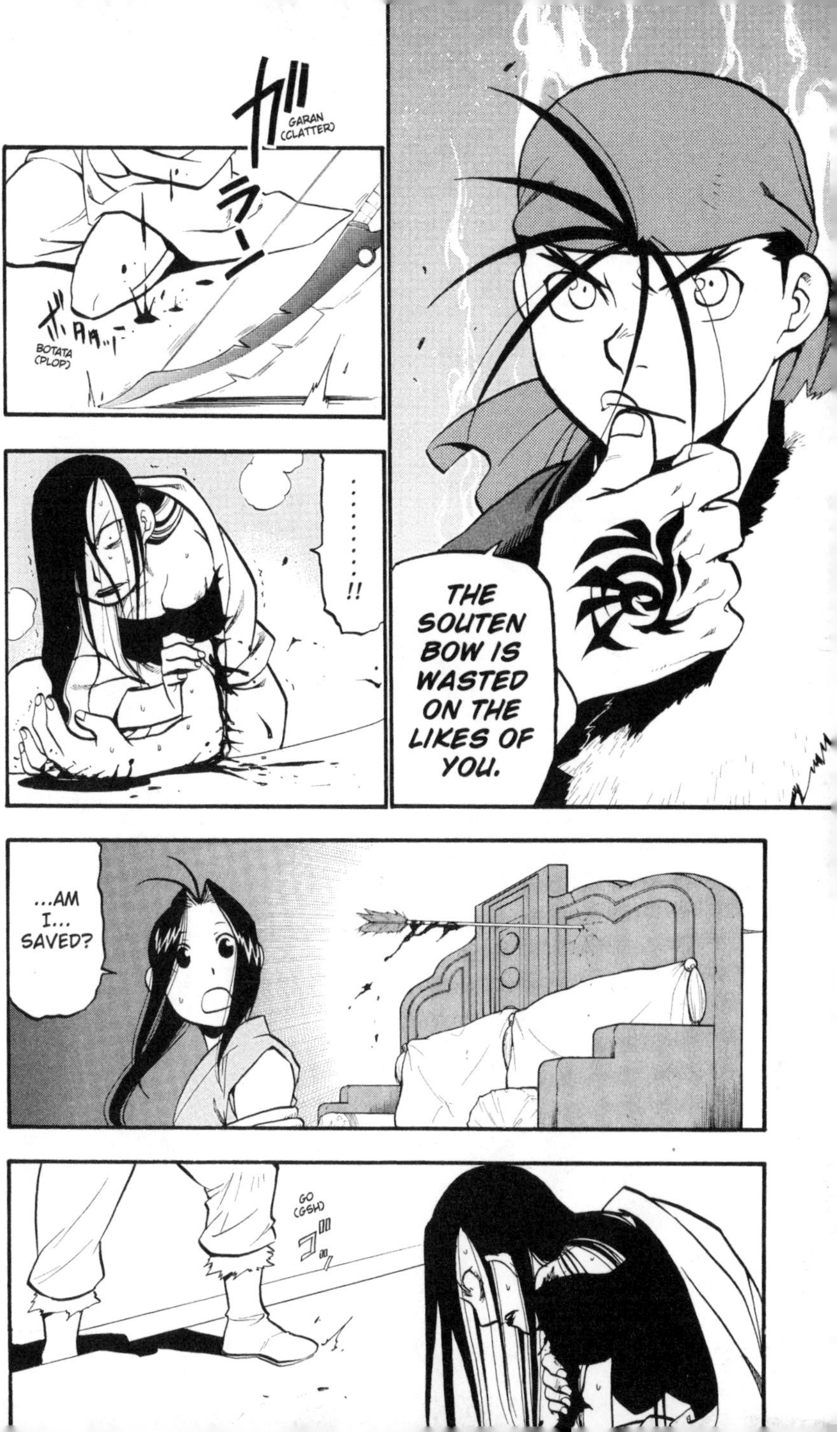
THE SOUTEN BOW IS WASTED ON THE LIKES OF YOU.
GARAN (CLATTER)
BOTATA (PLOP)
......!!
...AM I... SAVED?
GO (GSH)

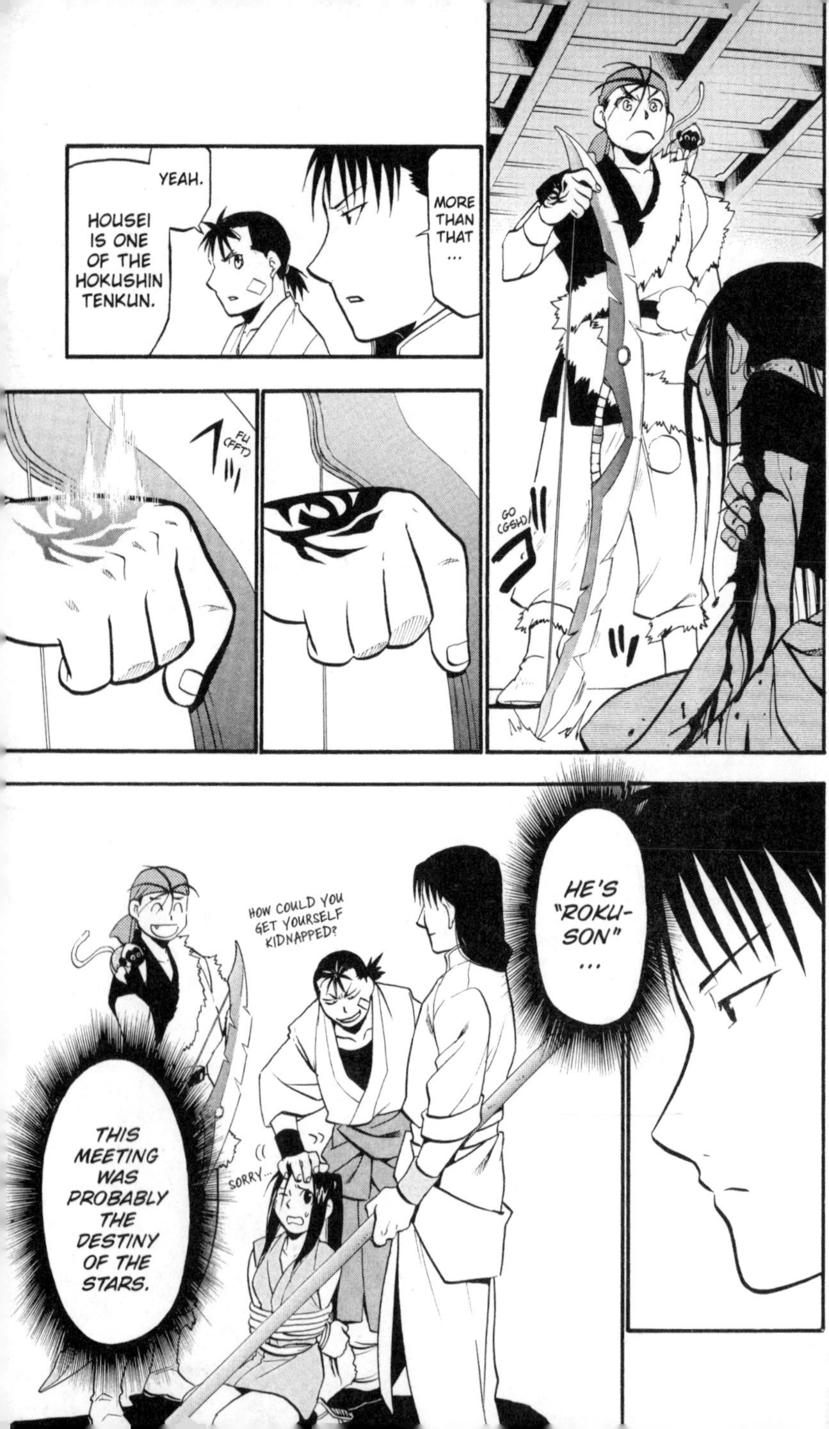

GO (GSH)
MORE THAN THAT ...
YEAH.
HOUSEI IS ONE OF THE HOKUSHIN TENKUN.
FU (FFT)
HE'S "ROKU-SON" ...
HOW COULD YOU GET YOURSELF KIDNAPPED?
SORRY...
THIS MEETING WAS PROBABLY THE DESTINY OF THE STARS.

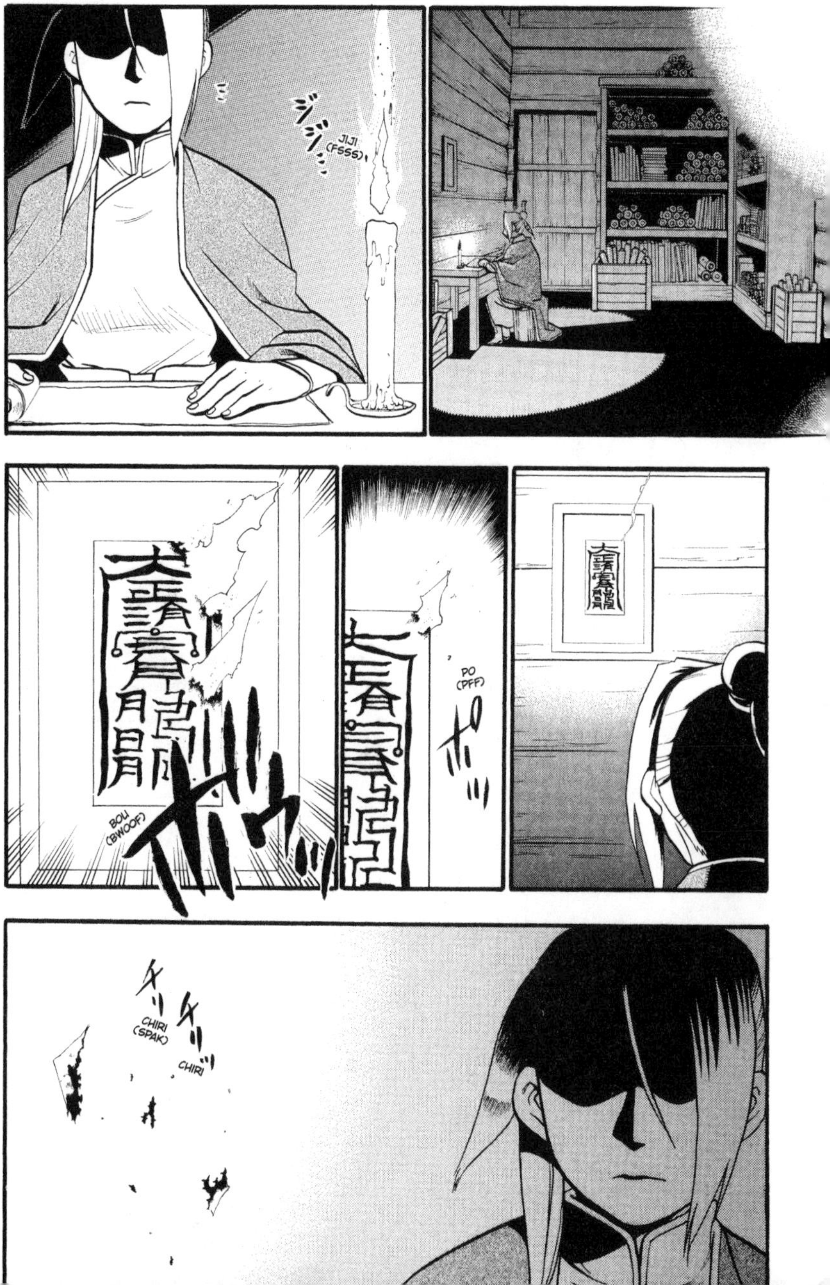
JIJI (FSSS)
PO (PFF)
BOU (BWOOF)
CHIRI (SPAK)
CHIRI

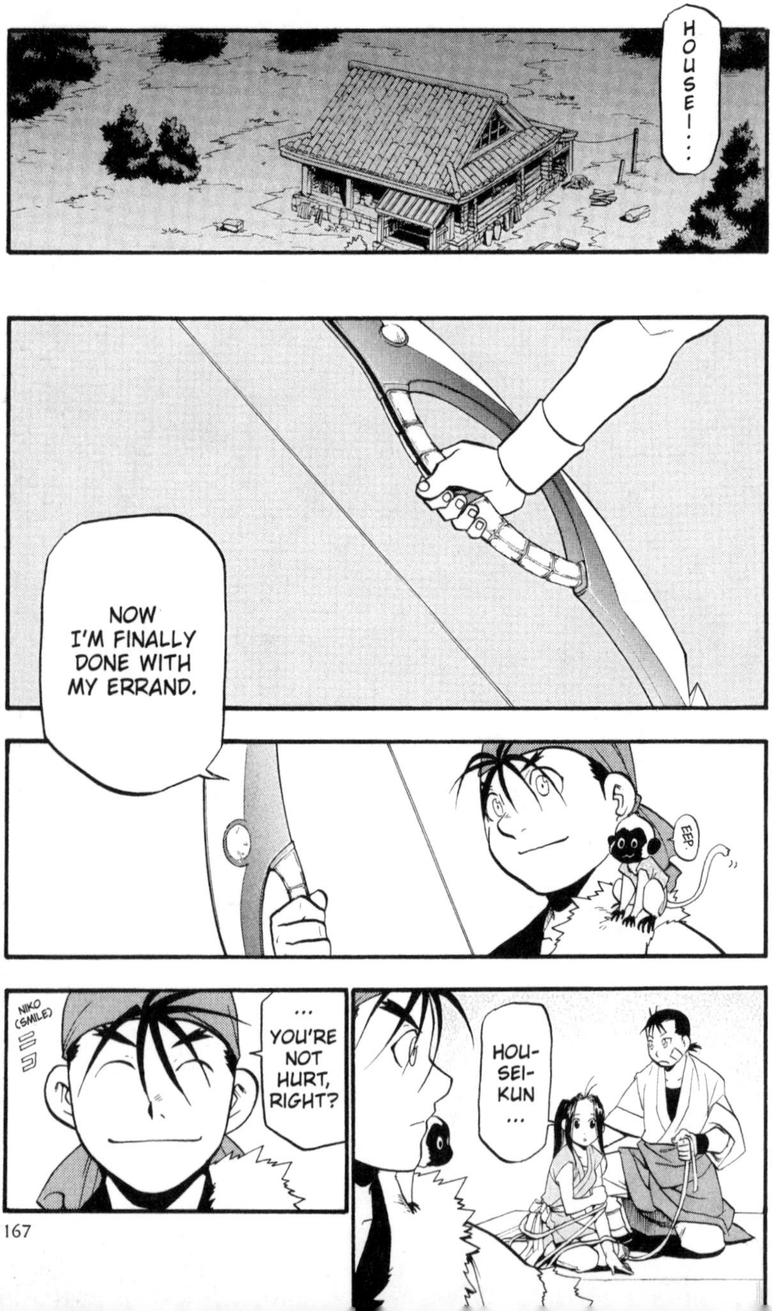
HOUSE!...
NOW I'M FINALLY DONE WITH MY ERRAND.
EEP.
HOU-SEI-KUN...
NIKO (SMILE)
...YOU'RE NOT HURT, RIGHT?

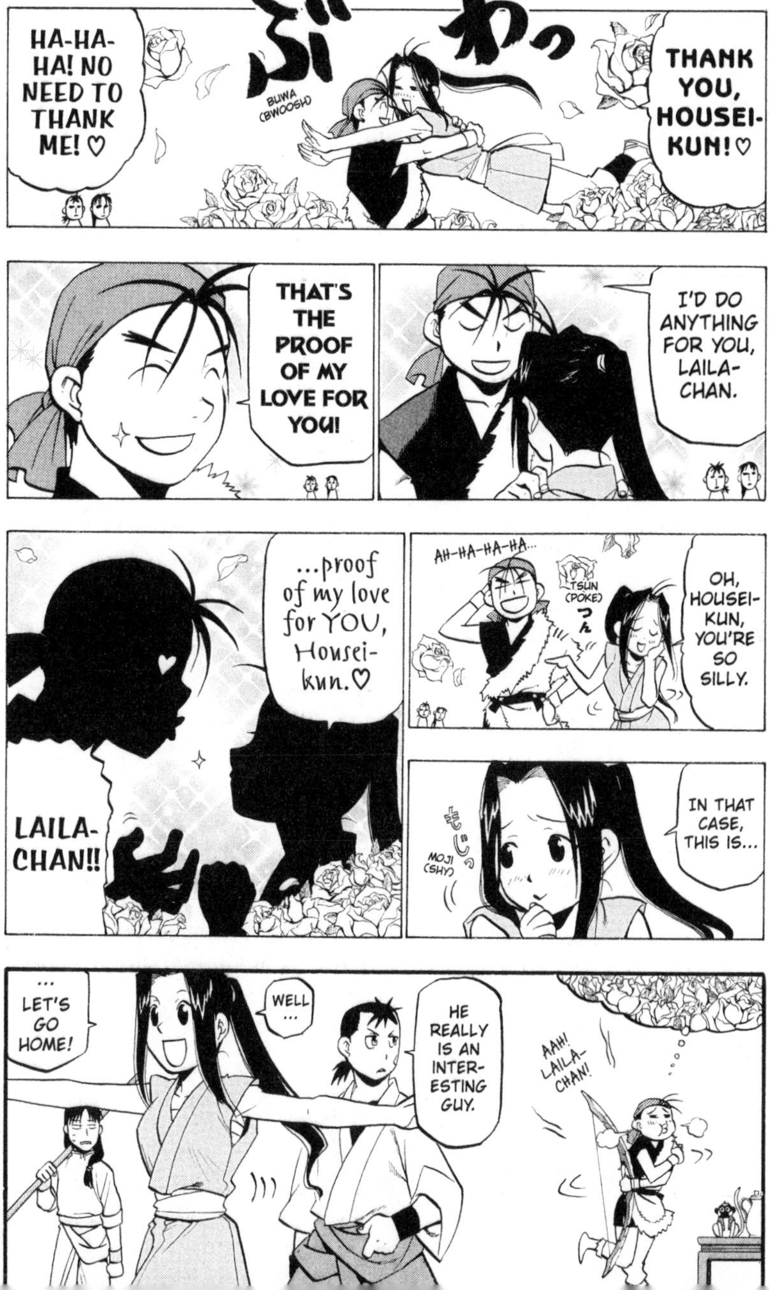
THANK YOU, HOUSEI-KUN!♡
ぶわっ
BUWA (BWOOSH)
HA-HA-HA! NO NEED TO THANK ME!♡
I'D DO ANYTHING FOR YOU, LAILA-CHAN.
THAT'S THE PROOF OF MY LOVE FOR YOU!
OH, HOUSEI-KUN, YOU'RE SO SILLY.
AH-HA-HA-HA...
つん
TSUN (POKE)
IN THAT CASE, THIS IS...
もじっ
MOJI (SHY)
...proof of my love for YOU, Housei-kun.♡
LAILA-CHAN!!
AAH! LAILA-CHAN!
HE REALLY IS AN INTERESTING GUY.
WELL...
... LET'S GO HOME!

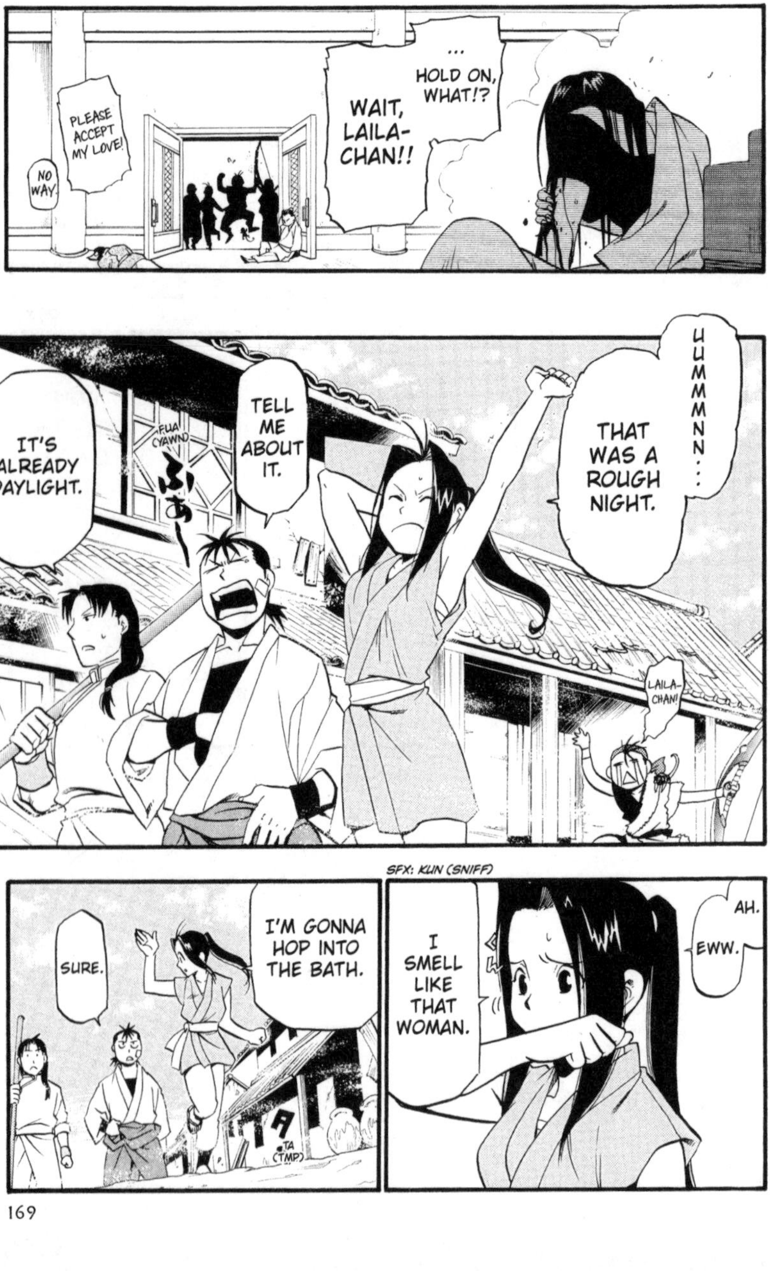
... HOLD ON, WHAT!?
WAIT, LAILA-CHAN!!
PLEASE ACCEPT MY LOVE!
NO WAY.
UMMMNN...
THAT WAS A ROUGH NIGHT.
LAILA-CHAN!
TELL ME ABOUT IT.
FUA CYAWND
IT'S ALREADY DAYLIGHT.
SFX: KUN (SNIFF)
AH.
EWW.
I SMELL LIKE THAT WOMAN.
I'M GONNA HOP INTO THE BATH.
SURE.
TA (TMP)

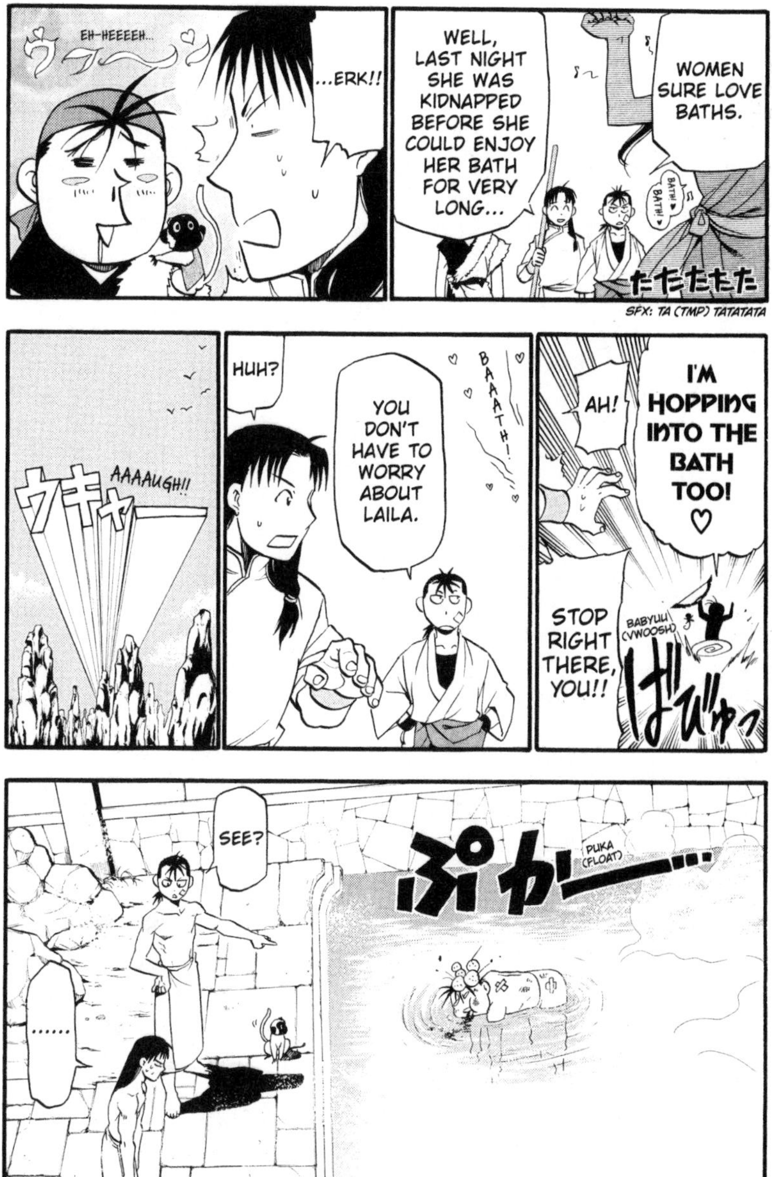
WOMEN SURE LOVE BATHS.
BATH! ♥ BATH! ♥
WELL, LAST NIGHT SHE WAS KIDNAPPED BEFORE SHE COULD ENJOY HER BATH FOR VERY LONG...
たたたたた
SFX: TA (TMP) TATATATA
...ERK!!
ウフ～ン
EH-HEEEEH...
I'M HOPPING INTO THE BATH TOO! ♡
AH!
STOP RIGHT THERE, YOU!!
ばびゅっ
BABYUU (VWOOSH)
BAAAATH!
HUH?
YOU DON'T HAVE TO WORRY ABOUT LAILA.
ウキャー
AAAAUGH!!
SEE?
ぷかー...
PUKA (FLOAT)
......

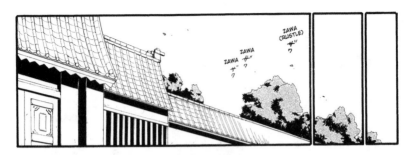

ZAWA
(RUSTLE)

ZAWA

ZAWA

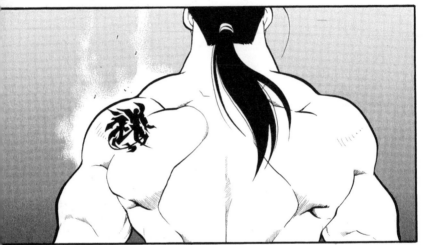

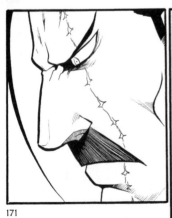

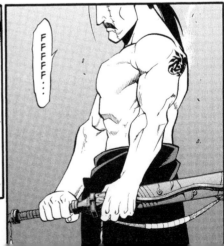

FFFF...

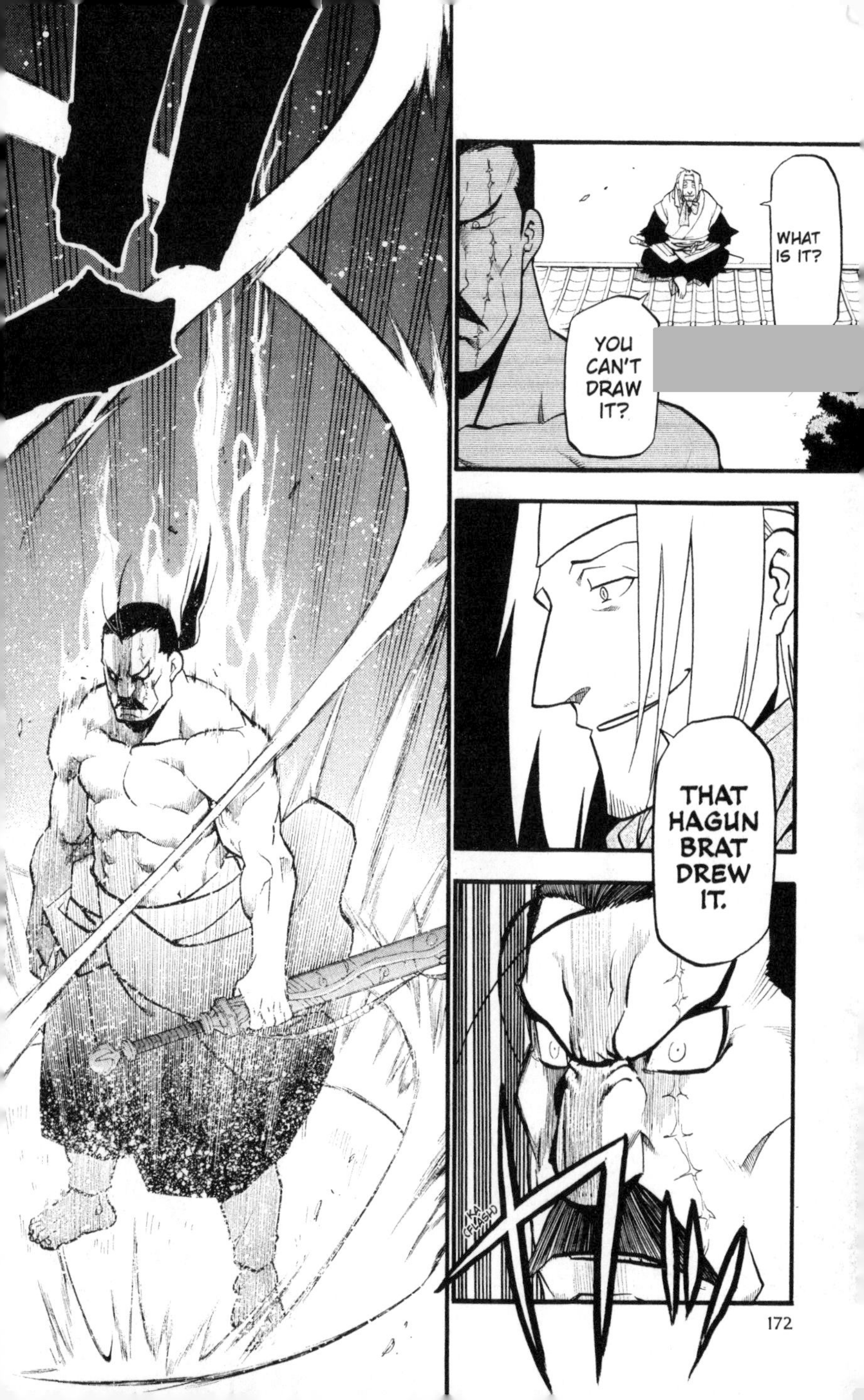
WHAT IS IT?
YOU CAN'T DRAW IT?
THAT HAGUN BRAT DREW IT.
KA (FLASH)

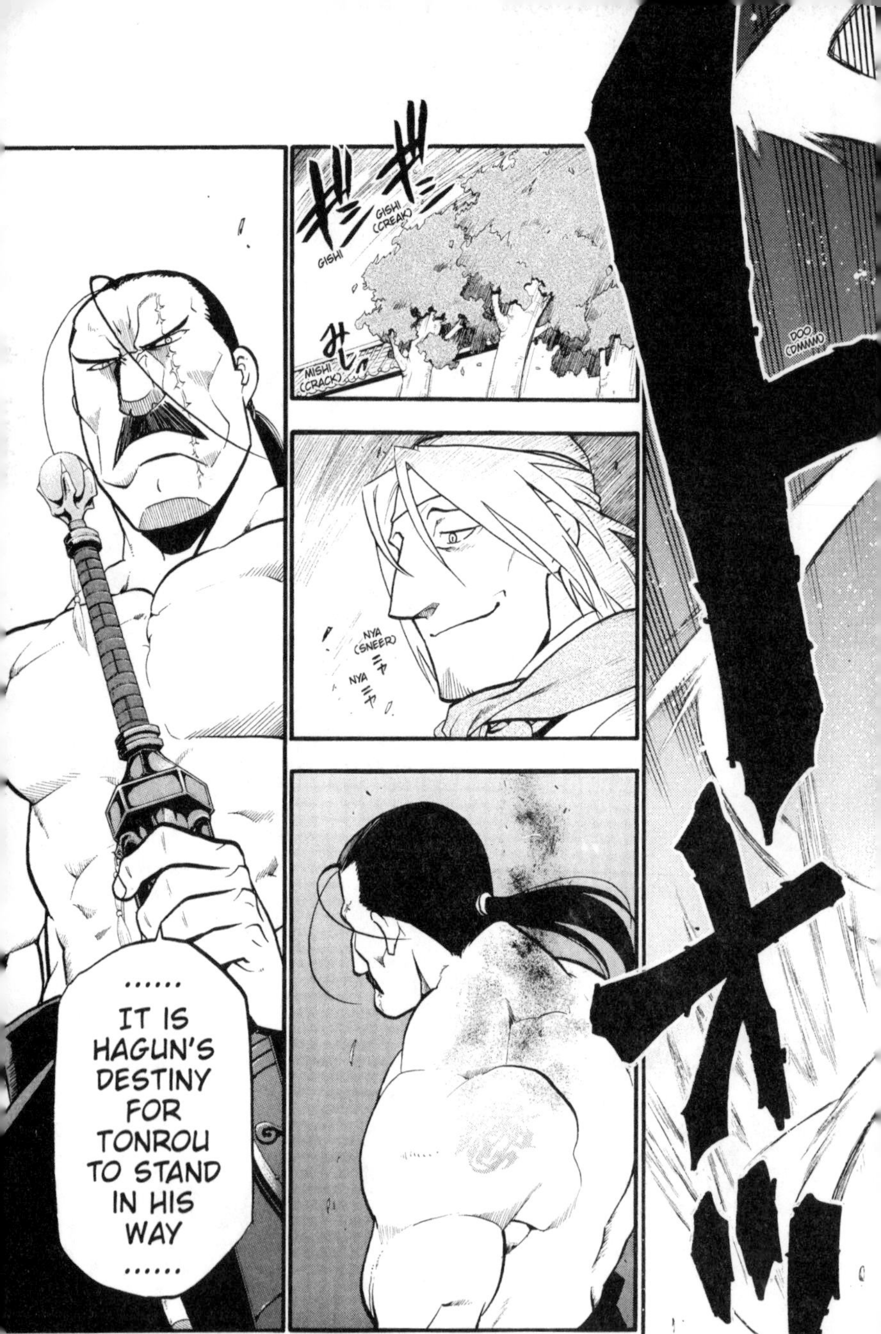
DOO (DMMMM)
GISHI
GISHI (CREAK)
MISHI (CRACK)
NYA (SNEER)
NYA
...... IT IS HAGUN'S DESTINY FOR TONROU TO STAND IN HIS WAY ......

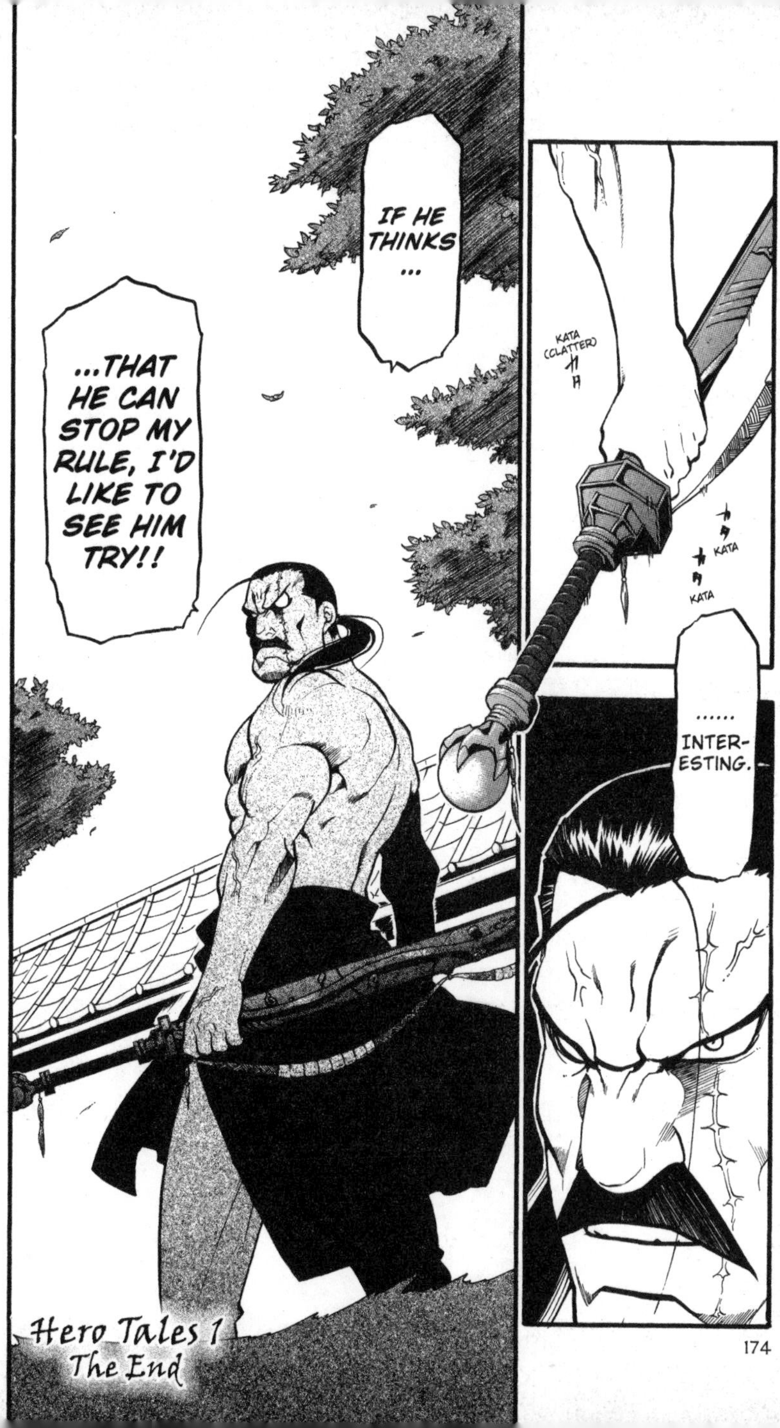
KATA (CLATTER)
KATA
KATA
......INTER-ESTING.
IF HE THINKS...
...THAT HE CAN STOP MY RULE, I'D LIKE TO SEE HIM TRY!!
Hero Tales 1 The End

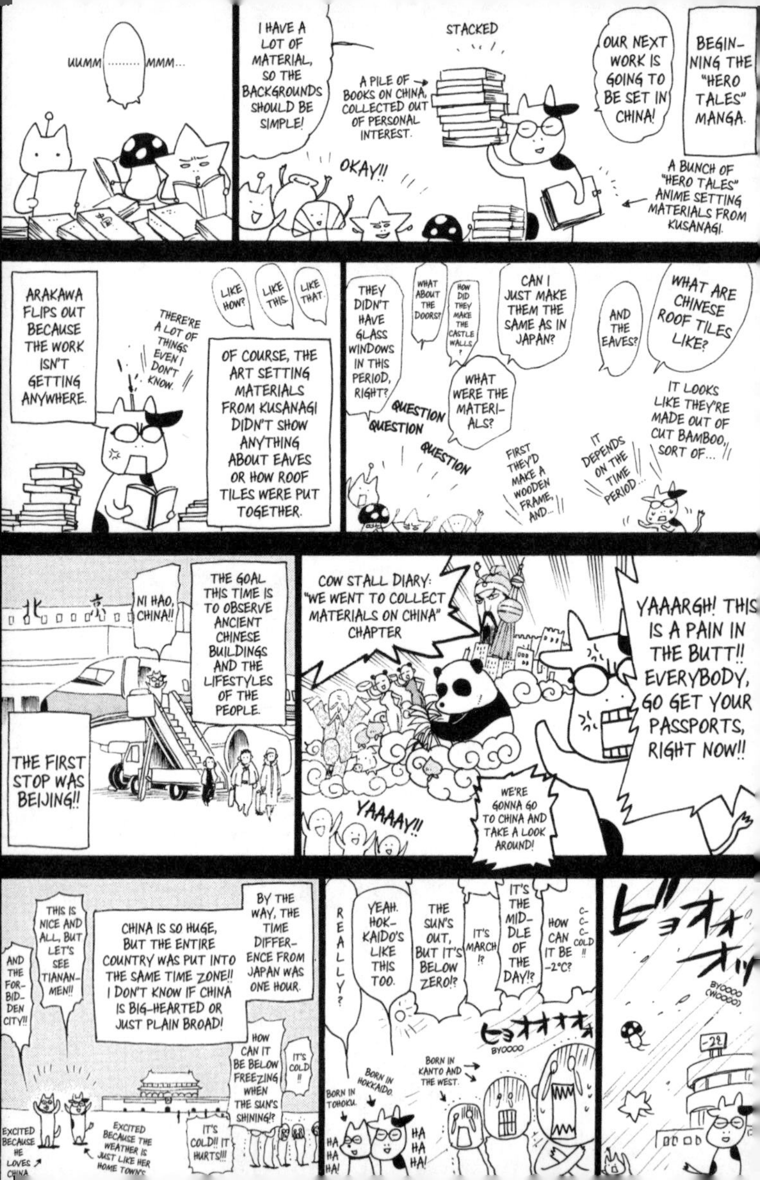
BEGINNING THE "HERO TALES" MANGA.
OUR NEXT WORK IS GOING TO BE SET IN CHINA!
A BUNCH OF "HERO TALES" ANIME SETTING MATERIALS FROM KUSANAGI.
STACKED
A PILE OF BOOKS ON CHINA, COLLECTED OUT OF PERSONAL INTEREST.
I HAVE A LOT OF MATERIAL, SO THE BACKGROUNDS SHOULD BE SIMPLE!
OKAY!!
UUMM.........MMM...
WHAT ARE CHINESE ROOF TILES LIKE?
AND THE EAVES?
CAN I JUST MAKE THEM THE SAME AS IN JAPAN?
HOW DID THEY MAKE THE CASTLE WALLS?
WHAT ABOUT THE DOORS?
THEY DIDN'T HAVE GLASS WINDOWS IN THIS PERIOD, RIGHT?
WHAT WERE THE MATERIALS?
QUESTION
QUESTION
QUESTION
IT LOOKS LIKE THEY'RE MADE OUT OF CUT BAMBOO, SORT OF...
IT DEPENDS ON THE TIME PERIOD...
FIRST THEY'D MAKE A WOODEN FRAME, AND...
LIKE THAT.
LIKE THIS.
LIKE HOW?
THERE'RE A LOT OF THINGS EVEN I DON'T KNOW.
OF COURSE, THE ART SETTING MATERIALS FROM KUSANAGI DIDN'T SHOW ANYTHING ABOUT EAVES OR HOW ROOF TILES WERE PUT TOGETHER.
ARAKAWA FLIPS OUT BECAUSE THE WORK ISN'T GETTING ANYWHERE.
COW STALL DIARY: "WE WENT TO COLLECT MATERIALS ON CHINA" CHAPTER
YAAARGH! THIS IS A PAIN IN THE BUTT!! EVERYBODY, GO GET YOUR PASSPORTS, RIGHT NOW!!
WE'RE GONNA GO TO CHINA AND TAKE A LOOK AROUND!
YAAAAY!!
THE GOAL THIS TIME IS TO OBSERVE ANCIENT CHINESE BUILDINGS AND THE LIFESTYLES OF THE PEOPLE.
北京
NI HAO, CHINA!!
THE FIRST STOP WAS BEIJING!!
ビュオオオッ
BYOOOO (WOOOO)
C-C-C-COLD!!
HOW CAN IT BE -2°C?
IT'S THE MIDDLE OF THE DAY!?
IT'S MARCH!?
THE SUN'S OUT, BUT IT'S BELOW ZERO!?
YEAH. HOKKAIDO'S LIKE THIS TOO.
REALLY?
ヒョオオオオ
BYOOOO
BORN IN KANTO AND THE WEST.
BORN IN HOKKAIDO.
BORN IN TOHOKU.
HA HA HA!
HA HA HA!
BY THE WAY, THE TIME DIFFERENCE FROM JAPAN WAS ONE HOUR.
CHINA IS SO HUGE, BUT THE ENTIRE COUNTRY WAS PUT INTO THE SAME TIME ZONE!! I DON'T KNOW IF CHINA IS BIG-HEARTED OR JUST PLAIN BROAD!
THIS IS NICE AND ALL, BUT LET'S SEE TIANANMEN!!
AND THE FORBIDDEN CITY!!
HOW CAN IT BE BELOW FREEZING WHEN THE SUN'S SHINING!?
IT'S COLD!!
IT'S COLD!! IT HURTS!!!
EXCITED BECAUSE THE WEATHER IS JUST LIKE HER HOME TOWN'S
EXCITED BECAUSE HE LOVES CHINA

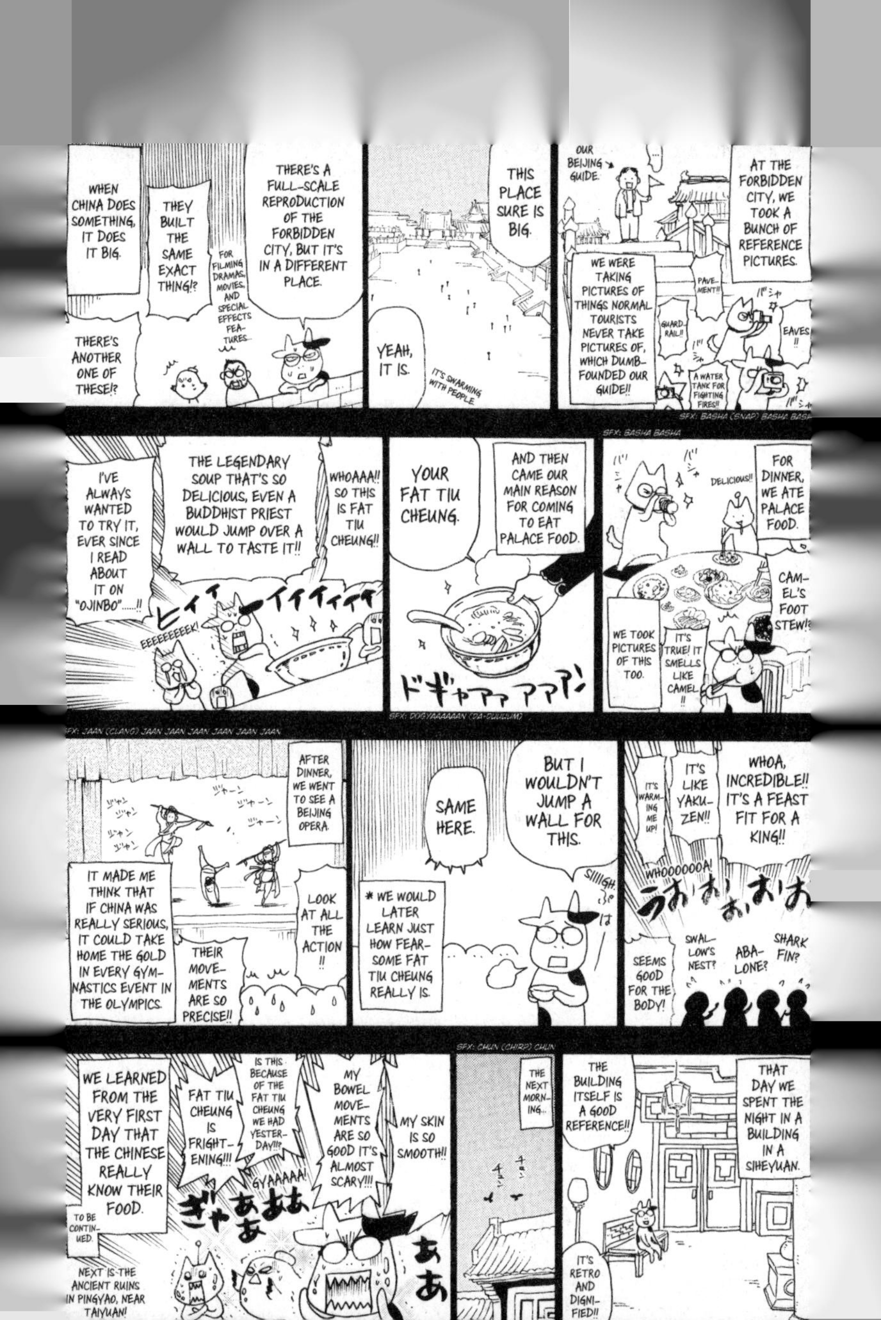
AT THE FORBIDDEN CITY, WE TOOK A BUNCH OF REFERENCE PICTURES.
...
OUR BEIJING GUIDE
PAVEMENT!!
EAVES!!
GUARDRAIL!!
WE WERE TAKING PICTURES OF THINGS NORMAL TOURISTS NEVER TAKE PICTURES OF, WHICH DUMBFOUNDED OUR GUIDE!!
A WATER TANK FOR FIGHTING FIRES!!
SFX: BASHA (SNAP) BASHA BASHA
SFX: BASHA BASHA
THIS PLACE SURE IS BIG.
YEAH, IT IS.
IT'S SWARMING WITH PEOPLE
THERE'S A FULL-SCALE REPRODUCTION OF THE FORBIDDEN CITY, BUT IT'S IN A DIFFERENT PLACE.
FOR FILMING DRAMAS, MOVIES, AND SPECIAL EFFECTS FEATURES...
THEY BUILT THE SAME EXACT THING!?
WHEN CHINA DOES SOMETHING, IT DOES IT BIG.
THERE'S ANOTHER ONE OF THESE!?
FOR DINNER, WE ATE PALACE FOOD.
DELICIOUS!!
CAMEL'S FOOT STEW!!
IT'S TRUE! IT SMELLS LIKE CAMEL!!
WE TOOK PICTURES OF THIS TOO.
AND THEN CAME OUR MAIN REASON FOR COMING TO EAT PALACE FOOD.
YOUR FAT TIU CHEUNG.
ドギャアァアァアン!
SFX: DOGYAAAAAAN (DA-DUUUUM)
WHOAAA!! SO THIS IS FAT TIU CHEUNG!!
THE LEGENDARY SOUP THAT'S SO DELICIOUS, EVEN A BUDDHIST PRIEST WOULD JUMP OVER A WALL TO TASTE IT!!
I'VE ALWAYS WANTED TO TRY IT, EVER SINCE I READ ABOUT IT ON "OJINBO"......!!
ヒイイイイイイイイ
EEEEEEEEEK!
SFX: JAAN (CLANG) JAAN JAAN JAAN JAAN JAAN JAAN
WHOA, INCREDIBLE!! IT'S A FEAST FIT FOR A KING!!
IT'S LIKE YAKUZEN!!
IT'S WARMING ME UP!
WHOOOOOOA!
うおおおおお
SHARK FIN?
ABALONE?
SWALLOW'S NEST?
SEEMS GOOD FOR THE BODY!
BUT I WOULDN'T JUMP A WALL FOR THIS.
SAME HERE.
SIIIIGH.
* WE WOULD LATER LEARN JUST HOW FEARSOME FAT TIU CHEUNG REALLY IS.
AFTER DINNER, WE WENT TO SEE A BEIJING OPERA.
ジャーン ジャーン ジャーン
ジャン ジャン ジャン ジャン
LOOK AT ALL THE ACTION!!
THEIR MOVEMENTS ARE SO PRECISE!!
IT MADE ME THINK THAT IF CHINA WAS REALLY SERIOUS, IT COULD TAKE HOME THE GOLD IN EVERY GYMNASTICS EVENT IN THE OLYMPICS.
SFX: CHUN (CHIRP) CHUN
THAT DAY WE SPENT THE NIGHT IN A BUILDING IN A SIHEYUAN.
THE BUILDING ITSELF IS A GOOD REFERENCE!!
IT'S RETRO AND DIGNIFIED!!
THE NEXT MORNING...
チュン チュン
MY SKIN IS SO SMOOTH!!
MY BOWEL MOVEMENTS ARE SO GOOD IT'S ALMOST SCARY!!!
IS THIS BECAUSE OF THE FAT TIU CHEUNG WE HAD YESTERDAY!!?
FAT TIU CHEUNG IS FRIGHTENING!!!
GYAAAAA!
ぎゃあああああ
WE LEARNED FROM THE VERY FIRST DAY THAT THE CHINESE REALLY KNOW THEIR FOOD.
TO BE CONTINUED.
NEXT IS THE ANCIENT RUINS IN PINGYAO, NEAR TAIYUAN!

Special Thanks

Original Story: Huang Jin Zhou

Scenario: Ryou Yashiro

Original Story Assistance: Shinya Oohara, Tetsuya Hayasaka

Art Setting: Kusanagi

Weapon Design: Takahiro Yamada

Production Assistants:
Sankichi Hinodeya   Jun Tokou
Aiyaabooru   Nono
Youichi Katouno   Mashi Mizutani
Sakamaki   Kuupon
Noriko Tsubota   Haruhi Nakamura
Atsushi Baba   Masanari Yuzuka

Editor: Yuichi Shimomura

AND YOU!!

Common Honorifics:

No honorific: Indicates familiarity or closeness; if used without permission or reason, addresssing someone in this manner would constitute an insult.

-san: The Japanese equivalent of Mr./Mrs./Miss. If a situation calls for politeness, this is the fail-safe honorific.

-sama: Conveys great respect; may also indicate that the social status of the speaker is lower than that of the addressee.

-kun: Used most often when referring to boys, this indicates affection or familiarity. Occasionally used by older men among their peers, but it may also be used by anyone referring to a person of lower standing.

-chan: An affectionate honorific indicating familiarity used mostly in reference to girls; also used in reference to cute persons or animals of either gender.

-sensei: A respectful term for teachers, artists, or high-level professionals.

Pg. 5
Manju
Manju is a pastry/bun with some sort of filling inside, usually *an* (sweet red bean paste). It was originally a Chinese confection and was later brought over to Japan.

Pg. 9
Son-jii
The old man's actual name is Sonnei. Here, Laila shortens it to Son and adds *jii*, which means "old man" or "grandpa."

Shifu, Shikei
Shifu is a term of respect for an elder master, particularly one who is like a father to you. *Shikei* can refer to an elder disciple and may also be a polite way to refer to an older brother (or older brother-like figure).

Pg. 16
Soukihou
Soukihou can be translated as "Ki (spirit) manipulation technique/method."

Pg. 72
Rikka sect
Rikka is a sect of Buddhism.

Pg. 75
-dono
The suffix "-*dono*" is polite and formal. Taitou quite naturally thinks it sounds stuffy and uptight when someone older than himself like Ryuukou uses it with him.

Pg. 137
Shouka-neesan
Neesan means "older sister" and is used to refer to either your actual older sister or a woman who is like an older sister to you.

Pg. 139
"A companion eases the journey, and satisfaction eases the way through life."
There is a common Japanese saying, "*Tabi wa michizure yo wa nasake*," which means, "A companion eases the journey, and compassion eases the way through life." In this case, however, Housei bungles the word "*nasake*" (compassion) and replaces it with "*manzoku*" (satisfaction).

Pg. 158
"History is written by the victor."
The Japanese have a proverb that says "*Kateba kangun*," which literally means, "If you win, you become the government army." This is sometimes followed by "*makereba zokugun*," which means "if you lose, you become armed rebels." The English equivalent is "History is written by the victor."

Pg. 175
Ni Hao
Ni Hao is "Hello" in Chinese.

"Hokkaido's like this too."
Hokkaido is an island in the northernmost part of Japan and is known for being cold.

Kanto
The Kanto region of Japan includes the eastern central part of Honshu, Japan's largest island. It is where Tokyo is located.

Tohoku
The Tohoku region of Japan includes the northern part of Honshu, Japan's largest island.

Big-hearted or just plain broad
In Japanese, the word for "big-hearted" (*ooraka*) is close to the word for "broad, rough, not precise" (*oozappa*).

Pg. 176
Fat Tiu Cheung
This Chinese dish is called "Buddha Jumps Over the Wall" in English, supposedly because it is so good that even though it contains meat, even a vegetarian like the Buddha would jump over the monastery wall to taste it. It is a highly complex soup or stew that can take from one to two days to complete.

Yakuzen
Yakuzen is a uniquely Chinese form of therapy which seeks to both prevent and treat illness through diet.

Siheyuan
Siheyuan (Chinese Quadrangle) refers to a historical type of residence found throughout China. A typical Siheyuan has a central courtyard surrounded by four buildings. It is the basic architectural style that forms the basis for many other Chinese architectural styles.

The ancient ruins in Pingyao, near Taiyuan
Pingyao is a city in the province of Shanxi near the provincial capital of Taiyuan. It is known for its ancient ruins and some of the most well-preserved city walls in China.

W9-CTK-100

HERO TALES ①

HUANG JIN ZHOU
HIROMU ARAKAWA

Translation: Amy Forsyth

Lettering: Abigail Blackman

HERO TALES: JUUSHIN ENBU Vol. 1 © HUANG JIN-ZHOU • GENCO •
FLAG ©2007 HERO TALES PRODUCTION PARTNERS © 2007 Hiromu
Arakawa / SQUARE ENIX. All rights reserved. First published Japan in
2007 by SQUARE ENIX CO. LTD. English translation rights arranged with
SQUARE ENIX CO. LTD. and Hachette Book Group through Tuttle-Mori
Agency, Inc. Translation © 2009 by SQUARE ENIX CO., LTD.

Yen Press
Hachette Book Group
237 Park Avenue, New York, NY 10017

Visit our Web sites at www.HachetteBookGroup.com and
www.YenPress.com.

Yen Press is an imprint of Hachette Book Group, Inc. The Yen Press name
and logo are trademarks of Hachette Book Group, Inc.

First Yen Press Edition: October 2009

ISBN: 978-0-7595-3116-1

10 9 8 7 6 5 4 3 2 1

BVG

Printed in the United States of America